ISBN 978-0-267-91463-0
PIBN 10596199

Manwood, John

Manwood's Treatise
OF THE
Forest Laws:

SHEWING

Not only the LAWS now in Force, but the Original of FORESTS, what they are, and how they differ from Chases, Parks, and Warrens; with all such Things as are incident to either:

TOGETHER WITH

The proper TERMS of ART, collected out of the Common and Statute Laws of this Realm; as also from the *Assises* and *Iters* of *Pickering* and *Lancaster*, and several other ancient and learned Authors.

Treating also of the Office of Agistors, Beadles, Foresters, Keepers, Rangers, Verderors and Wood wards, and of the Courts of Attachment, *&c.* With all the Variety of CASES relating to Forests, Chases, Parks, and Warrens; and all the LAWS concerning the Game made, adjudged or repealed, since the Year 1665.

The whole digested under proper Titles in an ALPHABETICAL ORDER.

The Fourth Edition, Corrected and Enlarged.

By William Nelson, of the *Middle-Temple*, Esq;

In the *SAVOY*:
Printed by E. Nutt, (Executrix of J. Nutt, Assignee of *Edward Sayer* Esq;) for B. Lintott at the *Cross-Keys*, R. Gosling at the *Mitre* and *Crown*, J. Pemberton at the *Buck* and *Sun*, all in *Fleet-street*; and T. Ward in the *Inner-Temple-Lane*. 1717.

[illegible]

[illegible]

[illegible]

[illegible]

[illegible]

[illegible]

THE PREFACE.

THIS Treatise of the Forest-Laws was first published about the later End of the Reign of Queen *Elizabeth*, and hath been so well received as to admit several Impressions; but 'tis now so very scarce, that it may be very necessary to send it (once more) to the Press, for 'tis the only valuable Book written on that Subject; the Author having perused the Records of the *Assises* of the Forest of *Sherwood*, kept in *Nottingham Castle*, and the Proceedings of the *Iters* of the Forests of *Pickering* and *Lancaster*, out of which he hath extracted many useful

A ful

ful Things, not to be found in any other Law-Book whatsoever.

I have thought fit to make some Alterations in the *Orthography*; for our Language being very much refined since the Author wrote, which is now above One hundred Years, I thought it proper to express his Matter in Words more adapted to the present Times, but without the least Alteration of the Sense, which I have been so nicely scrupulous in observing, that in many Places I have transposed whole Sentences and Paragraphs to make the same Matter cohere, and that it might be the more clearly understood.

To this Impression there are added all the Judgments and Resolutions in the *Assizes* and *Iters* of the Forests of *Dean*, *Waltham*, *Windsor*, &c. and all other Cases relating to *Forests*, *Chases*, *Parks*, *Warrens*, and the *Game*, published or adjudged since the Year 1665; and the whole is divided into several Titles, in an Alphabetical Order, which

which is a moſt approved Method for the ready finding any thing in the Book; under which Titles, and to ſuch only as they properly relate, I have placed the ſeveral Notes of the *Aſſiſes* and *Iters* of *Pickering* and *Lancaſter*, the ſeveral Judgments and Entries of thoſe *Aſſiſes*, and other Judgments taken out of the Records of the Foreſts; together with the Petition of the Biſhop of *Lichfield* and *Coventry* againſt the Juſtices of the Foreſt.

And, as an Appendix to the whole, I have added all the Laws of *Canutus*, the Charter and Ordinances, and all other Statutes relating to Foreſts, Parks and Chaſes, in order of Time as they were made; ſome of which were printed in a confuſed manner at the Beginning, and ſome as improperly at the End of the laſt Edition.

A

A TREATISE OF THE Forest Laws, &c.

Agistment in Forests.

See { *Charge, in Chief Justice*, 56. 57. 64.
Common 64.
Pannage 11.
Appendix, Ch. Forestæ, 91 }

1. THE Word *Agistment* signifies the feeding Cattle with Herbage; 'tis derived from *Agito*, to drive or to feed, and the Lawyers, by adding the Letter S, have made it a Term of Art.

2. From hence comes the Word *Agistator* or *Agistor*, who is an Officer that taketh Beasts to Pasture within the Forest; and this, my Lord *Coke* tells us, comes from the *French* Word *Gyser*, *i. e.* to lie down, because the Cattle, which feed there, are *Levant* and *Couchant*: He likewise tells us, that this Officer is constituted by the King's Letters Patent, and that his Office consists *Agistando, recipiendo, imbreviando & certificando*; and that there are Four in Num-

ber in such Forests where there is any Pannage, 4 *Inst*. 293.

3. *Agistment* is of Two Sorts; *viz*. of the Herbage of Woods, Lands and Pastures; and of Woods alone, that is, of the Masts of the Trees, which is properly call'd *Pannage*.

4. For where the King hath any Forests, he hath there Demesne Woods and Lands which are enclosed; he hath also *Waste* Ground not enclosed, but lies open and in common for the Benefit of the Inhabitants of the Forests; and 'tis the Business of the *Agistors* to look after those Woods and Lands, and to receive and take in the Cattle of such Persons who dwell within the Forest, who are to pay for the Herbage of such Cattle as are commonable within a Forest: And because these Officers are answerable to the King, as well for the Rule and Government of these Places, as for the Money and Profit which shall arise or be made thereof, they are called the Kings *Agistors* of the Forest.

5. But *Agistment*, in the proper Signification of the Word, is the Herbage of Land or Woods, or the Money received or due for the same. And of this Opinion was Mr. *Hesket*, in his Reading on the Laws of the Forest; *viz*. That the Pasture or Herbage of any Ground, or the Money that is taken for the same, is properly call'd *Agistment*. *Hesket*, *fo*. 48.

6. This appears by the Book of *Entries*, where an Action of Trespass was brought for breaking and entring the Plantiff's Close in *Dale*, and spoiling and eating his Pasture there with Cattle, *&c*.

7. The Defendant pleaded not Guilty, as to the breaking the Close; and as to the spoiling and eating his Pasture, he justified, that one *I. S*. was seised of the said Close in Fee *tempore quo*, *&c*. and that the Defendant, by the Appointment of the said *I. S*. did put his Cattle therein to *agist*, paying unto the said

said *I. S.* for the *Agistment* of every Beast there, *Three Half-pence* for every Week, *&c.* By which it appears, that the Pasture of the Ground, and the Money for the same, are called *Agistment. Lib. Intration. fo.* 549.

8. So in the same Book of *Entries*, an Action of Debt was brought against the Defendant for *agisting* his Cattle in the Plaintiff's Land; which likewise proves, that as well the *Pasturing* the Cattle, as the Money for the same, is call'd *Agistment. Lib. Intration. fo.* 149.

9. So in 22 *Assisarum, placito* 84, it was the Opinion of *Mowbray, Banke* and *Thorp*, that if a Man hath *Common* by Specialty in a certain Place, and Cattle of his own to put in, he may not agist other Mens Cattle there to use his *Common*; so that they declared what *Agistment* is. 44 *Ed.* 3. *fo.* 25. *placito* 38.

10. And in *Dyer, fo.* 80. *placito* 56, the Bishop of *Lincoln* made a Lease of the *Herbage* and *Agistment* of *Stow Park* unto *B*, which was confirmed by the Chapter; and that the Lessee surcharged the Park with so many Cattle, that the Deer could have no Pasture there, by Reason of *agisting* the Cattle, *&c.*

11. But those who have a Right of Common in the Waste of the Forest, and to agist their Cattle there, may not have *Agistment* for all Manner of Cattle; *viz.* not for Geese, Goats, Sheep or Swine, but only for such Beasts as are commonable.

Who shall agist in the King's Woods.

12. The King's Demesne Woods and Lands must always be agisted by his Foresters and Verderors; this appears by the Assises of *H.* 2. call'd the *Assises of Woodstock*; viz. *Item Rex præcipit quòd in quolibet Comitatu in quo habet Venationem, ponentur*

tur duodecim milites ad custodiendum venationem suam; & viridarii cum Forestariis & quatuor militibus, ad agistandum Boscos suos, & ad recipiendum pannagium suum.

13. By which it appeareth, that the agisting the King's Demesne Lands and Woods must be made by the Verderors, Foresters and Agistors, that is, it must be made by their Privity and Consent; and for that Purpose the *Swanimote* Courts were appointed by the Charter to be held at such Days and Times when the agisting the King's Demesne Woods and Lands doth begin, that all those Officers may meet there and join together about it; and when that expires they may meet again to receive the King's Money for *Agistments*, and likewise for agisting the King's Woods and receiving the Pannage Money.

14. Such *Agistments* being made in Manner as aforesaid, by the Privity of the Foresters and Verderors, they must be enroll'd in the Verderor's Roll, which Roll must agree with the Agistor's Accompts; for the Verderor's Roll of the *Swanimote*-Courts is the King's Record to charge his Agistors with the Receipts of his Money, which they, alone, are to receive for the *Agistment* of his Demesne Lands and Woods, and they are only chargeable to the King to answer for the same.

15. This appears by the *Assises of the Forest of Pickering*, *fo.* 7, 8, 9. *Anno* 8. *Ed.* 3. where it was adjudged; *viz.* As concerning the Agistors of the King's Demesne Woods and Lands, every Agistor in the King's Forest must bring before the Lord Chief Justice in Eyre of the Forest at the Justice-Seat, a true and just Accompt what Money he hath received for any *Agistment* or Pannage of the King's Woods and Lands, and the Entry thereof is thus; *viz. Rogerus M. unus Agistatorum istius Forestæ, respondebat de Agistamento Herbagii de Eastwood,*

wood, 3 *l.* 4 *s.* & *de pannagio porcorum de Eastwood*, 23 *s.* 4 *d.*

16. It appears likewise by the Charter of the Forest, *articulo* 8. *viz. Et circa festum Sancti Martini in hyeme, quando Agistatores nostri debent recipere pannagium nostrum*, at which Time one of the three Swanimotes is to be held.

17. So that though the agisting the King's Woods and Lands must be made by the Foresters, Verderors, and Agistors, yet the *Agistors* alone are to receive the Money for Agistments and Pannage; and therefore they only are answerable to the King and not the Verderors or Foresters; for the Verderors are only answerable to the King for the keeping of such Things which concern the Forests.

18. And if any *Stranger*, living out of the Bounds of the Forest, drives his Cattle into the Forest, and agists them in the King's Woods and Lands, without the Licence or Consent of the Officers of the Forest, or some other good Authority; then the Foresters and Agistors shall take the said Beasts and appraise them, and deliver them to the Verderors to answer the King the Value thereof, for by the Laws of the Forest such Beasts are *forfeited.*

19. But if an *Inhabitant* within the Bounds of the Forest do agist his Beasts in the King's Demesne Woods and Lands in the Forest, without any Agreement with those Officers, in such Case the Beasts so agisted are not *forfeited*, but the Party is to be *fined* for such Offence; and Mr. *Hesket*, *fo.* 23. and Mr. *Treherne*, *fo.* 8. are of Opinion, that such Offence is determinable before the Verderors in their Court of Attachments.

20. Common of Herbage is Matter of Agistment, but no Man may agist his Beasts within the King's Waste of the Forest, but he who is an *Inhabitant* in the Forest, or who hath Common appendant or

appurtenant there, by Reason of his Land lying within the Forest.

21. And if a Man, who dwelleth within the Forest, and who hath Common in the Waste there, will take the Beasts of *Strangers* to agist, this is an Offence fineable to the King: The Form of the Entry of the Record is thus;

22. *Item præsentant quòd* A. B. *agistat averia extraneorum apud* F. *infra forestam, ad dumnum Domini Regis & ad nocumentum ferarum: Et nesciunt quo Warranto: Ideo præceptum est Vicecomiti quòd venire faciat eum: Et postea testatum est per ministros forestarum quòd ipse nihil habet infra forestam. Ideo pro agistamento prædicto in misericordia, & remaneat agistamentum in manu Domini Regis. Itin. Pickering, fo.* 10.

23. *In Assisa Forestæ Pickering, fo.* 10. there is the like Entry in the like Case of the Prior of St. *John*, for agisting the Cattle of *Strangers* in the King's Forest, *ad nocumentum ferarum*, &c. *& ad damnum Domini Regis; & nesciunt quo Warranto. Ideo præceptum est Vicecomiti quòd venire faciat eum: Postea venit prædictus Prior & dicit quòd ipse virtute chartarum progenitorum Regis nunc factarum prædecessoribus suis agistare in loco prædicto; & petit quòd possit admitti ad finem faciendum cum Domino Rege pro clameo suo faciendo, licèt primo die itineris non fecit: Et admittitur ad finem* 13 *s.* 4 *d. per plegios, R. & N.*

Who shall agist the Woods and Lands of other Men.

24. The Words *in Charta Forestæ, Articulo* 9. are, *viz. Unusquisque liber homo agistet Boscum suum, &c.* That every Freeman, who hath any Woods or Lands within the Forest, either in Fee-simple or Fee-tail, for Term of Life or Years, either in his own Right, or in the Right of another, may, by himself, his Servants or Tenants, agist his

his Woods and Lands, and take the Herbage; and likewise the Pannage thereof, at seasonable Times, by his Beasts; but he must not agist Goats or Sheep there, though they are his own, without he hath a Licence so to do: *Quia præbent exilium ferarum Forestæ*; that is, They so taint the Pasture where they feed, that the Beasts of the Forest will not depasture there; so that they do, as it were, banish them from every Place where they are.

Of the Time of agisting the King's Woods and Lands.

25. The *Time* for taking in Agistments of all manner of commonable Beasts, in the King's Demesne Woods and Lands, for *Herbage* only, doth begin 15 Days before *Midsummer*, and doth end on *Holy-Rood-Day*.

26. This appears by the Charter of the Forest, *Articul.* 8. *viz. Tertium Swanimotum teneatur initio 15 dierum ante Festum Sancti Johannis Baptistæ, quando Agistatores nostri conveniunt pro feopatione bestiarum nostrarum.*

27. This Court of Swanimote is held at that Time for Two Causes; *viz.* That Care may be taken throughout the Forest to preserve the Wild Beasts in their Time of Fawning, which is usually 15 Days before *Midsummer*, and 15 Days after; and this is called the *Fence-Month.*

28. The other Cause is, That the Agistors of the King's Forests do then begin to agist the King's Demesne Lands, Woods and Pastures for *Herbage*, and for that Purpose do take in all manner of commonable Beasts to depasture the Herbage of the Forest; and this continueth till *Holy-Rood-Day*, which is 15 Days before *Michaelmas*, and then the next Court of *Swanimote* is to be held; this likewise appears by *Charta Forestæ*, *Art.* 8.

29. *Nullum Swanimotum de cætero teneatur in regno nostro, nisi ter in Anno; viz. in principio 15 dierum ante festum Sancti Michaelis, quando Agistatores nostri conveniunt ad agistandum Dominicos Boscos nostros, &c.*

30. In this Court, when the Agistors have done agisting for Herbage, then they receive the Money due for the same, in the Presence of the Foresters and Verderors, that they may record it in the Verderors Rolls.

31. And now at this Court the Agistors do begin to agist the King's *Woods* for *Mast*, which Agistment may be for Beasts not *commonable*; *viz.* for Swine and Hogs; and it begins 15 Days before *Michaelmas*, and ends 40 Days after, *viz.* about the Feast of St. *Martin*.

32. The next *Swanimote* Court is held about that Time, as appears *in Charta Forestæ, Artic.* 8. *viz. Et circa festum Sancti Martini in Hyeme quando Agistatores nostri debent recipere pannagium nostrum, &c.*

33. So that as the King's Agistors do begin to take in Swine and Hogs at the *Swanimote* holden on *Holy-Rood-Day*, to feed on the *Mast*; so at the next *Swanimote* afterwards held on the Feast of St. *Martin*, (at which Time the agisting of Hogs is ended) then they likewise, in the Presence of the Foresters and Verderors, receive the Money for the same, which is called *Pannage*, which is likewise entered on the Verderors Rolls.

34. But previous to all this, when the Times and Seasons are come to agist the King's Demesne Woods and Lands, as well for *Herbage* as *Pannage*, then the Agistors, Foresters and Verderors, must certify the Lord Chief Justice in Eyre thereof, who thereupon will direct a Commission to them, signifying what he will have done in this Matter, and how they are to proceed in taking Agist-

ments; which Commission must be returned to the said Chief Justice at the next Justice-Seat to be holden for the said Forest, together with a true Certificate how they have executed the same.

35. This appears by *the Assises and Customs of the Forest, Artic.* 14. *in Rastal, titulo Forest.* 21. viz. *Sciendum est quòd tempore Pannagii, quando Agistamentum debet fieri, debent Forestarii, Viridarii & Agistatores assensum intimare Justitiarius Forestæ Domini Regis, & inquirere voluntatem suam, & fiat Agistamentum tam in Dominicis Haiis & boscis, quàm in forinsecis; & secundùm mandatum suum & tenorem literarum debet fieri Agistamentum; quas literas debent habere coram Justitiariis de Forestâ prox. itinerantibus, &c.*

Of the Time of Agisting other Mens Woods and Lands.

36. Every Man, who hath Woods and Lands within the Regard of the Forest, may agist them, for the *Herbage* only, with his Beasts and Cattle, at all convenient Times of the Year; but it must be with his *own Cattle*; so that the Woods and Underwoods be carefully preserved to grow again for the Covert of the Beasts.

37. For, by the Laws of the Forest, no particular time is appointed for Men, who have Woods or Lands within the Forest, to agist them with their commonable Cattle; but they may do it at any time when they please, that is, they may depasture their *own Cattle* with the Herbage there.

38. This appears *in Charta Forestæ, Articul.* 9. viz. *Unusquisque liber homo agistet boscum suum in Forestâ pro voluntate suâ & habeat pannagium suum:* So that he is not only entituled to the *Herbage* of his Woods and Lands, but to the *Pannage*, that is, to the *Mast* of the Trees.

39. But if a Man hath Woods or Hedge-rows, near or adjoining to the King's Demesne Woods, in such Case the Owner must not agist his Woods or Hedge-rows with Swine or Hogs, until the King hath agisted his Woods, because they are not to prejudice or hinder the King's Agistment.

40. This is evident by *the Assises and Customs of the Forest*, *Articul.* 13. *Rastal. Titul. Forest.* 21. viz. *Si quis habuerit boscum juxta Dominicum boscum Domini Regis, licitum est ei, postquam Dominicæ haiæ agistatæ sunt, habere tempore Paunagii tot porcos, quot Boscus per visum Forestariorum, Viridariorum, Regardatorum, Agistatorum, & aliorum proborum hominum, possit pati: Et hoc fiat de exitu porcorum, &c.*

41. And as men may agist their own Woods, within the Regard of the Forest, at any Time, for the *Herbage* thereof, with their *own Cattle*; so they may, for the *Paunage* thereof, with their *own Hogs*, at any time, except their Woods and Hedge-rows are contiguous to the King's Woods, as aforesaid; and those they must not agist till after the King's Woods are agisted, which is about the Feast of St. *Martin*, and afterwards they may do it when they will. *In Clameo Abbatis de Ryval. Itin. Pickering, fo.* 166. 10. *Ed.* 3.

42. But notwithstanding the Words before-mention'd, *in Charta Forestæ, Articul.* 9. viz. *Unusquisque liber homo agistet boscum suum, &c.* he must not agist his Woods with the Cattle of *Strangers* for the *Herbage* thereof, unless he hath *Licence* so to do; for if he doth, 'tis fineable to the King at the next Justice-Seat.

43. For, by the Laws of the Forest, they may agist their *own* Lands with their *own* Cattle, but not with the Cattle of *Strangers*, for the *Herbage* only; but, by the same Laws, they are allowed to agist their own *Woods* and *Lands* within the Regard of the Forest, for the *Pawnage* thereof, as well

well with the Hogs and Swine of *Strangers*, as their *own*. *Assisæ & consuetud. Forestæ, Artic.* 13. *Hesket, fo.* 16. This appears in *Assisa Forestæ Pickering, fo.* 166. *Charta Forestæ Articul.* 9.

44. And the Reason of this Difference is, *viz.* If the Charter of the Forest gave Men Liberty to agist their Woods and Lands within the Forest, for the *Herbage* thereof, with the Cattle of *Strangers* as well as with their *own*, then they would agist their Lands and Pasture so bare, that it might be very prejudicial to the Deer for want of Food.

45. Every Agistor of the King's Woods in his Forests, must bring, before the Justice-Seat, a true Accompt what Money he hath receiv'd for *Pannage*, and the Form of the Entry is thus; *viz. Robertus M. respondebat de VI s. de pannagio porcorum de Eastwood, &c.*

Agistor, see *Rolls* 5.

46. The Office of an Agistor is to present Trespasses done by Cattle; and if he present any Thing which doth not belong to his Charge, the Presentment is void: And therefore one *Finch* was fin'd 10 *l.* at the Justice-Seat, *in Itinere Windsor*, for making the Agistors present Things which did not belong to them, and for perswading them to withdraw their Presentments. *Jones* 280.

47. There may be some Forests where there are no Agistors, because the King may have no Woods there to agist; but in every Forest where the King hath Woods, these Officers are very necessary, not only to look after such Woods, but to answer the Profits of Agistment to the King.

Amerciament, see *Distress*, 1. 4.

Appearance at the Justice-Seat.

See { *Boundaries*, 18.
Charge, in Chief Justice, 13.
Distress, 3, 4.
Forester, 58. }

1. BEfore the making of *Charta de Foresta*, all Men *within the County*, of what Quality soever, were bound to appear at the Justice-Seat, upon a *General Summons*.

2. This appears *in Assisa Forestæ, fact. tempore H.* 2. *Cap.* 19. viz. *Comites, Barones, Milites & liberi Tenentes, & omnes homines de Com' veniant ad Summon. nostri Forest', sicut se voluerint defendi, ne incidant in manus Regis, ad placitanda placita de forestis suis, vel ad alia negotia facienda in Com', &c.*

3. But it being found inconvenient for Men living out of the Forest, to appear upon such a Summons, it was therefore remedied by *Charta Forestæ, Articulo* 2. viz. *Homines verò qui manent extra forestam non veniant de cætero coram Justitiar. nostris de foresta per Communes Summonitiones, ni sint implacitati vel plegij alicujus vel aliquorum qui attachiati sunt propter forestam*: Where, by the Words *de cætero*, 'tis implied, that, before the making that Statute, all the Inhabitants in the County were bound to appear before the Justices of the Forest upon a *General Summons*; which was a very great Trouble to those who liv'd at a great Distance from the Forest, and which was remedied by this Statute.

4. The chief Reason of this Clause was, that King *H.* 2. having afforested the Woods and Lands of several of his Subjects, to which he had no manner of Title, and which afterwards were appointed to be dis-afforested; this Branch of the

Statute was chiefly intended for their Ease, who formerly had lived within such Parts of the Forest, which now, by this Statute, were dis-afforested, that they might not be compell'd to appear at the Justice-Seat; and 'tis divided into Two Parts;

1. *Concerning those who dwell without the Forest.*

2. *Concerning those who dwell within.*

5. As concerning those who dwell without the Forest, in some Cases they ought to appear before the Justices of the Forest upon a *General Summons*, notwithstanding the Words of the Statute; *viz. If they have any* Liberty or Franchise within the Forest, by Reason whereof they are to put in their *Claim* before the Justice in Eyre; then, though they dwell out of the Forest, they must necessarily appear at the First Day of the Sessions, as aforesaid, otherwise their Liberties will be seised into the Hands of the King, as forfeited, for not claiming the same.

6. So if one, who dwelleth out of the Forest, hath a *Profit apprender* out of any Land, or any Office within the Forest, or any other Privilege or Liberty there, he must appear on the first Day of the *Sessions*, and put in his Claim; otherwise, such Office, Privilege or Liberty will be seised into the King's Hands for Non-claimer.

7. And in these Cases he is bound to take Notice of a General Summons, though he live out of the Forest.

8. For, if a Man hath two Houses, one within, and the other without, the Forest, and the Owner dwelleth sometimes in one and sometimes in the other, and probably may be dwelling in that *out* of the Forest, at the Time when the *General Summons* is made; yet he must appear before the Justices of the Forest upon such *General Summons*;

mons; and this was the Opinion of Mr. *Hesket* in his Reading.

9. 2d. In some Cases those who dwell within the Forest are not compellable to appear upon such *General Summons*; *viz.* All those who are under the Age of 12 Years, though they have likewise Lands of Inheritance within the Forest. *Stat.* 52. *H.* 3. *cap.* 26.

10. So those who are sick or blind, those who are 70 Years of Age, or upwards, *Stat. W.* 2. *cap.* 38. Those who are employed in the Service of the King in any other Place; in such Cases they may have the Writ *Warrantia diei* to excuse their Appearance.

11. So though an Archbishop or Bishop hath Lands within the Forest, he is not bound to appear upon the *General Summons*. *Hesket*, *fo.* 8.

12. And yet the Words of the Summons are, *viz. Præcipio quòd summoneas per bonos Summonitores omnes Archiepiscopos, Episcopos, Comites, Barones, Milites & eorum liberos Tenentes, qui terras aut tenementa habent infra metas forestæ Domini Regis, &c.*

13. But all *Spiritual Persons* are exempted, by the Statute of *Marlbridge*, to serve on Juries; yet their Tenants shall appear upon this *General Summons*, if they dwell in the Forest; and if they neglect, they shall be amerced. *Treberne*, *fo.* 8.

14. Neither shall *Earls and Barons*, who have Lands within the Forest, and *dwell out* of it, be compelled to appear upon this *General Summons*, because they are not to be put upon any *Enquests*.

15. But *Archbishops*, *Bishops*, *Earls*, and other *Noblemen*, who *claim* any Liberties, Freedoms or Privileges within the Forest, must appear upon such *General Summons* to claim the same: Otherwise such Privileges, *&c.* will be seised into the King's Hands for *Non-Claimer*; but they need not appear in *Person*, but by *Attorney*.

16. The

16. The Tenants of ſuch Noblemen and Knights, and all other free Tenants, who dwell within the Foreſt, muſt appear; but Women who are free Tenants, and the Servants of thoſe who dwell in the Foreſt, ſhall not appear; for 'tis ſufficient if the Maſter appear, and not his Servant. *Quia ille eſt ſub manupaſtu alterius*, &c.

17. So that Knights, as aforeſaid, and thoſe who are Freeholders dwelling within the Bounds of the Foreſt, although they are Spiritual Perſons and dwell out of the Foreſt, yet they muſt appear on the Firſt Day, before the Chief Juſtice in Eyre, at the Seſſions of the Foreſt, upon ſuch *General Summons*, notwithſtanding the Words of the Statute; *viz. Qui manent extra foreſtam*, &c. For though they dwell out of the Foreſt, yet becauſe they have Lands within the Foreſt, the Law doth account them reſiant where their Lands are; for otherwiſe the Seſſions could not be held, nor Juſtice done in Trials of Liberties and other Things concerning the Foreſt. *Itin. Pick. fo.* 6.

18. So that all Perſons who have to do within the Foreſt, as well Spiritual as Temporal, muſt appear; and for not appearing, the *Abbot of Weſtminſter* was amerced; and ſo was *Jiffery Lucy*, a great Lord. *Jones Rep.* 275. and the Americiament ſhall be affeered. *Itin. Pick. fo.* 6.

19. The Reeve of every Town in the Foreſt, and four Men with him, muſt appear likewiſe on the Firſt Day, or they ſhall be amerced, and their Americiaments ſhall be affeered.

Of Appearance in Proper Perſon, by Attorney, by Guardian, &c.

20. All Perſons who are bound to appear upon a *General Summons*, in reſpect of their *Lands* which they

they have in the Forest, to serve there upon Enquests, must appear in *proper Person.*

21. But those who are bound to appear, in respect of any Claim of *Liberties* or *Privileges*, may appear, either in proper Person, or *by Attorney.*

22. It appeareth by the *Assises and Iters of the Forests of Lancaster and Pickering*, that those who are impleaded for Trespasses done within the Forest may appear,

1. *In proper Person*,	3. *By Guardian*,
2. *By Attorney*,	4. *By Procbein Amy.*

23. It was Mr. *Hesket*'s Opinion, That upon a Bill, Presentment, or Indictment, for a Trespass done in the Forest, the Defendant may appear either in proper Person or by Attorney; but this Appearance by Attorney must be enter'd at the Court of *Attachments*, or at the *Swanimote*, and not at the *Justice-Seat.*

24. For every Offender, who is bound to appear there, to answer any *Trespass* done in the Forest, must appear in *proper Person*, because, in such Trespasses, the King is Party, that is, he is Plaintiff; and therefore it is holden for Law in 20 *Ed.* 3. That in Trespass, where the King is Party, the Defendant must appear in *proper Person*, and not by Attorney; and so must all Offenders who have been presented at the *Swanimote Court.*

25. In many Cases the Defendant may appear in proper Person or by Attorney; as for instance, If a Man commit a Trespass in the Forest *after* the Court of Swanimote is holden, and *before* the Justice-Seat is kept, and is there presented, he may appear either in Person or by Attorney, and traverse the Presentment; for this shall not be said to be *Præsentatum per Forestarios, & convict. per Viridarios*,

Viridarios, unless the same was presented at the *Swanimote* according to the Ordinance of the Forest, *Anno* 34. *Ed.* 1. 4 *Inst.* 297. 20 *Ed.* 3.

26. For any Person who makes any Claim to Privileges or Liberties in the Forest, may, at the First Day of the Eyre, appear in Person or by Attorney. *F. N. B.* 26. *G.*

27. But all those who are mainprised or bail'd until the General Sessions of the Forest, must appear in Person, and not by Attorney.

28. In some Cases the Appearance may be by *Guardian* or *Prochein Amy*; as if an Infant is impleaded before the Chief Justice in Eyre for a Trespass done in the Forest, he may appear in proper Person and shew that he is under Age, and pray the Chief Justice that *I. P.* may be assigned for his Guardian, or if he doth not appear in Person, but the said *I. P.* appeareth for him, and sheweth he is an Infant, and prayeth he may be admitted as Guardian, the Court will admit him accordingly.

29. And if an Infant hath chosen his Guardian, who is afterwards sick, or will not appear before the Justice-Seat; yet if the Infant appears and prayeth that *I. S.* may be admitted for him as *Prochein Amy*, he will also be admitted according to that Prayer.

30. If a Man is attached for a Trespass in the Forest, and finds *Pledges* to appear at the next General Sessions; there the Defendant as well as the *Pledges* must appear in *Person*, according to the Opinion of Mr. *Hesket*, *fo.* 11. *Quia principales debitores & plegii sunt equales ad debitum Regis, sed aliter de aliis debitoribus*: And if the *Pledges* appear, and not the Defendant, they shall be imprisoned for his Default until they have made Fine for it; but if the Defendant himself appear, and is ready to

receive his Judgment and pay his Fine, the *Pledges* are excused.

31. But if he doth not appear, and if the *Pledges* are bound in a certain Sum for his Appearance, then, though the *Pledges* appear, yet the Sum in which they were bound, is forfeited for the Default of the Defendant.

32. But in such Case the King cannot have Execution against them presently for the Sum so forfeited; but there must be a *Sci' Fa'* against them, to shew Cause, why the King should not have Execution of the said Sum; to which they may appear, and plead either in Bar, though the Default doth appear by Matter of Record, or any other Matter, to save the Default of the Defendant.

33. For in every Case, upon a *Sci' fa'*, the Defendant may plead *special Matter* in Avoidance thereof, as well as upon any Original Process.

34. If the *Pledges* do not appear, in such Case they shall be *amerced*, but not *fined*.

35. If the 4 Men and the Reeve of any Town make Default in appearing upon the first Sitting of the Justice Seat, the whole Vill shall be amerced; but if, after *Appearance* and an *Adjournment*, they or any of them, make Default, then he or those who made such Default, shall be *amerced*. *Jones*, 279.

36. If any Officer make a *Deputy*, he ought to appear at the Justice Seat; and it must be enquired, if such *Deputy* make Default. *Jones's Rep.* 275.

37. A Forester in Fee *in jure uxoris*, may appear by Attorney, at the Justice Seat, *ad faciendum omnia quae Forestario incumbunt durante itinere*; *Assis. Pickering*, *fo.* 2.

38. Note, the *Prior of St. John of Jerusalem* did make his Claim by one of his Confriers, whom he made his Attorney, being a *dead Person in Law*.

Assart.

Assart.

See { *Charge, in Chief Justice*, 4, 47.
Nusance, 9.
Purpresture, 43, 44.
Regarders, 28.
Assisa Forestæ, 4. }

1. THis Word was first used in *England*, by *William the Conqueror*; 'tis a *French* Word, and comes from *Assartir*, or, as my Lord *Coke* tells us, *Essarter*, which signifies, to make plain, or grub up; and from hence is derived the barbarous *Latin* Word *Assarto*, which is, to pull up by the Roots, *Assartare enim est densas Silvas eradicare & in culturam redigere*; so that *Assart* is to destroy any Covert, by the rooting it up and to make it plain Ground. The *French* Word now is *Arracher*, which is *Eradicare* or *Eruncare*: In the Writ of *ad quod damnum*, in the Register, 'tis *Assertare*, and not *Assartare*, as 'tis in *Budæus in* 2 *Lib. Philologiæ*: And some are of Opinion it comes from *Ad* and *Sero*, to Sow.

2. *Assart* of the Forest is described *in Libro Rubro Scaccarii*; viz. *Quando forestæ nemora vel dumeta, pascuis & latibulis ferarum opportuna, succiduntur, quibus succisis, & radicibus evulsis, terra subvertitur & excolitur. Hesket*, *fo.* 20.

3. So in the *Register*, *fo.* 257. *Assart* is, where a Man doth fell and destroy his Woods, and convert the Soil, where they did grow, into Tillage: The Words are, *viz. Mandamus vobis, quod per Sacramentum, &c. Inquiratis, si sit ad dampnum, seu nocumentum forestæ nostræ prædictæ, aut alicujus alterius, si concedamus A. quòd ipse arbores in Bosco suo de M. qui est infra metas forestæ nostræ prædictæ, succidere, & eas, quo voluerit, cariare, ac commodum*

 suum

suum inde facere, & solum illud postmodum assertare, & in culturam redigere, ac parvo fossato & bassâ hayâ, secundum Assisam forestæ includere.

4. So that if a Man hath any Woods or Underwoods, or any other Coverts in the Forest, as Heath, Broom, Fern, and he cut it down, or pull it up by the Roots, that the Land is made plain, or converted into Arable or Pasture, then 'tis called *Assart* of the Forest, or Land assarted, though the Owner receive no Profit by it. *Hesket*, *fo.* 20, 21.

5. Mr. *Hesket* was of Opinion, That if a Man hath Meadow or Pasture Ground in the Forest, which is surrounded with thick Coverts where the Wild Beasts of the Forest frequent, if the Owner or Tenant, or other Occupier thereof, convert the same into Tillage, 'tis an *Assart* of the Forest, or Land assarted. *Hesket*, *fo*. 20.

6. And the Difference between a *Waste* of the Forest and an *Assart* is this; *viz.* A *Waste* is the *felling* or cutting down any *Covert* of the Forest without *Licence*; but an *Assart* is the *destroying* a Covert, and converting it into Plain or Arable Land.

The Forfeiture and Punishment of Assarting his OWN *Woods and Lands in the Forest.*

7. As no Man may *assart* without the King's Warrant, so the Ground, so *assarted*, is not *forfeited* to the King; but it shall be *seised* into his Hands, until redeemed by a Fine. *Hesket*, *fo*. 30.

8. So if a Man do assart a Covert, without Licence of the King, or the Chief Justice in Eyre; and, afterwards, if the Owner die before 'tis presented, the Land so assarted shall be *seised* into the King's Hands, until the Heir redeem it by a Fine: But if neither the Owner, whilst living, or his Heir

Heir afterwards, will redeem it, it shall remain with the King for ever.

9. In the *Assises of Pickering*, 8 *Ed.* 3. it appeareth, that Lands assarted were *seised* into the King's Hands, but afterwards redeemed by the Owners paying a Fine.

10. But the Laws of the Forest appoint no certain Sum for a *Fine*; therefore 'tis arbitrary at the Discretion of the King, or the Chief Justice in Eyre; but usually he doth assess the *Fine* according to the Number, Goodness and Value of the Acres assarted; therefore in every Indictment or Presentment made of any *Assart* or *Waste* in the Forest, the Number and Value of the Acres ought to be expressed.

11. In the new Assizes of the Forest, *Anno* 6. *Ed.* 1. *cap.* 4. *& in Rastall. Tit. Forest.* 21. it is ordained, *Quòd si quis inventus fuerit in Dominico Domini Regis assertando vel purpresturam faciendo, Corpus debet protinus retineri; si autem extra dominicum infra Rewardum, debet poni per sex plegios; si autem aliàs inveniatur, debet duplicare ejus plegios; si tertio, corpus debet retineri*; and such an Offender, for the third Offence, is not, by the Laws of the Forest, bailable by any Man, but only by the Lord Chief Justice in Eyre, or his Deputy.

12. By the Assises last mentioned, it appears, that there is a difference between *assarting* the King's Woods and Lands, and the *assarting* those of other Men; for he who is found assarting the *King's Lands*, is to be committed for the first Offence without Bail, (except delivered by the Chief Justice in Eyre, or his Deputy) till he hath paid a Fine to the King; but he who is found assarting the Lands of a *Common Person* in the regard of the Forest, is bailable for the first and second Offences, but not for the third; for in such case his Body shall be imprisoned until he hath paid a Fine to the

King, unless the Chief Justice in Eyre will bail him as aforesaid.

13. It was adjudged in the *Assizes of the Forest of Pickering*, 8 *Ed*. 3. in fo. 25. and 18. of the said Assizes, and in the case of the *Prior of St*. John *of* Jerusalem, That no man may assart his own Lands in the Regard of the Forest, without a special *Licence* from the King so to do; and if he doth assart them without such Licence, he shall pay a grievous Fine to the King; and if he will still continue them so assarted, then he must compound with the King or Chief Justice in Eyre, to pay a yearly Rent to the King for the same, which must be entered on Record at the time the Rent is set.

14. And likewise, fo. 7. and 11. of the said Assizes, it was adjudged, That he who is presented to have assarted or inclosed any Lands in the Forest out of the King's Lands, either is his own Fee, or in the Fee of any other Man, shall be fined for this Offence; and if he will compound with the King or Chief Justice, he may continue them so assarted, paying an yearly Rent, which must be entred in manner as aforesaid.

The Forfeiture or Punishment for assarting the King's Lands.

15. By the New Assizes of the Forest made 6 *Ed*. 1. *Artic*. 4. and in *Rastal*, *tit*. *forest*, *fo*. 21. 'tis ordained, *Quod si quis inventus fuerit in dominico Domini Regis assertando, vel purpresturam faciendo, corpus debit protinus retineri*, &c. as aforesaid.

16. That is, He shall be committed to Prison, there to remain till he hath paid a *Fine* to the King; and by the ancient *Iters* of the Forests of *Pickering and Lancaster*, *fo*. 35. 8 *Ed*. 3. in the case of *Gilbert de Acton*, the Fine, in such cases, shall be double as much as for the like Offence in his *own Woods* or Lands, and

yet,

yet, in both cases, the Fine is arbitrary; for 'tis a bolder Offence to make an Assart or Purpresture in the King's Lands, than in his *own*, and therefore to be more severely punished; which is the reason, that he who is actually taken, either in making Assart or Purpresture in the King's Lands, shall not be bailed for the first Offence; but he who assarts his own Lands, shall be bailed, both for the first and second Offence, but not for the the third, as aforesaid.

Attachment Court.

See *Presentment*, 1, 2, 3.
Regarders, 28.
Assisa Forestæ, 4.

1. THIS is one of the three Courts of the Forest, and 'tis held for the Foresters to bring in their Attachments, concerning any Hurt or Injury done *in viridi & venatione* in the Forest; and for the Verderers to receive and enroll the same; and this Court being held by the *Charter* of the Forest, *ad videndum Attachiamenta*, 'tis therefore called, *The Court of Attachments*.

2. By the aforesaid *Charter*, this Court is not to intermeddle with any thing but such which concerns an Injury or Hurt done, or to be done, to the *Vert* or *Venison*; for their Authority is *tàm de viridi quàm de venatione*; and the Foresters bring in their Attachments as well of the one as the other, which the Verderors are to receive and enroll.

3. But this is only a Court of *Enquest*; for an Offender cannot be *convicted* here, neither can he be attached by his *Body*, but by his *Goods*, unless he

he is actually taken committing the Offence in the Forest. 1. *inst*, 289.

When and how often this Court is to be kept.

4. Before the making *Charta Foresta*, this Court of Attachments was held very often, but at no certain time, only at the Will and Pleasure of the chief Officers of the Forest.

5. To remedy this Inconveniency, 'tis provided by that Charter, That, *singulis quadraginta diebus per totum Annum conveniant Forestarii & Viridarii*, to hold this Court; and therefore 'tis by some called *the Forty Days Court*, which before was called *the Woodmote-Court*, *Charta de Foresta cap*, 8. *Co.* 4, *Inst*. 289.

6. So that the time of holding this Court being limited by this *Charter* or Statute, *viz*. That it shall be kept every *Forty Days* throughout the Year, it hath been adjudged, that if 'tis kept at any other time, either sooner or later, then the keeping such Court is void.

7. Yet I am of Opinion, that the Proceedings in such Court are not void in Law; for if there are Presentments then made, and afterwards those Presentments do proceed to the Swanimote-Court, and then the Defendant takes Exception to them, because they were first made at a Court of Attachment not held according to the time limited by the Statute, such Exception shall not be allowed; because the Court of Attachment doth not proceed *judicially*, but only to receive the Presentments and cause them to be enrolled, in order to deliver them to the next Swanimote-Court; So that the receiving a Presentment or Attachment at such an irregular Court will not make it void; for if it had not been made there, 'tis still good in Law,

Law, though 'tis not presented until the next Swanimote-Court, and not before.

8. But if a Court of Attachments is held contrary to the Statute, and a Forester hath attached an Offender in the Forest, either by an Ox or Horse, to appear at such Court before the Verderors, and he doth not appear, so that the Court doth adjudge the Beast forfeited for this Default, and appoints it to be sold, and the Money paid to the King, this Proceeding is void in Law, because the Court did proceed *judicially*, which they ought not to do. *Hesket*, *fo.* 13.

9. Yet, in some cases, this Court of Attachments may be kept either sooner or later than the *Forty Days*, and yet, according to the Statute; as if the fortieth Day is upon *Christmas*-Day, or on a *Sunday*; in such case it may be held on the Day following.

10. But where it is said, that the Court of Attachments doth not proceed in a Cause *judicially*, it must be intended where the Value of the Trespass is above 4 *d.* for in such case it must be enrolled in that Court by the *Verderors*, and sent from thence to the *Swanimote*, to be tried there according to the Laws of the Forest; but if the Trespass is *under* the Value of 4 *d.* the Court of Attachments may determine the same, that is, the Verderors may assess the Fine, and cause the same to be levied to the use of the King, which must be entered on the Roll.

Of

Of the several Kinds of Attachments of the Forest.

11. There are Three manners of Attachments of the Forest.

Either { 1. *By Goods and Chattels.* 2. *By the Body, Pledges and Mainprise.* 3. *By the Body without Pledges.* }

12. If any Offence is done in the Forest, in any manner of *Underwood, Bushes, Furze,* or other thing called *Nether-Vert,* the Forester may attach the Offender by his Goods, to appear at the next Court of Attachment, in the same manner as the Sheriff doth attach the Goods of any Person at Common-Law, either in an Action of Debt, or Trespass, to appear at the County-Court.

13. After the Attachment is made, the Forester must acquaint the Owner of the Goods, for what cause they are attached, and require him to appear at the next Court of Attachments, and to find *Pledges* to answer the Offence; and in the mean time the Forester must keep the Goods attached until the next Court of Attachments, and then he is to bring them before the Verderors, and to present the Offence, and to shew them the Goods attached.

14. And if the Defendant doth not then appear, the Goods so attached are forfeited, and shall be sold, and the Value answered to the King; and the offender shall be attached again *in infinitum,* until he appear and put in Sureties to answer the Offence at the next Justice-Seat of the Forest, and then his Goods must be re-delivered to him.

15. The like Attachments of Goods may be made for all manner of small Trespasses in the Forest, and for most Trespasses in *Vert* or *Venison,* if

if the Defendant is not *actually* taken committing the Offence; for in such case the Forester may attach the Body, and compel the Offender to come before the Verderors at the said Court of Attachments, there to find Sureties to answer the same at the next Justice-Seat of the Forest, before the Chief Justice in Eyre.

16. (2) The Second manner of Attachment is, by the *Body*, by *Pledges*, and by *Mainprise*; and this is where the Forester doth take an Offender *actually* committing any Offence in *Vert*.

17. So if he is making Assarts or Purprestures in the King's Lands or Woods, there the Forester may attach him by *his Body*, and make him find *Pledges* to answer the Offence at the next Court of Attachments, and upon his Appearance there, to be *mainprised* until the coming of the Chief Justice in Eyre.

18. This manner of Attachment is warranted *per Consuetudines & Assisas Forestæ, Articulo* 1. viz. *Si forestarius invenerit aliquem attachiabilem pro viridi in forestâ nostrâ, primò debet ipsum attachiare per duos plegios, &c.* And if the same Offender is taken the second time, then the Forester shall attach him by the *Body*, and cause him to find four *Pledges* to appear at the next Court of Attachments, then and there to be *mainprised* until the General Sessions of the Lord Chief Justice in Eyre.

19. The Words are these; viz. *Si idem inveniatur aliàs, debet ipsum attachiare per quatuor plegios*; And if the third *time*, then the Forester shall attach him by *the Body*, and cause him to be brought before the Verderors, there to be mainprised by eight Pledges.

20. And in all cases where the Offender is to be attached by the *Body and Pledges*, he must be taken *actually* doing the Offence: This appears by the Statute 1 *Ed*. 3. *Cap*. 8. which hath made some

Alteration

Alteration in the Statute 6 *Ed.* 1. *de Assisis & Consuetudinibus forestæ*; viz. It directs in what Manner and Form the Offender, either in *Vert* or *Venison*, shall be indicted, and before whom, and that if any Man is indicted in other manner, that the Indictment shall be void. 7 *R.* 2. *Cap*, 4.

21. And further, 'tis by the same Statute enacted, That no Man shall be taken or imprisoned for *Vert* or *Venison*, unless he be taken *with the Manner*, or indicted after the Form therein specified.

22. So that now, by these Statutes, 1 *Ed.* 3. *cap.* 8, & 7 *R.* 2. *Cap.* 4. If the Offender is not taken *actually* doing the Trespass, then the Forester cannot attach him by *the Body*, or imprison him to find Sureties; but he may be attached by his *Goods* in such manner as before is mentioned.

23. (3) The third manner of Attachment for Offences in the Forest, is to attach the Offender by *the Body only*, without any Pledges or Mainprise; and this is warranted *per Assisas & Consuetudines Forestæ*, and confirmed by the Statute 1 *Ed.* 3. *cap.* 8, and 'tis there declared, that Offenders may be so attached in Six Degrees of Offences in Forests.

24. The First Degree is mentioned *in Assisa & Consuetudine Forestæ*, *Art.* 1. viz. *Postea, post tertium Attachiamentum corpus debet attachiari & retineri, & memoria habeatur quid sit Virid.* &c. For that if an Offender hath been taken *actually* doing an Offence in the *Vert* in the Forest, and hath been delivered by two Pledges, and for the second Offence hath been delivered by four Pledges, and for the third Offence by double that Number; then, if he be taken the fourth time, he shall be attached by *the Body, and imprisoned without Bail*, except he hath the King's Warrant to be bailed, or be delivered out of Prison by the Lord Chief Justice in Eyre, or the chief Warden of the Forest.

25. The

25. The Second Offence for which a Man is to be attached by *his Body without Bail* is mentioned in the said *Assises, Articulo* 4. viz. *Si quis inventus fuerit in Dominico Domini Regis assartando vel purpresturam faciendo, corpus debet protinus retineri.*

26. So that if he is taken *actually* making any Purpresture in the King's Woods, *his Body* shall be taken and detained in Priso nwithout Bail, unless delivered by the King's special Warrant, or by the Chief Justice in Eyre, or chief Warden of the Forest.

27. The Third Offence is likewise mentioned in the said Assizes, and in the 4th Article; *viz. Si autem extra dominicum infra rewardum, debet poni per sex plegios; & si aliàs inveniatur, debet duplicare ejus Plegios; si tertiò, corpus debet retineri*: So that if a Man is found in the Forest the third time assarting, or making any Purpresture in the King's Woods or Lands, he shall be attached by *his Body*, and committed without *Bail* until delivered as aforesaid.

28. The fourth Offence in *in Assisa & Consuetudine Forestæ, Articulo* 5. viz. *Si quis attachiabilis fuerit contra vadios & plegios, debet distringi per catalla sua infra metas Forestæ inventa; si autem defecerint, corpus ejus detineatur quousque fecerit quod debuerit*: So that if a Man hath been an Offender in the Forest in *Vert*, and bound to his good Behaviour, and afterwards is taken *actually* committing the like Offence, and hath no Cattle in the Forest by which he may be attached for the same, then *his Body* shall be attached and detained in Prison, till he hath done what he ought to do by Law.

29. And such an Offender is called *contra Vadios & Plegios*, because he offends contrary to his Sureties and Pledges, and he shall not be delivered out of Prison, but as aforesaid.

30. The Fifth Offence is for *Venison*, and 'tis mentioned in the said *Assises, Articulo* 10. viz. *Si quis ceperit feram sine Warranto in Foresta, corpus*

suum

suum arrestetur, ubicunque inveniatur infra metas Forestæ; & quando captus fuerit, non deliberetur sine speciali præcepto Domini Regis, vel capitalis Justiciarii Forestarum suarum.

31. And in the same *Assises*, *Articulo* 11. viz *Si quis viderit aliquos malefactores infra metas Forestæ aliquam feram capere vel asportare, debet illos capere secundum posse suum, & si non possit, debet levare hutesium & clamorem, &c.* So that a Person killing a Deer in the Forest, or carrying it away, without Warrant so to do, he shall be attached by *his Body*, and imprisoned as aforesaid, without Bail, *&c.* until he is delivered as aforesaid.

32. The Sixth Offence is mentioned in the Statute 1 *Ed.* 3 *cap.* 8. and this is either in *Vert* or *Venison*, the Words are; *viz. No Man shall be taken nor imprisoned for Vert or Venison*, unless he be taken *with the Manner*, or else *indicted* after the Form specified in the same Statute.

33. This is a Negative pregnant; for that if the Offender be indicted after the Form therein mentioned, and before such Officers as therein appointed, then, if such Offender is attached by *his Body*, either by the Forester or Sheriff, having a Warrant for that purpose from the Lord Chief Justice in Eyre, or from the chief Warden of the Forest, or his Deputy, he shall be committed without Bail, until delivered as aforesaid.

34 The same Law where an Offender in the Forest is *outlawed* for the like Offence, and *his Body* is afterwards attached by the Sheriff by vertue of a *Capias Utlagatum.*

35. And the Law is, That in every case where the Offender is to be attached by *the Body only*, without Pledges or Mainprise, he is not to be bailed by the Verderors, nor by the Foresters, or any other Officer of the Forest, without the King's special Command, or by the Lord Chief Justice in Eyre, or

or the Chief Warden of the Forest: The Words of the Statute are,

36. "No Man shall be taken or imprisoned for "Vert or Venison, unless he be taken with the "manner, or else indicted after the Form before "specified; and then the Chief Warden of the "Forest shall let him to Mainprise till the Eyre of "the Forest, without taking any thing for his De- "liverance: And if the Chief Warden will not do "so, he shall have a Writ out of the Chancery, "which hath been, in old time, ordained for such "Persons indicted, to be at Mainprise till the "Eyre; and if such Chief Warden, after he hath "received the Writ, do not incontinently deliver "such Persons indicted to Mainprise, without ta- "king any thing, then the Plaintiff shall have a "Writ out of Chancery to the Sheriff, to attach the "said Warden to be before the King at a certain "Day to answer, wherefore he hath not replevied "him who is so taken; and the Sheriff and the "Verderors being called to him, shall deliver him "so taken by good Pledges in the Presence of the "Verderors, and shall deliver the Names of the "Mainpernors to the same Verderors to answer "to the Eyre of the Justices; and if the Chief "Warden be thereof attainted, the Plaintiff shall "recover his treble Damages, and the said Warden "be committed to Prison, and ransomed at the "King's Will; and from henceforth it shall be "written to them as to the chief Warden of the "Forest, because they may not be Justices, nor "have any Record.

37. 'Tis to be observed upon this Statute, That the Sheriff is to let him to *Mainprise* by the *King's Command*, that is, by the *King's Writ*, for otherwise he cannot do it.

38. And

38. And the Verderors in this case are but Assistants to the Sheriff; for they have not a joint Authority with him to let the Person to Mainprise, because the Writ is not directed to them, but to the Sheriff alone.

39. 'Tis true, the Writ is, That the Sheriff shall let him to Mainprise *in presentiâ Viridariorum*, because that the Verderors being Judges of Record, the Names of the Mainpernors must be delivered to them.

Bail.

See { *Attachment*, 35. *Swanimote*, 6, 7. *Appendix*, Stat. 1. Ed. 3.

1. THE Words *Bail and Mainprise* being often mentioned in the *Assises of the Forest*, it may be proper to shew the Difference between those Words.

2. *Bail* is where an Offender *traditur in Ballivum ad salvum custodiend. semper in eorum custodiâ quibus traditur usque ad diem, &c.* Now in such case the Person is always accounted in Law to be in their actual Custody till that time, and they may keep him so in Custody if they will; for he cannot properly be said to be at Large or at Liberty.

3. And this manner of *Bail* is when any Man is *attainted of a Trespass* in the Forest, and is taken in Execution of the same; then the Lord Chief Justice in Eyre may let him to *Bail*, and the Entry is, *I. S. traditur in Ballivum* O. S. *corpus pro corpore usque*, &c. and in this case *Mainprise* doth not lie, and the Person thus bailed must be in proper Person; and none can let such an Offender to *Bail*,

but the Chief Justice in Eyre; 'tis true the *Chief Warden* may let a Trespasser in the Forest to *Mainprise* by virtue of the Statute, 1 *Ed*. 3. *cap*. 8. but not a *Man attainted* of a Trespass there. *Hesket*, *fo*. 11.

4. *Mainprise* is *quasi manucaptus & liberatus ad largum usque ad diem*, *&c*. and in such case the Offender is always said to be at large until the Day of Appearance.

How and before whom the Person is to be bailed.

5. In all cases where a Man is to be attached by his *Goods* or Chattels, which is the first manner of Attachment, or by his *Body*, *by Pledges and Mainprise*, which is the second manner of Attachment, the Verderors are the proper Officers to take the *Recognizance*, because they are Judges of Record, and have the keeping the Rolls for Matters of the Forest till the coming of the Lord Chief Justice in Eyre; and such *Recognizance*, with Pledges, is not to be taken by the Foresters, because they are not Judges of Record; their Office is to accuse the Offenders, and to present their Offences before the Verderors.

6. Besides, the Verderors are usually Men of Learning in the Laws of the Forest, and it seems necessary they should be so, because Offenders are to be bailed and mainprised according to the Quality of their several Offences; in some cases by two Pledges, and in some by four or more, and in some cases no Bail at all is to be taken, as may be seen in the precedent Title.

7. Now if the Foresters, or other Officers, who are ignorant of the Laws of the Forest, should take upon them to bail such Offenders, great Inconveniences might follow by letting those to *Bail* who are not bailable by the Laws of the Forest, and by

denying *Bail* to those who are bailable; therefore the Law hath provided a Steward, who must be learned in those Laws, to join with the Verderors, and to direct them in their Proceedings.

8. When the Persons are thus bailed by the Verderors, they are to keep the *Recognizance* for the use of the King till the coming of the Lord Chief Justice in Eyre; they are likewise to cause the Foresters to present the Offence in the same Nature it was done, and to enter such Presentments on the Rolls.

9. The Verderors may likewise, if they think fit, take an Obligation or Bond of the Offender with Sureties; which Bond being made to the King's use shall have the same Force and Efficacy, as any Recognizance acknowledged according to the Statute of 33 *H.* 8. *cap.* 39.

10. Likewise, if the Foresters might bail such Offenders, there would be great Partiality therein, and many Trespasses concealed from the King, and no Presentments made thereof, either before the Verderors at the Court of Attachment, or at the Swanimote-Court.

11. Upon the whole matter, he who is taken *actually* doing *Assart* or *Purpresture* in the King's Woods or Lands, is not *bailable* even for the first Offence; but he who doth the like Trespass in his own Freehold or Land, may be bailed for the first or second Offence, but not for the third.

12. If an Offender or Trespasser in a Forest is apprehended by a Forester *in the manner*, either chasing or killing a Deer, he may be arrested and committed to Prison, but he may be bailed upon giving sufficient Sureties to appear at the next Eyre, and if such Bail is refused, he may, if in Term-time, move the Court of *King's-Bench* for an *Habeas Corpus*, which will be granted *ex merito justitiæ*, or he may move the Court of *Common-*

Pleas, or *Exchequer* (if privileged) or the Court of *Chancery*, either in or out of Term, and upon this Writ he may be bailed to appear at the next Eyre to be holden for the Forest.

The Entry of the Bail is in this manner;

13. *Compert. est per rotulos Viridar. istius Forestæ quòd Edmundus Hastings postquam transgressus est de Venatione in Forestâ illâ dimissus fuit coram eis per Manucaptores, &c. qui manuceperunt habend. eum hic, &c. primo die itineris, qui modo eum non habent, &c. Ideo, &c.*

14. But though a Forester cannot take Bail, he may detain a Man till he gets Bail. *Pasch.* 45. *Ed.* 3. *fo.* 7. *placito* 8. *viz.* An Action of Trespass was brought against a *Forester* for taking and imprisoning the Plaintiff at such a Place; the Defendant pleaded, That he was *a Forester in Fee* of the Forest of *W.* and that at a certain Court of Swanimote holden for that Forest, the Plaintiff was presented by the Foresters, Verderors, Regarders and Agistors, *&c.* for chasing and taking a Deer in the Forest; whereupon the Defendant came to the Plaintiff, and desired him to find Pledges to answer the said Offence in Eyre, which he refused; by reason whereof he detained him in his Custody *quousque*, *&c.* and Issue being taken upon this Plea, it was found for the Defendant.

15. He may likewise be bailed by virtue of a Writ, *De homine replegiando*, directed *Custodi Forestæ*, if he was arrested by the Officers of the Forest for *hunting*, &c. and was indicted or presented for the same, as taken *with the manner*; and in this case he must find twelve Pledges, but if he is adjudged by the Justices in Eyre, he cannot be bailed by that Writ.

16. Where a *Writ de homine replegiando* is directed to the *Sheriff*, he is restrained by the Statute, *W.* 1. *cap.* 15. to replevy any Man imprisoned for the Forest, being taken *with the Manner*; which Statute doth not extend to the *Writ de homine replegiando*, directed *Custod. Forestæ*, *&c.*

Beadle.

See { *Distress*, 1. 8. *Forester*, 25. *Scotale*, 2. }

1. IN *Chartá de Forestâ*, *cap.* 7. there are these Words, *Nullus forestarius nec Bedellus*, *&c.* which imply, that the Beadle is an Officer of the Forest; his Business is to give notice of the time when the Courts of the Forest are to be kept, and also to make all manner of Proclamations as well in Court as out of it, and also to execute all the Process of the Forest; he is like a Sheriff's Bailiff in the County, for his Office is almost the same in the Forest.

2. And although this Statute mentions only a Forester and Beadle, yet it extends to all other Officers of the Forest; for it was made to redress a general Mischief, and therefore it shall not relate only to part, but to the whole, like the Statute which mentions only the Warden of the Fleet, yet the same extends to all other Prison-Keepers as well as to him, because it was made to redress a general Mischief.

Boundaries of the Forest.

See { *Chief Justice*, 15.
Charge, in Chief Justice, 7.
Hunting, 60, 61.
Appendix, in Stat. 17. Car. 1.
Appendix, Assisa Forestæ, 19.

1. FOrests must be meered and bounded with *unremoveable Marks, Meers and Boundaries*, either known by matter of Record, or by Prescription; for though a Forest doth lie open and not enclosed with Hedge, Ditch, Pale or Wall, yet in the Eye of the Law it hath as strong an Enclosure by these Marks, Meers and Boundaries as if it was enclosed with a Wall.

2. These Marks, Meers and Boundaries are unremoveable, because the King hath an Interest in them; for 'tis established as a Law, *Secundùm assisam Forestæ quòd omnes meræ Forestæ sunt integræ domino Regi*; so that they who remove them are punishable for the same by *the Assises of the Forest*.

3. Besides, some of these Boundaries are unremoveable in themselves, because they are such things which cannot be removed, as *Rivers*, *High-ways*, *Hills*, and such like; and for want of such Boundaries, great and remarkable Trees have been used for the same, but that is very seldom.

4. These Words, *Marks*, *Meers and Boundaries*, are often used in the old Perambulations of the Forest made *Anno* 29. *Ed*. 1. which were made by Men of great Judgment and Learning; and to signify the difference of such things as are Boundaries of the Forest, they used these Words, *Secundùm metas, bundas & meras pred.* where, by the Word *Meta*, they seem to understand a *Mark*; for any thing which ascends upward in height they

called a *Mark*, as, for instance, a Hill, a Church, a Tree, or such like; by the Word *Bunda* they understand any thing by which the Forest is bounded, which is a Level, and not higher in View than the Soil of the Forest itself, as a *River* or *Highway*, or the like.

5. By the Word *Mera*, they understand the Distance between the Forest and the Soil of other Men, whereon any thing stands which is a Mark of the Forest, in which *Mark* the King hath no Interest in the thing itself; for notwithstanding it is said that *omnes metæ Forestæ sunt integræ domino Regi*, yet that must be understood of such things which give any Shelter or Succour to the Wild Beasts of the Forest, and not otherwise.

6. For if a Dwelling-house, or a Mill, or such like, be a Mark of the Forest, yet the King shall have no Interest in it, because those are Marks rather *in Terrorem*, than any Succour, Covert or Relief for the Wild Beasts.

7. Wherefore there must necessarily be a Distance and Place between the Forest and such things; which Distance is called a *Meer* of the Forest.

8. In some Preambulations they use only these Words; *viz. Per Metas & Bundas*; by which is understood all manner of *Marks*, *Meers and Boundaries* whatsoever.

9. These *Marks*, *Meers and Boundaries* of the Forest are known either by Prescription or by matter of Record, or both.

10. For all those Forests which were newly enlarged by the Afforestation of *H.* 2. *R.* 1. or King *John*, have their Marks, Meers or Boundaries known by matter of Record, because Perambulations were made of them in the Reign of *Ed.* 1. in order to be disafforested.

11. But all such which were antient Forests before the Reign of *H.* 2. and where no Perambulations

tions were made since that time, because the People who dwell near such Forests had no Cause to complain that their Lands were afforested as the other had, the Marks, Meers and Boundaries of such antient Forests are known only by *Prescription.*

12. If it should be objected, that the King cannot make a Forest, but by matter of *Record*, 'tis true he cannot, but he may have a Forest by matter of Record whose *Boundaries* are known only by *Prescription*; for when these antient Forests were made, the Boundaries were known by matter of *Record*; but that being so long since, and the Nation having been often involved in many Wars and Troubles, the Records are all lost.

13. The newest Forest in *England*, except that of *Hampton-Court*, is in *Hampshire*, and 'tis called the *New Forest*, and yet that Forest was made in the Reign of *W.* 1. and there is no other of which the Beginning is mentioned in any History or Record.

14. The Forest Laws are likewise as antient as the Forests, except some few which have been altered and made more beneficial to the Subject by *Charta de Foresta*, and other later Statutes.

15. My *Lord Coke*, 2 *Inst.* 318. gives us a different Account of *Meets*, *Meers and Boundaries*, for he tells us, That *Meets* are either inclusive as *Ways*, *Rivers*, &c. or exclusive, as *Churches*, &c. that *Mera* is derived from the *Greek* Word Μείρω, which is to divide or bound; that *Bunda* is derived from the *Saxon Bunna*, which signifies a higher Thing, as *Hills*, *Houses*, *Trees*, &c. and *Marchia* is derived likewise from *March*, *Saxonicè*, now called a *Mark*, *sed meta accipitur pro quocunque termino, limite seu fine.*

16. And as 'tis necessary that every Forest should be bounded, so 'tis very requisite that the Boundaries should be generally known, especially

by those who are Officers of the Forest; for if a Man is presented for killing a Beast, 'tis very material that the Place should be distinctly known where the same was killed; for though it might be a Wild Beast of the Forest, yet if it was killed out of the Limits thereof, it may be no Offence against the Forest Laws.

17. So when the *Regarders* proceed to view the Forest, and to see whether any Spoil is made in the Woods and Coverts, and to enquire of all such Articles which they are bound by their Oaths, and by the Duty of their Office to do, 'tis necessary they should know the Limits of the Forest, for otherwise they may make Inquisitions where they ought not to come.

18. *In Charta Forestæ, Artic.* 2. there are these Words; viz. *Homines verò, qui manent* Extra Forestam, *non veniant de cætero coram Justiciariis nostris de foresta, per communes summonitiones*, &c. where by these Words *Extra Forestam*, it may be inferred, That every Forest must have certain *Boundaries*, that it may appear who dwell within those Limits, and who not.

19. So in Statute 21. *Ed.* 1. there are these Words; viz. *Si quis forestarius* in Balliuâ suâ *malefactores aliquos invenerit vagantes*, &c. if they would not yield themselves, but fly or resist, and are killed, the Forester shall not be guilty of Murder; for, in this Case, the Limits of the Forest are issuable, because the killing of the Offender within the Limits of the Forest, or without, makes it Felony or not; therefore the Boundaries ought to be certainly known. *Magna Charta* 117. *b. Rast. Tit. Forest.* 19.

20. But now, by the Statute 17 *Car.* 1. *cap* 16. the *Meets*, *Limits*, *Meers* and *Boundaries* of all Forests shall be taken, adjudged and deemed to extend no farther than they were commonly re-

puted

puted, known, used or taken to be, &c. in the 20th Year of King *James*, and not beyond in any wise, any Perambulations, Presentments, Extents, Surveys, Judgments, Records, Decrees or other Matter or Thing to the contrary notwithstanding.

That all Meers and Bounds of the Forest do belong to the King.

21. 'Tis established as a Law, *Secundùm assisam Forestæ, Anno* 6. *Ed.* 1. *Quòd omnes metæ forestæ integræ sunt Domino Regi. Articulo* 21.

22. But my Lord *Coke* tells us, this must be understood *quoad jurisdictionem & imperium, & non quoad Dominium*, 2 *Inst*. 318. Therefore as the Boundaries must be apparently known, so the Law hath vested an Interest in the King, that they should not be removed or defaced by Fraud.

23. In the *Assises of Pickering*, *Anno* 8. *Ed*. 3. *fo*. 11. it was adjudged, that a Man may not fish in a River which is a Boundary or Meer of the Forest, without a Warrant for that Purpose, because 'tis Parcel of the Forest, and because 'tis a Meer, therefore it belongeth to the King.

24. The *Abbot of Whitby* killed an Hart within the River of *Derwent*, which was within the Meers of the Forest of *Pickering*; and he and his Company being indicted, *Quia ceperunt unum cervum in aqua de Dervent, quæ est Marchia forestæ, & venationem illam secum asportavit*, he was fined and bound to his good abearing of the Forest.

25. If a Deer is chased in the *Purlieus*, and gets into a *Meer* of the Forest and is there kill'd, the Owner of the Dog must not have the Deer, because the *Meer* of the Forest is Parcel thereof, and the Deer was there privileged before the Dog did seise or kill it; for as soon as his Feet were within the *Meers* of the Forest, and before the Dog had hold

hold of it, 'tis the King's Deer and in his Protection, and whoever meddles with it is a Trespasser of the Forest.)

26. So if any Man hunt or kill the King's Deer in any part of a *River*, *Highway*, &c. being an inclusive Boundary of the Forest, he is as great an Offender as if he had hunted and killed in the midst of the Forest, though the Estate or Interest of the Soil of the Highway be in other men. 2 *Inst*. 318.

The Difference between infra Regardum Forestæ *and* infra Metas Forestæ.

27. These Words are often mentioned in the new Ordinances of the Forest, made *Anno* 6 *Ed*. 1, *Rastall Ab. Tit. Forest*. 21. but there is a wide Difference between them.

28. For a thing may be done, *infra metas forestæ*, and yet *extra Regardum*; but it cannot be done *infra Regardum*, but the same must necessarily be *infra metas forestæ*, as for Instance;

29. In the 3d *Article* of the said Ordinances, the Words are, *Si quis inventus fuerit extra dominicum boscum, & infra regardum*, cutting down an Oak standing out of the King's Woods, *& infra Regardum, &c.* There those Words cannot be taken in any other Sense, but that the Oak must stand *infra metas forestæ*.

30. But in the 5th *Article* the Words are, *viz. Si quis attachiabilis fuerit contra vad. & pleg', debet distringi per catalla sua* infra metas *forestæ inventa, &c.* Now in such case an Offender may have Cattle distrainable, which are *infra metas*, and yet *extra Regardum forestæ*; as if the Cattle were in Woods or Grounds, which the King, by some Grant or Charter, had exempted from the Charge of the Forest. See the Ordinances *in Tit. forestæ*, 3, 4, 5, 10, 11, 12, 15, 17.

31. For

31. For in the Time of *Ed.* 1. when *Hugh De Spenser* was Chief Justice in Eyre of all the King's Forests, *Ultra Trentam*, when the Perambulations of the Forests were made, there were several Woods within the Limits of the Forest exempted out of the *Regard*,: This appears by the Claims and Charters shewed and pleaded in several *Iters*.

32. And I have seen the like of several Forests, *Citra Trentam*, in the Reign of *Ed.* 1. when *Adam de Valentia*, Earl of *Pembroke*, was Chief Justice in Eyre of all those Forests: So that there are some Woods within the Bounds and Limits of the Forest which are not part of the Forest itself.

33. As for instance, *Walwood* in *Essex* was formerly within the Forest of *Waltham*, and yet no part of the Forest, nor within the *Regard* thereof.

34. So likewise *Havering* Park is *infra metas forestæ de Waltham*, but yet out of the *Regard* thereof, and no part of the same.

35. So if a Man hath a Manor to which a Wood doth belong, which is *infra metas forestæ*, or inclosed in the Forest, and yet such Wood is out of the *Regard* of the Forest, in this case he must make his Claim in these Words; viz. *Gilbertus de Acton clamat tenere Boscum suum de Trovesdale, pertinen' ad manerium suum de B. extra regardum forestæ*, viz. *illum Boscum, qui est ex parte Boreali*, &c. And so recite all the Limits and Boundaries thereof.

36. But all such Woods and Lands which are *Parcel* of the Forest, are within the *Regard* thereof, and all such as are within the *Bounds* of the Forest, and no part thereof, are out of the Regard.

37. *Docent nos mensores agrorum tria esse agrorum genera.* 1. *Divisum & assignatum quem limitatum vocat Florentius jurisconsultus, quia manufactos limites pro finibus habet.* 2. *Assignatum per universitatem sive mensurâ comprehensum, putà per Centurias & jugera.* 3. *Arcifinium qui inde dictus, docente Varrone, quòd fines*

fines habet arcendis hostibus idoneas, id est, naturales, ut sunt flumina & montes : Grot. de jure Belli & pacis. Lib. 2. *pag.* 3. *sect.* 16.

38. The Grand Jury, Verderors, Regarders and other Officers of the Forest of *Waltham*, had formerly *presented* the Meets and Bounds of that Forest to be from *Bow-Bridge* to *Lateward-Bridge*, and from *Stanes-Street* to the *Thames*; and, many Years afterwards, there being some Controversie about the *Boundaries* of the Forest, a Justice-Seat was held at *Stratford-Langton, Anno* 10. *Car.* 1. before the Earl of *Holland*, Chief Justice in Eyre, assisted by the Lord Chief Justice *Fynch*, Justice *Jones* and *Vernon*, and *Barkeley*, and Baron *Trevor*; and upon due Consideration had of several Records, it was adjudged, That the *Meets* and *Bounds* ought to be settled according to that *Presentment*, not meerly because they were presented so to be, for they all agreed, that the *Presentment* might be *traversed*; but for the Reasons following, they were of Opinion, that a *Traverse* was not to be allowed against them.

39. *ss.* 'Tis enacted by the Statute, *Charta de Forestâ*, That all other Mens Woods (but the King's) which were afforested before the Coronation of *H.* 2. were to be viewed by good and lawful Men, and then *statim disafforestentur.*

40. So that before the Disafforestation 'tis expresly required, that the Woods should be viewed by good and lawful Men: This was essential and necessary in order to the Disafforestation.

41. Now upon the Construction of the Statute, it was requisite there should be a Commission out of Chancery; and by vertue thereof, a Verdict being found, upon the Oath of twelve men, or more, which were the *Meets* and *Bounds* of the Forest, and that Commission and Verdict being returned into Chancery, and confirmed by the King,

King, and a Proclamation being made for the Disafforestation according to the Inquisition; then such Lands and Woods which were other Mens Lands and Woods, and which were afforested, *statim disafforestentur*, and until that was done the Lands continued Forest still.

42. But if, at the Time of the Afforestation, any Lands were the King's, and afterwards aliened from the Crown, before that Statute was made, they were not to be disafforested.

43. Now since the Statute enacts, that other Men's Lands shall be disafforested, and that to be upon a Perambulation and View as aforesaid, the Subject may demand a Writ of Perambulation *de jure*, and the King in Justice cannot deny it; for when a Thing is granted, all Things which conduce to the obtaining it, are in like manner granted.

44. So that when a Perambulation is duly made, returned and proclaimed, the same is peremptory and binding against the Subject; and if it was not right and truly made, the Subject would not, *de jure*, claim, or demand another, but the King might grant another, *ex gratia*; and after the same was executed, it would take away the Force of the first, though it was against the King himself; but if there had been no Perambulation at all, the same continueth Forest still, and the Subject may, at this very Time, demand a Writ of Perambulation *de jure*.

45. The Judges having agreed upon these Preliminaries, declared their Opinion, with Application to the Case in Question.

46. *ff*. There was a *Perambulation* of this Forest duly made and returned, *Anno* 12. *H.* 3. within three Years after the making of *Charta de forestâ*; which Perambulation did agree with this very *Presentment*; and this is binding to the Subject until

set

set aside by a subsequent Perambulation duly made and returned.

47. 'Tis true, there was another Perambulation made *Anno* 28. *Ed.* 1. and returned into *Chancery*, which took away from the Forest many things contained in the first Perambulation, and this was confirmed in Parliament; but by a subsequent Statute made *Anno* 34. *Ed.* 1. which was now produced and exemplified under the Great Seal, that second Perambulation was repealed and revoked: And for a further Confirmation thereof, a Judgment was produced in *B. R. Anno* 2. *R.* 2. in a case between the Bishop of *Winton* and others, where, in the Pleadings, it appeareth, that the Statute 34 *Ed.* did repeal the former Statute, *Anno* 28. *Ed.* 1. and then consequently the former Perambulation, *Anno* 12. *H.* 3. must be revived and continue in Force, and is peremptory, and cannot be traversed.

48. Neither can the Subject demand a new Perambulation *de jure*, but the King may grant one *de gratiâ*; so Judgment was given by the Chief Justice in Eyre, that the Meets and Bounds of this Forest should be according to the Perambulation of 12 *H.* 3.

49. Some Discourses there were amongst the Judges, whether a Perambulation allowed by the King, was not peremptory, as well to him as to the Subject, but they differed in Opinion as to that Matter.

Bridges in Forests.

See { *Nusance*, 3. 13.
Wood, 51.

IN *Itinere Windsor, Jones Rep.* 279. one *Clifton* was presented for selling and carrying away seven Timber-Trees: He shew'd to the Court, That they were felled to repair some Bridges in the Forest which the King ought to repair, and that the Lops were sold to pay for the Workmanship, which was affirmed by the Verderors to be so employed; and yet for the undue way of taking them he was fined 5 *s.*

In eodem itinere, fo. 273. it was presented, that *Lodden Bridge* in the Manor of *Sunningbill* was in decay, which the King used to repair as Lord of the said Manor, the greatest part whereof was conveyed to Mr. *Halstead*; and the Attorney-General *Noy* moved, that he might be indicted to make him repair it *ratione tenuræ*, for the King doing it before as Lord of the Manor, they that have the said Manor now must do it.

Mr. *Halstead* shewed that many others had purchased part of the Manor Lands which are liable to these Repairs, and desired he might have Contribution of them; and then he would repair; but it was answered, That the Court might compell him alone, and he is to seek his Remedy at Law for Contribution, and they are not to suffer the Bridge to be out of Repair till it be disputed and determined between him and others, whether they are to be contributary or not: And this was Mr. *Newly*'s Case for *Bow-Bridge* in *Waltham*-Forest, who was fined 100 *l.* for his Neglect, and ordered to repair it, and committed till he paid his Fine, which was ordered towards the Repair of the

the Bridge, though there was, at that very Time, an Order in the Court of *Exchequer* for him to have Contribution, and Suits likewise depending there for that Purpose, for Bridges are of Necessity, and may not expect Ends of Suits, but must have present Repairs.

Mr. *Halstead* offered to enter into Bond to repair it sufficiently by a certain Day, which the Court accepted, and ordered the Verderors to view the Repairs, and gave him leave to sell Timber in his own Woods for that purpose.

Buck.

The Buck is the first Beast of Chase, and is called,

1	*Year*	*a Fawn.*	4	*Year*	*a Sore.*
2	*Year*	*a Pricket.*	5	*Year*	*a Buck of the first Head.*
3	*Year*	*a Sorel.*	6	*Year*	*a Buck.*

THIS Season beginneth at *Midsummer*, and lasteth till *Holy-Rood*-Day.

The Terms of Hunting are,

A Brace or Lear of Bucks.
Dislodge the Buck.
A Buck groaneth.
A Buck goeth to Rut.

His Treading or Footing is called, the View.

His Tail is called, the Single.

The round Roll of the Horn next the Head is called the Burr.

The main Horn is called, the Beam.

The lowest Antler is called, the Branch.

The

The next are Advancers.
The next Palm.
And the top is called Spellers.
The Ordure is called Feumets or Feumishing.

Chase.

See { *Buck*, 1.
Common, 13.
Dogs, 41, 42, 43.
Forest, 7, 8, 33, 37, 38, 39, 43, 83, 87, 90, 92, 93, 95.
Hunting, 28.
Wood, 23, 31.

1. A Chase, in one Degree, is the same as a *Park*, only a Park is enclosed, and a Chase is always open: It differs from a *Forest* in three Things; *viz.* in particular Laws, in particular Officers, and in certain Courts, which are incident to a Forest, for the better Execution of those Laws.

2. For a *Chase* hath no particular Laws proper to it alone; and therefore all Offenders in Chases are punishable by the Common Law, and not by the Laws of the Forest.

3. Neither hath a Chase any such Officers as a Forest, for it hath neither *Verderors*, *Foresters*, *Regarders* or *Agistors*, but only Keepers and Woodwards.

4. Neither hath it any Courts of Attachment, Swanimote nor Justice-Seat, and those Officers which are called Keepers in a Chase, are called Foresters in a Forest.

5. And those Chases which never were any part of the Forest can have no Purlieus, and consequent-

ly the Case in *Dyer* 326. must be mistaken. 4 *Inst.* 303.

6. The Liberty of a *Free Chase* is next in degree to a *Forest*, but that being the highest and greatest Franchise, doth comprehend a *Chase*, a *Park*, and a *Warren*; and for that Cause the Beasts of Chase, and the Beasts and Fowls of a Warren, are privileged within the Forest; but a Chase is not a Forest, 'tis only a part of it; and therefore the killing, hurting or hunting any of those Beasts or Fowls of Chase, Park or Warren within the Boundaries of the Forest, is a Trespass against the Laws thereof, and to be punished by those Laws only.

Which are Beasts of Chase.

7. The Book called, *Antiquitas Britannia*, fo. 43. tells us, That there are five Wild Beasts called Beasts of Chase; *viz.* The Buck, the Doe, the Fox, and formerly the Martern and the Roe, of which there are none now in *England*.

8. *Hollingshed*, in his Description of *England*, *fo.* 206. *b.* and the Book of St. *Alban's*, *fo.* 30. and Serjeant *Fleetwood* in that Collection which he publish'd of the *Forest Laws*, all agree in this.

The Difference between Beasts of Chase, and those of the Forest.

9. As there is a Difference between a Forest and a Chase, so there is between the Beasts of Forest and of the Chase.

10. The Beasts of the Forest are *tantum sylvestres*, but those of the Chase are *Campestres tantum*. *Treberne*, fo. 8. *Hesket*, fo. 8. 11.

11. The Beasts of the Forest frequent the Coverts in the Day, and feed on the Lawns, Meadows and Pasture-Grounds in the Night, and therefore they

they are called *Sylvestres*, because they are oftner in the Woods and Coverts, than in the Plains.

12. The Beasts of the Chase frequent the Fields, Hills and Mountains in the Day-time, and the Valleys, Corn-Fields and Meadows in the Night; and therefore they are called *Campestres*, because they frequent the *Fields* more than the Woods.

13. As there may be a Liberty within a Liberty, so a Man may have a Chase in the Forest; and if the Owner of such Chase kill or hunt any Stag or Red Deer, or any other Beast which is a proper Beast of the Forest, he is finable. *Jus* 1274.

14. And if a Man hath a Chase adjoining to a Forest, if he deny the Keepers of the Forest to fetch back the Hunted Stag, this is finable: but Red Deer may be in a Chase by special Claim.

The Petition of the Bishop of Coventry *and* Litchfield *against the Justices of the Forest, and Judgment for a Free Chase.*

" Rogerus Covent' & Litchfield' Episcopus queritur Domino Regi de hoc, quod in ultimo itinere Roger' extran', & sociorum suorum Justic' Domini Regis de Foresta, in Com' Stafford; iidem Justic' boscos ipsius Episc' de maneriis suis de Cannock & Ruggelegh, in manu Domini Regis seisire fecerunt, & in manum Domini Regis adhuc detinent injuste, & ad gravamen per num suum, & exhaeredationem Ecclesiarum suarum de Covent' & Litchfield manifestam, &c.

" Et Rogerus, & alii Justic' socii sui, hoc Recordantur quod in itinere praedict' per viridar' forestar', & alios fideles Domini Regis, quam eis praesentatum fuit, quod praedict' Episcopi per Dominum Regem, & progenitores suos per ipsum

" sum Episc' & prædecessores suos purprestabantur,
" & à tempore quo, &c. bene licet Justic' de forestâ in itineribus suis purpresturas super Dominum Regem aut progenitores suos factas infra bundas Forestæ suæ per Assisam Forestæ in fine itineris sui capere in manum Domini Regis, & retinere, & ea ratione boscos præd' eò quod non sunt infra bundas Forestæ, & super Dominum Regem & Progenitores suos purprestabantur, ut præd. est, in manum Domini Regis seisire fecerunt, &c.

" Et Episc' bene cognoscit quod bosci præd' sunt infra metas Forestæ, sed dicit quod Dominus Rex Ricardus consanguineus Domini Regis nunc dedit, & chartâ suâ confirmavit Ecclesiæ beatæ Mariæ, & beati Cedde de Litchfield, & Hug' quondam Episc' Coventr' prædec' suo & successoribus suis Villam de Ruggelegh, & Villam de Cannock, cum Ecclesiis hundr' & omnibus aliis libertatibus & pertin' suis, habend' & tenend, in liberam puram & perpetuam eleemosynam per chartam suam quam profert in hæc verba.

" Ricardus Dei Gratia Rex Angliæ, &c. Archiepisc' Sciatis nos dedisse, & hac præsenti chartâ nostrâ confirmasse, pro Redemptione peccatorum nostrorum, &c. & pro anima Patris nostri, & Parentum nostrorum, Ecclesiæ beat' Mariæ & beati Cedde de Litchfield, parchamentum primum & Hug. Episc' Coventr' & successoribus suis Episcopis Coventr' Villam de Ruggelegh, & Villam de Cannock, cum Ecclesiis, hundredis, & omnibus libertatibus, & pertin' suis, habend' & tenend' in liberam puram & perpetuam eleemosynam. Quare volumus & firmiter præcipimus quod præfatus Episc' & omnes sui successores post eum habeant & teneant præd' Villas in puram & perpetuam eleemosynam

" cum

"cum Ecclesiis, hundredis, & omnibus aliis pertin'
"suis cum sacha & socha, thol & theim infangene-
"thief, & benè, purè, liberè, quietè, integrè &
"plenariè & honorificè in bosco & plano in pratis
"& pascuis, & pastur' vivar' & stagnis, & mares-
"cis in aquis, & molendinis, in viis, in semitis, in
"homagiis & releviis, in serviciis & omnibus aliis
"rebus, & locis in burgis, & extra burgam, &
"cum omnibus libertatibus, & liberis consuetud'
"suis. Testibus, &c. Dat' per manum Willi. Eliensis
"electi, 4. die Decemb. Anno Regn nostri primo.

"Præterea, idem Dominus Rex Ricard' con-
"cessit, & chartâ suâ confirmavit præd' Hug' præ-
"dic', &c. Ut omnia maneria sua, & omnes ter-
"ræ suæ, & omnes homines sui, & omnia ma-
"neria, & omnes terræ, & omnes feodi Ecclesiæ
"Coventr' & Litchfield, de Cestr' & Salop, & de
"Gnowesal, & omnium Ecclesiarum suarum libera
"essent in perpetuum, & quieta de Foresta, & de
"placitis Forestæ, de vastis, & assartis regardis Fo-
"restæ, per quandam aliam chartam quam profert
"in hæc verba.

"Ricardus Dei Gratia Rex Angliæ, &c Archie-
"pis', &c. Sciatis nos concessiisse, & præsenti Char-
"tâ nostrâ confirmasse dilecto, & familliari nostro
"Hug. Coventr. Episcopo, & succ' suis Episc.
"Coventr' ut omnia maneria sua, & omnes terræ
"suæ, & omnes homines sui, & omnia maneria
"omnes terræ & omnes feodi Ecclesiæ de Co-
"ventria & Litchfield, & de Cestria & de Sa-
"lop. & de Gnowesal, & omnium Ecclesiarum
"suarum in perpetuum libera sint & quieta de
"murdro, & latrocinio, & Shir' & hundr' & de
"sectis Shir' & hundr' & auxiliis vic' de Foresta, &
"placitis Forestæ de vastis & assartis rewardis Fo-
"restæ, & omn' aliis operibus tam Castellorum
"quam vivariorum & stagnorum, & omnibus placi-
"tis, & omnibus querelis. Quare volumus, & firmi-

"percipimus ut omnia maneria, & omnes terræ, "& omnes feodi præd' Episc. & successorum ejus, "ac præd' Ecclesiarum inde in perpetuum libera "sint, & quieta. Testibus, &c. Dat. per manum "Will' Eliensis Electi Cancellarii, Anno Regni "nostri primo apud Cantuar. 30 die Novembris.

"Unde dic' quod ipse & prædec. sui à tempore "præd' Hug' & post confectionem præd' carta- "rum tenuer' præd' boscos quietos de Forestâ, "Forestariis, Viridariis & aliis ministris Forestæ "Domini Regis, usque ad ultimum iter præd'. "Idem etiam Episcopus quæsitus siquid clamet in "venatione præd' boscorum dicit, quod omnes "prædec' sui, & ipse similiter post confectionem "præd' Chartarum, venari solebant in præd' boscis, "& capere & fugare pro voluntate sua feras in "eisdem boscis de Foresta Domini Regis venient' "usque ad prox. iter præd' & petit quod Domi- "nus Rex velit permittere ipsum & Ecclesias suas, "uti & gaudere statu, & libertatibus quibus hacte- "nus ipse & prædecessores sui, ut de jure Eccle- "siarum suarum usi sunt, & per præd. concessiones "prædicti Regis Ricardi antecessoris sui, &c.

"Et præd' Justiciarii dicunt quod Dominus "Henricus Pater Domini Regis nunc, post con- "fectionem præd' Chartarum Domini Regis Ri- "cardi fuit in seisina præd' maneriorum & bosco- "rum; & super hoc scrutatis rotulis & brevibus de "Scaccario de tempore præd' Henrici Regis inve- "niunt brevia subscripta, &c.

"Henricus Dei Gratiâ Rex Angl' Dominus "Hib' & Dux Norman' & Aquit' Comes Ande- "gaviæ Vic. Staff' salutem. Scias, quod reddimus "venerabili Patr. à Coventr. & Litchfield Episc' "maneria Cannock & Ruggelegh, quæ Rex Ri- "card' Avunculus nost' dedit bonæ memoriæ Hug. "de Nonant quondam Coventr. Episc, & ideo tibi "præcipimus, quod de præd. maneriis ipsi Episc'

"plenam

" plenam seisinam habere facias. Teste me ipso
" apud Waltham, 17 die Aprilis, Anno Regni,
" nostri quartodecimo.

" Henricus Dei Gratia, Rex Ang. Dominus, Hib'
" & dux Norman' & Aquit' & Comes, Ande-
" gaviæ Baronibus suis de scaccar' salutem Com-
" putate Vic' nostri Stafford in firma Com' sui tri-
" ginta solidos, & sex denar. Blanc' de mediet'
" Anno Regni, 14. pro manerio de Cannock, &
" de Ruggelegh, quæ reddimus venerabili Patri
" à Coventr. & Litchfield Episc. Computate etiam
" eidem Vic' sexag & unum solid' blanc' de
" Regn. nostro 15. pro eisdem maneriis, & sic de
" anno de cætero, &c. Teste meipso apud Wal-
" tham 17. die Aprilis, Anno Regni nostri quarto-
" decimo.

" Et quia præd. Charta per quam præd. Rex
" Ricardus dedit præd. maneria de Ruggelegh, &
" Cannock præd. Hug. Episc & successoribus suis
" posterioris datæ est, quam sit Charta ejusdem
" Regis, per quam ipse Episcopus clamat ipsa, &
" omnia maneria sua, terras & homines suos esse
" quietos de Foresta, prout per datas earundem
" patet; Nec idem Episcopus alia maneria sua seu
" terras clamare potest esse quieta de Foresta
" quàm illa quæ tempore confectionis illius Char-
" tæ fuerunt in seisina præd. Hug. Episcopi datus
" est dies præd. Episc' de audiend' judicio suo à die
" Paschæ in unum mensem ad Parliamentum, &c.
" Et idem Episcopus ponit loco suo Gilbertum de
" Kirkby, vel Robertum de Pipe. Et præceptum
" est per Dominum Regem, quod Regin. de
" Grey, Bogo de Knovil, & Ricardus de Hole-
" brook, interim inquirant per quas metas & di-
" visus prædicti bosci prædict maneriorum divi-
" duntur ab aliis boscis qui sunt Baronia ipsius
" Episc. & similiter à Foresta Domini Regis di-

" stinct' & appert', & planè certificent Dominum
" Regem ad eundem terminum, &c. Et Dominus
" Rex præcipit quod bosci præd' interim remane-
" ant in eodem statu quo nunc sunt, &c. Postea ad
" Parliamentum ipsius Domini Regis apud West-
" mon' post Pascha, Anno Regni nunc Regis de-
" cimo octavo, venit præd' Episcopus in propriâ
" personâ suâ, & reddidit ipsi Domino Regi præd'
" boscos, ut jus Domini Regis, & idem Dominus
" Rex de gratiâ suâ speciali concessit & dedit eos-
" dem boscos præd' Episc' per easdem metas bun-
" das & divisus, per quas ipse Episcopus & prædec'
" sui à tempore confectionis præd. Chartæ præd'
" Domini Regis Ricardi boscos illos tenuerit, ha-
" bend' & tenend' eidem Episc. & succes' suis, &
" Ecclesiæ suæ, sci' Cedde de Litchfield, in libe-
" ram, puram, & perpetuam eleemosynam, ut li-
" beram Chaceam in perpetuum. Ita quòd bene
" licet ipsi Episc' & succes' suis boscos illos inclu-
" dere, & inclusos tenere, & parcos inde facere
" pro voluntate suâ absque hoc quod saltatoria
" faciant in iisdem, seu rechia habeant ad vena-
" tionem ipsius Domini Regis de Foresta sua ca-
" piend' & ita quod bosci illi omnino quieti sint
" de Foresta, & de placitis Forestæ, & quòd nec
" Justic' ipsius Domini Regis seu Sen. de Foresta
" qui pro tempore fuerint Forestarii, Virida-
" rii, Agistatores, Regardatores seu alii ministri
" quicunqne fuerint in Boscis præd' per metas,
" bundas & divisus supradictas se aliqualiter intro-
" mittant seu officium suum exerceant quoquo mo-
" do, licèt præd' bosci sub suis metis, bundis, &
" divisis præd' fuerint infra antiquas metas Forestæ
" ipsius Domini Regis de Cannock: Et pro hac,
" &c. idem Episcopus cognovit se tenere Domino
" Regi in mille libris stirlingorum. 4 *Inst*. 302.

Chief

Chief Justice in Eyre.

1. THE Chief Justice of the Forest is an Officer of great Honour and Authority, and the Office is to be executed by a *Peer* who is always of the Privy Council.

2. There is but One Chief Justice on this side *Trent*, and he is called *Justiciarius itinerans Forestæ, &c. citra Trentam*; and there is another called, *Itinerans omnium Forestarum, &c. ultra Trentam*, who, as my Lord *Coke* tells us, is commonly a Man of greater Dignity than Knowledge in the Laws of the Forest; and therefore where Justice Seats are to be held, some other Persons, whom the King shall appoint, are associated to him, who, together, are to determine *omnia placita Forestæ*, with a Patent of *si non omnes*, and a Writ *de admittendo*, and then the Chief Justice in Eyre and those Associates are *Capitales Justiciarii Forestæ*, so called in respect of the Verderors and others, who, to some Purposes, have judicial Places. 4 *Inst*. 314.

3. *Anno* 10 *Car*. 1. a Justice-Seat was held at *Dean* for the Forest of *Dean* in *Gloucestershire*, before Justice *Jones*, Baron *Trevor*, and Serjeant *Bridgman*, being deputed by the Earl of *Holland* Chief Justice in Eyre, and at the Return of the Summons *Bridgman* adjourned the Court to *Gloucester-Castle*, and the Chief Justice in Eyre being there present, and the said Judges and Serjeant being commanded by the King, by a Letter under his Sign manual, to attend to give their Advice in Matters of Law, the Earl's Commission was read and the Letters enrolled, and the Officers of the Forest, and the Reeve and the four Men were called, who, together with the Foresters, were of the Petty-Jury, and a Grand-Jury was sworn of the County, and *Jones* gave the Charge, and the Verderors presented their

Rolls,

Rolls, and the Offenders were fin'd by the Chief Justice according to their Offences

4. When any such Peer is made Chief Justice in Eyre of the Forest by the King's Commission, he hath as great Authority as any other Justice in Oyer, and more; for then he may punish all Trespasses of the Forest according to the Laws of the Forest, and may hear and determine all Claims of Liberties and Franchises, as to have Parks, Warrens, *&c.*

5. He may also determine all Claims to be quit of *Assarts*, and *Purprestures*, the Claims of Leets, Hundreds, Felons Goods, Waifs and Fugitives, and all other Liberties within the Forest, and likewise of those who claim to kill Hares and other Beasts of *Chase* there, for Men may justifie the doing many Things in the Forest by lawful Claims, which would be otherwise unlawful for them to do; but then those Claims must be such which have been allowed before the Justice in Eyre within the time of Prescription: And if a Justice-Seat do Wrong or any Injustice, by allowing a Claim where it ought not, the Record may be removed by *Certiorari*, (which, in the Forest Law, is called a *venire facias Recordum*) into the *King's-Bench*, there to be determined. 4. *Inst*. 294. And if the Court will not allow a lawful Claim, the Party grieved may have a Writ *de Libertatibus allocandis* directed to the Justices of the Forest. 4 *Inst*. 237. and in case of an erroneous Judgment, a Writ of Error lies.

6. The Justices of the Forest may punish those who are indicted at the Swanimote, and presented before them at the Sessions, and this by Fine and Imprisonment at their Discretion.

7. And such an Indictment shall not be traversed because it is presented by more than twelve Persons.

8. But

8. But other Justices in Oyer and Justices of Peace, cannot determine Trespasses done in Forests, though such Trespasses are presented before them by way of Indictment; so if they intermeddle in such Cases, the Party may traverse the Indictment, which he could not do if it was taken in the *Swanimote*.

9. He hath likewise an absolute Authority to determine all Offences either in *Vert* or *Venison*; and those cannot be determined before any other Justices, excepting those who have a Commission under the Great Seal to assist the Chief Justice in Eyre in that Place.

10. This appeareth by *Charta Forestæ cap.* 16. viz. *Nullus Constabularius, Castellanus vel Ballivus teneat placita de Foresta, sive de viridi, sive de venatione; sed quilibet forestarius de feodo attachiet placita de Foresta, tam de viridi quam de venatione, & ea præsentet viridariis provinciarum, & cum irrotulata fuerint, & sub sigillis viridariorum inclusa, præsententur capitalibus Justiciariis nostris de Foresta, cum in partes illas venerint ad tenendum placita forestæ, &* coram eis terminentur: By which last Words all other Justices are prohibited to hear and determine Offences of the Forest.

11. For this Statute is in the *Negative* of the Common Law, and so taken by all the Judges, *Anno* 21. *H* 7. *fo.* 22. where the Case was thus.

12. ¶. In Trespass *de Malefactoribus in parcis*, the Plaintiff declared, that the Defendant *intravit in quandam forestam*: And it was the Opinion of the Court, that the Action did not lie, unless the Trespass had been done in a Park; for the Statute of *W.* 1. *cap.* 20. extends only to *Parks*, and must be taken in the strictest Sense.

13. So Trespasses which are done in a *Forest* are punishable only by *Charta Forestæ*, and by no other manner.

14. From

14. From which it may be inferred, That the Statute *de Malefactoribus in parcis* doth not extend to a *Forest*; and therefore that Statute which was made to reform Injuries done in the one, doth not extend to punish Trespasses done in the other; and if Trespasses done in a *Forest* are punishable only by *Charta Forestæ*, and not in any other manner, as it appears in *cap*. 16. then Offenders in the Forest must be punished according to that Statute.

15. So likewise, *Anno* 21. *H*. 7. *fo*. 30. a Man was indicted before the Justices of Peace for killing an *Hart proclaimed*; and the Indictment was challenged, because it did not set forth in what Place the Proclamation was made, nor in what Place the Hart was kill'd; for if it was kill'd without the *Boundaries* of the Forest, it was no Offence, but lawful for him to do it: And *Fineux*, Chief Justice, who gave the Rule of the Court, was of Opinion that this Matter might be pleaded to the Jurisdiction of the Court, because it was to be determined by the Justices of the Forest, and not elsewhere.

16. From which it may be likewise inferred, that Offences committed in the Forest are to be tried by the Justices of the Forest, and the Offenders are to be punished by the Forest-Laws *only*; because those Laws are appointed for that Purpose, and differ from all other Laws.

17. (2) If a Man hath committed an Offence in the Forest, either in *Vert* or *Venison*, and is indicted for it before any other Justices than the Justices of the Forest, or in any other Place, then he may plead that Matter to the Jurisdiction of the Court, and shew that the Offence was done in such a Forest, and that 'tis determinable before the Justices of the Forest, and not elsewhere.

18. Moreover, by the Statute *de Ordinatione Forestæ*, it appeareth, That all Proceedings against Offenders for Things done in the Forest, are void, if such Proceedings are had in any other Place

 than

than before the *Chief Justices* of the Forest. See *Kellewey*, *fo.* 150.

19. He is to make out his Warrant or Precept directed to the Sheriff of the County in which the Forest is, and where the *Justice-Seat* is to be holden; thereby commanding him to *summon* all Archbishops, Bishops, Earls, Barons, Knights and other their free Tenants who have any Lands or Tenements within the Bounds of the Forest; and to summon four Men and the Reeve, and also out of every antient Borough within the Bounds of the Forest, twelve good Men and other Freeholders, who ought to appear before the Chief Justice in Eyre, that they should accordingly appear on a particular Day.

20. He is likewise to command the Sheriff openly to proclaim in all Boroughs, Towns, Fairs, Markets and other publick Places throughout the County, that all Persons who *Claim* to have any Grants of *Liberties*, *Franchises* or free Customs in the Forest, to appear before the Chief Justice in Eyre, or his Deputy, at the said Day and Place, to shew what Liberties they claim; and that all Persons who are attached for *Vert* or *Venison* in the Forest after the last Court, and all Pledges and Manucaptors who were bound to appear, that they should appear accordingly: And that the Sheriff with his Bailiffs be there also to certifie what they had done, and also to execute the Office of a Sheriff in these and such like Matters concerning the same, the Form of which Precept is as follows:

The Form of the Precept or Warrant of the Chief Justice in Eyre.

21. *ss. Thomas Lovell nobilis ordinis Garterii miles, Justiciarius Itinerans omnium forestarum Domini Regis in Angliâ, tam citra Trentam quàm ultra, Vic. Essex Salutem: Ex parte dicti Domini Regis tibi*

præcipio,

præcipio, quòd summoneas per bonos summonitores, omnes Archiepiscopos, Episcopos, Abbates, Priores, Comites, Barones, Milites, & eorum liberos tenentes, qui terr' aut tenementa habent infra metas forestæ Domini Regis de Waltham in Com' Essex, & de qualibet villa & villata infr' easdem metas, quatuor homines, & propositum, & de quolibet burgo infra metas ejusdem forestæ duodecim probos & legales homines, & omnes alios qui coram Justiciariis placita forestæ ten' venire solent & debent, quòd sint apud Waltham die Lunæ prox' post festum sancti Petri Apostoli proxim' futur', coram me præfat' Justic' Itinerante, vel meo in hac parte deputato, audituri & facturi ea quæ ad placita forestæ ibidem pertinent. Et ulterius tibi præcipio, quòd per totam ballivam tuam, viz. tàm in Burgis & aliis Villis, quàm in feriis, mercatis, & aliis locis publicis, publicè proclamari facias, Quòd omnes illæ quicunque qui per Chartas dicti Domini Regis & antecessorum suis progenitor' suor', aut alio modo aliquas libertates, franchesias, aut liberas Consuetud' forestæ infra dictam forestam habere clamant, sint coram me præfat' Justiciar' aut meo in hac parte deputato, die & loco prædictis, ostensuri quas libertates habere clamant. Et omnes attachiat' pro viridi & venatione infra forestam prædictam post ultim' placit' forestæ tantùm ac eorum pleg' & manucapt' qui habuerunt diem per manucaptionem coram Justic' Domini Regis Itinerant' proxim' illic venient. quòd adtunc sint ibi coràm me præf. Justic' ad stand' rectè, & ad faciendum ea quæ secundùm legem forestæ facere debent: Et quòd tu sis ipse ibidem cum ballivis tuis ad exequend' & certiorand' me super his & aliis negotia illa tangentibus: Et habeas ibi summonit' & hoc breve, Teste, &c.

22. This is the General Summons mentioned *in Charta de Foresta*, and there ought to be forty Days Notice between the *Teste* and the Day of Appearance or first Day of the Sessions, in the same Manner as the Justices in Eyre at large do make, and they

they may hold Pleas of *Quo Warranto* as the other Justices do.

23. He is likewise to issue out a Writ before he holds his General Sessions, directed to the Sheriff as aforesaid, together with a short Abstract of all such Matters as the Regarders of the Forest shall enquire into; and when they have made their Range, and affirmed at the Swanimote, or Court of Attachments, all such Things which they found in their Survey, they are to present the same under their Hands and Seals unto the Chief Justice in Eyre. The Form of this Writ see in Title *Regarder.*

24. There is also another Form of General Summons, which the Justices of the Forest may make, directed to the Chief Warden of the Forest in this Manner:

25. *Thomas Lovell nobilis ordinis Garterii miles, Justiciarius Itinerans omnium forestarum Domini Regis in Anglia, tam citra Trentam quàm ultra, Johan' de Vere Com' Oxon' custod' forestæ Dom' Regis vel ejus locumtenenti in eadem foresta salutem: Ex parte dicti Domini Regis vobis mando, firmitèr injungendo, quòd venire facias coram me præfat' Justiciar' apud Waltham de Lane proximo post festum Sancti Petri Apostoli prox' futur' omnes Forestarios, Viridarios, Regardatores, Woodwardos, ac alios ministros ejusdem forestæ qui nunc sunt & qui post ultimum placitum forestæ prædict' tent' fuerunt & eorum quemlibet, cum omnibus rotulis scriptis, monumentis, & attachiamentis forestæ tam de viridi quàm de venatione, que post ultim' placitum illud emersa, & non determinat' extiterunt: faciat Regardatores Forestæ qui sunt & qui post ultimum placitum prædict' tent' ibidem fuerunt, cum omnibus regardis suis per idem tempus factis & irrotulatis: faciasque insuper adtunc & ibidem omnes Agistatores ejusdem forestæ qui nunc sunt & qui post tempus prædict' fuerunt, & eorum quemlibet, cum omnibus attachiamentis suis & rotulis agistamentor' ad standum inde*

recte & ad faciend' ea quæ ei & eorum cuilibet secundùm legem forestæ injungentur, aut quæ facere debent: facias etiam venire omnes illos qui clamant habere aliquas libertates aut franchesias infra forestam prædictam, quòd sint coram me aut locum meum tenente ad prædict' diem & locum ostensur' quomodo clamant habere libertates, franchesias, seu privilegia, & quo Warranto: Et quod vos sitis adtunc & ibidem cum nominibus omnium prædict' ministrorum, & hoc breve nobis remittentes, Teste, &c.

26. It appeareth by this Writ, that the Authority of the Chief Justice of the Forest differs from the Authority of other Justices in Eyre; because those of the Forest may make a Deputy to execute their Office, which other Justices cannot do; but this is by virtue of the Statute of 32 *H.* 8. *cap.* 35. for before the making that Statute, they could not make a Deputy because their Office is judicial; and yet all the Writs of Summons, before the making that Statute, are to appear *coram Justiciar. Itinerant. aut ejus Deputat.* 4. *Inst.* 291.

27. In former Days this great Officer was created by Writ as other Justices in Eyre are; but now, by the Statute of 27 *H.* 8. *cap.* 24. he is made by Letters Patent. *Co.* 4. *Inst.* 291.

The Manner of holding the Court, and what Offences are punishable there.

28. This Court cannot be kept oftner than every third Year, 4 *Inst.* 291. and though the Trespasses of Offenders are presented at the *Court of Attachments*, and afterwards those Offenders are upon such Presentments indicted at the Court of *Swanimote*, according to the Statute of 1 *Ed.* 3. *cap.* 8. and according to the Statute *de Ordinatione Forestæ*; yet those Courts cannot give Judgment or assess any Fine; for that must be done at the Justice-Seat: And therefore the Rolls of such Offences, in both those

those Courts, are to be sealed with the Seals of the Verderors, who are to keep them until the Justice-Seat, and then they are to present them to the Chief Justice in Eyre.

29. After forty Days Notice given by the Sheriff by Proclamation, as aforesaid, of holding this Court, and after the Chief Justice in Eyre, and those in Commission with him, are come to the Place appointed, then first the Commission must be read, and the Officers called, and the Freeholders and all other Persons who were summon'd to appear; then there must be a substantial Jury of 24, 20 or 18, chosen out of those Freeholders and others there present, who must be sworn truly to inquire and true Presentment make, of all such Matters and Things which shall be given to them in Charge.

30. And because the King may be better certify'd what Offences have been done in the Forest since the last Court, and also how and in what Manner those Offenders have been prosecuted, favour'd or punish'd, and that he may likewise know what Officers have faithfully discharged themselves in their Office as they ought to do, the Chief Justice in Eyre, or some Person learned in the Laws of the Forest, and appointed by him, must give the Jury a Charge to this Effect following.

The CHARGE.

1. FIrst, to enquire of all Attachments as well of *Vert* as *Venison* since the last Sessions, either in the King's Woods or in any Place within the Limits of the Forest, and by whom and how such Attachments were made, and whether there hath been any Hunting within such Limits, and if any, then by whom, and whether the Foresters, or what other Person, consented to such Hunting,

and who hunted with Warrant, and who without, and how often, when and where.

2. Whether any *Attachment* hath been made by Night and who, and by whom were they attached.

3. What *Attachments* have been made in Fence-time, as well of those who have offended, as those who were suspected, and of all others found in the Forest searching and going in a suspected Manner.

4. If any *Assarts*, Wastes or Purprestures have been made since the last Sessions, or before, and not presented, in whose Fee the same are or were made, whether in the Lands of the King or any other Person, and by whom, and who now possesses the same, and how they are enclosed, and what number of Acres.

5. To present the Names of such Persons who have enclosed any Ground adjoining to the Forest, and who have enlarged their own Grounds, and streightened the Forest by setting out their Hedges or Ditches, and to inquire what quantity of Ground is so enclosed.

6. If any Person hath taken away or destroy'd any Mark or Bound of the Forest, and who, and when it was done.

7. To inquire of the Bounds and Limits of all Bailiwicks in the Forest, and how and in what manner they are bounded; and how the Bailiffs and Foresters have kept their Walks, and what they claim as belonging to their respective Offices, and what they take by vertue thereof, and by what Warrant.

8. If any Mine, Delf of Coal, Stone, Clay, Marle, Turf, Iron or any other Mine, hath been made, and who made it, and where.

9. If any Tanner or White Tawer dwelleth within the Forest, and uses his Trade there.

10. If any Mine hath been made in the Forest since the last Sessions, or before, and hath not

been presented, and to present the Name or Names of the Persons who made it.

11. If any Church, Town or House hath been built in the Limits of the Forest since the last Sessions, and not yet presented, and by whom built, and how long since, and how many Beasts are pastured in the Forest by reason thereof, to the Prejudice, Hurt and overcharging of the same.

12. If any Swine-House, Neat-House, Sheep-House, or any other House or Inclosure, hath been built within the Bounds of the Forest to the Annoyance thereof, by whom, and on how much Ground, and what it containeth, and how much of the Pasture for the Deer is thereby surcharged and impaired by the Beasts which go in and out of such Houses.

13. If all the Inhabitants within the Forest, as well the Clergy who have Lay-Fees as others, being of the Age of 22 Years, be sworn to be true to the Forest or not, and of their Appearance and Defaults here.

14. If any Foresters, Keepers or other Officers of the Forest, who have any Walks, and are not sworn, to present their Names, and whether they are there or not.

15. If there are any Parks within the Limits of the *Forest* or near it, and how they are enclosed, and what Saltaries and Leaps they have which are prejudicial to the same; or what common Trespassers there are in any of the King's Parks in the County, either with Bows, Arrows, or any other Engine; or whether any Ground hath been ploughed there without Leave, and how much, and by whom.

16. If there have been Waifs or Strays in the Forest since the last Sessions, or before, and not presented, and who had the same, or what Person, and by what Title or Warrant.

17. If any Person hath taken any Swarm of Bees, or any Honey, or Wax in the Forest, how many, how much, and the Value, and who of Right ought to have the same.

18. To inquire who maketh or taketh any Profit of Turbary, if any be within the Forest, and what Ground it is, and whether any Rent ought to be paid for it, and how much the Forest is injured thereby.

19. If any River, Haven or Creek was newly made, by which Wood, Timber, or Venison hath been conveyed by Boat, Barge or Ship, and by whom, and by whose Assistance and Consent.

20. If any Officer hath made any *Scotales*, or gathered any Sheaves of Corn, or done any Extortion or Oppression by colour of his Office, and who, and what is his Offence.

21. If any Person came into the Forest in the Fence-Month to look after Sheep, Hogs or other Cattle, being not sworn to the Assise of the Forest, and who.

22. If the Steward hath kept the Swanimote-Court three Times every Year according to the Laws of the Forest, and taken Presentments, and caused them to be affirmed by the Verdict of 12 indifferent Men, and sealed by the Verderors and other Officers according to the said Laws, or not; and whether the Forty-Day Court hath been kept or not according to the Statute.

23. If the Keeper, Bailiff or Steward hath taken Fines or Amerciaments of Trespassers, or of those who were indicted or suspected for *Vert* or *Venison*; and if they did, then of whom, how much, and what it was; and whether they have caused any Person to be falsly indicted, how, when, and in what Manner.

24. If the Foresters, Verderors, Regarders, Agistors, or others, have concealed any Trespassers, indicted

indicted or suspected, or made any Attachments for their own Lucre, or for Favour, or for either of those Causes have concealed Purprestures, or any other Thing appertaining to their Office to discover, or whether they have appropriated any thing to themselves which belongs to the King.

25. If any Foresters in Fee, or other Officers, have taken any Fine or Reward, or Chiminage, or Passage, which did not belong to his Bailiwick, or who, by coulour of their Office, make any Collections which are prohibited by the Laws of the Forest.

26. If any Person doth usually resort to the House of any Forester to haunt the Forest, and what he doth take or receive of the Forester, and whether such Person is suspended for any Trespass or Offence done in the Forest, and who he is.

27. To inquire how the Foresters have behaved themselves in their several Bailiwicks and Offices, and who are profitable to the King, and who not; and for what Cause, and if they gave any thing for their Bailiwicks, and to whom; and whether any Forester hath been removed by the Steward or Verderor, for what Cause and who they were; whether there are more Foresters in any Bailiwicks than ought to be, or who are not necessary for keeping the Bailiwick; and whether they or any of them do surcharge their Bailiwicks by undue or too often lodging any Person, and who kept their Horses there three Days and Nights in other Mens Houses within their Bailiwicks, or without, by reason of their Office; and which of the Foresters have any lewd, mischievous or troublesome walking Servant under him to the Charge or Burthen of the Country; and which of them hath made or introduced any new Custom or Innovation in the Forest, to the Damage of the King and Burthen of the Country.

28. To enquire, by what Warrant Bailiffs, who are Foresters in Fee, do hold their Bailiwicks, and which of them pay any yearly Rent or Annuity to the King, and how much for the same, and what, of Right, they ought to take and enjoy in the Forest to pay the said Rent, and by what Meets and Bounds they ought to hold their Bailiwicks, and what Lands the King hath in each of the said Bailiwicks, and how they are inclosed.

29. If any Forester of Fee or any other hath taken any Reward of a Forester for his Office, and afterwards removed him and put another in his Place for a new Reward.

30. If any Person hath inclosed his Ground, Woods or Warren to the Damage of the Forest, or hath afforested any of his own Woods without the King's Warrant.

31. Whether any Deer have been found newly dead or wounded past Recovery, and whether the flesh of such Deer hath been given to Hospitals adjoining, and if there are none then to the poor, and whether the Verderors or Country can testify the same.

32. Whether the Head and Skin have been given to the Freemen of the next Town.

33. If any Arrow or Arrows have been found within the Forest, and due Presentment made to the Verderors thereof, that he might enter the same in his Roll.

34. If any Greyhounds have been found running in the Forest to the Disturbance of the King's Game, whether the same hath been presented in the Presentments of the Verderors, to the intent the same should be sent to the Chief Justice in Eyre.

35. If all the Dogs within the Limits of the Forest have been lawed as they ought to be.

36. If any Man in Harvest time, hath kept a Mastiff or great Dog in the said Forest to the Hurt of the Deer.

37 If any Person who hath a Grant from the King of free chasing in the Forest, hath, by colour thereof, done any Prejudice to the King.

38. If the King hath granted Liberty to hunt Vermin of Chase, *viz.* Foxes, Wild Cats, Polecats or Squirrels in the Forest, and by colour thereof any Deer hath been killed.

39. If any Man hath seen another taking Deer, and hath not raised Hue and Cry to apprehend him.

40. Who keepeth Dogs in the Bounds of the Forest, or without, which will kill Deer, Hares or other Beasts of Chase, or doth keep any Engine to take Deer or other Beasts, and who are Receivers, aiding and consenting to the same.

41. Whether any Deer are or have been taken, and by whom, and whether by Warrant or without.

42. If any have been Offenders in Warrens and Fish-pools within the Forest.

43. Who hath any Bows, Shafts, Hounds or any other Engines in the Forest to the Prejudice of the Beasts of Chase, and who doth usually enter into the Forest with Bows and Shafts.

44. If any Person (to whom, by reason of his Office, the King hath given any Deer) hath taken more Deer than he ought, and what Forester, Officer or other Person hath been assisting to the same, and whether it was taken in the Sight of the Foresters or Verderors; who hath taken any Hawks, Pheasants, Partridge or other Fowl of Warren within the Forest, contrary to the Laws thereof.

45. If any hath hunted the King's Deer within seven Miles of the Forest, at any time within forty Days next before the King's hunting, or forty Days

after; for that the King, before such hunting, or his Commissioners appointed to to view the Game, should see where the Deer haunt, and because, after hunting, they having been disturbed with Horns and Men, may return to their Haunts in the Forest.

46. If any Purlieu Hunter do disorderly hunt, to the Destruction of the King's Game in the Forest, or kill Deer, or hunt before the rising of the Sun, or after Sun-set, or with any other than his own menial Servants, or hunted on Sundays.

47. If any Purlieu-Hunter forestalled the King's Deer, by dead Hay or live Hay; for they may not forestall, but let slip at the Tail; and if he hath hunted in the Fence-Month.

48. If any Man cometh into the Purlieu, and finding a Deer feeding, goeth against the Wind and killeth him with Bow, Greyhound or other Engine, or waiteth for him at any Gap or Pitch where the Deer usually walk, or taketh his Flight.

49. If any Man who hath long running Hounds, and rideth or goeth in the Highways of the Forest, and doth not take up his said Hounds with a fast Knot, so that they follow the Scent of the Deer and kill it, either within the Forest or without, what Deer was so killed, by whom, and where he dwelleth.

50. If any Man hath taken Deer with Nets, Cords, Ropes, double *Pater-noster*, or other Engine, contrary to the Statute of 3 *Jac.* 1. *cap.* 13.

51. If any Man chase or course, or set any Net or Engine to kill Deer, though he doth not kill the same.

52. If any Man killeth any Fox Hare, Cony or other Beast or Fowl of Warren without Authority.

53. If

53. If any Man dwellling about the Borders of the Forest, and keeping any strange Grey-hounds, and watcheth the King's Deer out of the Forest, and way-layeth it that it cannot return home, and by that Means perisheth, to present the Name of such Person, and who is Owner of the Greyhound, and the Place where it was done.

54. If any Man hath killed a Deer in the Forest, and what Deer, and who it was.

55. If any Man, not worth 10 *l.* a Year in Land of Inheritance, or 30*l.* *a Year of Freehold* Land above all Charges, keepeth any *Greyhound* contrary to the Statute of 13 *R.* 2. *cap.* 13. or who is not possess'd of Goods or Chattels *worth* 200 *l.* contrary to the State of 1 *Jac.* 27. or is not the Son of a Knight or Baron, or some other Person of higher Degree, or the Son and Heir apparent of an Esquire, and hunteth in the Purlieus without any Authority, you are to make Presentment of his Name and hunting, for otherwise he ought not to hunt.

56. If the Foresters, or any other Officers, have agisted any other Cattle in the King's Hays, and several Woods wherein no Person hath Right of Common; and if they have mowed any of the King's Lands, and taken Grass and Hay thereof to their own Use, or sold the same to the Hurt of the Deer, and how much it was worth, or what they received for the same.

57. If the King's Agistors have faithfully agisted his Woods, and levied and received the Pannage and accompted for it, or if not fully accompted, then how much remains in their Hands.

58. If any Man, who hath Woods adjoining to the Forest, and hath put his Hogs therein in Pannage time, and hath made Gaps for his Hogs to pass out of his Woods into the Forest to eat the King's Pannage.

59. If any Man hath Swine coming into the Forest in Pannage-Time, or any other Time, either unringed, rooting or turning up the Soil, to the injury, and making lean of the King's Deer.

60. If any Man hath a Grant from the King, or any Specialty confirmed before the Chief Justice in Eyre, for a certain number of Hogs in the Forest, if he hath more there than he ought to have, and the Number and Value of them.

61. If any Hogs unring'd, or Goats, have been attached since last Sessions in the Forest, and the Number and Price of them, they being forfeited by the first Attachment, because they are no Beasts of Common; if any Sheep have been in the Forest, or the Covert, and have been three times attached since the last Sessions, the Number and Value thereof.

62. If any Stranger hath put his Horses, Mares, Beasts or other Cattle in the Forest, by reason whereof the Pasture of the King's Deer hath been surcharged to their Hurt, and the Annoyance of them who have Right of Common therein.

63. If any Man hath put a Stone-horse to feed in the Forest or to be commoned therein, and of the Age of two Years, and not fifteen Hands high by the Standard; or whether there are any Mares, Fillies or Foles not likely to bear Foles of reasonable Stature, depasturing therein, contrary to the Statute of 33. *H.* 8. *cap.* 5. and whether the Headboroughs and Tithing men of every of the Townships within the Forest, have duly executed that Statute on every drift Day.

64. If any Officer hath taken any Fines for agisting strange Cattle in the Forest, to hinder the Pasture of the King's Wild Beasts, and of such who have Common in the same, and what and how much the Pasture of such Beasts hath been hindered thereby.

65. If.

65. If any Man hath spoiled or destroyed any Brush or Fern, or any other Covert or Defence, in such Places where the King's Deer haunt, calve or fawn.

66. If any Man, who hath a Grant of Estovers for his own Use, hath, by colour thereof, given or sold any to other Persons, and who hath any, and what Warrant for such Estovers, and how much the Forest is thereby hurt, and the Names of those who have done the same.

67. If any Person, dwelling in the Forest, hath surcharged the same, or the Pasture or Meadow thereof, and how it hath been surcharged, and to what Hurt and Loss, &c.

68. If any Person hath fell'd or cut down any Underwood, Thorns or Rods in the Forest, and carried away the same unattach'd, and the Names of such Persons, and the Price of the Underwood, &c.

69. If any Person hath felled or cut down any of the King's great Oaks in the Forest, and carry'd them away, and the Price of the Horses and Cart, and of the Trees carried away.

70. If any Forester, or his Deputy, browsed any Mast, Boughs, or great Oaks in the Winter-time, more for his own Advantage to sell, than for the Food of the Deer, his Name, and the Value thereof.

71. If any, who take Wood by the King's Licence, hath exceeded their Authority, and who, how much, and by whose Assent.

72. If any Man, who hath a Warrant to take some Trees, hath taken more than he ought, or if he hath taken them without View of the Verderors or Foresters.

73. If a Warrant hath been granted to fell Oaks for the King's Use, and any Man hath taken them for

for his own Use, or otherwise given away or sold the same, and the Value thereof, &c.

74. If any Commissions have been directed to Wood-fellers to take a certain quantity of Wood or Underwood, and they have well made the Hedges of the Coppice to preserve the King's Covert, and if they have concealed any Profit which the King ought to have; if they have inclosed any Moors, great Plains or Wastes to the Damage of the Commoners, or put in any Cattle to hurt or crop the young Sprouts.

75. What Oaks or other Wood hath been given, sold or taken by the Foresters, who hath consented to the same, and the Quantity and Value thereof.

76. If any Man hath made any Spoil or Waste in the Forest, of Vert, in the King's Woods, or in the Woods of any Person, and what, and how much the said Foresters have given, sold or suffered to be given, or taken to their own Use, of any Wood within their Bailiwick, and if, through Favour of any Person, the said Officers have suffered them, or any of them, to make any Spoil or Waste in their Woods in the Forest, what and how much the Spoil was, and if they have taken any thing, and how much, for the same.

77. How much the Vesture and Covering of any Woods, and the Shade of the same, which were assarted, were worth before they were so assarted, as well of the King's Grounds as of other Men, and who hath received the Profits thereof, and how much the Corn thereof is worth which is now sowed on the Ground so assarted.

78. If any Person other than the Keepers or Officers of the Forest doth walk out of the Highways with Bows and Arrows contrary to the Assise of the same, and who it is.

79. If the respective Foresters have, early every Morning, walked within their Walk and Limits, and diligently

diligently performed their Duty at other times in the Day, by looking after the King's Deer and other Beasts of Chase, and in watching after Offenders who shall come into the Forest.

80. If any Person hath stopped or streightned any Church-way, Mill-way or other Ways within the Forest and Purlieu, &c.

81. If any Person hath gathered any Acorns, Crabs or other Mast, and sold the same to the Hurt of the Deer, and the Commoners there.

82. If any Man hath made any Coppice or Inclosure in the Purlieu, streightening the King's Deer from the Forest, to the Hurt of the Owners, or impounded the Beasts of any Commoners out of the Shire, and not put them in open Pounds, whether in Pannage-time or not.

83. Whether all Rents and Duties, which ought to be paid and done to the King or his Foresters, have been duly answered and done.

84. And, lastly, if any Person hath sued in another Court, any Plea arising within the Jurisdiction of the Forest, and to be determined by the Chief Justice in Eyre; and if any Person hath taken a Fine for killing Hares, or for keeping unprofitable Dogs in the Forest contrary to the Assise of the same, or for any other Trespass whatsoever, &c.

The Oath of the Inhabitants of the Forest, being of the Age of twelve Years, used antiently in these old Rhymes.

You shall true Liege-man be,
Unto the King's Majestie:
Unto the Beasts of the Forest you shall no hurt do,
Nor to any thing that doth belong thereunto:
The Offences of others you shall not conceal,
But, to the utmost of your Power, you shall them reveal
Unto the Officers of the Forest,
Or to them who may see them redrest:
All these things you shall see done,
So help you GOD at his Holy Doom.

If a Justice-Seat be discontinued by the not coming of the Chief Justice, it may be reviv'd by the King's Writ; for if the Pleas of the Forest are discontinued, they may be revived by the King's Writ of Re-summons, by which all things will be *in pristino Statu.*

The Court may set a Fine for any Mis-behaviour or abusive Words; as where a Man was indicted because discoursing with others before the Justice-Seat about an Indictment, he said, *If you complain of me for cutting Wood within the Forest, I will be reveng'd of you and make you smoak for it:* He confess'd the Indictment, and was fin'd 100*l.* and committed 'till he found Sureties for his good Behaviour. *Jones Rep.* 274.

So Sir *Charles Howard* was indicted, because, at the last Swanimote held before the Justice-Seat, there being some Discourse to the Jurors to present, that he felled several Trees, he said, *The Business is carried against me with a high Hand, but I care not for it, and when they that prosecute me have done, I will begin and have the Matter heard in another Place, and*

I will

I will stick close to them. He confessed the Indictment and was fined 100 *l.* and committed till he paid it. *Jones Rep.* 274.

Claims in Forests.

See { *Appearance*, 5, 6. *Common*, 39. *Dogs*, 18, 19. *Officer*, 6. }

1. BY good and lawful Claims Men may justify the doing several things in the Forest, which otherwise would be unlawful; but then such Claims must be allowed in Eyre within the Time of Prescription.

2. And if the Chief Justice in Eyre should refuse to allow the Liberties claimed, then the Party grieved may have a Writ of Allowance directed to the Chief Justice of the Forest, commanding him to allow the same; and so he may if the Chief Justice should neglect or delay to allow the Claim, and where any Liberties are allowed at one Justice-Seat, the same may be pleaded at another time, and the Record of the Allowance of the Claim shall be transmitted unto the Justices, and whatever was not allowed in the last Eyre, cannot be claimed or allowed in the next Eyre before 'tis replevied. *Jones Rep.* 285.

3. But if he who claims doth afterwards make Default, the Liberty shall be seised into the King's Hands; for a Default is a good Cause of Seisure. *Itin. Lanc. fo.* 59, 65. *Itin. Pickering*, 16, 23, 116.

4. A Woman who was Tenant for Life of a Park in the Forest of *Lancaster*, called *Knoghsly Park*, claimed the same, and also free Warren, and afterwards

wards made Default; whereupon one *Latham*, Tenant in Reversion, was received, and claimed both the Park and Warren; and because he did not produce a good Title, it was adjudged *quòd clausus præd. prosternetur & remaneat foresta, ut prius, & quod Warrena præd. capiatur in manus Domini.*

5 But for a *false Claim*, there is to be no *Seisure*, the Punishment is only to be fined Thus the Prior of *Lancaster* claimed the Tithe of all the Venison in the Forest, *tam in Carne quàm in Corio*, when he could not make out any Title to the Venison *in Corio*, and therefore he was *in misericordia de decima Venationis suæ in Corio non percipiendo.*

6. Now, by the *Assises of the Forest*, those who claim ought to make it on the *first Day of the Justice-Seat*, otherwise their Claim shall not be received without paying a Fine; for if once 'tis put in, and afterwards it should appear to be faulty, 'tis not to be amended without a Fine. *Assis. Pick.* 15. Or if put in and not prosecuted to get an Allowance, Judgment shall be entered against them for Default of Prosecution. *Jones Rep.* 297.

7. As to Trials of Claims, 'tis to be observed, if a Man claim to be a Forester in Fee, either by *Prescription*, *Grant* or *Tenure*, and prayeth, that it may be enquired by the Ministers of the Forest, in this Case the Verderors, Regarders and Agistors shall try the Title; but if a Man claim by *Inheritance*, or otherwise, any Profit *Apprender*, as Common of Estovers, or Common of Pasture, in this Case the Tryal shall be by the Foresters, Verderors and Regarders, and not by Agistors.

8. If the Claim require a Tryal by the Country, then the Conclusion of the Plea is *& hoc peratus est verificare prout Curia, &c. inde inquiratur inde veritas per ministros ejusdem forestæ*; and in such Case the Verperors, Regarders and Agistors, shall only try it; but there are many Precedents where the

Entry

Entry hath been as before mentioned, that these Words immediately have followed; *viz. Et quia videtur Curiæ hic quod expedit. & necesse est ad inquirend. tam per ministros forestæ prædictæ quàm per alios probos & legales homines.* And there are few or no Precedents where the Countrey alone, without any Officers of the Forest have tried Claims. *Itin. Lanc. fo.* 2, 3, 4.

9. Then as to the matter of pleading where there is no Tryal, 'tis to be noted, that there may be a Demurrer in Law upon a Claim before the Justices of the Forest. *Itin. Picker. fo.* 21.

10. And this was affirmed by the Chief Justice *Richardson, in Itin. Windsor.* 8 *Car. Jones* 272. *viz.* That the Court could not adjudge a Claim without some Plea or *Demurrer* on the King's side: But Mr. Attorney *Noy* said, There never was any Demurrer in Eyre, neither is the Attorney-General to attend there; but when the Claim is made, it is read to the Court, and the Allowance or Disallowance is *Quibus lectis, &c.* And when there is an Issue, the Entry is, *Qui sequitur pro Domino Rege petit quòd inquiratur, &c.* And there was a Person who, in the antient Eyres, attended in the nature of the King's special Attorney, but not his Attorney-General, who could not confess any Plea, but only said, *Visis præmissis non dedicit.*

11. If a Man claim any Liberty or Franchise by *Grant*, and if the King's Counsel demand *Oyer* of it, he must produce it, otherwise Judgment shall be entered against him, *quia non ostendit chartam*; and if, in the *King's Bench* or *Exchequer*, the King's Attorney desire *Oyer* of it at any time in that Term in which it was pleaded, if the Party do not produce it, the King shall have Judgment. *Jones Rep.* 274.

12. Tenants in Antient Demesne may not join in one Claim for a Common, because the King cannot claim for them; but Copyholders, who are Tenants to one Lord, may join in a Claim, or the Lord may prescribe for himself and them, because the Freehold of their Land is in him by Law; but he cannot prescribe for any of his Freeholders, but every one of them must put in several Claims. *Jones Rep.* 276.

13. A Claim, *quòd nullus forestarius, vicecomes, &c. intromittat* is void, if he doth not make Title to himself to do Justice; for no Place can be exempted from the King's Law, and therefore a Grant from the King to exclude his Officers from such a Place is void, unless he appoint some Body to do Justice there.

Common in Forests.

See { *Charge, in Chief Justice*, 61. *Nusance*, 15. *Prescription*, 19. *Woods*, 27. *Appendix*, Stat. 33. Ed. 1. *Appendix*, Ordinatio forestæ, 6.

1. IT appeareth, *in Chartâ de forestâ, Artic.* 1. That where the King hath afforested his *own Woods or Lands*, the same shall remain a Forest, but *salvâ communiâ de herbagio, & aliis in eadem forestâ, illis qui prius eam habere consueverunt*: So that by the Afforestation, he doth not abridge or prejudice any Man to have *Common* who had a Right before; but the same is reserved as it was at Common Law; *à fortiori*, where he afforests the *Woods or Lands of another Man*, he doth not abridge their Right

Right to have Common in any waste Soil or other Place in the Forest, where they used to have Common before, and with such Cattle which are commonable there.

2. And by the Statute called *Ordinatio Forestæ*, made *Anno* 33. *Ed.* 1. *cap.* 5. long after he had confirmed the *Charter* of the Forest, 'tis explain'd who shall have *Common*, and who not, and for what Cause, in the Forest, in these Words:

'3. *ff.* The Intent and Will of the King is, 'That from henceforth, where *Purlieu* is (that is 'to say) where Woods and Lands are disafforested, they may claim to be quit of the Charge 'and Burthen of the Forest: And whereas the 'King's Wild Beasts of the Forest cannot haunt 'and repair unto those Woods and Lands disafforested, as they might have done so long as the 'same were within the Bounds of the Forest; such 'Persons, who were put out of the Forest by *Disafforestation*, shall not have *Common* or other Easement within the Woods or Lands which remain 'in the Bounds of the Forest.

'4. But if any of them who have been disafforested by the Purlieu, would rather be within 'the Forest, as they were before, they shall be 'received and remain in their antient State, and 'shall have Common and other Easement as well 'as they had before.

5. So that the King, by the Afforestation of the Woods or Lands of *other Men*, doth not restrain them from the Right of Common within the Forest, but leaves that still as it was at Common Law.

6. And it seems by the whole scope of this Statute, that the Intent of the King is, That every Man, who is a Tenant of Land within the Forest, shall have and enjoy Common in respect of the Charge and Burthen, which, by the Laws of the

Forest, he is subject unto; for the King's Wild Beasts have their continual Haunt, quietly to feed in every part of their Woods and Lands in the Forest, which is a Burthen and Charge to the Tenants; therefore, if the King makes an Afforestation of any Place, he doth not restrain them from Right of Common, either in his waste Soil, or in that of any other Person; but by this Statute doth seem to inlarge their Common in his waste Soil only, or at least doth leave every Man's Right of Common in all Forests as it was before at Common Law; it may therefore be necessary to mention what is Common.

What is Common, and why it is so called.

7. Common is properly the Right or Interest which a Man hath to feed or pasture his Beasts or Cattle in another Man's Soil or Land; and 'tis called Common *a Communitate, viz.* From the Community or Number of Men who have a Right to it, or from the Number of Beasts who participate of the Herbage; for where Men have Common of Pasture for their Cattle or Beasts, many Mens Cattle do usually depasture there; and therefore *Budæus* calls such Common of Pasture, *Compascuum, viz.* A Place wherein several Mens Cattle feed in Community.

How

How many Sorts of Common there are, and in what Manner used.

At Common Law there are Four Sorts of Common.

Common { *Appendant.* *Appurtenant.* *In Gross.* *By Vicinage.*

8. *Common Appendant* is where a Man hath arable Land, unto which he hath *Common Appendant*; for it cannot be appendant unto any other than arable Land. 26. *H.* 8. *fo.* 4. *Plac'* 15. It cannot be appendant to a House, neither can he who hath such Common enjoy it with all manner of Beasts, but only with such which are Commonable; *viz.* with such as do feed on the Land unto which the Common is appendant, for Geese, Goats, Sheep and Swine must not common there.

9. *Common Appurtenant* is, where a Man is seised of a *Messuage* and certain Land unto which the Common appertaineth. *Hill* 10. *H.* 7. *fo.* 12. *Plac'* 1.

10. At Common Law *Common Appurtenant* was to have Common for all manner of Beasts and Cattle whatsoever, as well for such as were Commonable, as for those which were not; *viz.* for Geese, Goats, Sheep and Hogs; but for uncommonable Cattle, a Man cannot have *Common Appurtenant* in a Forest, without a special Grant from the King or Owner thereof. *Pas.* 9. *Ed.* 4. *fo.* 3. *Plac'* 13. *Dyer*, *fo.* 70. *Plac'* 39. But he may have *Common Appurtenant* in a Forest for all Beasts which are commonable. 25. *Assis.* *Plac'* 8. 37. *H.* 6 *fo.* 34. *Plac'* 20.

11. *Common in Gross* is, where a Man, by Deed, granteth unto another to have Common in a certain Place, with certain Beasts *only*; and such Common a Man may have in a Forest, either by the King's Grant, or by the Owner of the Forest, 22 *Assisa Plac'* 16. in the Case of the Prior of *Napleton*: 36 *Assisa, Plac'* 3.

12. *Common by Vicinage* is, where the Tenants of two Lords, who are seised of two Towns lying near to one another, and every one of them, Time out of Mind, had Common in each Town for all manner of commonable Beasts; and such Common may likewise be in a Forest by *Prescription*. 13. *H.* 7. *fo.* 13. *Plac'* 3. *Dyer, fo.* 47. *Plac'* 13.

13. In a *Chase* the Owner of the Soil may prescribe to have Common for Sheep, and Warren for Conies, either by Grant or Prescription; but he cannot surcharge with more than have been used Time out of Mind; nor make new Borows in other Places, unless he hath Warren by Grant, and then he may use it according to his Grant. 12 *Co. fo.* 22.

14. But no Man can have any Profit or Pleasure in a Forest which tends to the Destruction thereof; which is the true Reason why no Person can prescribe to have Common in a Forest for Sheep, Goats, Geese or Swine, for 'tis *ad magnum nocumentum ferarum forestæ*.

15. Sir *Edmund Sawyer* being seised in Fee of the Manor of *West Waltham*, alias *Heywood*, claimed Common of Pasture belonging to the said Manor in all open Places in the Forest of *Windsor*, within the Bailiwick of *Fynes*, and that he might *Stuff-herd* there, and derived a Title by a Grant of *R.* 1. to the Abbot of *Waltham Holy Cross* in *Essex*, and shewed the Dissolution of the Abbey, and the Possessions thereof came to the Crown; and a Grant of the said Manor to *J. Norris*, Esq; with these Words,

Tot, tanta, talia, libertates, privilegia & franches, &c. quot, &c. aliquis Abbas, &c. And so, by several Mesne Conveyances, brought down a Title to himself, and pleaded the Statute for reviving the Liberties in the Crown. See *Postea Dogs*, 39.

16. It was adjudged, *in Itinere Windsor, Jones Rep.* 286. That admitting a good Title in the Abbot; yet, by the Dissolution, there was an *Unity of Possession* in the Crown, which destroyeth the Common, and it shall not be revived by those general Words, *tot, tanta, talia, &c.* because a *Common* is neither a *Liberty, Privilege* or *Franchise*; and so it was adjudged for Land in *Braydon-Forest*, which was formerly the Possessions of the Abbot of *Malmsbury*. See *postea, par.* 25. of this Chapter.

17. But if the King had granted *tot, tanta, talia privilegia, &c. & communias, &c. quot aliquis Abbas Monasterii, &c.* in such Case, if there was any *Common, Appendant* or *Appurtenant* to that Manor or Lands in the Abbot's Hands, it shall be revived.

18. But if an Abbot had *Common in Gross*, and the King grants Parcel of his Possessions, with the Words *tot, tanta, talia, &c.* this shall not revive the Common in the Hands of the Grantee; because then every Man, who hath any part of the Abbot's Possessions, will have as much Common as the Abbot himself had whilst they were all in his Hands, and so the Forest would be infinitely surcharged.

19. But in case of *Common Appendant* or *Appurtenant*, there is no such Prejudice; because there each Man can keep a Number of Cattle only proportionable to his Land, and no more; for he cannot common with more than the Land, to which his Common belongeth, will keep in Winter.

20. He likewise prescribed for himself and all his Tenants, to have Common, &c. and that the Lands of his Copyhold-Tenants not being in the Crown, their Common was not gone.

21. But it was adjudged, that if so, then the Prescription for the Copyholders ought to be laid in some of the Abbots in whom the Possessions were severed, and then have shewed the coming of the Manor to the Crown, and from that have claimed specially by making a Title to themselves to their Copyholds by the Court Rolls of the Manor, as in *Swayne's Case*, 8 *Rep.* 64. But though the Claim was not good, yet the Court gave Direction to the Officers of the Forest to find the usage of the Tenants, which was accordingly done, and so the Common was allowed to them, but not to Sir *Edmund Sawyer*.

22. By the Statute of 17 *Car.* 1. *cap.* 16. The Tenants, Owners and Occupiers of Lands and Tenements which shall be excluded and left out of the Meets and Boundaries of the Forest (to be returned and certified by virtue of the Commissions which are to be granted by that Statute) shall use and enjoy their Commons, and other Profits and Easements within the Forest, as antiently or accustomably they have used and enjoyed the same, any thing in that Statute contained, or any Act or Ordinance made *Anno* 33 *Ed.* 1. or any Custom or Law of the Forest, or any other Matter or Thing to the contrary notwithstanding.

23. At a Justice-Seat held for the Forest of *Waltham*, *Anno* 10 *Car.* 1. at *Stratford-Langhton* in *Essex*, before the Earl of *Holland*, Chief Justice in Eyre, and Justice *Jones*, and Baron *Trevor*, by several Letters directed to them under the King's Privy-Signet, to be Assistant to the said Chief Justice in Matters of Law, it was resolved;

24. That if an Abbot, Lord of a Manor, hath Common for himself and his Tenants Copyholders of Inheritance in the King's Waste in the Forest, and in the Waste of other Freeholders there, and afterwards the Manor comes to the King by the

Dissolution

Dissolution of the Abbey, and then the King grants the Manor to another; That, in this Case, the Common is extinct in the King's Waste, as to the Lord of the Manor; but not as to the Copyholders, neither is it extinct as to the Lands of the Freeholders; but if the King had granted the Common as the Abbot had it before, there it shall enure as a new Grant of the Common in the King's Waste.

25. And at the same time it was held, That if a Liberty be reassum'd by Act of Parliament, which was vested in a Corporation before the Act of Resumption, and afterwards the Lands come to the King, and he grants the same, together with these Words, *Tot, talia privilegia & libertates, &c.* generally as the Corporation had before the Grant, the Liberties so reassumed shall not pass without special Words to grant them *de novo*. See abo e, *par.* 16.

26. And that if an Abbot was seised of a Manor, which had Waifs and Strays belonging to it, and likewise *catalla felonum & utlagat.* and the Manor afterwards comes to the King, and he grants the same over to another generally, with these Words, *Tot, talia privilegia, &c.* in such Case the Grantee shall have the Waifs and Strays as belonging to the Manor; but not *bona felonum & utlagat.* without special Words in the Grant. *Jones, Rep.* 349.

Who ought to have Common in the Forest.

27. Every Inhabitant in a Forest, who hath Common Appurtenant, that is, who can prescribe to the same, in the King's waste Soil, or in the waste Soil of any other, as belonging to his Dwelling-house only, or to his House and Lands, may have Common in a Forest; and such Prescription is good at Common Law, and likewise by the Forest Law, for there is no Law or Ordinance of the

the Forest against it; and therefore he who can so prescribe, may have Common there.

28. Likewise a Man may prescribe to have Common, by reason he is an Inhabitant in an antient Town, in which there is a Custom, Time out of Mind, That all the Inhabitants have Common within a certain Place, for all manner of commonable Beasts, Levant and Couchant within the same Town; and this is a good Prescription, both at Common-Law, and by the Law of the Forest. 20. *Ed.* 4. *fo.* 3. *Plac'* 15. 15 *Ed.* 4. *fo.* 32. *Plac'* 16. *fo.* 29. *Plac'* 7.

29. But a Man cannot prescribe to have Common there, if he dwelleth in a new House, that is, an House newly built; for all such new built Houses are Purprestures by the Laws of the Forest; and therefore those who dwell in them cannot prescribe, by reason of such Inhabitancy only.

30. *Anno* 10. *Ed.* 1. the Burgesses of *Lancaster* did claim to have Common of Pasture within the Forest of *Lancaster* for such Beasts which are commonable in a Forest; and this was held a good Claim, as appears *in Assisa foresta Lancastr. fo.* 13. & 30.

31. And in that Case, it was held for Law, That Sheep, Swine and Goats, are not commonable, *Quia præbent exilium ferarum in foresta.*

32. The like Claim was there made by the Burgesses of *Preston*; *viz.* To have Common of Pasture within the same Forest, by reason of their Inhabitancy, and it was allowed to be good; but it was adjudged in *the Assises of Pickering*, *fo.* 67. That a Man cannot have Common for Goats in a Forest without special Warrant, because they are neither *Bestiæ venationis neque forestæ.*

33. But many Things may be appurtenant, and not to a Messuage; for to be quit of Pannage, *tempore pannagii*, was adjudged good in the Claim of one

one Lawlesfoh, as appertaining to a Man's Free-hold.

34. So an Office of a Woodward, and likewise the Bark of Timber-Trees felled, was adjudged to appertain to a Manor. *Itin. Pickering, fo.* 16.

35. And in the same Folio, it was adjudged, That to be discharged of Pannage of Hogs in the Forest, may be appurtenant unto Lands.

36. To prescribe, that he and his Ancestors, *a tempore quo, &c.* had Common of Pasture, *&c.* is good, without saying, That he and his Ancestors, and *all those whose Estate* he hath in certain Lands, *&c. a tempore quo, &c.*

37. But no Man may have Common in a Forest for the Beasts of Strangers; but he must take the Common with his own Beasts. *Assisa Pickering, fo,* 10. in the Case of one *Gower.*

38. If the Foresters, or other Officers, disturb the Cattle of any Person or Township, in taking Common in the Forest, or extort any Money for the same, 'tis finable at the Justice-Seat. *Assisa Pickering, fo.* 10.

39. If the Chief of the Forest refuse to allow the Claim of those who prescribe to have a Common in a Forest, or any other Liberty, the Party may have a Writ of Allowance; and if he delay to allow such Claim, then he may have the King's Writ of Allowance directed to the Chief Justice of the Forest, commanding him to allow the same; the Tenor of which Writ may be seen, *Anno* 10. *Ed.* 3. *Itin. Lancastr. fo.* 9, *&* 69.

40. If a Claim is allowed at one Justice-Seat, the same may be pleaded at another Time; and the Record of the Allowance shall be sent down by the Writ unto the Justices.

41. And as a Man may claim *Common Appurtenant* in a Forest by Prescription, for all manner of Beasts which are commonable, so likewise he may pre-

scribe to have *Common of Vicinage* in a Forest, or to have *Common Appendant*.

42. As to Prescription for a Woodward, this Case happened *Anno* 21. *Ed.* 3. The Inhabitants of a Town, *&c.* made their Claim before the Chief Justice in Eyre of the Forest of *Pickering*, to choose their Woodward of a certain Wood within that Forest, and also to have the Windfall-Wood there, and reasonable Common of Estovers there, as appendant to the Inhabitants in that Town, and their Claim was allowed, *quod nota. Mich.* 21. *Ed.* 3. *fo.* 49, 70.

43. So that it seemeth, a Man may prescribe to have *Common Appendant* unto certain Land belonging unto the Inhabitants of a Town, for Beasts commonable in a Forest which are Levant and Couchant therein.

44. But this is contrary to *Gateward's* Case, 6 *Rep.* That Inhabitants, *&c.* cannot make a Claim for *Profit apprender*: And so it hath been since held in the Case of the Inhabitants of *Hiley*, who claim'd Common of Pasture in the Forest of *Windsor*; *viz.* That *Inhabitants* could not claim a *Profit apprender*, but an Easement they might. *Jones*, *Rep.* 297.

45. *In Itinere Eborac. Anno* 23. *H.* 3. There was a Claim for *Common in Gross*, in a Forest, the Case was thus; One *W.* who was Lord of a Forest, granted to an Abbot, Common of Pasture for forty Mares and eight Stallions, within the Forest of *L.* and because the Words of the Grant, *Quòd Abbas præd. habeat ubique pasturam in forestâ*, therefore it was adjudged, That the Grantor could not inclose any part thereof. *Fitz. Tit. Commun.* 25.

46. By which it appears, That a Man may have *Common in Gross* in a Forest; and he who hath such a Common, may use and enjoy it there according to the Purport of his Grant; for this sort of

of Common is by *Deed* only, and not by *Prescription*; but all the other three sorts of Common are by *Prescription only*, without *Deed*.

47. But in all these Cases, or any other, where Liberty is granted of any thing in a Forest, if the Grantee doth not use the same continually, and it appeareth so upon Enquiry, then the Liberty is to be seised, for *Non-user* is a good Cause of Seisure: This appears in the Case of the Abbot of *Rivall*, *Itin. Pickering*, *fo.* 15, 17, 18.

48. And no other Title can a Man have to a Common in a Forest, but either by *Prescription* or *Grant*, as aforesaid.

What Beasts are commonable in a Forest, and what not.

49. All manner of Beasts are commonable in a Forest, except *Goats*, *Geese*, *Sheep* and *Hogs*; and a Man cannot prescribe to have Common for them, because such a Prescription can have no lawful Beginning; for 'tis *ad magnum Nocumentum ferarum forestæ*, 25 *Assis. Placito* 8. 37. *H.* 6. 34 *Placito* 26. *Dyer*, *fo.* 70. *Placito* 39. But my Lord *Coke* tells us, A Man may prescribe to have Common for *Sheep* there, *Bulst.* 213. 4 *Inst.* 298.

50. And probably he might ground his Opinion upon the Case, 8. *Ed.* 3. *fo.* 31. where the Prioress of *Wickham* prescribed to have Common in the Forest of *Pickering*, *pro omnibus Bestiis suis exceptis Capreolis*; and this was before the Justice in Eyre, and the Claim was allowed.

51. But Common of Pasture for *Sheep* in a Forest, is good in two Cases; *viz.* Where an Officer of the Forest, who hath Land belonging to his Office, claims Common for *Sheep*, as belonging to his Land: And this was allowed in one *Blanchard's* Case, in the Reign of *R.* 2. who, by vertue of his Office, and the Land belonging to it, claimed

ed Common for *Sheep* in the Forest, by *Prescription*; and it was adjudged for him in Eyre, and also in *Chancery*, upon a *Monstrans de droit*, and afterwards in Parliament: And such another Case there was for *Clarendon Forest* in *Wiltshire*.

52. So where a Man prescribed to have Pasture for Sheep in his own open waste Grounds, but not in the Coverts on his own Land, nor on other Mens Lands, though it be in the open Places thereof.

53. And the Reason why 'tis good in the Case of an Officer of the Forest, is, because there is a Condition in Law annexed to his Estate, by reason of the Trust reposed in him; and if he put more in than he ought, 'tis a Surcharge, and a Forfeiture of his Office. *Jones, Rep.* 292.

Of Surcharges of the Forest.

54. If one who hath Common Appendant or Appurtenant in a Forest for a certain Number of Beasts, doth common there with more than his Number, then he surcharges the Forest, and is a Trespasser, punishable by the Law of the Forest, as well as by the Common Law; for by such Surcharge, the Wild Beasts are driven to find Pasture in other Places. *Assis.* 22. *p.* 65.

55. The Case is the same where a Man hath *Common in Gross* in a Forest, and he surcharges it.

56. And in this Matter the Forest-Law differs from the Common Law; for by that Law, if a Man hath *Common Appurtenant* or *Common in Gross*, in a certain place *sans Number*, he cannot surcharge such Common; and in such Case the Writ of Admeasurement will not lie: But, by the Forest-Law, if he hath Common *sans Number*, and surcharges it with so many Cattle, that the Wild Beasts of the Forest cannot have sufficient Pasture there,

there, he shall be accounted a Surcharger of the King's Forest, and shall be punished accordingly.

57. So that if a Man hath a Grant to common there *sans Number*, those Words must be understood, that he may have Common there with any Number of Cattle, so that the Wild Beasts may have sufficient Pasture left.

58. *Trin* 12. *H.* 8. *fo.* 2. *Brook*, one of the Judges of the *Common Pleas*, held, That where a Grant is made of a Common *sans Number*, yet the Grantee may not put in so many Cattle, but that the Grantor may have sufficient Pasture for his own Beasts in the same Lands: *Pari Ratione*, he who hath *Common in Gross sans Number* in a Forest, must not put in so many Cattle, but that the Wild Beasts of the Forest may still have sufficient Herbage left to depasture on, otherwise he shall be accounted a Surcharger. *Dyer*, *fo.* 80. *p.* 59.

59. The same Law where a Man claims *Common Appurtenant* in a Forest, or any other sort of Common there.

The Means to know who is a Surcharger is thus;

60. ¶. First, to make a true Estimate of the Number of Acres which the Place where the Common is surcharged doth contain; then to set down how many Parishes, Villages or Hamlets, have Right of Common there; then to number the Messuages and Cottages in those Towns and Parishes, *&c.* and what Land belongeth to each of them: So that by knowing the Certainty of the Number of Beasts which are usually fed on the Common so surcharged, a perfect Estimate may be made rateably, what Number of Beasts may be kept by every Man who hath Right of Common there, according to the Quantity of Land he enjoyeth, leaving sufficient Food and Pasture for the Wild Beasts; so that he who is found to have more

Beasts

Beasts there than this Rate doth allow him to keep, is a Surcharger.

61. The same Course is observed at Common Law to avoid surcharging a Common, by the Writ *de Admensuratione pasturæ, Lib. Intr. fo.* 13. which Writ is directed to the Sheriff of the County where the Commoners claim their Right of Common, that each of them may be admeasured; so that they may common with no more Beasts than they ought.

62. In like manner, upon Complaint of the Officers of the Forest, that the same is so much surcharged that there is not sufficient Pasture left for the Deer; in such Case a Commission may be directed out of the *Chancery* to the King's Lieutenant of the Forest, and the Verderors and Chief Foresters there, commanding them to inquire, by the Oaths of good and lawful Men, what Number of Acres the Place doth contain, wherein the Surcharge is supposed to be made; and what number of Beasts are commoning therein, and whose they are; and what Parishes, Villages and Hamlets ought, of Right, to have any Common there; and how many Messuages and Cottages there are in each of them; and how many Acres of Land do belong to every House: And then, by computing how many Beasts may common in the same, leaving sufficient Pasture for the Deer, they shall rate and apportion every Man what Number of Beasts, and of what sort, every Man may keep; and he who keeps more is a Surcharger of the Forest.

How a Surcharger is to be punished by the Laws of the Forest.

63. At Common-Law, if a Man surchargeth the Common, and the Writ *de Admensuratione pasturæ* is brought, every Commoner shall be admeasured

hereby, and rated to a certain Number of Beasts, and what Beasts; and if any of the Commoners do afterwards surcharge the Common, then any other Commoner may bring a Writ *de secundâ superoneratione pasturæ*, directed likewise to the Sheriff, reciting therein the first Admeasurement, and commanding him to go to the Common where the Surcharge is suppos'd to be, to inquire into the same by the Oath of good and lawful Men; and if, upon such inquiry, the Sheriff shall find a second Surcharge, then the Offender shall pay Damages to the Party grieved, and the supernumerary Beasts shall be forfeited to the King by the Statute *W.* 2. *cap.* 8. *F N. B. fo* 126.

64. This is the Punishment at Common-Law for Surcharge; but 'tis a *Quære* whether such supernumerary Cattle, commoning in a Forest, are *forfeited* to the King, by the Forest-Law; for, in all the *Iters of Pickering and Lancaster*, I find no such *Forfeiture*.

65. But, in the *Assises of Pickering Anno* 10. *Ed.* 3. *sect.* 12. it appears, That a Surcharger of a Forest shall be indicted and fined for the same to the King, and imprisoned till paid.

66. Yet it seems reasonable, That, after such a Commission, as aforesaid, is issued out of *Chancery*, in nature of a Writ *de admensuratione* at Common-Law, and every Man is rated according to his Portion, and that afterwards a Man surcharges the Common; that in such case the supernumerary Cattle should be *forfeited*; but 'tis plain, that he ought to be indicted as aforesaid.

67 'Tis true, in the Case of *Stow-Park*, *Dyer*, *fo.* 80. *Plac'* 59. the Grantee of that Park had likewise the Agistment thereof, and he put in more Beasts than he ought to agist, by reason whereof he surcharged the Park, so that the Deer had not

sufficient Pasture; it was not fully agreed what remedy the Grantor should have for this Offence.

68. But it seems very reasonable, that the Common should be seised into the King's Hands for a Surcharge; because, by the Forest-Law, whoever hath, or claimeth to have, any Liberty or Profit in a Forest, either by Grant or Prescription, and abuseth the same by using it in another Manner than what is warranted by his Title, as in the Case of the Prior of *Lancaster*, who took *viridem Boscum pro mortuo Bosco*, this is good Cause of Seisure, and the same must be seised into the King's Hands, and, after a Fine paid, must be restored to him again.

69. Now it cannot be denyed but that a Surcharge is *Abuser*, and for that Reason it ought to be seised; *tamen Quære*.

70. The Dean and Chapter of *Salisbury*, being Proprietors of the Rectory of *Winckfield*, claimed Common of Pasture for their Cattle, *Levant* and *Couchant* on the Rectory, in the open Places of the Forest of *Windsor*; and this was by Prescription.

71. Now it ought to be inquired, whether those who claim a Right of Common in a Forest, do use *Staff-herding* or not; that is, the Ministers of the Forest are to inquire, whether they use to have one follow their Cattle; for that is not allowable of Common Right, because, by that means, the Deer are frighted, which would otherwise feed with the Cattle; besides he who looks after the Cattle will drive them into the best Pasture, and so the Deer will have only what is left: Therefore if any Man hath Right of Common, and under Colour thereof, useth *Staff-herding*, his Common ought to be seised till he hath paid a Fine for the Abuse. *Jones* 282.

72. George

72. *George Tatersall* claimed Common of Pasture in the Forest of *Windsor*, *tanquam ad manerium suum de Finchamsted spectan.* and this was by Prescription; it appeared that the Manor had been in the Crown, and so, in strictness of Law, the Common was gone by Unity of Possession; but because it came from the Crown in the Reign of King *John*, such a long Possession was not questioned. *Jones* 285.

73. The Claim of commoning differs from all other Claims in a Forest, so 'tis good without an Allowance in Eyre, which no other Liberty is, that goes to Destruction of the Vert or the Game; and the Reason is, because a Prescription to have Common is an equitable Prescription, and upon the matter of Common Right; for since the Deer have fed on their Grounds, 'tis reasonable they should have Common. *Jones Rep.* 291.

Deer, see Doe.
Deputy, see Swanimote, 4, 5, 6, 7.

Distress.

See *Appendix*, Assisa forestæ, 5, 15.

Who may be compelled to appear by Distress, and how to be taken.

1. IN *Chartâ forestæ*, *cap.* 8. there are these Words; viz. *Nulli alii per districtionem*, &c. By which must be understood, That if any of the Officers of the Forest, or others, who ought to appear at the Court of Swanimote, make Default, the same shall be inrolled in the Rolls of the Court; and thereupon the Verderors and Steward thereof, or his Clerk or Deputy, by the Oath of other Officers

of that Court, shall amerce the Defaulters, which Amerciament shall be forthwith assess'd, and estreated to the Chief Warden of the Forest, or to his Deputy, or to the Beadle, to be levied by Distress; which Beadle is an Officer of the Forest to go throughout the same like a Sheriff's special Bailiff.

2. But in this Case the Verderors may choose whether they will estreat the Amerciament presently by Distress, or otherwise certify the Defaults in the Rolls of the Court to the Justices of the Forest; who thereupon will issue forth Writs directed to the Chief Warden of the Forest, or to the Sheriff of the County where the Defaulters live, to levy the same by Distress; or the Verderors may certify the Defaults into the Court of *Exchequer*, out of which Court Process will issue to the Sheriff to levy the same; and there are many good Precedents to warrant each of these proceedings.

3. The Default for not appearing at a Court of Swanimote being recorded, the Defaulters may be distrained to appear at the next Court; like as upon an Original where a Man is summoned and doth not appear, he shall be forthwith distrained; and if he shall make Default again, he shall be distrained in double the Sum, that is to say, one Distress for the Amerciament, by reason of his not appearing, *pro sectâ suâ non factâ*, and another for a new Appearance at the next Swanimote, be it Suit-Service or Suit-real, or else by direct Process of Common-Right, like a Distress against a Juror, to distrain him to come to the next Swanimote.

4. If an Officer of the Forest doth not appear, as aforesaid, at a Court of Swanimote, then the Chief Warden of the Forest, or his Lieutenant, or the Beadle of the Forest, may distrain him for that Amerciament in three Shillings, more or less, on any Land he hath, by reason of his Office, and, in like manner, he may distrain on any other

Land

Land he hath in the Forest, although he hath it not in Right of his Office; but he cannot take a Distress in any Lands out of the Forest; he may distrain the Goods of that Officer who makes Default, though they are in the Lands of any other Man in the Forest.

5. The same Law of any other Man who ought to appear at the Swanimote, besides an Officer of a Forest, as a *Bailiff*, *Constable*, *Tythingman*, *Freeholder* or *Juror*, who is summoned to appear at that Court, either to be of the Jury, or to do any Service there.

6. If no Distress can be found in the Forest, it ought to be certified by the proper Officer to the Chief Justice in Eyre; and upon a *Testatum* there that such a Person who ought to appear, did make Default, and was amerced for the same, and that he had not any Goods or Lands in the Forest that he might be distrained, but that he hath Lands out of the Forest, and in such a County; then there shall issue a Precept to the Sheriff where the Lands are, *ad distringendum terras & tenementa cujusdam, A. B. in Comitatu illo, &c.* by vertue whereof the Sheriff may distrain there for the Amerciament.

7. Now tho' the Justices of the Forest are not Justices in the County, yet, upon such a *Testatum*, they may cause a Precept to be directed to the Sheriff of a Foreign County out of the Forest, to levy the Amerciament; and this is affirmed by the Opinion of Mr. *Hesket*, *fo.* 37.

8. And if the Beadle or other Officer, coming to distrain, is prevented by the Owner of the Cattle, by conveying them out of the Forest, or otherwise, in such Case, though the Officer freshly pursue them, yet he cannot lawfully take them, being out of the Bounds of the Forest; but if such Cattle had once been distrained for the Amerciament, and then the Owner had, by Force, taken them

away, and driven them out of the Forest, in such Case he may retake them in any place out of the Forest.

9. The same Law if a Stranger take the Cattle from the Officer after the Distress made of them, and delivers them to the Owner, who drives them out of the Forest, the Officer may lawfully retake them any where; but if the Cattle so distrained, return to the Land of the Owner, by the Neglect of the Officer who ought to have impounded them, then, if the Land is out of the Forest, he cannot retake them there; for now the first Distress is determined by the return of the Cattle to the Owner, without his Account or Privity; for 'tis not like a *Rescous*, where the Owner comes to the Possession by his own Wrong.

10. But if the Officer hath distrained, and afterwards delivers the Distress to a Stranger to keep for his own Use, who drives them to his own Land within the Forest, and then the Owner takes them from thence and drives them out of the Forest; in this Case the *Beadle* or other Officer cannot retake them being out of the Forest.

11. But 'tis otherwise if the Officer had taken the Distress, and delivered it to a Stranger to keep as a Distress; in this Case, if the Owner take them and drive them out of the Forest, the Officer may pursue them and take them again any where out of the Forest, and in any foreign County; so that there is a Difference where such Cattle are delivered to be kept as a Distress, and where to be kept for his own Use.

12. If he who ought to appear at the Swanimote, hath Land in the Forest, and the Beasts of a Stranger are on those Lands, and the Tenant of the Lands distrains them and impounds them on the same Land, and the Beadle of the Forest finds them Levant and Couchant there; he may distrain the

the same Cattle for an Amerciament, in Default of not appearing; but he cannot distrain them if they were not Levant and Couchant there.

13. But he cannot break the Lock of a Gate of any inclosed Ground to distrain for an Amerciament on the Tenant of that Land or Ground; he may distrain in the Highway within the Forest, out of any Close or Inclosure.

14. If a Man, who is amerced, doth afterwards pawn or pledge the Cattle, which be in the Forest, to another, in such case the Beadle cannot distrain the same so long as they are in pawn.

15. But if Issues are returned upon the Lands of a Freeholder in the Forest, who hath made Default, and he afterwards sells those Lands, the Beadle may distrain on those very Lands for the Issues lost, though they are actually sold to another.

16. You may see, in *Register of Writs, Tit. Distresses*, of what Things Distresses may be lawfully taken.

Doe.

See { *Vert*, 14. *Appendix*, Ch. Forestæ, 10. *Appendix*, Assisa Forestæ, 7, 10. }

1. A *Doe* is the Second Beast of Chase, a Buck being the First; and 'tis called, the First Year,

1. *A Fawn.*
2. *A Pricket's Sister.*
3. *A Doe.*

2. The Season of the *Doe* beginneth on *Holy-Rood-Day*, and lasteth till *Candlemas*.

3. The proper Terms of hunting the *Doe* are the same as in hunting the Buck.

4. And every Justice-Seat, the Number of Deer must be presented which have been given away by Warrant, and all such which have died, or have been otherwise killed, since the last Court. *Itin. Lanc. fo.* 8.

5. There are several Statutes which relate to Deer-stealing, made in order of Time, as followeth:

6. *SS.* By 13 *R.* 2. *cap.* 13. A Lay-man, not having 40 *l. per Annum*, and a Clerk, not having 10 *l. per Annum*, are prohibited to keep *Dogs* to destroy Deer; the Punishment is Imprisonment for a Year. See *Postea, Dogs*, 72.

7. By 5 *Eliz. cap.* 11. He who enters into a *Park* to *chase* Deer, without the Licence of the Owner, must suffer three Months Imprisonment, and be bound to his good Behaviour for seven Years, which the Party grieved may release in the Sessions; but he might likewise recover treble Damages there.

8. These Laws are still in Force, but they did not prevent Offences of this Nature; therefore, by the Statute 3 *Jac.* 1. *cap.* 13. 'tis enacted, That where a Person is convicted at the Sessions of unlawful *Chasing* or *Killing* any Deer, he should pay treble Damages to the Party grieved, be committed for three Months, and afterwards to remain there till he found Sureties for his good Behaviour for seven Years.

9. These Damages were to be assessed by the Justices, after three Months Imprisonment were expired; but, by the Statute of 7 *Jac.* 1. *cap.* 13. the Party had Liberty, either to take those Damages, or 10 *l.* and when he was satisfied, the Justices, in Sessions, might release the good Behaviour.

10. But

10. But this Statute hath been construed to extend only to the *Chasing* and *Killing* in *Parks*, or Grounds *inclosed* to keep Deer, and not to *Forests*, and the Informer had no manner of Reward; therefore, by the Statute of 13 *Car.* 2. *cap.* 10. not only *Chasing*, *Coursing* and *Killing*, but *Hunting* or *taking* away any Deer in Grounds where they are kept, is punishable by the Payment of 20 *l.* a Moiety thereof to the Informer, and the other Moiety to the Owner of the Deer, if the Offence was committed against his Consent, or the Consent of the Keeper: The Conviction must be before one Justice of Peace, either by Confession of the Offender, or the Oath of one Witness. This Penalty is to be levied by Distress, by Warrant of the Justice before whom the Conviction was made; and if no Distress can be taken, then the Offender is to be committed, by the Justice, to the House of Correction for six Months, or to the common Gaol for a Year, and not to be discharged afterwards, till he can find Security for his good Behaviour for a Year after his Inlargement.

11. Those who are *aiding* or *assisting*, incur the like Punishment. This Penalty of 20 *l.* was too little to be inflicted on Offenders of this Nature; for they would kill and wound many Deer at the same time, and yet the Forfeiture or Punishment was no more than 20 *l.* Therefore, by the Statute of 3 & 4 *W.* & *M.* for *coursing* or *hunting*, the Offender forfeits 20 *l.* for taking in *Toils*, *killing* and *wounding*, he forfeits 30 *l.* for *every Deer*, one Third to the Informer, another to the Poor of the Parish where the Offence was commited, the other to the Owner of the Deer.

12. The Prosecution must be within a Year after the Offence; the Conviction before one Justice of the County where it was done, or where the Offender was taken; and if no Distress can be had,

had, then he is to be committed for a Year, and to ſtand in the Pillory one Hour on a Market-Day, in a Town next adjoining to the Place where the Offence was done.

13. By the ſame Statute, a Conſtable may, by Warrant from one Juſtice, enter and ſearch the Houſes of ſuſpected Perſons; and if he find any Veniſon or Deer-Skins, or Toils, he ſhall carry the Party before a Juſtice, and if he do not give a good Account how he came by them, and produce the Perſon of whom he bought it, or prove the Sale upon Oath, he ſhall be convicted of the Offence, and be ſubject to the Penalties for *killing Deer*, and to be levied in the ſame manner.

14. If he do not immediately pay down the Money upon Conviction, the Conſtable may detain him in Cuſtody till a Return is made of the Warrant for the Diſtreſs; but he cannot detain him above two Days.

15. And no *Certiorari* ſhall be allowed to remove the Conviction or other Proceedings, until the Offender, thus convicted, ſhall enter into a Bond of 50 *l.* to the Proſecutor, with Sureties, to be approved by the Juſtice, to pay full Coſts, upon Oath, within one Month after the Conviction confirmed, or a *Procedendo* allowed.

16. *In Sid. fo.* 286. there is a Caſe of a Deerſtealer, convicted for that Offence at the Seſſions, and fined, and a Writ of Error brought in the *King's-Bench*; and the Court being moved to bail the Offender till the Errors ſhould be argued, the Motion was denied, becauſe he was in Execution for the Fine; but this was before the making the Statutes laſt mentioned.

17. The Statutes which relate to the Puniſhment of thoſe who keep *Guns* and *Engines* to kill Deer, are,

18. *ſſ.* 19 *H.* 7. *cap.* 11. He who keeps *Deer-Hays*, or *Buck-Stalls*, or *ſtalks* any Deer with *Buſh*, (except

(except in his own Park, forfeits 40 *s. per* Month for *keeping* such *Deer-Hays*, and 10 *l.* for *stalking*.

19. Two Justices in Sessions may examine the Offender, and commit him till he pay the Forfeiture; of which the Justices are to have the tenth Part.

20. By the Statute of 3. *Jac.* 1. *cap.* 13. He who keeps a Gun to kill Deer, not having 40 *s. per Annum*, in Lands, or worth 200 *l.* in Goods, any Person having 100 *l. per Annum*, may take away the Gun and keep it.

Dogs in a Forest.

See { *Charge in Chief Justice*, 34, 35, 36, 40, 45, 49.
Doe, 6.
Appendix, Ch. Canuti, 31.
Appendix, Ch. Forestæ, 6.
Appendix, Assisa Forestæ, 8, 16, 17.

1. THe Laws of the Forest do so much regard the necessary Use of Dogs, for the Safety of Mens Goods and Houses who live within the Boundaries thereof, that certain Dogs are suffered to be kept therein by any Person whatsoever: But some Sorts are not suffered to be kept there, but only by particular Men.

Who may keep Dogs in a Forest.

2. *ss.* Every Farmer and Freeholder, dwelling in a Forest, may keep a *Mastiff* about his House; but such *Mastiff* must be lawfully *expeditated* according to the Laws of the Forest; *viz.* by the *Assises of the Forest*, made in the Reign *H.* 2. *cap.* 6. called, *The Assises of Woodstock*, *Mastiffs* must be *expeditated* in a Forest, where the Wild Beasts have any Peace: From which

which it may be plainly inferred, That the Inhabitants of the Forest may keep *Mastiffs* if they are *expeditated*

3. This likewise appears by *Charta Forestæ, Artic.6. viz.* That the Inquiry for *lawing* and *expeditating* of Dogs or *Mastiffs* in a Forest, shall be made when the *Regard* is made, *viz.* every third Year; and then 'tis to be done by the View and Testimony of honest Men, and not otherwise: Therefore 'tis lawful for the Inhabitants in a Forest, to keep *Mastiffs expeditated.*

4. So likewise, in *the Assises and Customs of the Forest, Artic.* 9. made *Anno 6 Ed.* 1. 'tis ordain'd, *Quòd si quis Mastivus inventus fuerit super aliquam feram, & mutilatus fuerit, ipse cujus erat quietus erit de illo facto*: So that if the *Mastiff* be *expeditated*, though he is found on the Deer, yet the Owner shall not be punished.

5. The Word *Mutilatus* is not taken there for *muzzled*, as some affirm, but for *maimed, lamed*, or expeditated, according to the Laws of the Forest; for there is no Law for *muzzling* of Dogs.

6. And, in the same *Assises and Customs of the Forest, Artic.* 16. 'tis ordain'd, *Quòd nullus messarius ducat secum Mastivum magnum ad fugandum feras Domini Regis, &c.* By which it appears, That Men may keep *Mastiffs expeditated* about their Houses; but they must not bring them into the Field to hunt or fright the Deer.

7. So also, *in Charta Forestæ, Artic.* 6. 'tis ordain'd, *Et ille cujus Canis inventus fuerit tunc non expeditatus det pro misericordia tres solidos*; (*i. e.*) Shall be amerced three Shillings: By which it appears, That *Mastiffs* may be kept in a Forest, being *expeditated*, and not otherwise.

8. And this Law is to be understood of *Mastiffs*, only *in the Forest*, and not of those which are out; for there is no Occasion of expeditating any Dogs out

out of the Forest: Therefore the Law doth not extend to them.

9. Besides, the Words in the beginning of the said First Article, are, *viz. Inquisitio vel visus de expeditatione Canum existentium in foresta nostra, de cætero fiat quando fieri debet regardum*: By which it appears, That *Mastiffs*, being *expeditated*, may be kept in the Forest.

10. And, because there is no Law directing who may keep such *expeditated* Dogs, therefore it is generally to be understood, That every *Gentleman*, *Husbandman*, *Farmer* and *House-keeper*, of any Worth, dwelling *within the Forest*, may keep them for the Security of their Houses and Goods.

What Dogs may be kept within the Forest.

11. There are two Sorts of Dogs which, by the Laws of the Forest, are allowed to be kept therein; *viz.* The *Mastiff*, being *expeditated*, and the *little Dogs*, which are mentioned in the Laws of *Canutus*, 32. *Quia manifestè constat in iis nihil esse periculi*; therefore *cuilibet licebit sine genuscissione eos custodire.*

12. Such *little Dogs* are likewise mentioned in *the Assises and Customs of the Forest*, *Artic.* 16. *viz. Nullus messarius ducat secum Mastivum magnum ad fugandum feras Domini Regis, sed parvos catulos ad expectandum extra Coopertum*, ss. *little Dogs* to look after things out of the *Covert*: So that such *little Dogs* may be kept in the Forest, and the Mowers may bring them into the Field.

13. Likewise, *Greyhounds*, and Mastiffs not expeditated, may be kept by some Men, and in certain Places in the Forest.

14. In the *Assises of Pickering*, *Anno* 10. *Ed.* 3. A Man claimed to be quit of *Footgeld*, that is, to keep Dogs in the Forest, without being *expeditated*, and without any Amerciament, Fine or Forfeiture for

for it; and he producing a Grant for the same, his Claim was allowed; but, it seems, a Man cannot prescribe for the same, because such prescription cannot have any reasonable Commencement.

15. In the *Assises and Customs of the Forest*, *Artic.* 17. mention is made of keeping *Mastiffs* in a Forest, *unexpeditated*, and also of *Greyhounds*, in these Words; *viz. De his qui clamant habere libertates, sicut Canes inexpeditatos &* Leporarios *infra metas forestæ, nihil eis faciendum sine Warranto Domini Regis vel Justiciariorum suorum.* By which it appeareth, That he who hath a lawful Claim, by good Title, may keep *Mastiffs*, in a Forest, *unexpeditated*, and *Greyhounds* also; but such a *Claim* must be by vertue of a *Grant* from the King, rather than by Prescription: *Sed de hoc quære.*

What Dogs may be kept in a Forest.

16. *Mastiffs expeditated*, and *little Dogs* may be kept in a Forest; but no other Dogs, without a good *Claim*, by vertue of a *Grant* from the King, or the Owner of the Forest.

17. As for *Greyhounds*, there is no Law to *expeditate* them; and yet there is more Danger in those Dogs than in Mastiffs.

18 'Tis true, *Greyhounds* and *Spaniels* are generally forbid, that is, they are not to be kept in a Forest, but only by a *Grant* from the King. This appears in the *Assises and Customs of the Forest*, *Artic.* 17. before-mentioned; by which 'tis ordain'd, That those who claim to keep *Dogs unexpeditated*, and *Greyhounds*, in the Bounds of the Forest, nothing shall be done unto them, without the King's Warrant, or the Warrant of the Justices of the Forest: From which Words it may be inferred, That *Greyhounds* may not be kept there without a good Claim or Warrant; for if it was lawful to keep them there without a good Claim, it were needless

to make any Claim at all; and so, in like manner, for other things.) *Si Leporarii invent. sunt in forestâ currentes ad aliquod nocumentum ferarum, forestarius debet retinere eos & præsentare in præsentiâ viridariorum & mittere eos Domino Regi vel Capitali Justiciar. forestæ. Assis. forestæ, Artic.* 8.

19. It appeareth, by several Claims in the *Assises* and *Iters of Pickering, fo.* 12. That Men have *claimed* to hawk, hunt the Hare, and to keep *Spaniels*, within the Liberties of the Forest, which is unlawful without such *Claim*; for it would be in vain to claim the keeping a thing which was lawful to be kept without any Claim.

20. And even from the very beginning of the Forest-Laws, it appears, That it was unlawful to keep *Greyhounds* there; for, by the 31*st* of the Laws of *Canutus*, tis ordain'd, *Quòd nullus mediocris habebit, nec custodiet Canes quos Angli* Greyhounds *appellant.*

Of Expeditating or Hambling of Dogs in the Forest.

21. The Dogs which are allowed to be kept in the Forest, must be such which are not able of *themselves* to hurt the Deer; or such which are disabled, by the *Law of the Forest*, to hurt them; which *Disabling* or *Lawing* of Dogs, was called *Hambling* by the Antient Foresters; but now 'tis called *Expeditating*, and it was instituted for the Quiet and Safety of the Wild Beasts.

22. The *Regarders* of the Forest are every third Year, to see what Dogs are *Expeditated*, and what not; and if there are any such, the *Regarders* are to present the same, and who are the Owners; and upon such Presentment, the Dogs are to be *expeditated*, and the Owners amerced 3 *s.* and every third Year, there ought to be a General *Expeditation* of all the *Mastiffs* in every Ward and Bailiwick throughout

throughout the Forest, upon the Presentment and Testimony of the *Regarders*.

What Dogs shall be expeditated.

23. In the 6th *Artic. in Chartâ forestæ*, there are these Words; *viz. Inquisitio vel visus de expeditatione Canum existentium in Foresta*, and doth not mention what Dogs; and since the Word *Canis* may be taken for any sort of Dogs, it may be doubtful what Dogs are there intended.

24. And in the same *Article*, there are these Words; *viz. Et ille cujus canis inventus est*; and in another Place, *Nec expeditentur Canes, &c.* in all which Places the Word *Canis* may be taken for any Dog.

25. So in the *Assises and Customs of the Forest, Artic.* 17. *De his qui clamant libertates habere, sicut Canes inexpeditatos, &c.* there also the Word *Canes* may be indifferently taken for all sorts of Dogs; yet by the Law, it shall be intended for *Mastiffs* only. 4 *Inst.* 308.

26. The Reason is, because, after the Words *De Expeditatione Canum*, these Words follow; *viz. Talis autem expeditatio fiat per assisam communiter usitatam*, that is, by the *Assises* of *H.* 2. and then sets down the Manner how they shall be *expeditated*.

27. And farther, 'tis mentioned there in what Manner Dogs shall be *expeditated*, and in what Places; *viz.* where they have been used to be *expeditated* at the time when *H.* 2. was first crowned: So that all that Article relates only to the *Assises* of *H.* 2. called, *The Assises of Woodstock*, which were made before *Charta forestæ*; and in those Assises, it appeareth, that the Word *Canis* signifies *Mastiffs* only, and no other Dogs; for the Words are, *Item*

Rex præcipit quòd expeditatio Mastivorum fiat ubicunque feræ suæ pacem habent vel habere consueverunt.

28. So that here the Words *Expeditatio Canum* are explained, and 'tis shewed what Dogs are intended, *viz. Expeditatio Mastivorum.*

29. *Anno* 6 *Ed.* 1. *Artic.* 9. *in Assisa foresta* beforementioned, there are these Words; *viz. Si quis Mastivus inventus fuerit super aliquam feram & mutilatus fuerit, ipse, cujus Canis erit, quietus erit de illo facto: si non mutilatus fuerit, ipse cujus Mastivus, erit culpabilis tanquam de manu facta*: In which Sentence, the Words *Canis & Mastivus*, are synonymous, and the one is meant by the other.

30. So that though the Letter of the Law is general, yet it must be construed by the Word *Canis* to mean a *Mastiff*, and no other Dog.

31. *Budæus* calleth a *Mastiff*, *Molossus*; and, in the Old *British* Language, that and all other Barking Curs about Houses in the Night, were called *Masethefes*, because they maze and fright *Thieves* from their Masters; but the Word *Mastivus* is used in the old *Assises of the Forest*, made before *Charta forestæ*, and in those *Iters* and *Assises* which were made since, that every Man might the plainer understand, a *Mastiff* was meant by that barbarous Word.

Besides, the Word *Canis*, without any Addition, may be more properly taken for a *Mastiff*, than for any other Dog; for *Budæus* calleth a *Greyhound*, *Canis venaticus*, and *Canis venatorius*; and in another Place *Canis Leporarius*; and a *Spaniel* he calls, *Canis fugax*, and in another Place, *Canis odoriferus*; all which are Additions to the Word *Canis*; so that where 'tis used alone, 'tis rather taken for a *Mastiff*, than any other sort of Dog.

By

By whom Dogs shall be expeditated.

33. By *Charta forestæ, Artic. 6.* 'tis ordain'd, That the Inquiry of expeditating Dogs in the Forest shall be made every third Year when the *Regard* is made, but doth not say by whom the *Mastiffs* shall be expeditated; but 'tis to be done by the whole Regard and by the Foresters, who go with them, or by the Regarders themselves, without the Foresters.

34. This appears in the 13th *Article* of the Charge of the *Regard*, which was made and used in the Reign of *H.* 2. to which the Charter of the Forest relates; *viz. In Capitulo de Regardo faciend'. Art.* 13. The Regarders of the Forest shall view all the Mastiffs in the Forest whether they are expeditated, and to inquire who keep any not expeditated, and, at the next Swanimote after they have made their Regard, to present what Mastiffs are not expeditated, and who are their Owners.

35. But as yet there was no Law enjoining *who* shall expeditate Mastiffs, therefore it must be done according to the Charter and Laws of the Forest, *Artic. 6. viz. Et tunc fiat per visum & testimonium legalium hominum & non aliter*; that is, Such Course must be taken therein as at Common Law, or in any other like Case by the Forest-Laws, which is to proceed by judicial Sentence from the Court.

36. For, after the whole *Regard* have made such View and Inquiry about the Mastiffs in the Forest, and have made their Presentments to the Verderors, of all such which are kept there, and whose they are; then the Court of Swanimote, or Court of Attachments, may cause all those Mastiffs to be brought before them at the Forty Days Court; and there the Court may appoint a Person, with Instruments convenient for the Purpose, to expeditate

editate them according to Law; which being done in this Order, 'tis done *per visum & testimonium legalium hominum.* So that, in this Case, the Law of the Forest is like the Common Law; for if an Offender is to be punished, and no Person appointed by that Law who shall do it, it is always reserved to the Discretion of the Court, before whom he hath been convicted of the Offence.

37. As for Instance, King *Edward* the Confessor made this Law; *viz. Volo ut omnis homo abstineat à venariis meis ubicunque pacem eos habere volo super pœnam vitæ:* This is *in Libro Sancti Edwardi Confessoris in Scaccario*, where hunting in his Forests is punishable by Death; but the Law doth not declare who shall be the Executioner, for that is left to the Discretion of the Justices of the Forest before whom the Offender shall be convicted, who pronounce the Sentence, and appoint both the Person and Place for the Execution.

38. So likewise, in this Case of *expeditating Mastiffs*, since the Law hath appointed they shall be expeditated, there must be a Person for that Purpose; and since, by *Charta forestæ, Artic. 6.* 'tis ordain'd, it shall be done by the View and Testimony of lawful Men, and not otherwise; and the View and Inquiry being to be made by the *Regarders* of the Forest, who are twelve lawful Men, sworn and appointed for that Purpose; when they have given in their Verdict to the Court of Swanimote, what *Mastiffs* are in the Forest, *unexpeditated*, and to whom they belong, that Court may cause the Foresters, within whose Bailiwick the Owners of such Mastiffs dwell, to bring them thither, where the Court may appoint one to expeditate them according to the *Assises of the Forest*; or otherwise may order the Owners of those Mastiffs to bring them before the *Verderors* at the next Court of *Attachments* to be

held after the *Swanimote*, and after such Inquisition of the Regarders; and then that Court will appoint one to expeditate all such Mastiffs which are returned by that Inquisition to be expeditated: For the Verderors being the Judges of those Courts, they are to give Judgment, and to see that Execution be done; and they are likewise to see that 3*s.* are levied on the Goods and Chattels of those Men who have kept their Dogs unexpeditated, which is to be paid to the Verderors for the Use of the King: All which is to be entered in the Rolls of the Forest, and the Verderors are to accompt for the Money so received, before the Lord Chief Justice in Eyre, at the next Justice-Seat.

39. Some Men have claimed a Privilege to be free from expeditating Dogs; but this is only a Personal Privilege, and shall not be revived by general Words in a Grant, as, *tot*, *tanta*, *talia*, *&c.* for then every one who is now in the Land, will keep each of them a Dog, when there might be but one kept before, and so there might be as many Dogs as Deer. *Jones's Rep.* 271. See *antea Common*, 15.

In what Manner such Dogs shall be expeditated.

40. The Manner of expeditating Dogs is mentioned *in Chartâ forestæ, Artic.* 6. *viz. Talis autem expeditatio fiat per Assisam communiter usitatam*, viz. *Quòd tres Ortelli abscindantur sine pellota de pede anteriori*, that is, (Three Claws of the Fore-feet shall be cut off by the Skin: And accordingly the same is now used, by setting one of his Fore-feet upon a piece of Wood eight Inches thick, and a Foot square, and then setting a Chizel of two Inches broad upon the three Claws of his Fore-foot, to strike them off at one Blow; and this is the manner of *expeditating Mastiffs*.)

In

In what Places Dogs are to be expeditated.

41. In the *Assises of Woodstock*, *Artic*. 6. made in the Reign of *H*. 2. there are these Words; *Item Rex præcipit quòd expeditatio Mastivorum fiat, ubicunque feræ suæ pacem habent vel habere consueverunt.*

42. By which Law it may seem, that *Mastiffs* are to be expeditated in *Chases* as well as in Forests, because the Beasts are as undisturbed there, as in Forests; but it was never yet taken or understood in this Sense, because those *Assises of Woodstock* are, *Tantùm Assisa Forestæ non Chaseæ*, and therefore the Law extends only to *Forests*; and I never read of any Mastiffs expeditated in Chases.

43. Besides, there are no *Regarders* in Chases, and Mastiffs are not to be expeditated but where the *Regard* is to be made, and that is only in *Forests*. This is by the express Words of *Charta forestæ*, *Artic*. 6. by which it is likewise ordained, That *Inquisitio vel visus de expeditatione Canum existentium in foresta fiat, &c.* by which it appears, that Dogs are to be expeditated only in *Forests*, for the Laws of the Forest do not extend to *Chases*; and no Forest is exempted from this Law without the special Grant from the King for that Purpose.

44. 'Tis true, there have been some Opinions, That *Mastiffs* are not to be expeditated, but only in such *Forests* where it hath been *accustomed* so to do in the Reign of *H*. 2. and such Opinions were grounded upon the 6th Article *in Charta de forestâ*, viz. *Nec expeditentur Canes de cætero nisi in locis ubi consueverunt expeditari tempore primæ Coronationis præd Henrici Regis avi nostri, &c.*

45. But the Meaning of those Words is not to exempt the antient Forests from expediating Mastiffs, but only such Places which were once

Forests, and which, by the First and Second Article, were to be disafforested.

46. For in the Sixth Article of the *Assises of Woodstock*, 'tis expresly ordain'd, That *Expeditatio Mastivorum fiat ubicunque feræ pacem habent, &c.* So that though by the First and Third Article of the Charter, all the *New Afforestations* which were by *H.* 2. *R.* 1. or King *John*, were appointed to be *disafforested*; yet, because in those Places the Wild Beasts were once quiet as they were in Forests, the *Mastiffs* were still to be *expeditated*; and therefore, in that Article of the *Charter*, where the Manner of expeditating Dogs is expressed, this Exception was made, *viz. Nec expeditentur Canes de cætero nisi in locis ubi consueverunt, &c.* as if he should have said, *Mastiffs* should not be *expeditated* in any of those Places, which were once, or are still, *Forests*, and which are now to be *disafforested* by this Charter; but they shall be expeditated in all Forests which were Forests at the Coronation of *H.* 2. that is, in all the *Antient Forests*, which are to remain so still, notwithstanding that *Charter*.

47. For, by that Charter, all the new Forests were generally to be disafforested, and therefore there was no *expeditating Mastiffs* in those Places; but all the old Forests which were Forests at the Coronation of *H.* 2. were to remain so still, and in them Mastiffs were and are to be expeditated.

48. So that the Meaning of those Words, *Nec expeditentur canes, &c.* is, That *Mastiffs* shall not be expeditated in any Place but in the antient Forests, and which remain Forests after the Disafforestation of the new ones; for as in the 2d Article of *the Charter of the Forest*, a Clause is inserted to exempt those who were put out of the Forest by the Disafforestation, that they should appear no more before the Justices of the Forest upon the Common Summons, as formerly; so likewise this Clause, *Nec*

expedi-

expeditentur canes, &c. is put into the Charter only to exempt and free those Places which are disaf-forested from the Trouble of expeditating their Mastiffs, as they were wont to do, before the Dif-afforestation of the new Forests; and therefore, at this time, in all Places in *England*, where Forests are, the Mastiffs must be expeditated, unless they have a Charter or Grant from the King to the con-trary.

The Forfeiture for keeping Dogs not expeditated.

49. *In Charta forestæ, Artic.* 6. 'tis ordained, *Et ille cujus canis inventus fuerit tunc non expeditatus det pro misericordiâ tres solidos.*

50. So the Forfeiture for keeping a Mastiff not expeditated, is no more than 3 *s.* but if the Dog doth hurt or kill a Wild Beast of the Forest, then the Owner is to be punished according to the Quality of that Offence, and above the said For-feiture.

Who shall be chargeable with the Forfeiture, and in what Manner.

51. By the same Article 'tis provided, *Quod ille cujus Canis inventus fuerit*; that is, There must be an Inquisition taken by the *Regarders* of the Forest, to certify who is the Owner of the Dog so found, &c. which must be presented, upon their Oaths, to the *Verderors*; and then upon such Mat-ter of Record, the Court may award Process to levy the 3 *s.* and not before.

52. So that it seems plain, the Forfeiture cannot be levied before 'tis found by *Inquisition*, and certified to a Court of Record,

1. *What Dog it was.*
2. *Who is the Owner.*
3. *Who doth keep the Dog.*
4. *Where, and in what Place.*

53. That it may appear whether it was kept in the Forest or not, it must likewise be found by Inquisition, what Manner of Dog it is; for if 'tis not a *Mastiff*, the Owner is not liable to the Forfeiture, for no other Dog is to be *expeditated* by the Laws of the Forest.

54. It must also be found, who is the proper Owner of the Mastiff; for, according to the Opinion of Mr. *Hesket, fo.* 17. he only is chargeable to pay the 3 *s*. He is likewise of Opinion, that if the *Regarders* of the Forest, upon their View and Inquisition, do present, That a Mastiff is kept in the Forest not expeditated, *Et quòd ignorant cujus Canis ille est*, this is a void Presentment, because the Owner is not found.

55. But yet in such Case the Officers of the Forest may take away the Dog; and if he hath hurt any of the Wild Beasts, then he who *kept* the Dog, though he is not the *Owner*, shall be answerable for the same; and if an Action of Trespass or Replevin should be brought against the Defendant for taking and carrying away such Dog, and the Plaintiff should recover a Verdict, then, upon such Trial, and the first Presentment, the Plaintiff who now appears to be the Owner, shall pay the 3 *s*.

56. If the *Regarders* find and present that a Dog is kept in the Forest *unexpeditated*, and that 'tis the Dog of *A. B.* this is a good Presentment; and the said *A. B.* cannot disclaim, nor say, that the same is

is not his Dog generally; for that would be against the Presentment and Return of the Officers upon Oath, and against that which is found by matter of Record for the King.

57. If a Man is indicted for *keeping* a Dog of *T. R.* in the Forest not expeditated, and he pleads, that 'tis not his Dog, this is no Plea, without setting forth the Property to be in some certain Person; and if the Jury should find, that the Property is not in that Person, nor yet in *D. A.* this is no good Verdict, for it ought to find in whom the Property was.

58. 'Tis like the Case of an Indictment before the Coroner, *super visum Corporis*, to which the Defendant pleads, not guilty, and the Jury find him so: This is no good Verdict without presenting another Person who did the Murder; which Presentment shall be in nature of an Indictment against him.

59. If the *Regarders* find and present such a Dog kept at or in the House of *D. A.* in the Forest, he shall not be amerced upon this Presentment; but if they present, that *D. A.* kept the Dog, this is good, and he shall be fined 3 *s.*

60. But if they present, that *D. A.* did deliver a Dog to *A. D.* to keep in the Forest, and that he did keep that Dog there unexpeditated, in such Case *D. A.* who delivered the Dog, shall be charged with the 3 *s.* and not *A. D.* to whom it was delivered.

61. If they present, that *D. A.* delivered the Dog to *A. D.* to keep for a certain time only, and that he accordingly kept the Dog in the Forest unexpeditated, there, both the Deliverer, and he to whom it was delivered, shall be charged; but if *D. A.* delivered it only to be kept as a *Pawn* for Money, there he to whom it was delivered, shall be only charged.

62. If 'tis found, that *D. A.* as a Trespasser, *vi & armis*, did take the Dog of *A. D.* and kept him in the Forest unexpeditated; in such Case *A. D.* the Owner of the Dog, shall be charged with the 3 *s.* and not *D. A.* the Trespasser.

63. So it is if it be presented, that *D. A.* *vi & armis*, took the Dog of *A. D.* who brought a Replevin for such taking; and that *D. A.* kept the Dog in the Forest unexpeditated; in this Case the *Owner* of the Dog, and not he who *kept* him, shall be charged.

64. And if 'tis presented, that one *D. A.* hath kept two Mastiffs in the Forest unexpeditated, he shall not be amerced 3 *s.* for each Dog, but so much only for both; but if two Men have, jointly or in common, one *Mastiff*, each of them shall be severally amerced.

65. But 'tis otherwise if the Husband and Wife have kept one Dog; for the Husband only shall be amerced, they being but one Person in the Law: Neither shall the Wife be charged upon such a Presentment after the Husband's Death; but if they had the Dog in the Right of the Wife, as *Executrix* to another Person, in such Case, if she survive her Husband, she shall be charged upon that Presentment.

66. If a *Peer* of the Realm, or a *Bishop*, is presented for keeping such Dog, he shall pay only 3 *s.* and not according to his Quality; but if a Peer is presented and indicted before the Justices of the Forest for keeping a *Greyhound*, and hunting with him there, in such Case he may be amerced by the said Justices according to his Dignity and Estate.

67. The Words in *Charta de foresta, Artic.* 6. are, *viz. Det pro misericordiâ tres solidos*: Upon which Word *Det*, Mr. *Hesket* hath observed, that the Amerciament of 3 *s.* is to be levied presently by Distress,

Distress, and before the coming of the Justices in Eyre; and so it hath been usually done, as appears by the Rolls and Presentments of the Regarders in several Forests; for he is of Opinion, that this Case is like an Amerciament of a Leet.

68. This Article for the View and Inquisition of expeditating Dogs, differs from any other Article of the *Regard*, because the *Regarders* may assess the Fine themselves; and upon their Presentment certified and returned of Record before the Verderors, the Fine may be levied presently; and he who is presented and found to have, or kept a Dog in the Forest *unexpeditated*, shall pay 3 *s.* and if he will keep the Dog still, he must have him expeditated, or must not keep him in the Forest.

69. This is the Opinion of Mr. *Hesket*, in his reading on the Forest-Law; but whether 'tis Law or not in every Point, *quære*.

Why it is called expeditating or hamling.

70. The Word *Expeditor* is a *Latin* Word of Art, it signifies, to lame, or make one halt or unable to run, and 'tis used instead of *Mutilo*.

71. But in *the Assises and Customs of the Forest*, *Artic.* 9. made in the Reign of *Ed.* 1. the Word *Mutilatus* is used instead of *Expeditatus*, as a more proper and significant Word, and much better *Latin*.

72. In the 31st Canon of *Canutus*, the *lawing* of Dogs is called *Genuscissio*, which was a cutting or laming them in the *Hams*; and therefore the old Foresters called it *Hamling* or *Haxing*, and some called it *Hocksinewing*.

73. King *H.* 2. was the first who cut off the *Claws* of the Fore-feet of *Mastiffs*, and therefore he called it *expeditatio*, that is, by making them unable to run *ex pede*, *viz.* from the hurt of the Foot, by

by cutting off three Claws, *Assis. Woodstock, Artic.* 6. Serjeant *Fleetwood* was of Opinion, that 'tis called, *Expeditatio, quasi ex pede statio, viz.* a Let or Stay to run, and caused by that Hurt of the Foot; but this seems to be a Jingle.

74. By the Statute of 13 *R.* 2. *cap.* 13. it is enacted, That if any Artificer, Labourer, or other Layman, who hath not Lands to the Value of 40 *s. per Annum*, or any Priest or Clerk who hath not a Living to the Value of 10 *l.* a Year, will have or keep any Greyhound, Hound or other Dog to hunt, or Ferrets, Hays, Nets, Hare-pipes, Cords, or other Engines, to take or destroy Deer, Hares, Conies or other Game, he shall be committed for a Year.

75. By another Statute made 1 *Jac. cap.* 27. All Persons, except such who are seised in their own Right, or in the Right of their Wives, of Lands or Tenements of Inheritance to the Value of 10 *l.* by the Year, or of 30 *l.* for Life, or possessed of Goods or Chattels to the Value of 200 *l.* or the Son of a Knight or Baron, or of higher Degree, or the Son and Heir apparent of an Esquire, and who shall have or keep any Greyhound to course Deer or Hare, shall be committed to the common Gaol for three Months without Bail, except he forthwith pay 40 *s.* to the Churchwardens of the Parish where the Offence was committed, or the Party apprehended for the Use of the same Parish.

76. The Qualifications for keeping a Dog, by the Statute of 22 & 23 *Car.* 2. *cap.* 15.

1. He must either be Owner of a Free Warren.
2. A Lord of a Manor.
3. Or he must have an Estate of Inheritance of 100 *l. per Annum*, either in his own Right, or the Right of his Wife, or for Life.

4. Or

4. Or must have a Lease for 99 Years, of 150 *l.* *per Annum.*

5. Or must be the Son and Heir of an Esquire, or one of higher Degree.

77. The Forfeiture is any Sum not exceeding 20 *l.* for every Dog; a Moiety to the Informer, the other to the Poor of the Parish where the Offence was committed; and if the Sum cannot be levied by Distress, then the Offender is to be sent to the House of Correction for any Time under a Month, and there kept to hard Labour, *per* 4 *&* 5 *Will. & Mar. cap.* 23. And no *Certiorari* shall be allowed to remove the Conviction or other Proceedings, unless the Party convicted do become bound to the Prosecutor in 50 *l.* with Sureties, before such Allowance, to pay him all the Costs and Charges on Oath, within a Month after 'tis confirmed, or a *Procedendo.*

78. 'Tis likewise enacted by the Statute of 19 *H.* 7. *cap.* 11. That if any Person, having no Park, Chase or Forest of his own, doth keep or cause to be kept, any Nets called *Deer-Hays*, or *Buckstalls*, he shall forfeit, for every Month, 10 *l.* to any Person who shall sue for the same by an Action of Debt, wherein no Wager of Law, *&c.* shall be allowed.

79. And by the Statute 3 *Jac.* 1. *cap.* 13. If any Person not having Lands of 40 *l.* *per Annum*, or not worth 200 *l.* in Goods, shall keep any Buckstall, *&c.* or Cony-Dogs; then any Person having 100 *l.* *per Annum* of any Freehold Estate, may take away such Dogs, *&c.* to his own Use.

80. By the aforesaid Statute 1 *Jac.* 1. it is farther enacted, That no Person shall be punished by force of any former Statute or Law, for any Offences for which any Punishment shall be inflicted by force of that Law.

81. Now

81. Now these Statutes may very well extend to prohibit such Trespassers who shall commit any Offences in the King's *Forests*, *Chases*, or *Parks*; yet they seem rather to relate to those who are Trespassers in other Men's Parks, *&c.* and not in the King's Forests, *&c.* because the Forest-Laws, which were made long before these Statutes, had provided against all such Offenders in *Forests*, *Chases*, and *Parks*.

82. But these Statutes being made in the Affirmance of the antient Law, the King may at his Pleasure proceed against such Offenders, according to the one or the other.

83. By the Statute 5 *Annæ*, he who keeps *Greyhounds*, *Lurchers*, *Setting-Dogs*, to kill the Game, being not qualified, forfeits 5 *l.* a Moiety to the Informer, the other to the Poor, and that Act is made perpetual by the Act 9 *Annæ*, *cap.* 25.

84. The Parson of *Skally* in *Yorkshire* was indicted, for that his Dogs were not *expeditated*; he pleaded, That *Ecclesia Anglicana sit libera & habeat omnes Libertates suas integras & illæsas*, and by this Plea he was discharged.

85. *Ministri forestæ dicunt quòd consuetum est ante hæc tempora præsentare quolibet tertio Anno de canibus non expeditatis.*

86. *Item dicunt quòd à tempore quo non extat memoria hominum, &c. præsentat. fuit per forestarios ad Attachiamenta istius forestæ de canibus prædicti Abbatis de Rivall, &c. in maneriis suis prædictis non expeditatis.*

87. The above mentioned are Forms of Entries *in placitis forestæ de Pickering*, *Anno* 8 *Ed.* 3. but a Claim to be privileged from expeditating Dogs, is a mere personal Privilege, and shall not be revived by general Words in a Grant, such as *tot*, *talia & tanta Privilegia*, *&c.* for then, where the Possessor kept but one or two Dogs, every one

one who hath a new Grant of any Part of his Lands, may keep a Dog; and this may multiply them to the Destruction of the Deer. *Jones, Rep.* 271.

88. 'Tis part of the Riding Forester's Office to have the care and view of Lawing Dogs.

Drifts of the Forest.

See {*Charge in Chief Justice,* 63. *Appendix in Stat.* 32 *H.* 8.}

1. THE Officers of the Forest do usual *drive* it where there is commoning with Beasts, that the same may not be surcharged by those who have a Right of Common; and also to avoid the Commoning of *Foreigners*, who have no right to common there. 4 *Inst.* 309.

At what Time of the Year the Forest shall be driven.

2. By the Assises of the Forests of *Pickering* and *Lancaster, fo.* 123. the Officers of the Forest *there* did usually make two Drifts of their Forest every Year, (*viz.*) fifteen Days before *Midsummer*, at the beginning of the *Fence-Month*, because at that Time no Man might have any Beasts commoning there; so that by this Drift the Forest was cleared of all Cattle during that Month only; for every Man who had any Cattle at that Time commoning in the Forest, was to take them away when that Drift was made, otherwise the Officers of the Forest might *seize* them to the King's Use, as *Estrays.*

3. And if the Cattle of any *Foreigners* dwelling out of the Limits of the Forest were found com-

moning, who had no right of Common there, in such case the Owners were to be punished according to the Laws of the Forest.

4. The next Drift of the Forest was usually made about *Holyrood-Day*, when the Officers began to agist the King's Woods, at which Time all manner of Cattle which were found commoning in the Forest, were taken by the said Officers and impounded in some convenient Place adjoining; and then the Under-Foresters, Walkers, and *Woodwards* of every Parish, Village, and Hamlet, gave Notice in every Ward that the Owners might come and fetch them away; and then, upon the Delivery of the said Cattle to the respective Owners, a perfect Roll was kept thereof, (*viz.*) What number of Cattle every Commoner had, and what Beasts they were, where the Owner dwelt, what Free-Land he had of his own, or of any other Person in his Tenure or Occupation; and this Order was every Year observed and kept, so that it was known who had right of Common there, and with what Number of Beasts, and who was a *Surcharger*, and also who did agist the Beasts of *Strangers* or *Foreigners* there, for by the Laws of the Forest no *Foreigner* may common there without a Grant from the King.

5. And if the Beasts of any *Foreigner* are found commoning there, tho' they came thither by *Chance*, yet the Owner shall be amerced for every Foot of those Beasts, one Penny for the first Offence, and in like manner for the second Offence, but the third Time they are *forfeited* to the King, and then the Foresters may *seize* them and deliver them to the *Verderors*, and they must enter it on the Forest-Rolls, that the King may be answered of the Value thereof: *Assis. Pickering*, *fo.* 15, 17, 19.

6. In

6. In the case before mentioned, the Beasts of such *Foreigners* must come into the Forest of *themselves* without the Procurement or Drift of the Owner; but if he will *voluntarily* drive them thither to common there, *Quære*, If they are not *forfeited* for the first Offence? See *Assis. & consuetud. Forestæ. Artic.* 15.

7. And it seems very reasonable that the Cattle of *Foreigners* who have no Free Land in the Forest, should have no manner of Common there, because of Right it belongeth to the Inhabitants, and to such who have Lands and Tenements in their Tenure and Occupation there; for they only are subject to the burthen and inconveniences of the Forest in their Corn, Meadows, and Pastures, where the Deer often feed; and for that cause they are to have the Benefit of the Common, for *Qui sentit onus sentire debet & commodum. In decretali Bonifacii*, 8.

How often in every Year the Forest shall be driven.

8. Tho' the Officers of the Forest of *Lancaster* did drive their Forest twice in a Year, yet they might have driven it oftner if they would, and as often as it shall be necessary so to do; but by the Statute 32 *H.* 8. *cap.* 13. 'tis enacted, That all Forests in *England* and *Wales*, and the *Marches* of the same, shall be driven every Year at *Michaelmas*, or within fifteen Days next after.

9. And it appeareth by the same Statute, That the aforesaid Forests may be driven at any other Time of the Year whensoever, and as often as it shall be convenient so to do: See the Statute in the *Appendix*.

For what cause the Forest shall be driven.

10. Forests are to be driven for several causes,

1. For avoiding *Surcharging* of Commons by such who have no right to Common there.
2. That *Foreigners* may be prevented to have any Common there.
3. That no Beasts be suffered there but such as are commonable.

11. By the aforesaid Statute 32 *H.* 8. *Stone-Horses* above two Years old are not to common in a Forest or Chase, unless they are fifteen Hands high, to be measured from the lowest Part of the Hoof of the Fore-foot, unto the highest Part of the Wither, and every Hand must be four Inches of the Standard; but this Statute extends only to Forests and Chases in *Norfolk*, *Suffolk*, *Cambridge*, *Buckingham*, *Huntingdon*, *Essex*, *Kent*, *Hampshire*, *North Wiltshire*, *Oxfordshire*, *Berkshire*, *Worcester*, *Gloucester*, *Somerset*, *North Wales*, *South Wales*, *Bedford*, *Northampton*, *Yorkshire*, *Cheshire*, and *Staffordshire*, the County of the City of *York*, the Town and Liberty of *Gloucester*, the County of the Town of *Kingston* upon *Hull*, the County Palatine of *Lancaster*, the Counties of *Salop*, *Leicester*, *Hertford*, and *Lincoln*.

12. So that by this Statute such Horses are not Beasts commonable in any Forest or Chase in those Counties; and if any such are found there upon any *Drift* made, or otherwise, they are forfeited: See Statute 8 *Eliz. cap.* 8.

By whom Forests are to be driven.

13. It appeareth by the *Assizes of Lancaster and Pickering*, *fo.* 82. That the Drifts of the Forests there were always made by the attending Officers, (*viz.*) by the *Foresters*, *Verderors*, *Regarders*, *Agisters*, *Woodwards*, by the Bailiff, or Bailiffs, and the four Men and Reeve of every Town.

14. And 'tis necessary that all those Officers should be at the Drift of the Forest, as well to be assisting in driving the Cattle, as also for giving Notice to each other, who are to have Common in every Town, and with what Number and what Sort of Beasts, and also who are *Foreigners*, and whose Cattle are found commoning there, that the Owners may have Notice thereof.

15. But by the Statute of 31 *H.* 8. the Drift is to be made by the Officers of every Forest and Chase, and by no other; and that all Drifts which are made at any other Time of the Year than at *Michaelmas*, shall be made and driven by the Officers of the Forest and Chase, and also by the Constable, Bailiffs, Headboroughs, Bursholders, and Tithingmen, and every of them, within the Limits of their Offices, *quod nota.*

In what manner the Drifts are to be made.

This is likewise declared by the *Assizes of the Forest of Lancaster*, *Anno* 10 *Ed.* 3. *fo.* 69. (*viz.*) That at a certain Day appointed by the general Agreement of all the Officers of the Forest, every *Verderor* goes to his own Ward and Precinct, and then calls every other Officer of that Division, and so they proceed in their Drifts thro' their several Precincts, until they are gone thro' the whole Forest, where any Common is taken by Cattle.

In what Places of Forests Drifts shall be so made.

17. This Course may be used in all Forests and Chases where there are any Deer or other Wild Beasts; and 'tis necessary, that Drifts should be made in this or in such Manner, which hath been usually made in every Forest and Chase where there are Wild Beasts of Venery or Chase; and this is for the better Government of the Commons and Herbage there.

Of what Cattle Drifts are to be made.

18. All Cattle whatsoever, which are found commoning, must be driven out of the Forest to some convenient Place adjoining, there to be impounded till the Owners shall claim them; and then every Man may put his Cattle to Pasture and Feeding again in the Common where they were before.

Escapes in a Forest: See **Amerciaments**.

Estovers.

See { *Charge in Chief Justice*, 66.
Wood, 48.

1. THe Prior of *Lancaster* had, by Charter, every Day two Cart-Loads of dead Wood to be burnt in his Priory; and because he took *viridem Boscum pro mortuo*, contrary to his Grant, his *Estovers* were seised into the Hands of the Lord of the Forest, and the Prior was fined, *pro Estoveriis rehabendis ad* 3 *l.* 6 *s.* 8 *d. & rehabuit Estoveria sua. Itin. Lancastr. Anno* 10. *Ed.* 3. *fo.* 65.

2. A

2. A Man may have *Estovers* as appurtenant to a House: This is proved by the Case last mentioned, where the Prior had a Grant of *Estovers* to be burnt in his Priory; and in such Case, if the *Estovers* are spent in any other House, 'tis a good Cause of Seisure of the same *Estovers*, for this is an *Abuser* which is a Cause of *Forfeiture*.

3. Every Man may take *Estovers* in his own Woods by the *View* of the Foresters, and not otherwise; and the Foresters must not take any thing for their *View*; if they do, 'tis Extortion. *Jones's Rep.* 277.

4. Sir *Charles Howard*, amongst other things, claimed Liberty to cut down as much Fir-Wood in any of the King's Woods in *Windsor-Forest*, as he shall *think convenient and sufficient* to burn in his *House* in *New Lodge*. Mr. Attorney *Noy* argued, That this was void, because he had made no Title to *New Lodge*; and if the King grant a Man as much Fire-Wood as he thinks fit to burn in *another Man's House*, 'tis a void Grant, which the Judges agreed.

5. Mr. Attorney also argued, That if he had laid a Seisin in the *New Lodge*, and made a Title to himself, yet the Grant had been void, because it was of as much Wood as he shall *think convenient* to burn there: So that he might take what he thought convenient to burn, and sell it when he had done, it was not of so much Wood as he *should burn in New-Lodge*, for that had been good. *Jones's Rep.* 294.

6. He likewise said, If a Man claim *Estovers* to his *House* by *Prescription*, in such Case 'tis sufficient to alledge a Seisin of the House in himself at that very time when he claimeth them; but if such Claim is by Grant, he must averr a Seisin of the House, *&c.* at the Time when the Grant was made.

7. And in the Case of Prescription, as aforesaid, he must averr, that the House in which the *Estovers* are

are to be burned, is an antient House, otherwise 'tis not good. See *Plus*, Title *Wood*.

Fence-Month.

See *Charge in Chief Justice*, 21.

1. MAny provident Laws have been made for the Preservation of Forests, and for replenishing them with Wild Beasts, especially in the Time of *Fawning*; and therefore since certain Officers are appointed to attend on Wild Beasts, and the Vert of the Forest at all times in the Year, they ought chiefly so to do in the time of *Fawning*, when the young ones are subject to the greatest Danger.

2. *Canutus*, in his 4th Canon, appointed Officers to watch the Deer in the *Night-time* throughout the whole Year: From which it may be inferred, If so much Care was taken to watch the Deer at all times in the Year, the Officers should be more careful in this dangerous Time.

3. King *H.* 2. in *the Assises of Woodstock*, *Artic.* 4. did appoint, That there should be twelve Knights in every Forest, to look after the Wild Beasts, and to see, that all other Officers of the Forest who have the Care of them, shall give their Attendance for their better Safety and Peace.

4. And King *H.* 3. by the Charter of the Forest, *Artic.* 8. did appoint, That the third Court of *Swanimote* should be kept fifteen Days before *Midsummer*, to the Intent, that all the Foresters, Verderors and Agistors, should meet together to make Provision for the Safety of the Wild Beasts during the Time of *Fawning*, which is called, the *Fence-Month*, or, *Tempus Vetitum*, or *Mensis Vetitus*, being the

the Month or Time wherein every Man is forbidden to wander up and down in the Forest, or otherwise to disquiet the Deer.) 4 *Inst*. 313.

5. And some antient Foresters call it the *Defence-Month*, because there ought to be Watch and Ward kept at this Time, to defend the Wild Beasts and their young ones from Danger.

When the Fence-Month first began to be kept.

6. 'Tis uncertain, when the keeping of the *Fence-Month* first began; 'tis probable it might be in the Reign of *Canutus*, because there were no particular Laws to be observed in Forests before that Time, and there hath been no Law since, enjoining the keeping this Month; and therefore Serjeant *Fleetwood*, in his Collection of Forest-Laws, *fo*. 5. tells us, that it hath been always kept in Forests since that Time; for though Forests are privileged Places for the Quiet and Preservation of Wild Beasts, yet, in the Time of *Fawning*, there ought to be very diligent Watch kept for that Purpose.

7. It appeareth by *the Assises of the Forest of Lancaster*, *fo*. 7. made *Anno* 8 *Ed*. 3. That the *Fence-Month* was then kept: And by *Charta Forestæ*, *Artic*. 8. That it it was kept before the Time of *H*. 3. For by that Charter, it was appointed to keep the third Swanimote, when the Agistors and other Officers of the Forest, do usually meet to look after the *fawning* of the Wild Beasts: So that it was kept before the making that Charter, and therefore 'tis probable, that it hath been observed ever since the first making the Forest-Laws, which was in the Reign of *Canutus*; and that when he made Laws for the Preservation of Forests, and the Wild Beasts therein, the *Fence Month* was included in those Laws.

When the Fence-Month begins, and when it ends.

8. The *Fence Month* is 31 Days, and always begins 15 Days before *Midsummer*, according to the Charter of the Forest; *viz. In initio quindecim dierum ante Festum Sancti Johannis Baptistæ, quando Agistatores nostri conveniunt pro feonatione Bestiarum nostrarum, &c.* and it endeth 15 Days after *Midsummer*, on St. *Cyrill's* Day.

9. This appears likewise *in Assisa forestæ Pickering, fo.* 20. and in *the Assises of the Forest of Lancaster, fo.* 7. in which last Assises 'tis mentioned, That if any Swine are found in the Forest, *tempore vetito*, they shall be forfeited to the King; and therefore they shall be delivered to the *Verderors* to answer the Value thereof.

10. The same Law concerning Sheep and Goats. Therefore, during this Month, there must be diligent Watch and Ward kept in every Bailiwick through the Forest, and no Man suffered to wander out of the Highway, nor to fetch or drive any Cattle out of such Highway, lest they should trouble or disquiet the Beasts in the Time of *Fawning*.

11. The Execution of the Laws of the Forest hath been so severely exacted in this Particular, that it appeareth by the antient *Assises of the Forest of Lancaster, fo.* 19. That no Person was suffered to come or pass near the Place where the Beasts did resort at this Time.

How every Officer ought to behave himself at this Time.

12. The Foresters, Verderors, Regarders, Agistors and Woodwards, are all to be assisting each other in this Service for the *Fence-Month*; and at the Court of Swanimote, which is to be held on

St. *Ed-*

St. *Edmund's* Day, *viz.* 15 Days before *Midsummer*, at which Time the *Fence-Month* begins, the Verderors, who are the Judges of that Court, and the chiefest Officers, are to give Directions to all other Officers of the Forest in their Course.

12 This appears by the *Iters of Lancaster, fo.* 59. *viz.* The Forest of *Lancaster* is divided into several Wards, and the Verderors there at the Swanimote Court held for the *Fence-Month*, do divide themselves to their respective Wards; and then each Verderor assembles all the other Officers in his proper Division, *viz.* The Foresters, Regarders, Agistors and Woodwards, and gives them Directions how and in what manner, and in what Places, and with what Company, Watch shall be kept in every Division by the Foresters: And this being done by the Privity and Consent of all the other Officers, 'tis usual for the Regarders and Agistors to join with the Foresters, and to be aiding and assisting them in any thing requisite or necessary to be done at this time; and likewise every Woodward doth usually attend within his own Charge, to watch with the Foresters.

13. And at this Time also, the Foresters do give publick Notice at every House in each Bailiwick in the Forest, that they keep in all manner of Dogs, and not suffer them to go out.

14. The Verderors likewise at this time, give a Charge to those who watch and ward, in this Manner:

1. *ss.* If they find any Person suspiciously wandering up and down out of the Highway in the Forest, they are to apprehend him, and to bring him before the Verderors.

2. If they find any Dogs running up and down, and likely to do any Hurt, or to fright the Deer, they

they shall inquire whose Dog it is, and apprehend the Owner and bring him before them.

3. If they see any Man hunting or coursing any Wild Beast in the Forest, they are to do the like by him, &c.

4. So likewise, if they see any Person taking or carrying away any young Fawn or Fawns.

5. If they find any Man out of the Highway with a Cross-bow, Long bow, Gun, or any other Engine, to hurt or destroy the Wild Beasts, they are to apprehend him, &c.

6. If they find any Person gathering Rushes or Bents, or such like, in the Forest, or in the King's Woods or Lands, or elsewhere, to the Hurt of the Wild Beasts at this Time, they shall apprehend him and bring him before the Verderors to find Pledges.

7. If they see any Person driving Swine to feed in the Forest, they shall apprehend him and the Swine, and carry him, and drive the Swine, to the Verderors.

8. If they shall find any Foreigner driving his Cattle to agist in the Forest, they shall likewise apprehend him, &c.

9. If they find any Deer hurt or dead, they shall inquire how it came, and give Notice thereof to the Verderors.

10. If they shall see any Offenders or Trespassers in the Forest, they shall apprehend them, if they can, and bring them before the Verderors; and if they cannot apprehend them, they shall make Hue and Cry till they are taken.

11. If any Man shall fetch or drive any Cattle through the Forest at this Time, to the Hurt or Disquiet of the Wild Beasts, they shall apprehend him, and bring him before the Verderors.

15. This very Course was observed and kept in every Point in the Reign of *Ed.* 3. as it appeareth by

by *the Assises of the Forests of Lancaster and Pickering*; and also by the Laws of the Forest, this Course is still to be kept in every Forest in the *Fence-Month*.

16. If any Hogs, Goats or Sheep are found in the Forest in this Month, they are forfeited to the King. *Itin. Lancastr. fo.* 7.

Forests.

See { *Boundaries*, 13.
Appendix, Charta Forestæ, 1.

BEfore this Nation was replenished with Inhabitants, there were many great Woods full of all sorts of Wild Beasts then known in *England*; and after the same came to be inhabited, the Woods were, by degrees, destroyed, especially near the Houses; and as the Land increased in People, so the Woods and Coverts were daily destroyed, and, by that means, the Wild Beasts retired to those Woods which were left standing, and which were remote from their Habitations.

2. But there were still, and even in the *Saxons* Time, many great Woods which were not destroyed, and those were called *Walds*, that is, Forests or Woods where Wolves and Foxes did harbour; which being afterwards destroyed by *Edgar*, a *Saxon* King, *Anno* 959. and very few remaining, the *Welchmen* paid him a Yearly Tribute of *Wolves-Skins*; and those and such like ravenous Beasts being thus destroyed, the residue being Beasts of Pleasure, as well as delicate Meat, the Kings of this Land began to be careful for the Preservation of them, and in order thereto to privilege certain Woods and Places, so that no Man may hurt or destroy

destroy them there; and thus the said Places became Forests.

3. *Canutus* the *Dane*, who was King here in the Year 1018, was the first who set Bounds and Limits to those Forests; and the better to have his own preserved from Offenders, he made this Law at *Winchester* in the first Year of his Reign, (*viz.*) *Volo ut omnis Liber homo pro libito suo habeat Venerem sive viridem in planis suis super terras suas, sine Chaceâ tamen, & devitent omnes meam ubicunque eam habere voluero:* Upon pain to forfeit as much as a Man may forfeit, which Law was afterwards confirmed by many succeeding Kings.

4. As this King made a Forest *ubicunque eam habere voluit*, as it appeareth by the aforesaid Law, so in after Ages, when any King intended to do the like, a Commission issued under the Great Seal, out of the Court of *Chancery*, directed to certain Persons, declaring his Will and Pleasure to make a Forest in such a Place, and in such a County, within so many Miles of such a Place, commanding them to perambulate and view the County within the Compass of so many Miles; and to bound and meet so much thereof as they should think convenient to make a Forest for his Delight and Recreation; and to encompass the same with such Marks and Boundaries, as the King may know and discern it from other Land which is not Forest; commanding them likewise to certify to the Court of *Chancery* their proceeding therein before such a Day.

5. When the Commissioners had viewed the Ground and considered how much was convenient for a Forest; then they made Perambulations round it, and bounded it with Hills, Rivers, Highways, and sometimes with remarkable Trees, that the same might be known to be a Forest; and having returned their Commission into *Chancery*, and there-

therewith certified the circuit and compass of the Ground so bounded, beginning at such a Bridge, at such a River, the Highway over the same leading from such a Place to such a Place, as the Highway there goeth, all on the right Hand of the same Highway, is Forest, and so directly from Mark to Mark, and all the Boundaries round the same, until they come to the same Place where they began the Perambulation; and this being retorned and certified as aforesaid, then the King is entituled to it by Matter of Record. 14 *Ed.* 4. *fo.* 2.

6. But as yet it was not a Forest, for after this another Writ issued out of the *Chancery*, directed to the Sheriff of the County where the Place was so retorned to be a Forest, which Writ recited all the Proceedings of the Commissioners; the circuit of Ground they had viewed and perambulated, and their Retorn and Certificate of the same; and that they had appointed so much as is contained in that Circuit, and encompassed with such Marks and Boundaries to be a Forest, and so recited the whole Circuit of the same by such Marks and Boundaries *Verbatim*, as they had retorned, commanding by the said Writ, That the Sheriff make Proclamation throughout the County, as well in Boroughs and Towns, as also in Fairs, Markets, and other publick Places, that the King had appointed that circuit of Ground so bounded and thus retorned into his Court of *Chancery* to be a Forest, and that no Person whatsoever after such a Day, should hunt or chase any wild Beasts of Venery or Chase there, *&c.*

7. And yet after such Proclamation made and retorned by the Sheriff into the Court of *Chancery*, 'tis not a Forest yet, but a Chase, for something more was to be done to make it a *Forest*; because neither the Perambulation, nor the Retorn and Certificate into the *Chancery*, tho' 'tis Matter of Record, with-

without any Proclamation, did make the same either a Forest or Chase, but only a Territory of Ground; for tho' by the Retorn of the Perambulation the King is entituled by Matter of Record, yet 'tis neither a Forest or Chase till 'tis proclaimed by the Sheriff, That the King's Pleasure may be known that it should be so: Neither doth that Proclamation make it a Forest, but only a Chase; for 'tis not a Forest after all this is done, nor until the King hath appointed Officers for the same, as *Verderors*, *Foresters*, *Regarders*, *Agistors*, and *Woodwards*.

8. And a Forest being thus made, and such Officers appointed, there are certain proper Laws and Courts which are incident to the same, just as a *Court-Baron* is incident to a Manor, or a Court of Pie-powders to a Fair, (*viz.*) as for Instance, the Court of *Attachments* or *Woodmote*, the Court of *Swanimote*, and the Court of the *Lord Chief Justice in Eyre*; so that until the same hath such Officers and Courts, the Place is but a *Chase* and not a Forest. *Hesket*, *fo.* 10. *Treherne*, *fo.* 5.

9. But it doth not appear either by Histories or Records, when the *old Forests* in *England* were made, and as antient are the Forest-Laws, except such which have been altered by *Charta de Foresta*, and other subsequent Statutes. 4 *Inst.* 319. *Ibid.* 293, 294.

10. 'Tis true, the Judges *in Pascha*, 5 *Jac.* 1. resolved, That 'tis not the Appellation of it by the Name of a *Forest* in Grants, Offices, and Conveyances, that makes it so in Law; but it must appear by Matter of Record, as by the Eyres of the Justices of Forests, Swanimotes, Officers of Forests, as Regarders, Agistors, Verderors, &c. 12 *Rep.* 22.

11. But this must be understood of the new Forests which were made by the Afforestation of *H.* 2. *R.* 1. and King *John*, and which were disafforested again by *Ed.* 1. for no Records do mention

tion the beginning of the ancient Forests which were made before that Time.

What a Forest is.

12. A *Forest* is a certain *Territory of woody Grounds* and fruitful Pastures, privileged for wild Beasts and Fowls of Forest, Chase, and Warren, to rest and abide there in the safe Protection of the King, for his Delight and Pleasure; which Territory of Ground so privileged is meered and bounded with unremoveable Marks, Meers and Boundaries, either known by Matter of Record or by Prescription; and also replenished with wild Beasts of Venery or Chase, and with great Coverts of Vert, for the Succour of the said Beasts there to abide; for the Preservation and Continuance of which said Place, together with the *Vert and Venison*, there are particular Officers, Laws, and Privileges belonging to the same, requisite for that purpose, and proper only to a Forest, and to no other Place.

13. And therefore a Forest doth chiefly consist of these four Things,

Of { *Vert*, *Venison*, } of { *Particular Laws*. *Proper Officers*. }

14. All which are appointed that the same may be the better preserved for a Place of Recreation for Kings and Princes.

But my Lord *Coke*, in 4 *Inst*. 289. tells us, That a Forest doth consist of eight Things, (*viz.*)

Of { *Soil*, *Covert*, *Laws*, *Courts*, } of { *Judges*. *Officers*. *Game*. *Bounds*. }

15. In

15. In the aforesaid Description of a Forest 'tis called a certain *Territory of Ground*, which word *Territory* is a Circuit of Ground, containing a Liberty within it self; and tho' several Men have Land in it, yet the Territory lies open, tho' likewise there may be several Inclosures in it.

16. The Word in its proper Signification signifies all the Fields and Country lying within the Bounds and Liberty of a City, extended round about to certain Meers and Boundaries, and with no other Inclosure.

17. And because a Forest doth lie open, and not inclosed, and is distinguished only by *Meers* and *Boundaries*, therefore the word *Territory* is a proper Word to express the same; and in the same Sense the *French* do use this Word, (*viz.*) *Territoire d'une Ville*, that is, the Territory or whole Circuit of Land belonging to a City or Town.

18. 'Tis likewise said, that a Forest is a *Territory* of *woody Grounds and fruitful Pastures*, the one for the Shelter, and the other to feed the Deer, without which it cannot be a Forest; and therefore to destroy the *Coverts*, or to destroy the Woods, is to destroy the Forest it self; and so 'tis to convert the Pasture into arable Lands.

19. It must also be *privileged for wild Beasts and Fowls*, because many other Places have Woods, Coverts, and fruitful Pastures, yet are no Forests; so that 'tis this Privilege that distinguishes a Forest from those Places.

20. But a Forest is not a privileged Place for all manner of wild Beasts or Fowls, but only for Beasts of *Forest*, *Chase*, and *Warren*, and no other, that is, for the *Hart*, the *Hind*, and the *Hare*, which are Beasts of the *Forest*; the *Buck*, the *Doe*, the *Fox*, which are Beasts of the *Chase*; the *Hare*, the *Cony*, the *Pheasant*, and the *Partridge*, which are Beasts and Fowls of *Warren*, and no other.

21. The Privilege which they have, is to rest and abide there without Disturbance; and the words (*In the safe Protection of the King*) are to shew by whom they are protected and privileged, (*viz.*) by the Royal Authority of the King, to rest and abide there without the Hurt, Disquiet, or Damage of any Person or Persons whatsoever.

22. By the following Words, *viz.* (*For his Princely Delight and Pleasure*); 'tis plain for what purpose the Beasts are so protected; therefore 'tis not sufferable for any other Person to Hunt or Hawk there without the King's Licence, or without the Licence of his Chief Justice in Eyre, or some other lawful Authority so to do.

23. And by the Words, *viz.* (*Which Territory of Ground, &c. is meered and bounded with unremoveable Marks, Meers and Boundaries*) is shewed by what Means the Forest is known from other Lands, for tho' it lies open and not inclosed with any Hedge, Ditch, Pale, or Stone-Wall, yet in Law 'tis as strongly inclosed by those Meets, Marks and Boundaries, as if it were with a brick Wall.

24. 'Tis farther said, That a Forest *must be replenished with wild Beasts of Venery or Chase*, for otherwise 'tis no Forest; and in such case Men may fell their Woods which they have in the Forest, and destroy their Coverts, because there are no Beasts to take Shelter there, and may also convert their Pasture into Arable.

25. But if there are Beasts of Venery or Chase in any Part of the Forest, the same remaineth so still, and then the Woods must neither be felled, nor the Pastures plowed, without special Licence for that purpose.

26. And by the Words, *viz.* (*Great Coverts of Vert for the Succour of the wild Beasts to have their Abode in*) is shewed the Necessity to preserve those Coverts; and even the Lord Chief Justice in Eyre him-

himself, cannot licence a Man to cut down his own Woods within the Forest, unless there is sufficient left unfelled to shelter the wild Beasts.

27. And these Coverts which Men have Licence to cut, the Springs thereof must be carefully preserved, that they may grow to be Coverts again; for tho' they may have Licence to fell their own Woods, they must not destroy them.

28. 'Tis farther shewed, what Coverts these must be, *viz.* (*Coverts of Vert*,) which word comprehends every Thing bearing green Leaves in the Forest.

29. And 'tis added, *viz.* (*For the Preservation of which said Place, &c. there are particular Laws, Privileges, and Officers, &c.*) which Words shew, That a Forest differs from all other Places, having particular Laws and Officers for the Government thereof; which Laws consist in three Things, *viz.* The Preservation of the Place, and of the *Vert*, which is the green Woods that are Coverts, and of the *Venison* which is every Beast of Forest and Chase; and there can be no Trespass done in the Forest, but it must be either to the Hurt of the Forest, or of the *Vert* or *Venison*, which last Word comprehends every Beast of Forest and Chase, and is a general Appellation for them all.

30. And these Laws of the Forest are called particular Laws, not because they relate to one Forest, and no more; for they are general to all Forests alike; but, because they are particular only, and proper to Forests, and not to any other Places.

31. 'Tis farther added in this Description, That *there are proper Officers belonging to the same*, by which the Jurisdiction of the Forest is set forth; for all Offences and Trespasses in a Forest must be tried before the Officers thereof.

32. The

32. The necessary Officers are these, (*viz.*) A Steward, Verderors, Foresters, Regarders, Agistors and Woodwards, and these hold the Courts of the Forest, for the due Execution of the said Laws.

The Difference between a Forest and a Chase.

33. A Forest differs from a Chase in three Things, (*viz.*) in particular Laws, in certain Officers, and in particular Courts which are incident to Forests, for the Execution of these Laws: And there are no particular Laws proper to a Chase alone; for all Offenders in a Chase are punishable by the Common Law, and not by the Forest-Law, or any other Law proper only, and peculiar to a Chase.

34. Neither are there any such Officers in a Chase as in a Forest, for there are neither *Verderors*, *Foresters*, *Regarders*, nor *Agistors*, but only *Keepers* and *Woodwards*.

35. Neither are there any Courts of *Attachments*, *Swanimote*, or *Justice-Seat* in a *Chase*; all which are held and kept in Forests; and those Officers which are called *Keepers* in a *Chase*, are called *Foresters* in a *Forest*.

36. Neither can Chases, which never were any Forests, have any *Purlieu*; and consequently the Case in *Dyer* 326, must be mistaken. 4 *Inst*. 303.

A Forest comprehends a Chase, a Park, and a Warren.

37. A Forest is in its Nature the highest Franchise of princely Pleasure, and the next to that is a Liberty of a *Free Chase*.

38. (A *Chase* is in one Degree the same Thing as a *Park*, only a Park is inclosed, and a Chase is always open.)

 39. The

39. The next in Degree to a free Chase, is a Park, and next unto a Park is the Franchise of a free Warren; and therefore, because a Forest is the highest and greatest Franchise, being also a general and compound Word, it comprehends both a Chase, Park, and Warren; and for that Reason the Beasts of Chase, and the Beasts and Fowls of Warren, are privileged in a Forest, as well as the Beasts of Forest; and therefore, if any such Beasts or Fowls of Chase, Park or Warren, are hunted or killed in a Forest, 'tis a Trespass of the Forest; and to be punished by the Laws thereof, and by no other Law whatsoever.

Of the Prerogative of the King to make Forests when he pleaseth.

40. The King having a continual Care for the Preservation of the Realm, and for the Peace and Quiet of his Subjects, he had therefore, amongst many Privileges, this Prerogative, *viz.* To have his Places of Recreation wheresoever he would appoint: But this must be understood to be before the making *Charta de foresta.* 4 *Inst.* 300.

41. As by Law he may enter the Grounds of any of his Subjects, where Mines of Gold or Silver are found, so he might keep Wild Beasts and Game to himself in such privileged Places where he will appoint. *Plowd.* 318 *B.* 17 *Car. cap.* 16.

42. For Wild Beasts of Venery, and Beasts and Fowls of Chase and Warren, being Things of Excellency, are, for that Reason, more proper for the Delight and Recreation of a Prince; and therefore they belong to him. *Bracton, Lib.* 2. *cap.* 1.

43. And this may be the Reason why 'tis not lawful for any Man to make a Chase, Park or Warren in his own Freehold; or elsewhere, to pre-

serve

serve such Beasts without the King's Grant or Warrant so to do. *Br. Action sur Stat.* 48.

44. The Punishment for making a Chase, Park or Warren, without such Licence, is by *Quo Warranto*, and the Franchise may be seised into the King's Hands, *Br. Quo Warr.* 7. 6 *Ed.* 2 *Assis. pag.* 34. *Lib. Intr. Quo Warr.* 2. for such Wild Beasts do belong to the King.

45. This appears in *Bracton*, *Lib.* 2. *cap.* 24. *viz. Habet enim Rex præ cæteris omnibus in regno suo de jure gentium, privilegia, quæ de jure naturali esse deberent inventoris, sicut Thesaurum, Wreccum Maris, crassum piscem, Sturgionem, Wayvium, quæ in nullius bonis esse dicuntur: Habet etiam de jure gentium in manu suâ, quæ de jure naturali deberent esse communia, sicut feras Bestias, & aves non domesticas, quæ deberent esse communia de jure naturali, & per apprehensionem & captionem & aucupationem propria, &c.*

46. And although men may kill such Beasts while they are wild and found out of any Forest, Chase, Park or Warren; yet no Man hath any Property in them until they have killed them; for during the Time of their Wildness, they are *nullius in bonis*; and they may properly, in such Case, be said to be *in manu Domini Regis*; and therefore he may prohibit any Man to kill or destroy them.

In what Places Forests should be made.

47. *In Libro Rubro in Scaccario*, it appeareth, *Non in quibuslibet locis est foresta Domini Regis, sed in certis*, viz. *In locis sylvestribus*; So that Forests were always made in Woody Places, where there was great Store of Coverts.

48. And, in the same Book, 'tis said, *In singulis Comitatibus foresta Regis non est, sed in nemorosis, ubi ferarum latibula sunt & uberiores pasturæ.* Here it

appears, that a Forest should have fruitful Pastures, as well as Coverts, for the Wild Beasts.

49. And, in another Place in the same Book, *Numquid in singulis Comitatibus foresta Regis est infra regnum? Non, sed in saltuosis locis*: And in another Place, *Foresta est tuta ferarum mansio, non quarumlibet, sed tantummodo sylvestrium.* By which it appeareth, That Forests were at first made for Beasts of the Woods, and that those are properly Beasts of the Forest which frequent the Woods; and therefore 'tis necessary, that Forests should be made where Woods are growing for the Covert of such Beasts.

50. In the first Article of *Charta de foresta*, it likewise appeareth where Forests should be made, *viz. Omnes forestæ quas Henricus avus noster afforestavit, videantur per bonos & legales homines, Et si Boscum aliquem alium quàm suum Dominii cum afforestaverit ad damnum illius cujus Boscus ille fuerit, statim deafferestetur.*

51. Here the Statute mentions the Woods of other Men; but the Meaning must be, that all the Lands and other Grounds which were before that Time afforested by *H* 2. should now, as well as the Woods, be disafforested by this Charter.

52. So likewise, in the 3d Article of the said Charter, *viz. Omnes autem Bosci qui fuerunt afforestati per Regum Ricardum avunculum nostrum, vel per Regem Johannem patrem nostrum, usque ad primam Coronationem nostram, statim disafforestentur, nisi sit Dominicus Boscus noster.*

53. From both which Places it may be inferred from the Word *Boscus*, that seldom any Lands were afforested, but Woods or Woody Grounds.

54. And because, in former Days, the Woody Countries not being inhabited, were full of Wild Beasts, therefore the Word *Sylva*, which in *Latin*

is

is a Wood, was commonly taken for a Forest, and so was the Word *Saltus*; and in the *Saxon* and *Celtick* Languages, great and vast Woods are called *Falor*, *i. e.* Woods or Forests, because Woods were then Forests.

Why it is called a Forest.

§ 55. Though the Word *Sylva* is often taken and translated for a Forest, and so is the Word *Saltus*, yet neither of them are proper Words for a Forest, but for a Wood. 'Tis true, they are taken for a Forest, because 'tis a Place full of Woods; and therefore a good Forester is called, a good Wood-ward, and was antiently called *Saltuarius*, which shews from whence his Name is derived, though now he is called *Forestarius*.

56. But it doth not follow from thence, that every Wood is a Forest, though there are Deer and other Wild Beasts there, unless the Place is privileged by the King for the Quiet and Protection of the Wild Beasts there.

57. Such a Wood so privileged is called, by *Budæus*, *in 2 Lib. de Philologia*, *Sylva sacrosancta*; and in another Place, *Saltus sacrosanctus*: So that a Wood privileged for Wild Beasts, and a Forest, are both the same Thing.

58. The same *Budæus* calls a Forest, *Saltuaria sacrosancta*: For, speaking of hunting, he saith, *In quibus saltibus ferarum greges sacrosancti sunt, legum regiarum sanctionibus, quos aquarias saltuariasque dicimus.*

59. And hereupon the *Latinists* have framed the Word *Foresta*, which is compounded of *Fera & Statio*, *i. e.* a safe Abode for Wild Beasts; And, in Imitation of the *Latinists*, we have made an *English* Word, Forest, which is compounded of *For* and *Rest*, the Name being derived from the Nature

of the Place which is privileged by the King for the Rest and Abode of the Wild Beasts.

What Benefit the King hath by the Preservation of Forests.

60. If the Officers, who have the Charge of the Forest committed to them, are diligent in the discharge of their Offices, the King would have Plenty and Increase of Deer, as well for the Provision of Venison for his Table, as for his Recreation in hunting.

61. Besides, the great Woods and Timber, as well of his own as of his Subjects, growing in the Forests, would, by this means, be preserved; which otherwise would be cut down and destroy'd.

62. For the Negligence in putting the Forest-Laws in Execution, hath not only been the great Decay and Destruction of the Deer almost in all the Forests of this Realm, but also the Destruction of the great Wood and Timber, the Want whereof, as well now as hereafter, will appear in the Navy.

63. Likewise, the Negligence of putting these Laws in Execution, hath induced a general Ignorance of them; so that they are not only grown out of Use in most Places, but into Contempt by the Inhabitants of the Forests.

64. I do not write this to have those Laws rigorously executed against Offenders; but to have them so executed, that the Forests may still be known to be Forests, and that the Game may be preserved for the King's Use: For otherwise it was much better to disafforest them all, and then the King will be discharged of those great Fees, which he yearly pays out of his Exchequer to the Officers of the Forests.

Who

Who may make a Forest.

65. 'Tis a general Opinion amongst the Learned in the Law, That the King only, *de jure Gentium*, or, as they say, at Common Law, may make a Forest. *Brook Lib.* 2. *cap.* 24. *Hesket*, *fo.* 8. *Treherne*, *fo.* 5.

66. So likewise 'tis a general Opinion, That no other Person whatsoever, but the King, or such who have Authority from him, can make a Forest.

Whether a Subject may have a Forest.

See *Appendix*, in Stat. 22 Ed. 4.

67. 'Tis likewise a common Opinion, that a Subject cannot be seised of a Forest, and that Franchise, which is a Forest in the Hands of the King, is but a Chase in the Hands of a Subject: The Reason is, because a Justice-Seat is incident to a Forest, and none can make a Justice in Eyre but the King. 2 *Bulst.* 295.

68. But this Opinion is not well grounded; for, by the Records of the Court of the Dutchy of *Lancaster*, it appeareth, That in the Reigns of *Ed.* 2. and *Ed.* 3. the Earl of *Lancaster* had a Forest in the Counties of *York* and *Lancaster*, and did execute the Forest-Laws there as largely as ever any King did before.

69. For it appeareth *in Itin. Lancastr. fo.* 64. in the 10th Year of *Ed.* 3. That the Earl of *Lancaster*, who was a Subject, was Lord and Owner of a Forest; and gave Licence unto another to make and inclose a Park within the Boundaries of that Forest; and to have and hold the Park so inclosed, with all such Venisons as the Grantee should put therein, to him and his Heirs for ever: And this was

adjudged to be a good Licence in a Claim made by the Grantee. By which it appeareth, That a Subject may be Owner of a Forest; and that it may be and remain a Forest still, though in the Hands of a Subject.

70. By the same Records it likewise appeareth, That the Earl of *Lancaster*, being Tenant in Tail of the Honour and Forest of *Lancaster*, did, by his Deed, grant unto *W. N.* Licence to make a Park within the said Forest, and afterwards the Earl died; and this Grant being not binding to his Heir, the Grantee compounded and paid a new Fine to the Heir, that he might suffer his Park to continue. *Itin. Lancastr. Anno* 10. *Ed.* 3. *fo.* 69.

71. *In* 26 *Assisarum placito* 60. King *H.* 3. being seised of the Honour of *Pickering*, to which a Forest was then appendant, did grant the said Honour, *cum pertinentiis suis*, unto *Edmund* Earl of *Lancaster*, and his Heirs; and it was adjudged, that by this Grant of the Honour, *cum pertinentiis*, the whole Royalty of the Forest did pass.

72. *In Hill.* 42. *Ed.* 3. *fo.* 2. it was held, That a Forest in the Hands of the King may be granted by him to a Subject, even by the Name of a Forest; and that the same shall be a Forest still in the Hands of the Grantee, being a Subject.

73. By the reciting Part of the Statute of 22 *Ed.* 4. *cap.* 7. which provides for those who had Woods in the Forests, that they might lawfully inclose such Woods after they were cut down, it appears, That the Statute relates as well to those who have Woods in the King's Forests, as to those who have Woods in the Forests of other Men, by express Words.

74. And the Statute of 27 *H.* 8. *cap.* 7. provides for the Reformation of several Disorders and Oppressions on the King's Subjects in *Wales*, by colour of the Forest Laws; *viz.* Within such Forests as

as were the Inheritance of the King, as in other Forests whereof Lords and other meaner Men were Owners.

75. By all which Cases and Statutes, it plainly appears, That a Subject may be Owner of a Forest.

76. And this is grounded upon the old Authorities, in *Bracton*, *Lib.* 2 *cap.* 24. where, writing of the Privileges of the King, and what Privileges he may grant, he hath these Words; *viz. Ea vero quæ dicuntur privilegia licèt pertineant ad Coronam, tamen à Coronâ separari possunt, et ad privatas personas transferri, sed de gratiâ ipsius Regis speciali.*

77. So that 'tis not to be doubted but that a Subject may have a Forest by the King's Grant under the Great Seal, as the Duke of *Norfolk* had formerly: The Lord *Abergavenny* had St. *Leonard's* Forest in *Sussex*; and the Duke of *Buckingham* had the Forests of *Brecknock-Hay* and *Causellay*; and though they were in their Hands, being Subjects, yet they were Forests still, and they punished Offenders therein by the Forest-Laws.

78. And even at this time there are some Noblemen who have Forests by Grants from the King to them or to some of their Ancestors; as the Lord *North* hath the Forests of *Weybridge* and *Sapley* in Fee. *Dyer*, 169.

How a Forest may be granted by the King to a Subject.

79. Mr. *Treherne*, *fo.* 5. and Mr. *Hesket*, *fo.* 7. tell us, That if the King is seised of a Forest, and by his Letters Patent, grants the same to a Subject, by the Name of a Forest, *Habendum sibi & hæredibus suis, cum omnibus incidentibus, appendiciis & pertinentiis*; that the Grantee, or his Heirs, shall have the same as a Forest by vertue of such Grant; and all Officers which belong to the Forest, must remain

remain as they were before, excepting only a Chief Justice in Eyre.

80. And such Grantee may hold a Court of Attachments every forty Days; and likewise, a Court of Swanimote, in such Manner as the Law appoints: But if he will hold a Court of Justice-Seat, to punish such who are presented in those Courts aforesaid, for Trespasses done in the Forest, then he must procure a special Commission from the King, under the Great Seal, directed to certain Persons therein to be named, giving them Authority to hold Plea of all Trespasses done in the Forest, and to hear and determine the same.

81. For though the Grantee hath the Place as a Forest, yet he cannot appoint a Justice in Eyre himself, unless the King, by special Words, had granted to him *Jura Regalia*; and then the Grantee may hold a Justice-Seat for that Forest, and appoint Justices to hear and determine Trespasses done there, and punish Offenders for the same.

82. And 'tis not an unusual Thing for the King to make such Grants; for several Abbots and Bishops had *Jura Regalia* in many things; as the Abbots of St. *Albans* and *Glastonbury*. *Lib. Intr. tit. Franches. fo.* 358. *Secretum Domini, fo.* 78.

Where a Forest, granted by a King to a Subject, shall still be a Chase.

83. It was the Opinion of the Lord Chief Justice *Thorp, Anno* 43 *Ed.* 3. That if the King purchaseth a Manor unto which a Forest is regardant, and afterwards gives the said Manor to another, *Simul cum libertatibus, ad illud spectantibus*, That, by such Grant, the Forest doth not pass; for, by the Purchase, all Royal Franchises and Liberties belonging

to

to the Manor, were annexed to the Crown. *Plowd.* 332.

84. But 'tis otherwise if he grant the Manor, *cum Libertate ad illud spectante tempore quo manerium fuit in manibus feoffatoris*; so that by the Purchase, the Franchise Royal is extinguished, and cannot pass without special Words, which amount to a new Grant.

85. *Treherne, fo.* 6. and *Hesket, fo.* 7. are of Opinion, That where the King is seised of a Forest, and by his Letters Patent grants the same to a Subject, by the Name of a *Forest*, *cum omnibus suis Parcellis*, yet the same is but a *Chase* in the Hands of the Grantee; for he cannot hold any *Court of Attachment* or *Swanimote*; neither can he make *Verderors*, *Regarders*, and other Officers, and without such Courts and Officers it cannot be a Forest. 42 *Ed.* 3. *fo.* 2. *Placito* 8. *Kelleway* 14. 2 *Bulst*. 298.

86. But if the King had granted, That he should have made a *Justice-Seat*, in such Case the Grantee would have a Forest. 2 *Bulst.* 297. 4 *Inst.* 314.

87. So that by the Book-Case 42 *Ed.* 3. as aforesaid, it appeareth, That a Forest which is such in the Hands of the King, may be granted by the Name of a *Forest* to a Subject, and yet shall be but a *Chase* in the Hands of the Grantee.

88. In *Dyer*, *fo.* 169. there is this Case, (*viz.*) *H.* 8. by Letters Patent, in the 33 Year of his Reign, granted to Sir *Richard Cromwell*, *forestas suas de Weybridge & Sapley in Com. Huntingdon, habendum sibi cum suis partibus, membris, parcellis & pertinentiis universis*; and this was for the Term of 80 *Years*, paying for the same yearly to the King, 6 *l.* 13 *s.* 4 *d.* with this Clause, (*viz.*) *Et prædict' Richardus Cromwell, Executores & Assignat. sui custodient, habebunt & manutenebunt in forestis prædictis de tempore in tempus durante termino prædicto Centum Damas*

Damas & easdem seu alias consimiles in numero in prædictis forestis in fine termini prædict. dimittent præfat. Regi, hæredibus & successoribus suis, without any other Reservation of the Game.

89. The Lord *North*, who had afterwards the Inheritance of the said Forests by a Grant from the King, gave out Warrants, and did take the Game there; and it was the Opinion of most part of the Justices, and the Serjeants of both Houses, and the King's Attorney, that he could not do it, because all the Game were included in the word *Forest*; and the hundred Deer, or any of them, were not reserved to be killed; for then it was impossible for the Lessee to perform his Covenant, but they were reserved for a Stock and Breed of more in the Forest.

90. It was likewise held, That Sir *Richard Cromwell* the Grantee might have the same as a *Forest* by the Words of that Grant; and that he might hold a Court of Attachments and Swanimote, but no Justice-Seat, without a special Commission for that purpose granted by the King; so that if a Trespass is committed in such Forest, the Grantee may punish it according to the Laws of the Forest, which he could not do if it was a Chase; for then he must bring an Action of Trespass at Common Law, *Quare Chaseam suam fregit*, or else indict the Offender; so that it plainly appears, That a Forest granted by the King to a Subject, by the Name of a Forest, shall remain and continue a Forest in the Hands of the Grantee.

91. *The last Prince* Henry *had a Forest granted to him with a Power also to make a Justice in Eyre, and also Licence to keep Courts; and the Duke of* Lancaster *likewise had such a Grant with a special Commission to make a Justice in Eyre for keeping Courts.* 2 Bulst. 295.

4 92. From

92. From the aforesaid Case in *Dyer* it may be inferred, That if the King had granted the said Forests of *Weybridge* and *Sapley* unto Sir *Rich. Cromwell*, *habendum Richardo Cromwell*, *&c.* leaving out the following Words, *Cum suis partibus, membris, parcellis & pertinentiis universis*; and tho' the Grant had contained all the other Words, and likewise the Covenant for maintaining the Deer; yet the Grantee should have those Forests but as *Chases*; for nothing is included in the Grant by the word *Forest*, but the Deer and Game.

93. Therefore, where the King is seised in Fee of the Royal Franchise of a *Forest*, and grants the same to a Subject by the Name of a *Forest*; yet if there are no Words which enable him to keep a Court of Attachments and Swainmote, he shall have it only as a free Chase, and not otherwise; so that without Words in the Grant to authorize him to keep such Courts which are incident to a Forest, the same is but a free Chase.

94. *King Ric.* 2. *granted to* Thomas *Duke of* Gloucester, *the Castle of* St. Briowell, *and the Forest of* Dean, *in special Tail*; *and it was afterwards enacted by the Parliament*, *That the Duke should hold the said Forest as a Forest*, *with Power to constitute such Justices and Officers*, &c. *as are incident and belonging to a Forest*. 4 Co. 315.

95. And according to the Cases before mentioned, all the Judges of *England* met together in *Serjeant's Inn*, where, amongst other Things it was resolved, That a *Forest* may be in the Hands of a Subject, and be used as a Forest, if the King gives Authority by express Words for the Administration of Justice there, and for his Justices to come there; and if the Grantee had a Commission to use and have Officers in the Forest, then it shall continue a Forest in the Hands of a Subject; otherwise, without such Liberties, it is but a Chase in the

 Hands

Hands of a common Person; and *Popham* said, That he had seen such Liberties of Forest granted in that manner. 2 *Co.* 155.

96. But in all the Cases where it is said a Subject may have a Forest, as 2 *Ed.* 2. *Tit. Trespass, fo.* 9. in the Time of *Ed.* 1. *Tit. Trespass, Plowd.* 239. *Dyer* 72, *&c.* it must be intended, if he hath Power to have *Swanimotes* and Justices in Eyre, and Foresters appendant to his Forest.

Which are Beasts of Forest, and the Difference between them and Beasts of Chase.

97. The Book called *Antiquitas Britannica, fo.* 48. which was written before the Conquest, mentions five wild Beasts of Venery, which are called Beasts of the Forest, (*viz.*) The *Hart*, the *Hind*, the *Hare*, the *Bear*, and the *Wolf*; and accordingly the antient Book of *St. Albans, fo.* 30. concerning *hunting* and *hawking*, written long since by a Monk, mentions those five Beasts to be Beasts of Forest, and no other; and with him agrees *Hollingshed*, in his Description of *England* 206; and old Sir *Tristram*, in his worthy Treatise of Hunting, saith the same Thing: and with them agreeth *Budæus*, in his second Book *De Philologia*, that those five *semper forestæ & veneris habentur Bestiæ*; and so likewise saith *Fleetwood, fo.* 9. and Mr. *Hesket, fo.* 20. tells us, those five are properly called Beasts of Forest or Beasts of Venery.

98. As for *Wolves* there are none now in *England*, but formerly there were many here; and all the antient Woodmen and Foresters did account them Beasts of Forest, and the Fox a Beast of Chase, because Kings and Princes took a Delight in hunting them; and therefore, if they were killed by any other Person without Leave, and within the Boundaries of the Forest, it was a Breach

of

of the King's Royal Franchise, and the Offender was to be punished.)

99. But the *Wolves* were almost destroyed by King *Edgar*, so that when *Canutus* began to reign, no care was taken to preserve those which were left, because they were dangerous and hurtful Beasts; and therefore in his Forest-Laws, *Canon* 27, they were not accounted Beasts of Forest; nor Foxes, Beasts of Chase, (viz.) *Vulpes & Lupi nec forestæ nec Veneris habentur, & proinde eorum interfectio nulli emendationi subjacet, si tamen infra limites occiduntur fractio sit Regalis Chasiæ & mitius emendatur*; so that tho' *Canutus* did not account the one a Beast of the *Forest*, nor the other a Beast of *Chase*, yet they were privileged in the Forest, and were not to be hurt there.

160. (The Difference between Beasts of Forest and Beasts of Chase, is, That Beasts of Forest are *Sylvestres tantùm*, and usually frequenting the Coverts, and the Beasts of Chase are *Campestres tantùm*.)

101. If any white Tawer live in a Forest, he shall be removed and pay a Fine, for they are the common Dressers of Skins of stoln Deer. *Irish Laws. fo.* 7.

Forester.

See { *Bail*, 5, 7, 13.
Charge in Chief Justice, 24, 25, 26, 27, 78, 79.
Hunting, 41.
Offender, 2, 3.
Presentment, 1.
Ranger, 4.
Regarder, 38.
Scotale, 3.
Venison, 6.
Warrants, 2.
Woods, 5.
Appendix, Charta Canuti, 4, 8.
Appendix, Charta Forestæ, 7.

1. A Forester is an Officer sworn to preserve the *Vert* and *Venison* in the Forest, and to attend upon the wild Beasts within his Bailiwick; and to attach Offenders there, either in *Vert* or *Venison*, and to present the same at the Courts of the Forest, that they may be punished according to the Quantity and Quality of their Offences and Trespasses.

The Oath.

2. ¶ *You shall truly execute the Office of a Forester, or Keeper of the King's wild Beasts, in the Walk called* P. *within the Forest of* W. *you shall be of good Behaviour your self towards his Majesty's wild Beasts, and the Vert and Venison of the same Forest; you shall not conceal the Offence of any other Person, either in Vert or Venison, that shall be done within your Charge, but as well the same Offence, as also all Attachments you shall present at the next Court of Attachments or Swanimote, which shall first happen to be*

holden for the same Forest; and you shall to the uttermost of your Power maintain and keep the Assise of the Forest, and in all Things the King's Right defend concerning the same, so long as you shall be Keeper there:

So help you God.

3. He is made by *Letters Patent* under the Great Seal, and some of them have their Offices in *Fee*, paying to the King a Fee-Farm Rent for the same, as it appeareth by the Assises of *Pickering* and *Lancaster*; and such Office in Fee may be forfeited, and this was the Case of *Roger Bigot*, Earl of *Norfolk*, in the Forest of *Pickering*; and a Man may be a Forester in Fee *in jure Uxoris*. 11 *Ed.* 3.

4. Some of them have their Office *for Life*, and some of them but only *durante beneplacito*, and in like manner it is of all other Foresters that are not Foresters to the King, and those who are Servants to such Officers are not properly called Foresters, but *Walkers* or *Under-Keepers*.

5. These Foresters must not *walk* or make any *Attachments* in the Forest before they are *sworn*, if they do 'tis *contra Assisam forestæ*, as appears by the *Iters* of *Lancaster*, *fo.* 7. and by the *Woodstock Assises* in the Reign of *H.* 2. where the Words are, *nec aliquis aliquem attachiet nisi sit forestarius juratus.*

6. His Office consists principally in these four Things,

To { *Preserve.* / *Watch.* / *Attach.* / *Present.* }

7. (1.) He must preserve the *Vert* and *Venison*, without which it cannot be a Forest; therefore he must be very careful to preserve the Coverts where the wild Beasts frequent, (*viz.*) Such which are

wild Beasts of Venery; and he must not destroy any such Beasts without good Warrant so to do; if he doth, 'tis a *Forfeiture* of his Office.

8. He must likewise take care that the Deer may have Food in the Winter; and for that purpose, by the *Assises* of *Pickering*, *fo.* 19. 'tis provided, That he may lop Trees in another Man's Land for *Browse*.

9. He must also be very diligent in looking after the Deer in the *Fence-Month*, and to preserve the young *Fawns* for the Increase of the Game, according to the *Assises* of the Forest.

10. He cannot give a Licence to any one to *hawk* or *hunt* in the Forest; for if he doth, both he, and all those who hawk or hunt there by his Warrant, are Trespassers, and punishable for the same by the Laws of the Forest.

11. *In long quinto, Ed.* 4. *fo.* 26. *B.* and also in *Trin.* 5 *Ed.* 4. *fo.* 5. *Placito* 64. it appeareth, That if Deer in a *Park* are destroyed by the Negligence of the *Keeper*, 'tis a *Forfeiture* of his Office; the Law is the same in case of a *Forester*.

12. Neither can he hunt there himself, or kill any Deer in the Forest without a lawful Warrant, for if he doth, he forfeiteth his Office; for he hath an Authority to preserve, and not to destroy, and therefore the Misuser or Abuser of his Authority will incur a Forfeiture.

13. (2.) Another Part of his Office is to *Watch* the *Vert* and *Venison* in the Forest, that it may not be destroyed; for as a Forester himself may not kill any wild Beasts of the Forest without good Warrant, nor cut down or destroy the *Vert* or *Venison*, so he must not suffer any other Person to do any manner of Hurt or Trespass to either; for it appeareth by the Laws of *Canutus*, *Canon* 2, That Foresters were at first appointed, *ad suscipiendum*

endam curam & onus tam de viridi quàm de Venatione.

14. (3.) Another Part of his Office is to *attach* Offenders or Trespassers in the Forest; for as he is to preserve the *Vert* and *Venison*, and to watch and attend the same, so he must *attach* all such Offenders and Trespassers as he shall find in the Forest, that they may be punished as the Laws of the Forest direct, but he must not do it before he is sworn. *Itin. Lancastr. fo.* 7.

15. And therefore, if he find any Man in the Forest, either with Bow and Arrows, or with *Greyhounds*, intending to offend there, he may arrest and imprison him as if he had actually done the Fact, but he cannot arrest the Body of such Offender, unless he is taken *with the Manner*, That is Dog, Draw, Stable-stand, Back bearing, Bloody-hand. 4 *Inst.* 294.

16. If such Offender fly, the Forester may pursue him with *fresh Suit*, and within his View *out of the Forest*, and may attach him there; but this is not justifiable, unless upon such a *fresh Pursuit*, and upon extream and forcible Means.

17. So that he is bound as well by his Oath as by his Office to apprehend the Offender's Trespassing in his Bailiwick, if he can by any means; and this upon the Peril of forfeiting his Office.

18. For if he is negligent in apprehending, or willingly suffers them to kill or destroy the Game, 'tis a Forfeiture of his Office; this appears *in long quinto of Ed.* 4. *fo.* 2[illegible] and *Trin.* 5 *Ed.* 4. *fo.* 5. *Placito* 64. before mentioned, and by the *Assises and Customs of the Forest. Anno* 6 *Ed.* 1. *Art.* 11. not only the Foresters, but all other Persons dwelling in the Forest must do what they can to apprehend such Trespassers and Offenders; the Words are, (viz.) *Si quis viderit aliquos Malefactores infra*

metas forestæ aliquam feram capere, vel asportare, debet illos capere secundùm posse suum.

19. But as it hath been already said, neither a Forester, or any other Person may apprehend an Offender, being without the Limits and Bounds of the Forest, unless he followed him out of the same, by a *fresh Pursuit*, always within his View; for in such Case he may apprehend him out of the Limits, but he may neither wound, beat, or kill him there, as in some Cases he may, if within the Forest, by vertue of the Statute 21 *Ed.* 1. and the Reason is, because, whilst the Offenders are within the Forest, the Officer hath a sufficient Authority, by vertue of his Office, to arrest them, that they might give Satisfaction to the King for their Offences.

20. So that in this Case the Authority of a Forester is like the Authority of a Sheriff, who having a Warrant to apprehend a Man in his Counry, and he flieth into another, in such Case the Sheriff may freshly pursue him within his View, and arrest him in that other County; but he must not assault or beat him for flying, or because he was not arrested before in the first County. *Pasch.* 2 *Ed.* 4. *fo.* 6. *Placito* 74. 13 *Ed.* 4 *fo.* 8 *&* 9. *Placito* 4.

21. And a Forester or Keeper of the King's Forest, may do the like, so as he follow and freshly pursue the Offender within his View, as aforesaid, or hath a special Warrant and Authority from the Lord Chief Justice in Eyre, to arrest him wheresoever he shall be found.

22. And this may be inferred from the 10th *Artic. Assisæ forestæ, Anno* 6 *Ed.* 1. (viz.) *Si quis ceperit feram sine Warranto in Foresta, Corpus suum arrestetur ubicunque inveniatur infra metas forestæ*; therefore the Forester may not arrest him *without* the Bounds, unless he is followed by a *fresh Pursuit* within the *View*, as aforesaid.

23.

23. (4) Another Part of the Office of a Forester, is to present; that is, He must not conceal any manner of Offence in the Forest, either in the Vert or Venison, nor any Attachments he hath made for any Offence or Trespass; but must present the same before the Verderors at the Forty-Days-Court, or at the Court of Swanimote, according to the Assises and Laws of the Forest, that the Vert and Venison may be the better preserved, and the Offenders, in such Cases, punished.

24. It may not be improper in the next place, to shew how Foresters ought to behave themselves towards the Inhabitants of the Forest, without any manner of Extortion and Oppression; for before the Statute *de Charta Forestæ* was made, it was a general Complaint, That Officers of the Forest did very much oppress those People who dwelt therein, or who had Lands adjoining; and these Oppressions were Two-fold, *viz.* by Extortions, and by a multitude of Officers, by whom the same were exacted.

25. Now as the Mischiefs were Two fold, so were the Remedies, *viz.* The first is a general Prohibition for avoiding all manner of Extortion by any Officer of the Forest, *viz. in Charta de Foresta, cap.* 7 *Nullus forestarius vel Bedellus de cætero faciat scotallas, vel colligat herbas, vel avenam, vel bladum aliquod, vel agnos, vel porcellos, nec aliquam Collectam faciat, nisi per visum & sacramentum duodecim Regardatorum, &c.*

26. The second Branch is likewise a general Prohibition to avoid all manner of surcharging the Forest, with too many Foresters and Walkers, and other Under-Officers: So that there should be no more than what are sufficient to look after the Wild Beasts, and by diminishing the Number of these Officers, their Extortions, of consequence, would be diminished: The Words are, *viz. Tot*

forestariis ponantur ad forestas custodiendum quot ad illas custodiend' rationabiliter viderint sufficere.

27. Now concerning the first Prohibition of the Statute which is for avoiding Extortion, 'tis to be considered, that there are seven Things forbidden in this Branch, wherein Extortions were in former Days committed by these Officers, *viz.*

In gathering of { *Scotale.* / *Hay.* / *Oats.* / Other *Corn.* / *Lamb.* / *Pigs.* }

Or any manner of *Gathering* whatsoever.

28. (1) A *Scotale* is where any Officer of the Forest keeps an Alehouse there, and, by colour of his Office, causeth Men to come thither to spend their Money, for fear of his Displeasure. This is an Offence to be inquired at the Swanimote; and at the general Sessions of the Forest, *per duodecim juratores*; and if such a Forester be attainted of this offence, he is to be punished and put out of his Office.

29. The like Law if any Forester or other Officer of the Forest keeps any Game, or sells any Ale at a certain Day, and by colour of his Office causeth People to spend their Money there, this is a *Scotale*.

30. But if such Forester or other Officer is robbed, or his House or Buildings are burnt by Misfortune, so that he is reduced to Poverty, and the People come and drink at his House, and give him Money in Charity; this is no *Scotale* nor Extortion, because *Scotale* is Extortion *colore Officii*, and not *virtute Officii*; for what he doth *virtute Officii*, is not Extortion.

31. The

31. The Words, *Nullus de cætero faciat scotallas, &c. Nisi per visum & sacramentum duodecim regardatorum quando faciunt Regardum*, do imply, That some sort of Scotales are lawful, *viz.* Such which had a lawful beginning; and those must be found and presented by the View of the Regarders, upon their Oaths, when they make their Regard, that they had a lawful Beginning, either by Tenure, Grant, or Prescription, so that it may appear that it was lawfully done, by good Right and Title, and not wrongfully exacted of the People, *colore Officii*.

32. So if a Forester or any other Officer of the Forest, by colour of his Office, doth oppress those who have any Right of Common there, by compelling them in a clandestine Manner, to give him Hay, Oats, or any other Corn, or Lambs, or Pigs; or make any manner of Collection for Money or other things, this is Extortion, and 'tis now prohibited by that Statute to be used for the Time to come, for the Words are, *de cætero*, that is, from henceforth, *viz.* from the making the Statute, such Things shall not be used.

33 But though the collecting Hay, Oats, Corn, Lambs and Pigs, or any thing whatsoever, is prohibited by the Statute where a Man hath no good Right or Title to the same; yet, in some Cases, 'tis lawful, *viz.* If such collecting commenced by good and lawful Title, which may be by these three Ways or Means.

1. *Tenure.*
2. *Grant.*
3. *Prescription.*

34. First, by Tenure, as where a Man holdeth Land in the King's Forest, to pay unto a Forester every Year, at his Scotale, 5 *s.* or one Sheep or

Lamb; this is not Extortion, for 'tis not paid, *colore Officii*, without any Right or Title.

35. So 'tis if one holds Land of another paying a certain Rent, and also paying to the Forester a certain Quantity of Oats and Corn: This is not Extortion.

36. So likewise, if a Man, by Bargain and Sale inrolled, intail his Land to find or give unto the Foresters a certain Collection every Year: In this Case, if the Donee will not pay or deliver the Collection, the Foresters have no Remedy in Law to compel him, but the King may; for he, in respect of the Right he hath in the Forest, may cause the Donee to be indicted, and the Donor likewise may compel the Payment by Distress; and if the Donee should pay it to the Donor, and not the Foresters, according to the Tenure, yet the Donee shall not be discharged by that Payment, but that the Donor may distrain him a-new for his Service not done.

37. (2) The Second is by Grant, as if one, dwelling in the Forest, grants unto the King a certain Collection or Profit for his Foresters to be received by them Yearly: In this Case they may lawfully collect the same.

38. So likewise, if one grant to an Officer in the Forest, any such Collection, Profit or other thing *in Sustentationem Officii*: This is a good Grant, and the Officers may lawfully collect it.

39. Therefore, in these Cases, First, as to the Donee, Though the Foresters have no Remedy against him, yet the King may compel him by Information at his Suit, before the Justices of the Forest, by a *Datum est curiæ intelligi*, That the Donee will not pay such a Collection according to his Grant; and, in the other Case, he shall be compelled to perform it by an Action of Covenant brought against him by the Donor.

40.

40. (3) The Third way of lawfully collecting is, by Prescription, and that is only where there hath been a Forest and Officers Time out of Memory; for to alledge, that the Forest was made after the Limitation of the Writ of Right, doth avoid such Prescription.

41. A Forester in Fee may prescribe in himself and his Ancestors, to have Three Half-pence every Day throughout the whole Year, *pro victu suo*; and according to the Opinion of Mr. *Hesket*, *fo.* 30. he may lawfully collect the same.

42. The Law is the same in all cases of Prescription, where the same is lawful; and therefore a Forester in Fee may prescribe to have all the Wind-fall Wood and dead Wood in the Forest, or throughout his Bailiwick, and all the Browse-Wood felled in the Winter for the Deer; and to have the Humbles, or one or both Shoulders of every Deer killed in his Baliwick, and likewise the Skin; and all these are good Prescriptions in Law.

43. Before the making the Statute of *Charta de Foresta*, the Foresters and all others who had Baliwicks in Fee, did appoint more Walkers and Under-keepers than were needful; so that the People were oppressed by the Extortions of a Multitude of unnecessary Officers, which were exacted by them in the Forest for the Maintenance of their Families, they having no other Wages but such which they got by Extortion by colour of their Office.

44. Therefore it was provided by that Statute before-said, *viz. Quod tot forestarii ponantur ad forestas custodiendum quot ad illas custodiendum rationabiliter viderint sufficere*; that is, No more than the Regarders shall think convenient when they make their Regard; for if they find more than are necessary, or more than have been accustomed in antient Times, then, upon their Presentment thereof, before

before the Justices of the Forest, they shall be removed, and the Offenders, in this behalf, shall be punished.

45. This appears *in Ordinatione forestæ*, made in 34 *Ed.* 1. *cap.* 3. *viz. Et si superoneratio forestariorum aut aliorum qui se gerant ut ministri forestæ inveniatur, amoveantur hujusmodi superonerantes, & imprisonentur secundùm discretionem Justiciarii forestæ vel ejus Locumtenentis, necnon & illi, per quos positi fuerant, ad voluntatem nostram similiter puniantur; & ad quodlibet Swanimotum inquiratur de superoneratione forestariorum & aliorum ministrorum forestæ, & de eorum oppressionibus populo nostro, & fiant inde emendæ & punitiones, sicut superius expressum, &c.*

46 By this Law, it appeareth likewise, That the Manner of surcharging the Forest is to be inquired at the Court of Swanimote; and then, if any such is found, 'tis to be certified to the Justices of the Forest, and they are to remove the Surchargers.

47. It seems, that by the Words aforesaid, *viz. Quòd ad illas custodiendum rationabiliter viderint sufficere*, That the Number of Foresters and other Officers of the Forest, is to be established by the Discretion and Oath of the Regarders; and the Words *viderint sufficere* seem to import, That it must be according to the Quantity of the Ground of the Forest; for if the Foresters have divers Bailiwicks and Walks, there ought to be one Forester or more in every Walk and Bailiwick. This is proved in *cap* 10. *de capitulis attachiamentorum, viz. Quòd forestarii manè surgant & in Ballivam eant & ibi moram faciant usque ad horam nonam & tunc eant ad prandium: Et citò post prandium redeant in Ballivam suam, viz. In partes illas ubi non fuerant ante prandium, & ibi eant audientes, & insidiantes, ne quis in eâ malum faciat, usque ad Vesperum: Et sic faciant singulis diebus.*

48. Every

48. Every Forester is bound to appear at the Justice Seat, and when he is first called, he ought to deliver his Horn upon his Knees to the Chief Justice in Eyre, which is then delivered to the Marshal, and he pays the Fine of 6 *s.* and 8 *d.* before 'tis redelivered. *Jones*, 266.

49. The Office of a Riding-Forester is to lead the King in his hunting. *Ibid.*

50. It has been observed before, that he is constituted by Letters Patent; but if it be, that he shall have *Officium custodis domus vocat.* the *New-Lodge*, &c. *alias, Dict. Officium unius forestariorum Domini Regis in foresta de Windsor.* This is void as to the Walk, for it doth not say of what Place in the Forest; so that 'tis uncertain, and therefore void. *Jones*, 281.

51. If he claim the Office, and no Fee for the Execution of it, he is removeable at Pleasure; and though the Words *Una cum Vadis & feodis eidem spectan. &c.* are in most Patents; yet he must averr some Fees certain in his Claim, or 'tis not Good, for he shall have no more allowed than is claimed.

Fox.

1. THis is the Third Beast of Chase, and there is very little Variety in the Terms of Foxes: 'Tis called,

The First Year, a Cub.
The Second Year, a Fox.

And so afterwards they are still called Foxes, without any other Distinction more than an Old Fox, and also a Litter of Cubs.

2. His

2. His Season of Hunting begins at *Christmas*; and lasteth till *Lady-day*.

The Terms are,

ſſ. A Brace or Leash of Foxes.
The Fox is Cased.
Unkennel the Fox.
A Fox backeth.
A Fox goeth to clicketing.
The Dung of a Fox is called Syants.
The treading is called, The Footing.
His Tail is called his Bush, or Holy-Water-Sprinkle.

Hampton-Court Forest.

1. THe newest Forest in *England*, is that of *Hampton-Court*, which was made by Act of Parliament, *Anno* 31. *H.* 8. *cap.* 5. 4. *Inst.* 301.

2. King *H.* 8. having made *Hampton-Court* a most beautiful and sumptuous Manor, and very convenient for a King, with Princely Parks, Gardens, Orchards, and other Things of Pleasure, requisite for his Royal Person; He limited a certain Territory of Ground, lying within the Precincts of *East-Mulsey*, *West-Mulsey*, *Walton* and *Esher*, contiguous to the said Manor, to be a Forest; and caused the same to be meered and bounded with certain Boundaries; and appointed it for the Increase and Pasture of Wild Beasts of Venery and Chase, and also for Beasts and Fowls of Warren, and made it a Forest by the said Act; which enacts, That the said Forest should have all such Laws and Officers necessary for the Punishment of Offenders in the same, as all other Forests in the Realm had, and

and used heretofore: So that hereby you may see, a Forest may be made by Act of Parliament.

3. After the King had made it a Forest, as aforesaid, he, by the same Act, made the Manor of *Hampton-Court* an Honour, and gave it the Name and Title of, *The Honour of Hampton-Court*.

4. And because that King had afforested the Lands of several Men to their Prejudice, he covenanted with the Owners of such Lands, to allow them certain Privileges in Recompence thereof; and also, That they might fell their Woods in the Precincts of that Forest, without Leave from him or any of his Officers; and that they might make great Fences and Hedges about their Corn, to keep it from the Deer.

Hare.

1. THe Hare is a Beast of Forest, and also of Warren. *Co. Lit.* 233.

2. And if a Man hunt and kill a Hare in the Forest, the Forester may apprehend him, because 'tis a Trespass in the Venison in the King's Forest: For Proof whereof, it appeareth in *the Assises of the Forest of Pickering*, *fo.* 13. That two Men were indicted, *viz.* one *Bulmer*, for striking a Hare in her Form; and another Man, for taking a Hare in the Forest: One of them was committed and fined for the said Offence, and was bound to his good Behaviour in the Forest; and the other was outlawed. So that Hares are Venison and Beasts of the Forest.

3. Before the making of *Charta de Foresta*, he who killed any Wild Beasts in the Forest, was not punishable by any certain Law, but at the Will of the King; and therefore he might have inflicted

the Loss of an Arm, or even of Life, on such Offenders: But in the said Charter, *Artic.* 10. 'tis enacted, That *Nullus de cætero amittat Vitam vel membra pro Venatione nostra, &c.* No Man, from henceforth, shall lose his Life or Member, *Pro Venatione nostra*, for killing Venison, that is, for killing any Beasts of Forest or Chase.

4. A Hare is called, by the old Foresters, the King of all Beasts of Venery; but there is little Variety of Terms concerning this Beast, only 'tis called,

The First Year, a Leveret.
The Second Year, a Hare.
The Third Year, a great Hare.

5. The Season for hunting the Hare, beginneth at *Michaelmas*, and lasteth till Midsummer.

6. The Terms of Hunting, and other Terms, are,

A Brace or Leash of Hares.
A Hare is seated or formed.
The Hare is cased.
Start the Hare.
A Hare beateth or tappeth.
A Hare goes to Buck.
The Tail is called a *Scut*.

7. The Dung of the Hare is called Crottels, and the Footing hath divers Appellations; for when she is in the plain Fields, she *soreth*; when she turns to deceive the Huntsmen, she *doubleth*; when she runs in the Highways, where her Footing may be perceived, she *pricketh*, and in the Snow 'tis *tracking*.

8. By the Statute of 14 & 15. *H.* 8. *cap.* 10. tracing, destroying and killing a Hare in the Snow, the

the Forfeiture is 6 *s.* 8 *d.* for each Hare: This is inquirable in Sessions and Leets, and the Fine goes to the King.

9. Any Person, not qualified, and being convicted by his own Confession, or the Oath of two Witnesses, before two Justices, of killing a *Hare*, he forfeits 20 *s.* to the Use of the Poor of the Parish where the Offence was committed, or where he was taken; if he cannot pay it, he must be committed for three Months, without Bail; but after he hath been in Prison one Month, he may be discharged, if he will be bound, with two Sureties, before two Justices, never to offend, in that Kind, any more. 3 *Jac.* 1. *cap.* 27.

10. *Selling a Hare* forfeits 10 *s.* to be divided between the Poor and the Prosecutor.

11. By the Statute of 5 *Annæ*, an *Alehouse-keeper*, *Carrier*, *Chapman*, *Higlar*, *Inn-keeper*, *Victualler*, having in his Custody, or who shall buy or sell, or offer to sell, a Hare after the 1st of *May*, 1707, forfeits 5 *l.* one Moiety to the Informer, and the other to the Poor of the Parish where the Offence was committed; and if he cannot pay it, he is to be sent to the House of Correction for three Months, without Bail, for the first Offence, and four Months for the next: The Conviction is to be before one Justice upon View or Oath of one Witness, within three Months after the Offence.

12. The aforesaid Statute is made perpetual by the Statute of 9 *Annæ*, *cap.* 25. And that if any Hare is found in the Shop, House or Possession of one not qualified or intitled under some Person qualified, it shall be adjudged an exposing to *Sale* within the former Act.

13. There must be but one Game-keeper in a Manor, and his Name must be enter'd with the Clerk of the Peace; and if any Game-keeper, whose Name is not so enter'd (or otherwise quali-

fy'd) do kill, he incurrs the same Forfeiture of 5 *l.* so if he kill a Hare in the Night.

14. Officer or Solder killing a Hare, without Leave of the Lord of the Manor, forfeits 5 *l.* or if not paid after Conviction, and within two Days after demanded by the Constable, his Commission is void; and the Officer must pay for every Soldier convicted, 20 *s.* both Sums to be distributed to the Poor.

Hart.

THE antient Charter of the Forest, made by *Canutus*, calls the Hart, *fera Regalis*, 'tis a Beast of the Forest, and called *Cervus*, in *Latin*; which *Isidore*, *in* 12 *Lib.* tells us, is derived from the *Greek* Word *κέρας*, signifying an Horn: And *Bartholomæus de proprietatibus rerum*, *fo.* 357. says, he is the most stately Beast which goeth on the Earth, having, as it were, a Majesty both in his Gate and Countenance.

2. *Budæus*, in his 2d Book *de Philologiâ*, writes, That *Exuvias illas anniversarias, quibus orbati latent cervi, quasi honore atque insigni amisso, non Cornua, ut Latini, sed caput, quasi decus ferinum appellant venatores.*

3. 'Tis true, the *Hart* and the *Hind* are Beasts of one Kind; but yet they are accounted several Beasts, because of the several *Seasons* of hunting them; for the Season of the Hind beginneth when that of the Hart endeth.

4. The Word *Hart* is a general Appellation for a *Stag*, *Staggard*, and every other Male Deer of that Sort, and so it is usually understood; and the

Beast

Beast itself is the most noble and the worthiest of all Beasts of Venery, and is called,

The First Year, a *Hind-Calf*, or *Calf*.
The Second Year, a *Bracket*.
The Third Year, a *Spayad*.
The Fourth Year, a *Staggard*.
The Fifth Year, a *Stag*.
The Sixth Year, a *Hart*.

5. The antient Writers tell us, That the Foresters and Wood-Men, in former Days, call'd him a *Stag*, and not a *Staggard*, in the fourth Year; and likewise they called him, the fifth Year, a *great Stag*; and some were of Opinion, that let his Age be what it will, it was not to be called a *Hart* until hunted by the King.

6. But this seems to be a Mistake, for after he is five Years old, he is always called a *Hart*. This appears in *Budæus*, 2 *Lib. de Philologia*, and that there are Three sorts of Harts.

1. A *Hart*, as aforesaid.
2. A *Hart-Royal*.
3. A *Hart-Royal* proclaimed

And yet all these may be but One Beast still.

7. For, at six Years old, he is called a *Hart*; and if afterwards he is hunted by the King, and escapes alive, he is called a *Hart-Royal*; and if, in hunting, he is driven out of the Forest so far, that he is not likely to return of himself, and the King giveth over hunting him, then, because he hath made such sport, the King causeth a *Proclamation* to be made in all the Towns and Villages near the Place to which he was pursued and hunted, that no Person should kill, hurt or hunt him, and appoints

 certain

certain Foresters to look after him till he returns to the Forest, and afterwards he is called a *Hart-Royal proclaim'd*; and by *Budæus*, *Eximius Cervus*, that it, a goodly Hart.

8. I have seen many antient Records in the Tower of *Nottingham Castle* very badly kept, and scarce legible; in which Castle the Court is usually kept for *Peverill-Fee*: Amongst which it appears, That in the Year 1194, King *Richard* being hunting in *Sherwood-Forest*, did chase a *Hart* out of that Forest into *Barnesdale* in *Yorkshire*; and because he could not recover him, he made Proclamation at *Tickill* in *Yorkshire*, and at several other Places thereabout, That no Person should kill, hurt or chase the said *Hart*; and this was afterwards called a *Hart-Royal proclaim'd*.

9. In the Book-Case of 21 *H*. 7. *fo*. 3. *Placito* 7. it appeareth, That a Man was indicted for killing a *Hart-Royal proclaim'd*; and Exception was taken to it, for that it was not set forth where, or in what Place, the Proclamation was made. 7 *H*. 6. *fo*. 36. *Placito* 41.

10. The Time of Grace or Season of a *Hart* beginneth at *Midsummer*, and lasteth till *Holy-Rood Day*.

The Terms are,

A Herd of Harts.
A Hart harboureth.
Rowse the Hart.
A Hart belloweth.
A Hart goeth to Rut.
His Fat is called Sewet.
His Dung is called Fewmits, or Fewmishing.
His Footing is called the *Slot*.

11. When a *Hart* is past his Sixth Year, he is called, a *Hart of Ten*; and afterwards according

to

o the Increase of his Head, whether he is *croched*, *almed* or *crowned*.

12. When he breaketh the Herd, and runneth to the Thicket or Coverts, the Foresters say, he then taketh his *Hold*.

13. They call the round Roll of the Horn next to his Head, the *Bur*; they call the main Horn, the *Beam*; the lowest Antler is called, the *Brow-Antler*, or *Bezantler*; the next is called, *Royal*; the next above that, the *Sur-royal*, and then the *Top*.

Hind.

1. THe *Hind* is the Female to the *Hart*; they are both of one Kind, yet are accounted several, because of the different *Seasons* of Hunting, for the Season of the Hind doth begin when that of the Hart ends; she is called,

The First Year, a *Calf*.
The Second Year, a *Brocket's Sister*.
The Third Year, a *Hind*.

2. The Season of the *Hind* or Doe, beginneth on *Holy Rood-Day*, and lasteth till *Candlemas*.

The Terms are,

ss. A Herd of Hinds.
Her Dung is called *Fewmets*, or *Fewmishing*.
Her Fat is called *Sewet*.

Hue and Cry.

See { *Charge in Chief Justice*, 39.
Offenders, 21.
Appendix, Assisa Forestæ, 11. }

1. WHen a Forester or any other Officer of the Forest shall find any Persons doing or intending to do any Hurt or Damage to the Forest, and they fly for the same, they are forthwith to make an Out-cry unto the Inhabitants and next Dwellers in the Forest, where such Persons were seen, requiring them in the King's Name to aid and assist them to pursue such Offenders from Town to Town, and from Village to Village, Place and Place, within the limits and bounds of the Forest, until they are taken.

2. This Hue and Cry of the Forest is properly to be made by the Forester himself, because he is usually a Person known in that Place, and the more likely to be followed: Yet any other Officer or Minister of the Forest may make it; as appears in *the Assises and Ordinances of the Forest, Anno* 6 *Ed.* 1. *Artic.* 11. *viz. Si quis viderit malefactores infra metas forestæ, &c. debet illos capere secundum posse suum & si non possit debet levare hutesium & clamorem.*

3. If after such *Hue and Cry* made as aforesaid, any Person is negligent or refuses to pursue the Offenders; then the Default of such Person, or Persons, or Village, or Township, so offending, shall be presented by the Forester of the same Bailiwick at the next Court of *Swanimote* or *Justice-Seat*, which shall first happen; and if after such Presentment the Offenders shall be duly convicted,

ac-

according to the Laws of the Forest, they shall be fined.) *Itin. Lanc. fo.* 7.

But such *Hue and Cry* is not to be made for every Trespass and Offence done in the Forest, but only for such as are done in hunting and destroying the wild Beasts of the Forest, as it doth appear in the same Assises of the Forest, *Artic.* 11. For it is, *Si quis viderit aliquos malefactores aliquam feram capere & asportare*; in such Case he is to make *Hue and Cry, viz.* after those who are Hunters and Takers of Venison, and not after such as commit Trespass in Vert.

5. (So that *Hue and Cry* is to be made for a Trespass in Venison only, and the Offence must be committed in the Forest, and not in the Purlieus,) and it cannot be pursued out of the Limits and Boundaries thereof. 4 *Inst*. 294.

6. (And if after such *Hue and Cry* made, and the People come to the Place where the Offenders are, if they resist and will not yield;) or if they fly, and any Person who came in Assistance to the Forester or other Officer, shall happen to kill one or more of them in the Bounds of the Forest, either in apprehending or taking them or any of them, he shall not be arraigned for the same before the King and his Justices, or before any other the King's Bailiffs, or any other within any Franchise or without; neither shall he for so doing lose either Life or Limb, or suffer any other Punishment, but shall enjoy the King's Peace as before.

7. But Care is to be taken, That if such Things happen, that the same be done within the Bounds and Limits of the Forest: For the Words of the Statute, *De malefactoribus in parcis* are, *If any Forester, &c. shall find any Trespasser within his Liberty*; so that if he kill an Offender out of his Liberty, he must be punished. *Magn. Chart.* 117. *B.*

N 4 8. For

8. For this and many other Causes 'tis necessary to know the true Bounds and Limits of every Forest.

9. If *Hue and Cry* be made by the Officers of a Forest, and if 'tis not pursued and followed with effect, the Township, which is faulty, shall be fined. *Itin. Lanc. fo.* 7.

Hunting.

See { *Charge in Chief Justice*, 1, 37, 38, 45. *Purlieu*, 102, 104, 105, 108, 114, &c. to the End of the Chapter. *Warren*, 7. }

1. THE Antiquity of Hunting is proved from *Nimrod* and *Esau*, but the Derivation of the Word is of a more modern Date, *viz.* Hunting and Hunter are derived from the *French*, *Haunter*, which signifies in *Latine*, *frequentare*. *Cicero* hath this Phrase, *Opes consectari*, which is greedily to hunt after Riches; and probably from hence *Budæus* calleth Hunters *Sectatores ferarum*: *Terence* also useth the Word, *viz. sectare belluas*; and *Ovid*, *feras persequi*: But the Foresters have another Derivation of the Word *Hunter*, *viz.* from *Haunt-Deer*, one who hunteth after Deer, and now used generally for Hunting all manner of wild Beasts.

2. Hunting in Forests is Sport for Kings and Princes, and therefore not to be used by every common Person, but only by such of the Nobility and others who have Authority from the King, or from his Justice in Eyre, or other Officers of the Forest, or by such who have some good and lawful Authority so to do, and no other may hunt there.

3. All

3. All such Persons who have any lawful Claim, allowed in Eyre, by reason of any Grant from the King, to hunt in the Forest, may use the same according to their Grant; that is, they must pursue their Authority in the same manner it was granted.

4. In the Assises and Customs of the Forest, *Anno* 6 *Ed*. 1. *Artic*. 20. the Abbot of *Peterborough* had a Grant from the King to hunt Hares and Foxes in certain Forests.

5. So likewise in the Assises of the Forests of *Pickering* and *Lancaster fo*. 59. several Persons had Grants from the King to hunt Hares and Foxes, and also to hawk and take Fowls and Birds of Warren in a certain Place in the Forest: By vertue of which Grants they did make their Claims in Eyre before the Justices of the Forest; so that without such Grants they could not hunt or hawk there.

6. And therefore by the Assises of *Pickering*, *fo*. 39. 'tis a Trespass for a Lord or Owner of a Manor in the Forest, or any other Freeholder dwelling in the Regard thereof, to hunt or hawk in his Manor within the Regard, unless he hath some lawful Authority.

In Charta de Foresta, *Artic*. 11. 'tis enacted, That any *Archbishop*, *Bishop*, *Earl* or *Baron* of the Realm, coming to the King by his Order or Command, and passing thro' any of his Forests, may kill one or two of his Deer there by the *View* of the Forester, if he is present, or otherwise to blow a Horn for him.

8. From whence it may be inferred, that before the making this Charter they could not hunt in the King's Forests without a Warrant so to do, neither can they now, but when they are sent for to the Court by the King's Command, and in their return home.

10.

10. And in this Case four Things are to be observed strictly.

Viz.
1. That he be either a *Lord Spiritual or Temporal*.
2. That he be *sent* for by the King.
3. That it be done by the *View* of the Forester, if present.
4. If he be *absent*, that a Horn be blown for him.

Of Licences and Warrants to hunt in the Forest, and how they must be used.

10. He who hath any Warrant to hunt in a Forest, must pursue his Authority very strictly; for if he doth not, he is a Trespasser *ab initio*, and must be punished accordingly. 12 *H. 7. fo.* 15, *Plac.* 5.

11. Therefore if he hath a Warrant to hunt and kill a Buck in a Forest, Chase or Park, he must not take it away when killed, neither may he hunt or kill any other Deer, but only one *Buck* and no more, for he must not abuse his Authority.

12. In *Mich.* 18. *Ed.* 4. *fo.* 14. *Plac.* 12. it was held for Law in one *Ashton's* Case, That where a Man hath a *Warrant* to hunt and kill three Bucks, and to dispose of them for the Honour of him who was the Owner of the Park, and from whom he had the *Warrant*; that in such Case his *Servant* might not hunt or kill those Bucks by vertue of that Warrant, neither might he to whom the same was granted hunt with any manner of Servant, or in any Company whatsoever, but only by himself; and that he could not assign or transfer that Warrant to another, because it was only a *Licence of Pleasure and not of Profit*; for the Grantee had not any Property in the Thing granted.

13.

13. So in the Case of the Dutchess of *Norfolk*, *Anno* 13 *H.* 7. *fo.* 13. *Plac.* 2. she granted a Licence to the Earl of *Suffolk* to *hunt* in her Park at *Lopham* at his Will and Pleasure, It was adjudged, that the Earl could not hunt with any of his *Servants* with him, nor with any more Company than himself, because it was only a *Licence of Pleasure*. *Trin.* 12 *H.* 7. *fo.* 25. *Plac.* 5. the like Case.

14. But 'tis otherwise where a Man hath a *Licence of Profit*, for there he may justify to hunt with others.

15. And therefore in the said Case of the Dutchess of *Norfolk*, the Court held, That the Earl having pleaded, that she gave him a Licence *to hunt*, *kill and carry away the Deer*, that he might justify to hunt with his *Servants* and other Friends, because it was *a Licence of Profit*, and he had a Property in the Thing granted.

16. So in the same Term and same Year, *fo.* 12. *Plac.* 1. in the Case of the Earl of *Suffolk*, who brought an Action of Trespass against *Ralph Berney* and *Richard Whitley*, for Hunting in his *Park*, *Whitley* pleaded in Bar, That the said Earl at a certain Day and Place did deliver a sufficient *Warrant* sealed with his Seal unto one *Robert Southwell*, directed to one *T.* the Keeper of the Park where the Trespass was supposed to be done, commanding him to deliver unto the said *Southwell* one *Buck* of the first Season; by vertue whereof the said *Southwell*, at the Time of the Trespass supposed, and the said *Whitley*, as his Servant, entered with him into the said Park, and there the said *Southwell* delivered the said Warrant unto the Keeper, and they required him to hunt, which he did, and killed one *Buck*; and that the said *Whitley* carried the same away, as it was lawful for him to do: And this was held a good Justification.

17.

17. In the Case of the Lord *Beaumont*, *Anno* 22 *H.* 6. *Pasch. fo.* 25. *Plac.* 23. it was held, That if a Man have a Licence for himself and *his Servants* to hunt in a *Chase*, *Park* or *Warren* at his Pleasure; this is a *Licence of Profit*; for by vertue of those Words for himself *and his Servants*, the Grantee hath a Property in the Thing hunted, because he may justify Hunting by *his Servants*, which is more than a *Licence of Pleasure*.

18. It hath been mentioned before, That where a Man hath a Licence to hunt in a Forest, his Authority must be strictly pursued, (that is) he must not exceed it in any Point; for if he do, he shall be punished, as if he had no Licence at all; as for Instance, if he hath a Licence to kill one *Buck in Season*, and he wilfully hunts and kills a *Hind out of Season*.

19. So likewise in the said *Book-Case*, 12 *H.* 7. *fo.* 25. if he hath a Licence for himself only to hunt in a *Chase* at his Pleasure, and he orders his *Servants* to hunt with him, and they hunt accordingly, both he and all his Servants are Trespassers, because he hath abused his Authority.

20. Lastly, 'tis to be observed, that whatsoever hath been said of Licences for Hunting in Chases and Parks, the same is to be understood of Licences for Hunting in Forests.

Who may grant Warrants to hunt in a Forest, and who not.

21. The King and all those who have special Authority from him under the Great Seal, may grant Warrants to hunt in the Forest: And the Lord Chief Justice in Eyre may licence a Gentleman to hunt there, in his own Lordship or Manor, or in his own Freehold.

22.

22. A Subject who is Owner of a Forest, may grant Warrants to hunt there; but no Man can give Licence to hunt in the King's Forests, but himself or his Ch. Justice in Eyre, being within his Jurisdiction, or those who by some Grant from the King have a special Authority so to do.

23. In *Easter Term, Anno,* 2 Ed. 4. *fo. plac.* 9. An Action of Trespass was brought against the Defendant for hunting in the Plaintiff's Park. The Defendant pleaded, That the Plaintiff made one *John at Styles Keeper of his Park*, where the Trespass was: And that at the same Day and Time of the supposed Trespass, the said Keeper did licence and pray the Defendant to kill two Deer for him: By vertue whereof he did kill two Deer, and so concludes, and prays Judgment, *si actio, &c.* And this was held no Bar, because the Keeper had no such Authority himself; for he was only to keep and preserve, and not to kill the Deer; and therefore it was held in that Case, that he cannot justify the killing without a Warrant for that purpose; and if so, he cannot licence another.

The difference between Warrants of Pleasure and Warrants of Profit.

24. This hath been in some measure explain'd before, *viz.* when a Man hath a Warrant *to kill and carry away* the Thing hunted and killed, in such Case he hath a Property in it, and 'tis a Warrant of *Profit*, and he may hunt with what *Company* he will.

25. But where he hath no Property in the Thing hunted or killed, 'tis only a Licence of *Pleasure*; and in such Case he must not hunt with any more but himself.

26. And therefore, in every Warrant for Hunting, these Five things ought to be observed.

1. By whom it was granted, and whether the Person had an Authority to grant it.
2. For what it was granted, and what is the Purport thereof.
3. For what Place it doth serve.
4. To whom it is granted, and for what Time.
5. Whether 'tis a Thing of Pleasure or Profit.

The Difference between a Licence in Law and a Licence in Fait.

27. Where a Man hath a Licence to hunt by *Word* only, without *Writing*, or where he *prescribes* to hunt, as belonging to his Office in the Forest; this is called, a *Licence in Law*.

28. And it was never doubted, but such a Licence, by *Word*, is good between Common Persons; and therefore, where a Lord and Owner of a free Chase, brought an Action of trespass for hunting and killing his Wild Beasts in the same, the Defendant pleaded, That he had a Licence from him by *Word* only, without Writing; and, for that Reason, *Fencot*, who was of Counsel for the Plaintiff, took Exception to this in Bar; but it was held good. *Hil.* 42. *Ed.* 3. *fo.* 2. *Placito* 8. 12 *H.* 7. *fo.* 25. *Placito* 5. 18 *Ed.* 4. *fo.* 14 *Placito* 12. 13 *H.* 7. *fo.* 14. *Placito* 2. 34 *H.* 6. *fo.* 43.

29. But it hath been a Question, Whether such a Licence, granted by the King to a Subject, is good without *Writing*; because, as he taketh nothing from any Man, but by matter of *Record*, so neither doth he grant any thing, but by the like matter of *Record*.

39. Yet

30. Yet there are some Opinions, That a Verbal Warrant from the King is good; *viz.* in *Anno* 4 *H.* 7. *fo.* 6. *Placito* 2. *Bryan* and *Shelley* held, That the King may give many things without any *Writing*, and that such Gift of Chattels shall be good.

31. And in *Mich.* 39. *H.* 6. *fo.* 17. *Placito* 21. in an Action of Trespass, the Defendant justified by pleading a Command of the King, by *Word* only, without *Writing*; and this was held a good Justification.

32. So that it seemeth, That if the King giveth a *Verbal Licence* to a Man to hunt in one of his Forests, and that if he hunt there by vertue of this Licence, this is justifiable; because the hunting is no more than a Trespass without such a Licence: And if a Man may plead the King's Command by *Word* only, in Bar of a Trespass, by the same Reason he may plead his *Verbal Licence* in Bar of the like Trespass.

He who abuseth his Warrant is a Trespasser ab initio.

33. He who abuseth or misuseth a Warrant or Licence to hunt, is a Trespasser *ab initio*, and so are all they who hunt with him.

34, *Anno* 11. *H.* 4. *fo.* 74. *Placito* 16. an Action of Trespass was brought, *Quare vi & armis domum suum fregit, &c.* The Defendant pleaded not Guilty to the Force; and to the rest, that he was seised in Fee of the said House, and did let it to the Plaintiff for a Term of Years; and so justified the coming into the House when the Doors were open, to view the Repairs, and what Waste was done; and this was held a good Plea, But the Plaintiff reply'd, That besides his coming into the House to see what Repairs were needful, *&c.* he did also commit certain Trespasses against the Will and Consent of the Plaintiff, for which Cause he was

adjudged

adjudged a Trespasser *ab initio*, and yet his coming into the House at first was justifiable; but because he did misuse his Authority, he was a Trespasser, as aforesaid.

35. In like manner, he who hath a lawful Authority to hunt in the Forest, and if, in his hunting, he misuseth that Authority, shall be accounted a Trespasser *ab initio*, and shall be punished as such.

How Hunters, without Licence, shall be punished.

36. If any Forester or Keeper shall take any one *in the Manner*, then he may carry him to Prison, from whence he shall not be delivered, without a special Warrant from the King, or from his Chief Justice in Eyre of the Forest.

37. This appears by the *Ordinance of the Forest*, made in 6 *Ed.* 1. *Artic.* 10. *viz. Si quis ceperit feram sine Warranto in foresta, corpus suum arrestetur ubicunque inveniatur infra metas forestæ, & quando captus fuerit, non deliberetur sine speciali præcepto Domini Regis vel capitalis Justiciarii forestarum.*

38. Now the Words are, *Si quis ceperit feram*; yet if a Man is apprehended *hunting* in the Forest, though he hath not *taken* a Wild Beast, he shall be punished as if he had actually *taken and killed one*, because, by *the Assises of the Forest*, *Voluntas reputabitur pro facto*.

39 In *the Assises of the Forest of Pickering*, *fo.* 3. it was adjudg'd, That he who enters the Forest with Bow and Arrows with an *intent* to offend there, is to be punished, though he do not act.

40. So where an *Abbot* lent a Bow and Arrows to another, to the *Intent* to kill the King's Deer, he was fined. And, *Anno* 1632. *Wheatley* was fined 50 *s.* being presented for carrying a Gun with *Intent* to kill the Deer. 1 *Jones* 275.

41. But the Forester must not arrest the Body of any Offender, except he take him *with the Manner*, that is, according to *the Assises of Lancaster*, *fo.* 13. either,

1. *Dog-draw.*
2. *Stable-stand.*
3. *Back-bare.*
4 *Bloody-hand.*

42. (1) *Dog-draw* is where a Man hath wounded a Wild Beast, and is found with a Hound or other Dog drawing after him to recover the Beast so wounded.

43. (2) *Stable-stand* is where one is found at his Standing ready to shoot at any Deer, or standing close by a Tree with Greyhounds in his Leash, ready to let slip.

44. (3) *Back-bare* is where a Man hath killed a Wild Beast in the Forest, and is found *carrying* him away.

45. (4) *Bloody hand* is where one is found in a Forest in any suspicious Manner, and is bloody.

46. All these are said to be taken *in the Manner*: The Punishment is by a judicial Sentence at the Justice-Seat, and to be fined at the Discretion of the Lord Chief Justice, and committed till he pay the Fine, and then and there to be bound to the Good Behaviour in the Forest for ever afterwards.

47. By the Statute of 1 *H.* 7. *cap.* 7 it was enacted, That upon Information given to any of the King's Council, or to any Justice of the Peace of the County, &c. of any unlawful *Hunting by Night*, or with *painted Faces*, in any Forest, Park or Warren, or of any Person suspected thereof, it shall be lawful for them to make a Warrant to the Sheriff, or to any Constable, &c. to apprehend such Person, and to bring him before them, and then to ex-

amine him of such hunting; and if he conceal the Offence or Offender, 'tis Felony; if he confess the Truth, then the Offence by him done in hunting, is finable at the next general Quarter-Sessions; and if any Rescous be made, so that the Warrant cannot be executed, 'tis Felony, to be inquired and determined as other Felonies are.

How far a Purlieu Man may pursue his Chase in Hunting.

48. A *Purlieu*-Man may not hunt in every Man's Lands within the *Purlieu*, but in his own Lands only; and therefore if he finds the Beasts of the Forest in his Woods or Lands in the *Purlieu*, in such Case he hath a *Property* in them against any other Man, *ratione soli*, (the King only excepted;) and if he kill them by hunting, without any *forestalling* before they recover the Forest, then they are absolutely the Property of him who killed them, and the King hath no Interest in them; but if they recover the Forest, so that they are *infra metas forestæ*, that is, within the Limits and Bounds thereof, then they are *in Statu quo prius*, and are the King's Wild Beasts again.

49. So that though they are out of the Forest, and in the *Purlieu*, yet the King hath, in some sort, a Property in them still, and that against every man but against the *Owner of the Lands* where they are.

50. But if the Owner of the Lands *beginneth the Hunting in his own Lands*, where he hath a lawful Interest and Property in the Beasts so long as they are there; then, by reason of that Property, he may pursue his Hunting through any Man's Woods or Lands, so as he doth not enter into any *Forest*, *Chase*, *Park* or *Warren*, which are Places privileged

by

by the Law, that no Man may enter there but the Owner.

51. And if he kill the Beast in another Man's Land, and out of such privileged Place, he may take and carry away the same by reason of the first Property, in respect of the *Soil* where it was when he *first* began hunting.

52. This appears in *Mich.* 12 *H.* 8. *fo.* 10. *viz.* If I find a Pheasant in my Lands, and I let my Hawk fly, I may follow the Flight into another Man's Land by reason of the first Property which I had in the Pheasant, *ratione soli*; and if my Hawk kill the Pheasant in another Man's Land, I may enter and take it by reason of that Property and Pursuit; for the Possession of the Hawk shall be accounted in Law my Possession; and in that Case, I shall not be punished as a Trespasser for taking and carrying away the Pheasant, but only for the entring the Ground: And the Law is the same in the Cases of all Wild Beasts of the Forest and Chase.

53. But though I may pursue the hunting *usque ad metas forestæ*, yet I must not enter there; for when the Wild Beast hath recovered the Forest, I must call the Dogs back, that is, as the old Foresters call it, I must blow a *Rechase* with my Horn, as loud as I can.

54. And if such *Purlieu*-Man doth not immediately call back and rebuke his Dogs, after the Beast hath recovered the Forest, and they happen to kill it *in the Forest*, then the Owner of the Dogs is a Trespasser of the Forest, and shall be punished as such, though he himself never came within the Bounds thereof.

55. But if he had called his Dogs back, and yet they had hunted and killed the Beast in the Forest, in such Case he shall not be punished, because he did

did his Endeavour *repellere & retorquere Canes*, and to restrain them from hunting there.

56. This appears in the Earl of *Arundel's* Case, *Hill.* 43 & 44 *Ed.* 3. *fo.* 8. *Placito* 23. *viz.* If a Man hath Lands sown with Corn adjoining to a free Chase or Forest, and the Wild Beasts come out on those sown Lands, and the Owner hunts them with his Dogs, but calls them back again before they enter the Forest; yet if they still pursue and enter the Forest or Chase, and kill them there, the Owner is not to be charged as a Trespasser.

57. From which Case it may be inferred, That if the Hunter had not called back his Dogs, he had been a Trespasser; and much more those are Trespassers, who hunt in the *Purlieus*, and are so far from recalling their Dogs, that they follow them into the Forest, and encourage them there, and kill and carry away the Deer as their own.

58. 'Tis probable, the Earl of *Arundel's* Case might be adjudged upon the Authority which happen'd six Years before that Time, *viz. Pasch.* 38 *Ed.* 3. *fo.* 10. *B* which was the Case of the *Pheasant* before-mentioned; *viz.* If a Man finds a *Pheasant* in his own Ground, and lets his Hawk fly, and she flieth after the Pheasant into a Warren (which is a privileged Place for Birds of Warren) and kills it there, the Falconer shall not have the Pheasant, but the Owner of the Warren; but if the Hawk had kill'd it out of a privileged Place, then 'tis otherwise: Which proves, That as soon as the Pheasant (which is naturally wild) was within the Bounds of the *Warren*, it belonged to the Owner; and therefore the killing it there could not vest any Property in another Man; for the Falconer should not have suffered his Hawk to fly into the Warren if he could, by any Means, have prevented it.

59. Both

59. Both which Cases before mentioned prove, That if any Wild Beasts are killed within the Meers or Bounds of the Forest, they belong to the King or to the Owners of the *Forests*, *Chases* or *Warrens*; and not unto him who killed them.

60. For if the Dogs of a *Purlieu*-Man follow a Deer towards the Forest, and before they fasten on it, or before he recall them from hunting, the Deer doth recover a Common High-way, or a River, which are *Meers* of the Forest, and being on or in the said *Meers*, the Dogs kill it there; in such Case the King, or the Owner of the Forest, ought to have the Deer, because all the *Meers* and *Bounds* are the King's, for they are Parcel of the Forest.

61. This appears by *the Assises and Customs of the Forest*, made *Anno* 6. *Ed.* 1. *Artic.* 19. *viz. Quòd secundùm assisam forestæ omnes Metæ forestæ sunt integræ Domino Regi*; though they stand on another Man's Land or Soil: So that he who kills a Deer there, kills it in the Forest.

62. Thus, in *the Assises of Pickering*, *Anno* 10. *Ed.* 3. the Abbot of *Whitby* killed a *Hart* in the River *Derwent*, which was a *Meer* of that Forest; and he and his Company were indicted, *Quia ceperunt unum Cervum in aquâ de Derwent quæ est marchia forestæ & venationem illam secum asportavit*; for which Fact he was fined and bound to his Good Behaviour in the Forest. *Assis. Pickering*, *fo.* 6, 41.

63. But yet, in some Cases, a *Purlieu* Man may lawfully pursue his Chase, and hunt and kill a Deer in the Forest; for if he find such Deer in his *Purlieu*, and, in hunting it towards the Forest, the Dogs fasten on it before 'tis within the Bounds thereof, and the Dogs still hanging on, are drawn by the Force of the Deer into the Forest, and 'tis killed there; in this Case, by reason of the first Property which he had, *ratione soli*, and also by the Pursuit

and Possession thereof by his Dogs, before the Deer entered the Forest, he may lawfully follow his Chase there, and take and carry away the Deer, because he was actually possessed thereof by his Dogs (which are his Servants) before it entered the Forest.

64. In the aforesaid Case, 12 *H.* 8. it appeâreth, That if a *Purlieu*-Man doth begin to hunt in another Man's Grounds in the *Purlieu*, and not in his own; this being an Injury to the Owner of those Grounds, if his Dogs fasten on a Wild Beast before it recovers the Bounds of the Forest, and are drawn in by Force, and then they kill the Deer there, the Owner of the Dogs must not enter into the Forest, nor take the Best so killed, because the *first* Hunting and Pursuit began by *Wrong*; for he never had any Property in the Beast, *ratione soli*; and therefore, though he doth not come himself into the Forest, yet he shall be a Trespasser of the Forest, because his Dogs enter'd it and killed a Wild Beast, in which he never had any manner of Property.

65. And in such case he cannot justify his Hunting, and say, that he is a lawful *Purlieu*-Man; and that he found the Beast on his own Lands within the *Purlieu*; which would be a good Justification by the Owner of the Land in which the Beast was found, but not by him where it was not found. *Hill.* 43 *Ed.* 3. *fo.* 8. *Placito* 23. 38 *Ed.* 3. *fo.* 10. *B. Hill.* 13 *H.* 7. *fo.* 16. *Placito* 14. *Pas.* 7 *H.* 6. *fo.* 36. *Placito* 41.

66. So in the Case of the *Hawk* and *Pheasant* before mentioned, which was found in the Land of the Owner of the Hawk, and kill'd in another Man's Land; the Owner of the Hawk shall have it, and not the Owner of the Ground where it was killed, because of the first Property which he had *ratione soli*: But if the Pheasant had been

found

found in another Man's Land, and pursued by the Hawk, and killed; in such Case it doth belong to him who is the Owner of the Ground where it was killed; for no Man shall take the Benefit of his own Wrong; for the Owner of the Hawk began his first Flight at the Pheasant by a Wrong: And in such Case, he cannot justify his Entry into another Man's Ground to make a Flight, nor the Pursuit of such Flight, and taking the Pheasant, as he might have done if he had first made his Flight in his own Ground.

67. *Presentatum est per forestarios, & convictum per Viridarios quòd Nicholaus Merill & aliis venerunt in forestam illam, &c. & cum arcubus, sagittis & Leporariis ibidem ceperunt duos cervos.* 8 Ed. 3. *in foresta Pickering.*

Inclosures in a Forest.

See { *Assart*, 14.
Charge in Chief Justice, 5, 30.
Cattimon, 48.
Purpresture, 14.
Wood, 45.
Appendix, Stat. 22 Ed. 4.

1. IF a Chief Justice in Eyre will grant a Licence to a Man to inclose his Ground in the Forest, paying a certain Rent, and such Licence is made *sedente Curiâ*, 'tis good for ever, but not otherwise; for if 'tis not granted in Court, it may be pulled down again. *Jones's Rep.* 277.

2. But then such Inclosures must be with *low Hedges*, which may not disturb the Game. This appears in the *Register*, fo. 257. ff. *Mandamus vobis quòd per Sacramentum, &c. inquiratis, &c. si sit ad*

damnum forestæ nostræ aut alicujus alterius si concedamus R. B. solum, &c. parvo fossato & bassâ baiâ secundum assisam forestæ includere, &c.

3. So that *arable* Land may be inclosed, not with high Hedges; but *cum parvo fossato & bassâ baiâ*, according to *the Assises of the Forest*; but Woods and Coverts in the Forest may be inclosed with *high Hedges and Ditches*, to preserve them from the Hurt and Cropping by the Cattle, until they are past all Danger.

4. If a Man claims a Liberty to inclose twelve Acres in a Forest, by vertue of Letters Patent from the King, it shall be inquired *per ministros forestæ*, whether it was inclosed *parvo fossato & bassâ baiâ secundum assisam forestæ*, or not; because the King's Licence shall be taken to a general and common Intent, *viz.* That he shall inclose within the Forest *secundum Assisas forestæ*, as he may; and therefore, without special Words in the Licence, he shall not inclose *magno fossato & altâ baiâ*. *Jones's Rep.* 278.

5. *Parks* being laid open to Forests for forty Years, may yet be inclosed again; and they may kill any Deer which come into those *Parks*: So though Inclosures have been continued for forty Years, if they were not before, they may be destroyed and laid open. 2 *Rep.* 155.

6. *In Itinere Windsor, Jones's Rep.* 296. *Thomas Cary* claimed *Sunninghill-Park, Fore extra forestam, & habere liberam Warrenam ibidem licet sit infra metas forestæ.* And this was by vertue of Letters Patent from King *Charles* the Second.

In this Case, the Officers of the Forest ought to inquire, Whether the Warren is inclosed with Pales? and whether there are any *Saltaries* in it, so that the King's Deer may get in? and whether there are Conies there? and if there are, whether the Park is so inclosed that they cannot get out, for all those are Causes of Seisure.

7. And

7. And it being found, that the Park was well paled, and that there were no *Saltaries*, and that the Conies could not get out, the Claim was allowed, *& insuper dictum est ei per Curiam quòd parcum præd. amodo includat, &c.*

8. And as a Man may have a Park in a Forest by *Grant*, so he may by Prescription; but then likewise it must be inclosed, that the Beasts of the Forest may not enter, otherwise 'tis a Forfeiture of the Park; and so it is if he have a *Saltary* or *Deer-Leap*, for the nature of a Park is to be inclos'd; and therefore, in 10 *H.* 7. *fo.* 6. it is said, That a Park consists in *Soil*, *Inclusures*, and *Game*: And in 15 *Ed.* 3. *Thomas* Earl of *Lancaster*, Lord of a Forest, gave Licence to one *John Harrington* to make a Park in his Forest; and there it was adjudged, That if the Grantee doth so slightly inclose the Park, that the Beasts of the Forest may get in, 'tis a Forfeiture, and the Owner of the Forest may enter and take the Deer.

9. An Action of Trespass was brought against the Defendant for breaking the Plaintiff's Close: He pleaded, That the Place where the Trespass was supposed to be, is called *B.* adjoining to the Forest of *G.* which is the King's Forest; and sets forth, That one *R* was Forester there, and lays a *Prescription* in himself and his Ancestors, *&c.* and then shews, that the Plaintiff, and all those whose Estate he had in a Place adjoining to the Forest, have constantly used to impale, *contiguè versus* the said Forest; and that, for want of paling it, Four Deer escaped out of the Forest, into the Place where the Trespass was supposed; and that the Defendant, as Servant to the said *R.* the Forester, and by his Command, drove them to the Forest again.

10. It was argued, that this Plea was not good; for though the Fault might be in the Plaintiff, for

not paling against the Forest; yet it was a Wrong done to the King, which he might punish: But 'tis unreasonable, that, because the Plaintiff had done an Injury to the King, therefore the Defendant might do the like to the Plaintiff.

11. And the better Opinion was, That the Plea was not good; for though the Fault was in the Plaintiff for not paling, it was not lawful for the Forester, or any Man, to drive the Deer out of the Ground, or to take them; and the Reason is, because the King had no Property in them; and if so, the Forester could not meddle with them when they were in another Man's Ground: And therefore the hunting them, by the Defendant, must be wrongful; for this is not like the Case of *tame* Cattle, where the Property still remains in the Owner, though they are out of his Grounds, for which Reason he may retake them where-ever he finds them: But 'tis not so where the Beasts are *wild*; for if a Man breaks a Park-Pale, and the Deer go out, you cannot pursue them into the Land of him who broke the Pales; because, when they are out of the Park, the Owner hath no Property in them; he is to take his Remedy by an Action *de parco fracto*. *Kellewey* 30.

12. *The Assises of the Forest* are, That a Man may not inclose any Ground within the Forest *ad nocumentum ferarum*; and that if any one hath a Licence to inclose, he may not do it *cum altâ haiâ & fossatâ nec cum alto palatio contra assisam forestæ. In Assis. Lancastr. fo.* 6.

12. He who is presented to have assarted or inclosed any Land in the Forest, either belonging to the King, or to any other Man, shall be fined; but if he will compound with the Justice, he may continue the same, paying a yearly Rent to the King, which must be enter'd of Record at that time. *Assis. Pick. fo.* 7.

In-

Indictment.

See { *Offenders.*
Appendix, Stat. 7 R. 2.

1. THe following is a very good Form of an Indictment.

Se Quòd B. R. est communis Malefactor venationis ubique in Foresta & Malefactoribus venationis consentiens.

2. For 'tis a good Indictment to alledge, *Quòd B. R. consuetus est ponere acutas Catbeas in berkis baiarum ad feras capiend.*

3. So tis, *Quòd R. B. venit in Parco de N. ad malefaciend. in venatione.*

4. An Abbot of *Whitby* kill'd a Hart in the River *Derwent*, which was the Meets of the Forest of *Pickering*; and he and his Company were indicted, *Quia ceperunt unum Cervum in aqua de Derwent, quæ est Marchia Forestæ; & venationem illam secum asportavit. Itin. Pickering. fo.* 6, 41.

Jury, See *Appendix*, Stat. 7 R. 2.

King.

1. THe King having a continual Care for the Preservation of the Community, the Law, amongst many other Privileges, gives him the Prerogative to have his Places of Recreation wheresoever he will direct; and therefore he may reserve the Wild Beasts to himself to hunt in such privileged Places where he will appoint; for he may, by Law, make

make a Forest at his Will and Pleasure (4 *Inst.* 300. 301. *contra.*) as he may enter the Grounds of any of his Subjects where any *Mines* of Gold or Silver are found, and carry the Metal away; for the Law gives the most excellent Things to the most excellent Person.

2. In like manner, because Wild Beasts of Venery, and Beasts and Fowls of Chase and Warren, are Things of great Excellency, therefore they are most proper for the Dignity of a Prince, and, in a peculiar Manner, belong to him only: And this is the Reason why 'tis not lawful for any Man to make a *Chase*, *Park* or *Warren*, on his own Freehold, to preserve any Wild Beasts or Birds of Forest, Chase, Park or Warren, without the King's Warrant so to do; and the Offender in such Case is to be punished in a *Quo Warranto* brought against him, and the Franchise is to be seised into the King's Hands, because such Beasts belong to the King, as 'tis in *Bracton, Lib.* 2 *cap.* 24.

3. ff. *Habet enim Rex præ cæteris omnibus in regno suo, de jure gentium, privilegia quæ de jure naturali esse deberent inventoris, sicut Thesaurum, Wreccum Maris, crassum piscem, Sturgionem, Wayvium, quæ in nullius bonis esse dicuntur: Habet etiam de jure gentium in manu suâ, quæ de jure naturali debent esse communia, sicut feras bestias, & aves non domesticas, quæ deberent esse communia de jure naturali, & per apprehensionem & captionem & aucupationem propria.* See *Commentar.* 318 Stat. 17 *Car.* 1 *cap.* 16. *Br. action sur Statute* 48. *Quo Warr.* 7. *Lib. Intration. Quo Warr.* 2 6 *Ed.* 2. 22 *Assisar. Placito* 34.

Laws

Laws of the Forest and Purlieus.

See *Boundaries*, 14.

1. THe Laws of the Forest are *general*, because they respect all Forests alike; they are likewise *particular*, because they relate to Forests, and to no other Places.

2. (They consist principally in three Things, *viz.* In the Preservation and Continuance of the Place to be a Forest; in the Preservation of the *Vert*, which are the Green Woods and Coverts there; and in the Preservation of the *Venison*, which is every Beast of the Forest and Chase, that being a general Word for all; and there can be no Trespass committed in the Forest, but it must be in one of these Particulars.)

3. By the Records of the Dutchy Court of *Lancaster*, it appears, That the Earl of *Lancaster* had a Forest in the Counties of *Lancaster* and *York* in the Reigns of *Ed.* 2. and *Ed.* 3. and did execute the Forest-Laws there, in as ample a Manner as ever any King did before him.

4. And even at this Day, there are no Records extant which are of that Validity relating to Forests as those Laws are; and therefore 'tis necessary for him who will be learned in the Forest-Laws, carefully to read *the Assises of the Forests of Lancaster* and *Pickering*; in which he will find many Precedents of Judgments and Resolutions, and almost every thing which may happen or relate to Forests; therefore those Assises are in the nature of Year-Books to the Forest Laws.

5. Before the making of *Charta de forestâ* there was no certain Law to punish Offences committed in Forests; for, at first, the King caused such Offenders to be punish'd in such manner as he thought fit, till King *Canutus*, and other Kings, made Canons

nons and Constitutions to preserve the *Vert* and *Venison*.)

6. These Constitutions afterwards, by continuance of Time, were taken for Laws, and even those Laws were not certain before the making the said Statute of *Charta de foresta*.

7. But the Laws of the Forest did always differ from the *Common Law*: This appears *in Libro Rubro*, in the Exchequer, in these Words:

8. ¶. *Sane forestarum Lex, ratio, pœna quoque vel absolutio delinquentium, sive pecuniaria fuerit, sive corporalis, seorsum ab aliis regni judiciis secernuntur: Et solius Regis arbitrio seu cujuslibet familiaris ad hæc specialiter deputati subjicitur: Legibus quidem propriis substitit, quæ non de Jure Communi sed voluntariâ principum Institutione subnixæ esse debent: Adeò ut quod per legem ejus factum fuerit non justum absolutè, sed justum secundùm Legem forestæ dicitur, quia in forestis penetralia Regum sunt, & eorum maximæ deliciæ, ad has quidem venandi causâ, curis quandoque depositis, accedunt, ut modicâ quiete recreentur illic, seriis simul & multis Curiæ tumultibus omissis, in naturalis libertatis gratiam, paulisper respirant; unde fit, ut delinquentes in ea soli Regiæ subjiceant animadversioni.*

9. As for the Laws and Ordinances of the *Purlieus*, they are more properly to be called, *The Laws of the Forest*, though they chiefly concern the disorderly hunting and Trespasses in the Purlieus, because they generally tend to the Preservation and Continuance of Forests.

10. Those Ordinances, for the most part, are no other than the Common Law, or such which are grounded thereon; and they began in the Reign of *H.* 3. who disafforested certain Places; but yet had such a special Care of the Wild Beasts of Venery and Chase, that he made Laws and Ordinances to preserve them in those Places.

11. This

11. This appears in *the Assises of Woodstock*, and likewise since the time of *H* 3. and the Statute *de Charta de foresta*, when all the new Afforestations were disafforested by the Perambulations, it would have been a difficult thing to preserve the Wild Beasts, which, in great Numbers, came to those disafforested Places, without certain Laws and Ordinances made for that purpose.

Manner, See Hunting, 41.

Nusances in a Forest.

1. WHatsoever tends to the Hurt or Destruction of the Forest, or of the *Vert* or *Venison*, or which tends to the breach of those Laws made for the Preservation of them, the same is and may be called a *Nusance* of the Forest; which is a Word that generally comprehends every Offence there, or which may be done against the Laws of the Forest.

How many Sorts of Nusances of the Forest there are.

2. There are three sorts of *Nusances* of the Forest:

3. The First is called, *Nocumentum Commune*; and this sort of *Nusance* is a general Hurt, as well to the Inhabitants, as to the Beasts of the Forest, as for Instance; If any Man, who ought to make or repair a Bridge over the River for a common Passage into a Highway leading through the Forest, and he suffers it to be in Decay, so that People cannot pass as they ought to do, but are forced to go through the Forest out of the way, both to the Trouble of themselves, and the Disquiet of the Deer; this is a *Nusance*, and this is to be presented

sented at the Justice-Seat before the Chief Justice in Eyre. *Itin. Lancastr. fo.* 7.

4. So it is if the common Highways in the Forest are suffered to be out of repair, that Men cannot pass as usually they have done.

5. So also it is if any *Foreigner*, who dwells out of the Boundaries of the Forest, doth surcharge the Common there, having neither Freehold, nor any manner of Right there; this is a Common *Nusance* as well to the Inhabitants of the Forest, who have Right of Common, as to the Wild Beasts there.

6. In like manner, the erecting a Water-Mill upon a River in the Forest, or making a Dam, or stopping a Water-course, so that the Water overflows, and drowneth any Meadow or Pasture Ground, or any common Highway there; this is a common *Nusance*, and punishable by the Chief Justice in Eyre at his Justice-Seat.

7. The Second Sort of *Nusance* is called *Nocumentum Speciale*, and this tends chiefly to the Hurt of the Wild Beasts of the Forest; it comprehends all manner of Hunters and Trespassers which, in any ways, offend against the *Venison* or the Wild Beasts, as by Hunting, or in any other manner, to take and destroy them, or intending so to do, either with Dogs, Greyhounds or otherwise.

8. The third sort of Nusance is called *nocumentum generale*, and this tends to the hurt of the whole Forest, and as it may happen to the wild Beasts, it comprehends all manner of Trespasses, which tend to the waste, hurt or destruction of the Vert; the Consequence whereof is the driving the Deer out of the Forest to other Coverts, which is a hurt to them; for whatever tends to the hurt of the *Vert or Venison*, tendeth to the general hurt of the Forest it self.

9. This *nocumentum generale* comprehends likewise all Surcharges of the *Commons*, all *Agistors* of

 their

their own Pasture Lands; by eating them so bare that the Deer can have little or no feeding there, all *Assarts* and *Purprestures*, and all manner of Trespasses, which tend to the hurt or destruction of the Herbage or Pasture in the Forest, or any unlawful disquieting the wild Beasts.

Who are to inquire of Nusances in the Forest.

10. The Regarders of the Forest are to inquire into all these *Nusances*, and to make their Presentments and Certificates to the *Verderors* at the next *Swanimote Court* to be holden for the Forest, that the Offenders may be tried according to *Ordinatio forestæ inde Anno* 34 *Ed.* 1.

11. After such Offences are tried, the Proceedings are to be sealed up and kept by the *Verderors*, until the coming of the Chief Justice in Eyre, and then they cannot be traversed.

How the Nusances shall be remedied, and in what manner the Offenders shall be punished.

12. At the coming of the Chief Justice in Eyre, the Nusances shall be thus remedied.

13. If 'tis a Common *Nusance*, as in not repairing Bridges, or such like, which is *Commune nocumentum*, the Offender being convicted, and bound to appear before the Chief Justice, he shall cause the Offender to be bound with sufficient Sureties to see the same repaired (as it ought) by a certain Day, or otherwise to forfeit his Bond, and also he may fine him for this Default.

14. But if he be convicted and adjudged to repair it, and afterwards neglects to do it, then, if he is bound to appear at the *Justice-Seat*, and refuseth to appear there, and Judgment is there given against him, that he ought to repair, and the

first Judgment affirmed; in such Case, if he doth not fulfill the same, his Lands and Tenements shall be seised into the King's Hands, until he hath repaired (as he ought) pursuant to the Judgment.

15. So likewise if any Foreigner, who hath neither Freehold or Right of *Common* in the Forest, do *Surcharge* the same, he shall be fined for the first Offence, and his Beasts forfeited for the third Offence: And he who erects a Water-Mill on a River as aforesaid, or makes any Dam to drown a Meadow, or stop any Passage, shall be fined at the Discretion of the Chief Justice in Eyre, and shall be bound in a great Sum of Money, with sufficient Sureties, to amend the Default before a Time then limited for that Purpose.

16. If an Offender be convicted of that which is called *Nocumentum speciale*, viz. of Hunting in the Forest, or Trespassing there to the hurt of the wild Beasts or Venison, he is to be committed, ransomed and bound to his Good Behaviour of the Forest; and all such who are convicted of destroying the *Vert*, or cutting down the Woods, Covert or Vert, within the Regard of the Forest, are to be committed and fined to the King, and bound to the Good Behaviour of the Forest.

17. 'Tis a general Rule, that for every Trespass and Offence in the Forest, either in *Vert or Venison*, the Offender must be committed, fined and bound to his Good Behaviour of the Forest.

18. But this Punishment cannot be executed in every one of those Particulars, but only by a judicial Sentence pronounced by the Chief Justice in Eyre of the Forest at his Justice Seat; in which Case the Party is always first convicted for the Offence, by a lawful Trial according to the Forest-Laws.

19. And all such who are convicted of any *Common Nusance* in the Forest, are to be committed,

ted, fined and bound to amend it by a certain Day; but not bound to the Good Behaviour of the Forest, for I find no Precedent for that in all the *Assises* of *Pickering* and *Lancaster*; for Wastes and Assarts of the Forest are comprehended in the Trespasses of *Vert*; and therefore they, who are Offenders therein, are to be committed, fined and bound to the Good Behaviour of the Forest.

20. And all such who are convicted of any *Purprestures* in the Forest are to be committed, fined and bound to pull down and destroy the same in a certain Time, or otherwise to pay a Yearly Rent to the King: But I do not find that any Man hath been bound to the Good Behaviour in the Forest for that Offence.

The difference between Nusance at Common Law and Nusance of the Forest.

21. *Nusance*, at *Common Law*, is that which tends to the general hurt of the People, or else to the hurt of some particular Man; but *Nusance* by the *Forest-Law* is that which tends to the hurt of the *Vert or Venison* in the Forest in any manner whatsoever.

22. So that what is a *Nusance* at *Common Law*, is not so by the *Forest-Law*, except it likewise tends to the hurt of the Forest.

Offenders in Forests.

See { *Attachment*, per totum.
Chief Justice, per totum.
Forester, 14, 15, 16.
Outlawry, per totum.
Purlieu, 120.
Regarder, 10. }

BY the Assises and Customs of the Forest, made *Anno* 6 *Ed.* 1. *Artic.* 11. it appeareth, That every Inhabitant in the Forest must use his utmost Endeavour to apprehend Offenders in Forests; for the Words are, *viz. Si quis viderit aliquos malefactores infra metas forestæ aliquam feram capere vel asportare, debet illos capere secundùm posse suum.*

2. And because every Inhabitant should be the more willing to put this Law in Execution, it is provided by the *Assises* of *H.* 2. call'd *The Assises of Woodstock, Artic.* 15. That every Man dwelling in the Forest shall be sworn to the Peace thereof, *viz. Item Rex præcipit quòd omnis homo habens ætatem duodecim annorum manens infra pacem venationis juret ejus pacem, ac Clerici laicum feodum habentes*; by which it appears that the Ancient Assises and Laws of the Forest are, That all the Inhabitants there must be sworn to keep the Peace of the Forest, and being sworn to keep the Peace himself, he ought not to suffer another to break it.

But the chiefest Care to take Offenders is incumbent on the Foresters; which if it cannot be done without some apparent Danger, then these Officers are to enquire out the Names and Habitations of the Offenders, and to present the same and the Offence at the next *Swanimote* or *Court* of *Attachment*, and upon that Presentment found and certified to the Chief Justice in Eyre by the Testimony of the *Verderors*, pursuant to the *Ordinances* of the Forest, made *Anno* 6 *Ed.* 1 *viz. Debet forestarius hoc intimare Justiciario per testimonium Viridar.* he may issue out a Special Warrant to apprehend such Offender in any Place in *England*, and to imprison him till he put in Sureties to answer the Offence.

3. And likewise upon such a Presentment, the Offender may be out-lawed in Trespass at the Suit of the King. This likewise appears, *Anno* 6 *Ed.* 1. *Artic.* 5. *Si quis attachiabilis fuerit, &c. debet distringi per catalla sua infra metas forestæ inventa; sin autem deficerent, corpus ejus detineatur quousque fecerit quod debuerit, & si extra metas forestæ fuerit manens nomen ejus & villa unde sit irrotulentur.*

4. *By the Statute of* 19 *H.* 7. *cap.* 11. 'tis enacted, If any Man *Stalk*, or causes any other to *Stalk*, with any *Bush* or *Beast*, to any Deer in a Park, Chase or Warren, or without, except in his own Ground, without Licence of the Owner, or the Master of the Game, or Keeper of the Forest, Chase or Park, he shall forfeit for every Time ten Pounds to any Person who will sue for the same by Action of Debt, *&c.*

5. This Statute is made in affirmance of the Common Law; so that the Law which was before is not abridged or taken away by it, and therefore such *Offenders* may be prosecuted either at the *Common Law* or by this *Statute.*

6. Yet there are some Opinions that the Statute doth not extend to such Offenders in the *King's Forests*, because he hath a Chief Justice in Eyre, who by the Laws of this Realm hath an absolute Authority to hear and determine all manner of Trespasses for *hunting*, and all Offences against *Vert* and *Venison* done in any of his *Forests*; and

therefore this Statute was never intended to diminish his Authority, and to give Power to Justices of Peace to punish Offenders of this Nature.

7. 'Tis farther objected, That the Statute was made only for a more speedy remedy and redress of *Trespasses* done in the Forests, Parks and Chases of several *Subjects*, who were *Owners* thereof, and not of *Trespasses* in the *King's Forests*.

8. But we see by daily Experience, and by the Proceedings of the Justices of *Assise* in their several *Circuits*, that this Statute doth extend as well to the *King's Forests* as to those of his *Subjects*, because they assess Fines upon those who offend therein.

9 A Man must not enter the Forest in the *Night-time*; therefore if his Horse is pasturing there, and he enter in the *Night* and take out his Horse, he shall be imprisoned, ransomed and bound to the Good Behaviour of the Forest.

10. The like Punishment for him who enters the *King's Forest* with Bows and Arrows, with an intent to offend there, tho' he doth no Act; for by the *Assises* of the Forest, *Voluntas reputabitur pro facto*, *Itin. Pickering fo.* 3, 7.

11. One *Nicholas Melvill*, and several others, were indicted for that they, with Bows and Arrows and Dogs, had killed 43 Stags and Hinds in the Forest, and had set their Heads on Stakes; they were committed and grievously fined, and according to the Charter of the Forest, were bound to their Good Behaviour; and so they must have been if they had been pardoned. *Itin Picker. fo.* 5.

12. In Trespasses in Forests all are *Principals*, for there are no *Accessaries*; and therefore he who *receiveth stoln Venison* shall be punished as a *Principal*. *Itin. Picker. fo.* 3.

13. Stripping or fleaing a Beast in the Forest, dead of the *Murrain*, is finable, if presented, and the

Of-

Offender shall pay the Value of the Skin besides. *Assis. Pick. fo.* 8.

14. In some cases Offenders in Forests may be guilty of *Felony*, as for instance; If a Forester hath killed a Deer, and leaves it in the Forest whilst he goes to his Lodge for a Horse, and in the mean time another Person carries it away; this is Felony, and the Offender is to suffer as in other cases of Felony.

15. *Anno* 12 *Assis. Placito* 32. A Forester was indicted for feloniously *cutting down* and carrying away several Trees; but the Judges would not suffer him to be arraigned for Felony upon that Indictment, because the Trees which are growing are annexed to the Freehold, of which a Man cannot commit Felony; but if they had been cut down by the Owner, and then the Forester had carried them away, this had been Felony.

16. So if Pigeons are taken abroad, or Fishes in a River, this is not Felony; but if taken in a Pigeon House, or if the Fish are taken in a Trunk, with a felonious Intent, 'tis Felony. 22 *Assis. Placito* 95. *Trin.* 12 *H* 8. *fo.* 3, 4.

17. So in 18 *H.* 8. *fo.* 2. *Placito* 11. If Apples, growing in an Orchard, or the Trees, are cut down and carried away, or Corn growing on the Ground is cut and carried away with a felonious Intent; this is not Felony, because, at the time of taking it, 'twas Parcel of the Freehold; but if the Apples had been gathered, or the Corn cut by the Owner, and afterwards carried away by another, this is Felony.

18. So if Deer are taken in a Forest, such taking is but a Trespass; but if killed by the Forester, and afterwards carried away by another, 'tis Felony.

19. As to these Cases of the Trees and Apples, *&c.* 'tis true the Law is so, but 'tis difficult to apprehend the Reason of it; for if a Man hath a

felonious Intention to steal Trees, and for that purpose unlawfully enters upon my Ground, and cuts them down, and afterwards carries them away; this seems to be one continued Act of Felony, begun by his unlawful Entry and cutting down, and accomplished by his carrying the Trees away when cut down.

20. 'Tis true, he would not commit Felony whilst they were actually growing on the Freehold, because it was impossible for him to remove them; but when once they were cut down (and to me it doth not seem material by whom) they were no longer any Parcel of the Freehold; 'tis the carrying them away which compleats the Felony, and not the cutting them down; but if cut down by the Felon, 'tis so far from extenuating, that I think 'tis an Aggravation of his Offence.

21. But to return, where Felony is committed in a Forest, *Hue and Cry* may pursue the Felon wheresoever he goes, as after a Felon at Common Law, till he is apprehended; but 'tis a Question, if the Offence had been only a *Trespass*, whether the Forester could pursue him with Hue and Cry *out of the Boundaries of the Forest*, because the Words of *the Assise of the Forest*, *Anno* 6 *Ed.* 1. *Artic.* 11. are, *Si quis viderit aliquos malefactor' infra metas forestæ aliquam feram capere vel asportare, debet illos capere secundum posse suum, & si non possit, debet levare Hutesium & clamorem, & si non fecerit, remaneat in misericordia Regis.*

22. Now some are of Opinion, that this *Hue and Cry* is limited to be *within the Bounds of the Forest*, because, in the precedent Article of the same *Assises, viz. Artic.* 10. the Words are, *Si quis ceperit feram sine Warranto in foresta corpus suum arrestetur ubicunque inveniatur infra metas forestæ.*

23. Therefore, without the Bounds the Forester cannot apprehend him, unless he follow him with

fresh Pursuit in his *View*; so that if he cannot arrest an Offender *without the Limits of the Forest*, by the same Reason he cannot pursue a Trespasser with *Hue and Cry out of the Boundaries*.

24. Mr. Attorney *Noy*, *in Itinere Windsor*, affirmed, That in the Reign of *H.* 2. the Inhabitants of that part of the Forest next *Surrey*, were fined an Hundred Marks for burning Heath in it; for it disturbeth and spoileth the Layer of the Deer, *Jones's Rep.* 276.

Officers in a Forest.

See { *Charge in Chief Justice*, 24.
Forests, 31, 32.

1. THere are Six Sorts of necessary Officers in a Forest; *ss.* A *Steward*, *Verderors*, *Foresters*, *Regarders*, *Agistors* and *Woodwards*.

2. All Offences and Trespasses in the Forest must be tried before these Officers, or by some of them, in those Courts which they hold for the due Execution of the Forest-Laws.

3. But it may happen that there may be Forests which have not every one of those Foresters; for there are some Forests which have no Agistors, because the King hath no Woods there to agist, but in every Forest where there are Woods, there must be Agistors.

4. These Officers must duly attend their respective Offices, and each of them must execute his own Office, and no more; for if several Offices are in one Hand, they may be seised, and the Reason is, *Quia habet plurima officia quæ intendere non potest.* *Jones's Rep.* 266. And to prove this, Mr. Attorney

Noy

Noy told the Court, that he had seen several Precedents. *Jones's Rep.* 295.

5. Therefore, if a *Forester*, or *Bailiff*, or *Keeper* of several Walks, hath afterwards the Office of a *Verderor*, all his other Offices are void, and may be seised, because they are all subordinate to the Office of a Verderor; and by the Acceptance of that Office the other are determined; like *Blage's* Case, who being a Remembrancer in the Exchequer, was afterwards made one of the Barons, and it was resolved, that his Office of Remembrancer was determined.

5. It is to be inquired how Officers have used their Offices; for there is a Trust implied in the Grant of an Office, *viz.* That the Grantee should use it well: Now if he hath broken that Trust, 'tis a Forfeiture of the Office, as if a *Woodward* hath fell'd Wood for his private Use; so that, by Law, there is a tacit Condition annexed to their Estates. *Jones's Rep.* 272.

6. If a Man claim the Office of a Keeper, and do not claim any Fees for the Execution thereof, this is but an Office of Burthen, and he is removeable at Will; and therefore, in most Grants of Offices, tis *Unà cum vadis & feodis eidem spectan.* And though there are no certain Fees expressed by those Words, yet in his Claim he must averr some certain Fees due to him, or else his Claim is not good. *Jones's Rep* 292.

Officers of the Forest as they have been returned by the Sheriff upon a Writ of Summons, to the Justice-Seat. Coke, 4 Inst. 310.

'EDwardus Dei gratiâ Rex Angliæ, Dominus
' Hiberniæ, & Dux Aquitaniæ, Vic' Ebor'
' salutem. Summon' per bonos summonitores
' Archiepiscopos, Episcopos, Abbates, Priores,
' Co-

'Comites, Barones, Milites, & omnes liberè tenentes qui terras seu tenementa habent infra metas Forestæ dilecti consanguinei & fidelis nostri Henrici Com' Lancastr' de Pickering in Com' præd' & de qualibet villa ejusdem Com' infra metas forestæ dilecti consanguinei & fidelis nostri Henrici Com' Lancastr' de Pickering in Com' præd' & de qualibet villa ejusdem Com' infra metas ejusdem forestæ existen' quatuor homines & præpositum & forestar. villarum & omnes alios qui coram Justiciariis ad placita forestæ venire solent & debent, quòd sint apud Pickering die Lunæ prox' post Festum Sancti Michaelis prox' futur' coram dilectis & fidelibus nostris Richardo de Willoughby, Jo. de Shardelow, Roberto de Hungerford, & Johanne de Hambury, tribus vel duobus eorum, quos ad requisitionem dicti consanguinei nostri constituimus Justiciarios ad itinerand' hac vice ad placita Forestæ ipsius Comitis in Com' præd' à tempore quo Edmundus nuper Com' Lanc', Pater prædicti Henrici, cujus hæres ipse est, placita forestæ in eadem foresta virtute concessionis sibi per Dominum Edwardum nuper Regem Angliæ, Avum nostrum, inde factum ultimum tenuit auditur' & factur' præceptum nostrum, iis quæ ad placita prædict' pertinen. Facias etiam venire coram Justiciar' prædict' omnes Forestarios & Viridarios forestæ prædict' in Com' præd post ultima placita prædict' cum omnibus attach' suis, tam de viridi quàm de venatione, quæ post ult' placita forestæ emersa & nondum terminat', viz. tam de attachiamentis quæ manent infra metas forestæ quàm de illis quæ manent extra forestam. Facias etiam venire coram eisdem Justiciariis, tribus vel duobus eorum, Regardatores ipsius Comitis in balliva tua. Ita quòd habeant ibi omnia Regarda sua sigillis suis signat' & omnes Agistatores præfati

'Com'

'Com' in eadem balliva sua cum omnibus At-
'tachiamentis: Et habeas ibi summon' & hoc Breve.'
'Teste meipso apud Westm' 17 die Augusti Anno
'regni nostri octavo.

The Return.

'Ad quod Breve Petrus de Saltmarsh, Vic'
'Ebor' retornavit quòd fecit plenum retornum
'istius brevis Hugoni de Nevill ballivo libertatis
'Henrici Comitis Lancastr' honoris de Pickering,
'cui executio istius Brevis restat faciend', qui sibi
'respond' quôd summoniri fecit Archiepiscopos,
'Episcopos, Abbates, Priores, Comites, Barones,
'Milites, & omnes liberè tenentes qui terras &
'tenementa habent infra metas forestæ & qualibet
'villâ ejusdem forestæ existen' quatuor homines &
'præposit' & forestar' & villar' & omnes alios qui
'coram Justiciar' ad placita venire solent & debent,
'quòd sint apud Pickering ad diem in Brevi præ-
'dict' content' coram præfat Justiciariis tribus vel
'duobus eorum auditur' & factur' præcept' Domi-
'ni Regis de iis quæ ad prædict' placita pertinent.
'Et quod venire fecit Forestarios, Viridarios, &
'omnes illos qui fuerunt Forestarii & Viridarii Fo-
'restæ præd' in balliva sua post ultima placita præd'
'cum omnibus attachiamentis prædict' tam de vi-
'ridi quàm de venatione, quæ post ultima placita
'Forestæ sunt emersa, & nondum terminata. Et
'etiam quòd venire fecit coram eisdem Justiciariis
'tribus vel duobus eorum Regardatores ipsius Co-
'mitis in balliva sua ita quòd haberent ibi omnia
'Regarda sua sigillis suis signat' & omnes agistato-
'res præfat' Comitis in eadem balliva sua cum
'omnibus Agistamentis prout patet in retorn' Sche-
'dulæ suo præd' attachiata.

Fo-

Forestarii de feodo in le Westward istius Forestæ de Pickering.
- *Willielmus de Percebay Miles.*
- *Petronilla de Kynthorpe, quæ posuit loco suo Edmundum de Hastings ad omnia faciend' quæ Forestar. incumbunt durante itinere & fecit Sacramentum.*

Forestarii Custod' Forestæ in le Eastward.
- *Rogerus de Leicester.*
- *Hugo de Yeland.*
- *Willielmus de Parker.*

A Woman may be a Forester in Fee, but she cannot execute the Office, as may be seen by this Return; but she may make a *Deputy* during the Eyre, which Deputy shall be sworn.

Viridarii Forestæ de Pickering.
- *Robertus Thurnese.*
- *Rogerus Brown.*
- *Robertus Playce.*
- *Johannes de Kilwardbye.*

Regardatores Forestæ de Pickering.
- *Willielmus de Everley.*
- *Rogerus de Long.*
- *Johannes Boye.*
- *Johannes Filius Alani.*
- *Galfridus de Knitborpe.*
- *Thomas Thurnese.*
- *Hugo de Nevil.*
- *Rogerus de Alveston.*
- *Johannes Filius Gladford.*
- *Rogerus de Stapleton.*
- *Rogerus Strutcock.*
- *Radulphus de Colloughton.*
- *Johannes de la Chemne.*

By this Return it appears there were *Thirteen Regarders* then of the Forest of *Pickering*, which are

are more than required by *the Charter of the Forest*, *Cap.* 7. where 'tis prohibited to make any Gathering but upon the Sight and upon the Oath of *Twelve Regarders*; which Number is necessary in every Forest.

Agistatores in le Westward.	*Johannes Dring.* *Richardus Russell.*
Agistatores in le Eastward.	*Willielmus de Roston.* *Willielmus Russell.*

Nomina Forestariorum istius Forestæ & eorum qui fuerunt Forestar' istius Forestæ, & eorum qui fuerunt viridarii istius Forestæ.

Capital. Forestar. *Willielmi de Pereebay, unius Forestar' de feodo Forestæ de Pick' in le Westward, ibidem.*	*Alanus de Newton.* *Johannes de Wardesden.*
Capital' Forestar' Petronillæ de Kynthorpe alterius Forestar' de feodo Forestæ de Pickering.	*Henry de Ripley.* *Thomas de Dalby.*
Capital' Forestar' Hugon' de Yealand Forest' Custodis Forestæ in le Eastward.	*David de Newton.* *Thomas de Ripley.*

Nomina Subforestariorum Forestæ prædict.

Forestarii Radulphi de Hastings, Custod' Forestæ præd.	*Johannes de Harley.* *Richardus de Aleintofetes.* *Willielmus Gower.* *Richardus de Halmesley.* *Johannes Munmewe.* *Johannes Scot.* *Willielmus Courtnan.*

Nomina Subforestariorum qui fuerunt in Foresta illa post ultimum iter'.

Galfridus de Hawley.	*Alanus fil. Radulphi.*
Robertus de Wigan.	*Adamus fil. Willielmi.*
Petrus Lilly.	*Johannes de Nevill.*
Johannes Ronceby.	*Thomas de Newton.*
Rogerus fil. Nich.	

Besides the Officers before mentioned, there is one called *Custos Totius Forestæ*, and another *Supervisor Forestariorum, quod nota*; the *Custos* is mentioned in the Statute of 1 *Ed.* 3. *cap.* 3.

The Names of the Officers of the Forest of *Lancaster*: *Willielmus Blount*, *Custos totius Forestæ & seneschallus*; *Robertus de Ratcliff, Magister Forestarius*; *Willielmus de Holland, Supervisor Forestariorum totius Forestæ*; *Johannes Balridge, Forestarius de feodo in warda de Lonsdale.*

Robertus Fowcher nunc Custos istius Forestæ venit, &c. et illo amoto Willielmus de Clapham juratus est, & efficitur' Custos ejusdem Forestæ.

Outlawry.

See { *Presentment*, 7. *Swanimote*, 24.

1. OFfenders in Forests may be prosecuted by way of *Outlawry*, *viz.* If a Man is indicted for any Offence done there, who lives in another County, and *out* of the Forest, so that he cannot be taken by the Foresters; in such Case the Offender may be *outlaw'd*, and the Proceedings against him are the same as at Common Law; that

that is, Proclamation must be made at five several County Courts; and after the *quinquies exact.* the *Coroner* gives Judgment for his Contempt in not appearing, so that he who is five Times proclaimed, and doth not appear, shall be out of the King's Peace, and by consequence an *Outlaw*, and then the Person is absolutely outlawed. *Fleetwood fo.* 8. *Hesket fo.* 16.

2. The Law is the same *per Assisam forestæ*, for he who is to be outlawed for any Offence in the Forest must be proclaimed in the same manner as at Common Law; and when he is *quinquies exact.* he is fully outlawed; and by vertue of that *Outlawry* his Goods and Chattels are forfeited to the King, and the *Profits* of his Lands by the *Inquisition* of the Sheriff and the Coroner.

3. If a Man is outlawed for an *Offence* either in the *Vert* or *Venison*, and afterwards taken by a *Capias utlagatum*, he shall be committed without *Bail*, to remain in Prison until delivered by a special Warrant from the King, or from the Chief Justice in Eyre, or Chief Warden of the *Forest*.

Parks in Forests.

See { *Charge in Chief Justice*, 15.
Forests, 38, 39.
Forester, 11.
Inclosures, 5, 8.
Appendix, Trespass in Parks.

1. IN many Forests, those are Parks which the Owners claim, either by *Grant* from the King or *Prescription*: Such Parks must be stored with *Game*, and the Woods must be preserved, and the *Pales* be kept, so that there are no *Inleaps* for the Deer.

And

And if a Subject is Owner of a Forest, he may give Licence to another to make and enclose a Park within the Meets of his *Forests*, and to hold the same so enclosed, with all such *Venison* as the *Grantee* shall put in, to him and his Heirs. And this was adjudged a good *Licence* in a Claim made in Eyre: But if such a *Park* is so slightly enclosed and fenced, that the *wild Beasts* of the Forest do enter, in such Case the Lord of the Forest may enter and hunt there at his pleasure. *Assis. Pickering fo.* 64.

2. The Owners of those *Parks* may divide any competent parcel thereof with Rails, Pales or Hedge, for the feeding the *Game* in *Winter*, and he who hath the Herbage cannot put any Cattle therein.

3. In a *Quo Warranto*, for that the Defendant, amongst other Things, did without Warrant use a Park with a Pale, Ditch and Hedge enclosed in the *King's Forest*, &c.

4. The Defendant prescribed, That *John Byron*, and all those whose Estate he had, were seised in Fee of seven hundred Acres, &c. and have accustomed to have therein, &c. Hedging, Ditching and Inclosing at their Will and Pleasure, with all Liberties, Privileges and Franchises to a Park belonging, and have used to keep Deer therein, and to appoint a Keeper, &c. to look after them, *Ac ad venandum, fugandum occidendum, capiendum & asportandum omnes & omnimodas Damas in eodem parco de tempore in tempus existentes, ita quod nullus forestarius Domini Regis forestæ præd' nec aliquæ aliæ personæ quæcunque intromittantur ad venandum & fugandum in parco præd' sine licentia præd' Johannis*, and so derives a Title to himself, &c.

5. In the Argument in this Case it was admitted, that a Man may have a *Park* in a Forest, either by *Prescription* or *Grant*: But then it must be so *inclosed*,

that the Beasts of the Forest cannot enter, for if there is any Deer-leap, or if the Park is not kept enclosed 'tis a Forfeiture of the Liberties thereof.

6. But it was argued, That the Defendant could not *prescribe* in such manner to have a *Park*, because 'tis contrary to the Nature of the Royal Franchise of the Forest, and tends to the destruction thereof; for 'tis not only *ad magnum nocumentum ferarum*, but to the destruction of all; for they are subject to be destroyed by the Defendant, because no Person whatsoever is to enter into his Park, besides himself or his Keepers.

7. If 'tis objected that this Park, claimed by the Defendant, is but a little part of the Forest, that will not be material; for if the Defendant may *prescribe* to have such an irregular Park in part of the Forest, other Men may make the like *Prescriptions* in other parts thereof; and so the King may lose all the Franchise of his Forest.

8. Besides, the Defendant may make his Fence or Ditch *very low* on the outside next the *Forest*, and *so high* within his Park, that the King's Deer cannot get out when they are once within, and so the Park would be in the nature of a *Trap* to catch them.

9. Neither hath the King so much Power in this *Land*, being in the midst of his *Forest*, as he hath in the *Lands* of any of his *Subjects* lying out of it; for if the Beasts of the *Forest* stray into the *Lands* of any *Subject*, the Foresters may lawfully enter those Lands and drive them back again. *Bridgman's Rep.* Sir *John Byron's* Case.

10. In the Reign of King *James* I. some Questions being moved between the Earl of *Nottingham*, Justice in Eyre of all the King's Forests, and the Earl of *Dorset*, then Lord *Treasurer*, concerning those Forests; the Judges of *England* were assembled, and upon Conference they resolved,

That he who hath the Herbage or Pannage of a Park by the *Grant* of the King or of any other Person, cannot take such Herbage or Pannage, but what is Surplusage and above the competent and sufficient Pasture and Feeding for the *Game*; and if the Owner of the *Game* suffer them to encrease, so that there is no Surplusage, then he who hath the Herbage and Pannage cannot put any Beast into the *Park*.

11. That the Owner of such *Park* may divide any competent parcel thereof with Rail, Pale or Hedge, to feed the *Game* in *Winter*, and he who hath the Herbage cannot put any Beast therein.

12. If the Pasture and Pannage of a *Park* be not sufficient to feed the Deer in *Winter* and *Summer*, the Owner thereof may drive out the Beasts of him who hath the Herbage and Pannage. *Rot. Parl.* 18 *Ed.* 1. *fo.* 16.

Pannage.

See *Agistment*, 23.
Charge in Chief Justice, 58.
Common, 33, 35.
Appendix, Charta Forestæ, 9.
Appendix, Assisa Forestæ, 13.

1. THE *Latine* Word *Pannagium* is derived from *Panegyris*, in *English Pannage*, which is a gathering of Money, or the Profits made of the Fruits of Trees. 'Tis true, the *Latinists* express all manner of Fruits by the Word *Fruges*; but the Common Lawyers and Civilians do use the Word *Pannagium*, for the Mast of such Trees only, which bear Fruit to feed Hogs, or else for the Money made of such Mast; and therefore it differs from

Agistment, for that is the Herbage of any Ground or the Profit made thereof; but *Pannage* is the *Agistment* of the *Mast* of Trees, or the Money paid for the same.)

2. The Word is often taken in the Sense beforementioned, but *Pannage* is properly the Money received for the *Agistment* of the *Mast*. This appears by *Charta Forestæ, Artic.* 8. *viz. Quando Agistatores nostri debent recipere pannagium nostrum, &c.* And in the same Article, *& habeat pannagium suum*, where by the Word *Pannagium* is understood *Money* for agisting the Wood, or the Profit of the Mast, *viz.* the Money received for the same.

3. So in *Assisa Forestæ, Artic.* 14. *viz. Quod deinceps capiatur pro quolibet porco quantum potest ad opus Domini Regis pro pannagio (i. e)* the Money which is due for the Mast.

4. *Heskct, fo.* 48. is of the same Opinion, *viz.* That *Pannage* is not properly the *Agistment* or *Mast* of the Hogs, but the *Money* or *Profit* which is due and ought to be paid for the same: And he cites a Case adjudged in the Reign of *Ed.* 1. where an Action of Trespass was brought against the Defendant for entering into his Park, and eating up his *Pannage* with his Cattle: And the Writ was abated, because it was for eating his *Pannage*, when it ought to have been for eating of his *Mast*; for *Pannage* is only the *Money* paid for the *Mast*, and not the *Mast* it self.

Quære of this Case, for I can find no such Case reported.

5. In the Book of *Entries, fo.* 595, *Trespass in Pannagio*, it appears that an Action of Trespass was brought against the Bishop of *Litchfield* and *Coventry*, for taking and driving away certain Hogs, *&c.*

6. The *Bishop* pleaded, That he was seised of a *Chase* in right of his Bishoprick, *&c.* in which

2 there

there was a great Wood, and that the Hogs were found there agisting the *Mast*, and then prescribes that he and all his Predecessors, *&c.* used to have the *Pannage* of the said Wood, *viz. unum denarium de pannagio cujuslibet porci tempore fugationis in eadem chasea proinde, &c.* And for the levying thereof, he and all his Predecessors, *&c.* had yearly, between *Michaelmas* and *Christmas*, driven the Hogs, then being in the said Chase, to some convenient place to pound and detain them, until he was paid the *Pannage* thereof, and so justifieth the taking, *&c.*

7. So that in this Case the Word *Pannagium* is rather taken for the *Money* or *Profit* made of the *Mast* or *Agistment* of the Wood, than the *Mast* or *Agistment* it self.

8. But in the same Book of *Entries, fo.* 605. Tit. *Toll.* there is a Case, where the Word may be indifferently taken in either Sense, *viz.* *A Prior and Convent* pleaded a Grant from the King to be quit *de pannagio*: There the Word *Pannagium* is understood to be discharged of payment of *Money* for *Pannage*, and may also be understood to be discharged of *feeding Hogs with Mast*.

9. So in the same Book, Tit. *Assis fo.* 75. *in Offices*; the Tenant pleaded a *Grant* from the King to keep a Park and to have Profits of the Woods there, and also the *Pannage*: The Words of the *Grant* are, *viz. Necnon pro quolibet porco in eodem parco ad pannagium posito pro eodem pannagio unum quadrantem.* There the Word *Pannagium* is rather understood for the feeding Hogs with *Mast*, than the *Money* for the same, and yet it may very well be taken for either,

40. In *Lynwood's Provincial Constitutions de pannagiis*, amongst the Tithes of Woods and wild Fruits, he mentions *pannagia sylvarum*, the *Mast* of Beech and Oak, or such like; and tells us, if 'tis

sold, then the Owner of the Woods must pay the Tenth Penny, *de pannagiis silvarum*: Here the Word *Pannagium* is understood properly for the Money paid for the Mast, but may likewise be taken for the Mast it self.

Of the Time of Pannage in the King's Woods, *and who is to receive it.*

11. The Time of *Pannage* in the *King's Woods*, begins on *Holy-Rood-Day*, which is fifteen Days before *Michaelmas*: This appears *in Charta Forestæ, Artic.* 8. *viz. Quando Agistatores nostri conveniunt ad agistandum Dominicos Boscos nostros, &c.* and it ends forty Days after *Michaelmas*, that is about the Feast of St. *Martin* the Bishop, *Quando Agistatores nostri debent recipere pannagium nostrum*: By which last Clause it appeareth, that the Agistors are to receive the *Pannage*; for tho' they ought not to agist the Woods without the Privity and Consent of the *Foresters* and *Verderors*; yet they only are chargeable for the *Pannage*; which appears likewise in the Entries in the Records and Assises and Iters of *Pickering* and *Lancaster, &c.*

Of the Times of Pannage of other Men's Woods *in the Forest, and who is to receive it.*

12. The Freeholders, and all other Men who have Woods and Lands within the regard of the Forest, may agist the same at convenient Times when the Mast is ripe, for tho' by the Assises of *Woodstock* Artic. 4. it was appointed, *Quod nullus agistet Boscos suos infra metas forestæ*, before the King's Woods were agisted; yet that Law is altered by *Charta forestæ, Artic.* 9. made long after the *Assises* of *Woodstock*, *viz. Unusquisque liber homo*

agistet

agistet boscum suum in foresta pro voluntate & habeat pannagium suum.

13. So that now Men may agist their own Woods at any Time *tempore pannagii*, when there is Mast; but when there is none, they must not put their Hogs there.

14. But they cannot agist all their Woods at all Times when there is Mast, for they are prohibited by the *Assises* of the Forest, made *Anno* 6 *Ed.* 1. *Rast. Forest.* 21. The Words are, *viz.* If any Man hath Woods lying within the Forest near the *King's Woods*, the Owners may not agist them till the King's Woods are agisted.

15. So that now the Law is, *viz.* Every Freeholder who hath any Woods or Hedge-rows within the Regard of the Forest, may agist them and take the *Pannage* thereof at any time *tempore pannagii*, excepting only such Woods and Hedge-rows which lie near the *King's Woods*; and those must not be agisted till the *King's Woods* are agisted, which will be about the Feast of St. *Martin* the Bishop, as aforesaid.

16. By the aforesaid Words *in Charta forestæ, viz. Unusquisque liber homo agistet boscum suum*, the *Freeholder* is not confined to agist his Woods with his *own Hogs*, but he may agist them with the Hogs of other Men; for the Copulative *& habeat pannagium suum*, imports, that he may agist them with such Hogs, and take the *Pannage* thereof, that is, the Money for the *Pannage*.

17. This is likewise proved by the Assises and Customs of the Forest, *Anno* 6 *Ed.* 1. *Artic.* 15. *viz. Et hoc fiat de exitu porcorum*; that is, This may may be done of the Profit of the Hogs; so that a Man may agist his Woods himself, and may likewise take and receive the *Pannage* of them by the agisting the Hogs of other Men; and this Liberty

is given to them by *the Charter of the Forest*, for it was otherwise before.

18. It was admitted and adjudged in the Claim of one *Lambeson*, *Itin. Pick. fo.* 16. That to be quit of Pannage, *tempore pannagii*, might be *appurtenant* to a Man's Freehold, that is, it may be by *Prescription* appurtenant to Lands.

19. At every Justice-Seat, the Profit of Pannage must be presented, and likewise the Profit of Rushes, Fern, Gorse, Sedge, and such like. *Itin. Lanc. fo.* 8.

Prescription.

See { *Common*, 14, 27, 28, 29, 36, 48.
Dogs, 14.
Estovers, 6, 7.
Forester, 41, 42.
Park, 6.
Pannage, 18.
Purlieu, 100.
Warrant, 1.
Warren, 4.
Woods, 5, 13, 18.

1. THe Form of a Prescription in the Forest, differs from a Prescription at Common-Law; for a Claim that he and his Ancestors, *tempore quo*, is good, without saying, that he and his Ancestors, and *all those whose Estate he hath* in certain Lands.

2. A Man cannot prescribe to fell *Wood* in a Forest, without the View of the Foresters, unless it be upon an Allowance in Eyre; and even in such Case it must be intended there was a *Charter*, upon which the first Allowance was made. *Jones's Rep.* 271.

3. Nei-

3. Neither is a Prescription good to fell Wood *per visum Forestariorum & Viridariorum*; it ought to be *per visum & allocationem Forestariorum & Viridariorum*; for if it should be good *per visum, &c.* only, then if the Foresters and Verderors are required to come and view it, and they refuse or neglect to come, the Person may cut it without View.

4. This is the Opinion of some; but it seems contrary to Sir *Thomas Palmer*'s Case, 5 *Rep.* 25. where my Lord *Coke* tells us, There is no manner of Difference between a Prescription *per Visum, &c.* only, and *per visum & allocationem, &c.* for upon a Request and Refusal the Party may take the Wood without View. *Jones*'s *Rep.* 276.

5. In the Case of the Tenants of the Manor of *Bray*, *Jones*'s *Rep.* 289. They prescribed to fell their Woods at Pleasure, *without View of the Foresters*, and to have Common of Pasture. Mr. Attorney *Noy* argued, That since the Statutes of *Charta Forestæ*, and *Consuetudines & Assisæ Forestæ*, a Man cannot prescribe to do Waste, or make Assarts, or cut the Wood *without View*; for by *Cap.* 4. 'tis ordain'd, *Quod liberatio de Housebote & Haybote, fiat prout Boscus pati potest in Statu quo est, & non ad exigentiam petentis, nec potest aliquis dare vel vendere de Bosco suo sine licentiâ Domini Regis.*

6. It was argued for the Tenants, That, notwithstanding those Statutes, the *Prescription* was good; for there is a Difference between a Negative Statute, which is only *declaratory* of the Common-Law, and a Negative Statute which is *introductory* of a new Law. *Co. Lit.* 115.

7. Against the last no *Prescription* is good; but 'tis otherwise where a Negative Statute is declaratory of the old Law; for in such case, no Alteration is made of the Law, and therefore a Prescription may be good notwithstanding such Statute.

8. And

8. And for this Reason a Man may prescribe to hold a Leet more than *twice* in a Year, though the Statute of *Magna Charta* is Negative, *viz.* that a Leet be *only* holden *twice*, *&c.*

9. And they cited a Case in 8 *Ed.* 3. *in Itin. Pick.* where *Thomas Wake* of *Lydham* prescribed to cut Wood without View, *&c.* and Issue was joined upon the Prescription.

10. And so are the Cases of *Gilbert Acton* and *Henry Piercy*, there adjudged on Issues joined upon the like *Prescriptions*, and afterwards allowed in the King's Bench.

11. And in *Hill.* 19 *Ed.* 1. *Rot.* 58. in a Case between a Prebend of *Chichester*, and the Earl of *Arundel*, Issue was joined upon the like Prescription; and *Anno* 6 *Eliz.* in another Case reported by the Chief Justice *Popham*, That a Prescription to cut down Wood *without View*, *&c.* was good.

12. To which it was answered, by *Noy* Attorney-General, first by denying the Difference taken by my Lord *Coke*, between a *Negative Statute introductory of a new Law*, and where 'tis *declaratory* of the old Law; for the Statute *de Sylvâ cæduâ* is only *declaratory* of the old Law, and 'tis a Negative Statute; and yet a Prescription to have Tithes of Timber is not good.

13. As for the Case in *Hill.* 19 *Ed.* 1. and the Statute *Consuetudines & Assisa Forestæ*, the one was of *Chases*, and the other of *Forests*; and he agreed, That a Prescription to cut down Wood in *Chases*, *without View*, was good: And so was the Case cited by my Lord *Popham*, for it was in a *Chase* of which the King was seised in Right of his Dutchy of *Lancaster*.

14. And as for *Piercy*'s Case, it did not concern the Case now in Question; for it was a Prescription to fell Woods in the *King's Forest*, without *View*, *&c.* But the Forest of *Pickering* was not then in

in the Hands of King; for *H.* 3. gave it to his Son *Edmund* Duke of *Lancaster*; so that it was out of the Crown and in the Possession of a Subject, when the Statute *de Consuetudinibus & Assis. foresta* was made; so that whatever a Man could prescribe for in that Forest, before the making that Statute, he might still prescribe for the same after 'twas made.

15. Therefore, excepting only in that Case of *Ed.* 1. in the Forest of *Pickering* aforesaid, and in the Cases of *Chases*, it cannot be shew'd, that ever a Prescription to fell *Wood* in the *King's Forests, without View of the Foresters*, was held good.

16. A Man cannot prescribe to have *Strays* in gross; but a Prescription may be good for *Strays, Tanquam ad manerium de C. pertinen.* *Jones's Rep.* 283.

17. A Prescription to *hunt* in a *Purlieu* is not good, because a *Purlieu* itself cannot be by Prescription. *Jones's Rep.* 278.

18. But a Prescription for Housebote and Haybote is good, because those are Things which must necessarily be had; and it may not be convenient at all times to look after the Foresters. *Jones's Rep.* 271.

19. A Prescription to have *Common* is good, without an Allowance in Eyre; because 'tis an equitable Prescription, and in the nature of a Common Right; for since the Deer have fed on my Grounds, 'tis reasonable I should have Common in the Forest.

20. But generally a Man cannot prescribe to any thing which goes to the Destruction of the *Vert* or *Venison*, without an Allowance in Eyre. *Jones's Rep.* 291.

21. A Man cannot prescribe to a *Warren* in a Forest, but if such Prescription hath been allowed in Eyre, 'tis good. And this was Sir *Richard Harrison's*

rison's Case, *Jones*'s *Rep*. 272, 280. But this seems contrary to the case of *Strata Marcella*, 9 *Rep* wherein it appeareth, That if any thing be claimed by Charter, leaving out, *before time of Memory*, tis not good, without an Allowance, in Time of Memory: But if Liberties be claimed by Charter since Time of Memory, or by Prescription, they need no Allowance; for, by the same Reason I might prescribe 300 Years ago, I may prescribe now.

22. But in 2 *Rep*. 155. it was adjudged, That a Man may prescribe to a *Warren*, or to keep Sheep in a Forest, although in the King's Hands, but it must be by a Special Prescription.

23. And in such Case of Prescription for *Warren*, though it hath not been used for several Years, yet a *Non-user* of *Fairs*, *Markets*, *Courts*, or such like Liberties, wherein the Subjects have an Interest either for their common Profit, or for the Administration of Justice, is a good Cause of *Seisure*; but the *Non-user* of *Parks* or *Warrens*, which are only for the *Profit* or *Pleasure* of the Owner, is neither a Cause of Seisure or Forfeiture.

24. And in this Case my Lord *Coke* cited the Lord *Hatton*'s Case, which was adjudg'd in *B. R. Anno* 18 *Ed.* 1. upon a Demurrer, *viz*. That one might prescribe to cut down Woods in a Forest, though it was in the King's Hands; which *Popham*, Chief Justice, affirm'd, but said, That not long after it was adjudged *otherwise* in the *Exchequer*.

25. *Continual Usage* is the Strength and Support of all *Customs* and *Prescriptions*; and therefore to *prescribe*, that he and all those, &c. *poterint succidere arbores*, &c. is not good, without laying an *actual Usage*; for a Man may do a Thing unlawfully, and be punished for doing it, *Jones*'s *Rep*. 291. And therefore, *Anno* 21 *Ed*. 4. *fo*. 28. the Defendant pleaded a *Custom*, &c. to turn his Ploughs on his Neighbour's Headlands; and it was adjudged not

not good, without laying an *Usage*: And as to this Matter, there is a Difference between a *Customreal*, which concerns Lands, and other Customs; for where a Custom was pleaded, That within such a Borough, *quilibet, &c. potest legare tenementa sua*, 'tis good, without laying an *Usage*; but 'tis otherwise of other *Customs*.

Presentments.

See { *Dogs*, 53, 54, 57, 58, 59.
Regarder, 53.
Waste, 14.
Appendix, Assisa Forestæ, 23.
Appendix, Ordinatio Forestæ, 1. }

1. MOst Presentments for Offences in Forests, are made by the *Foresters*, in the Court of *Attachments*, before the Verderors, and usually in this Form:

2. ss. *Ad istam Curiam Attachiamenti Dominæ Reginæ forestæ suæ de Waltham in Com' Essex tent. apud Chigwell in eodem Com' nono die Julii, Anno regni Dom' nostri Eliz. Dei Gratia, Angliæ, Franciæ, & Hiberniæ Reginæ, Fidei Defensoris, &c. primo.*

3. *Johannes Matthews forestarius jurat. de Warda de Woodford infra forestam illam præsentat, quòd Johannes West de Chinkford in Com' Essex, Yeoman, nono die Julii, Anno regni, &c. primo; intravit forestam illam cum arcubus & sagittis & ibidem in quodam loco vocat' Woodford Mead infra forestam præd versavit unam damam ad mortem & carnes cepit, & fecit inde voluntatem suam.*

4. This Presentment being made in the Court of *Attachments* before the *Verderors*, and inrolled by them in the Rolls of the Forest, must be by them trans-

transmitted to the Court of *Swanimote*; for the Court of Attachments cannot proceed to Conviction: But the Offender may traverse such Presentment before it comes to the *Swanimote*, but not after.

5. After 'tis transmitted thither, then they may proceed to Tryal and Conviction, but that Court cannot determine the Offence, or assess any Fine, or give any Judgment; but the Conviction must be certified by that Court to the Chief Justice in Eyre, at the next Justice-Seat, and so must all the Proceedings in those Courts; for this is according to *the Ordinance of the Forest*, *Artic.* 1. made *Anno* 34. *Ed.* 1. and according to *the Assises and Customs of the Forest*, made *Anno* 6. *Ed.* 1. *Artic.* 19. and according to *Charta de foresta*, *Artic.* 16. *viz. Et ea Presentet Viridariis Provinciarum, & cum irrotulata fuerint & sub sigillis viridariorum inclusa presententur capitalibus Justiciariis nostris de foresta cum in partes illas venerint ad tenenda placita de foresta, & coram eis terminentur.* So that it belongeth to the Lord Chief Justice in Eyre, at the High Court of Justice-Seat, or General Sessions of the Forest, to give Judgment for all Offences, and to assess the Fines, and to punish Offenders; but he can do nothing but upon the Presentments and Convictions in the other Courts. 2 *Bulst.* 297.

6. At every Court of *Swanimote*, all the *Presentments* of the Foresters for any Offence in the Forest, either in *Vert* or *Venison*, are delivered to the Jury, who are there sworn to inquire of the Truth thereof; and if they find the Presentments to be true, then the Offenders stand convicted thereof in Law; and they are not allowed by *the Assises of the Forest*, to *traverse* the same: And so is my Lord *Coke*'s Opinion, 4 *Inst.* 290. *viz.* That an Indictment in the *Swanimote* is not *traversable*. The Entry of the Record is thus:

Præsentat'

Praesentat' est per Forestarios & duodecim jurat' wardae praed', & convictum per viridarios, quòd A. B. vicesimo septimo die Januarii, Anno Regni, &c. secundo, intravit forestam de Windsor, cum arcubus & sagittis, & ibid. versavit unam Damam ad mortem, & carnes cepit, & inde fecit voluntatem suam. Et testatum est per Vicecomitem quòd praed. A. B. non est inventus, nec aliquid habet in Balliva sua per quod attachiari potest, nec prius se reddidit, nec scitur quo devenitur, ideo exigatur de comitatu in Comitatum quousque utlagetur si non comparuerit; & si comparuerit, tunc vicecomes eum capiat, & salvò, &c. ad satisfaciend' domino Regi de transgressione praed' unde per forestarios, viridarios & alios ministros forestae convictus est.

8. By which Form of Presentment you may see, that the Offences in *Swanimotes* are presented there by Foresters and the twelve sworn Men, and that the Offenders are convicted by the Verderors; so that an Indictment found in the *Swanimote*, is a Conviction in Law, and such an Indictment, by the Forest-Laws, cannot be *traversed.*

9. But all Presentments and Indictments made by the Foresters and the Jury, or twelve sworn Men, before the Justice in Eyre, for any Offence in *Vert* or *Venison*, are *traversable per Assisas forestae*; and so it was adjudged by the whole Court at the Justice-Seat holden at *Waltham Holy-Cross* in *Essex*, before the good Earl of *Bedford*, then Lord Chief Justice in Eyre of all the Forests on this side of *Trent*, *Anno* 24 *Eliz.* where certain Indictments were found by the Jury, upon the Presentments made by the Foresters against *John West*, and *William Fiswick*, and others; and they were all traversed, because the Presentments were not first made at the *Swanimote.*

10. So that an Indictment at the Justice-Seat is traversable; but an Indictment at the *Swanimote* cannot

cannot be traversed by the Laws of the Forest: And with this my Lord *Coke* agrees. 4 *Inst.* 290.

11. There is some Variance between the Form of an Entry of a *Presentment* in the *Swanimote*, and the Form of a *Presentment* in the Court of *Attachments*; for, in the *Swanimote*, the Words are, *viz. Præsentat' est per forestarios & duodecim juratores, & convict' per virdarios*; but the Words of a *Presentment* in the Court of *Attachments* are, *Præsentat' est per A. B. forestarium*, only: *Assis. Lancastr. fo.* 11. See *Ordinatio forestæ, Anno* 34. *Ed.* in what manner Offenders shall be indicted at the *Swanimote*.

12. And great Care must be taken, that every Presentment for an Offence done in the Forest, in *Vert* or *Venison*, be certain,

In respect of the { Person. Place. Thing. Instruments. Manner of the Act. Value of the Vert. }

13. In respect of the *Person* of the Offender; for it must set forth his Name and Surname, and the Place where he dwelleth.

14. In respect of the *Place* where the Offence was committed; for it must set forth, That it was done in such a *Place within the Forest*, that it may appear the Fact was committed therein.

15. In respect of the *Thing* itself, in which the Offence was committed, *viz.* It must set forth, That the Offender kill'd a *Buck* or *Doe*; or as the Case is.

In respect of the *Instruments* with which it was done, for those must be certainly named, because they

they are forfeited to the King; therefore it must set forth, that the Offender enter'd the Forest with a *Cross-bow*, *Long-bow*, *Gun*, *&c.* and did there kill a Deer.

17. In respect of the *Manner of doing it*, for that must be set forth, because the Punishment will be aggravated or extenuated thereby; for it may be either a voluntary or negligent Offence; as if a Man riding through a Forest with a *Greyhound* in a Slip, which, upon the Sight of the Deer, breaks loose against the Will of the Owner, and kills the Deer, this is an Offence by Negligence.

18. In every Presentment of Offences in *Vert*, the Value of it must be set forth; and it must be delivered to the Verderors upon the Oath of the Forester; for if it appears to be under the Value of 4 *d.* then 'tis too small for the Justice-Seat; and in such Case, the Verderors may determine it in the Court of *Attachments*, and assess the Fine and cause the same to be levied to the Use of the King.

19. And as every Presentment concerning *Vert* or *Venison* must be certain; so every other Presentment for any Offence ought to be in like manner very certain: And therefore Mr. Attorney *Noy* affirmed, That where a Presentment was made at a Justice-Seat held in the Forest of *Windsor*, that 42 Cottages were built there, and inhabited by poor Men; but did not set forth by whom they were built, nor on whose Land; and that the Regarders ought to be fined, for that imperfect Presentment; and Judgment was given against them all, *quòd prosternentur.* *Jones's Rep.* 273.

20. *In Itin. Windsor. Jones's Rep.* 275. Mr. Attorney *Noy* moved, That every Regarder might be fined *quia minùs plenè præsentaverunt & imperfectè:* Upon which the several *Regarders* of *Battell's Bailiwick* were fined 5 *l.* every *Regarder* of *Finch-*

hamsted-Bailiwick, 5 *l.* and every *Regarder* of *Fine's Bailiwick*, 10 *l.* *Jones's Rep.* 275.

21. *In eadem Itinere*, one *Finch* was fined 10 *l.* for drawing Presentments of the *Agistors*, and for making them present such things which did not belong to their Charge. *Jones's Rep.* 280.

Purlieu.

See { *Charge in Chief Justice*, 46, 47, 48. *Forests*, 36. *Hunting*, 48, 63. *Prescription*, 17. *Ranger*, per totum. *Swanimote*, 22. *Appendix*, Stat. 33. Ed. 1. }

1. THis is a certain Territory of Ground adjoining to a Forest, meered and bounded with immoveable Marks and Boundaries, and known by matter of Record only; which Territory of Ground was once Forest-Land, and afterwards disafforested by the *Perambulations* made for dividing the *new* afforested Lands from the *old*.

2. 'Tis derived from the *French Pur*, *i.e.* clear, intire, exempt, and *Lieu*, *i.e.* a Place; so that 'tis a Place exempt from the Forest.

3. The *Perambulation* by which the *Purlieu* is made, is called, in *French*, *Pourallee*, *i. e.* a *Perambulation*: So that the *Purlieu* and *Pourallee* are distinct Things; and the right Name of the Place disafforested is *Purlieu*. 4 *Co.* 303.

How the same did first begin.

4. When *H.* 2. commonly call'd *Fitz-Empress*, who was a *Frenchman* born, and Second Son of *Jeoffrey Plantagenet*, Earl of *Anjou*, came to be King, which was *Anno* 1154, he took so much Delight in the Forests, which were then here, that, in a few years afterwards, he inlarged them by the afforesting the Lands of the Nobility, Gentry, and others, which joined to those Forests; and thus it continued during all his Reign.

5. After his Decease, *Richard* his Second Son succeeded, who, in a short time afterwards, followed this Example of his Father, by afforesting more Lands adjoining to his Forests; so that during his Reign, they were likewise very much inlarged.

6. Afterwards *John*, the youngest Son of *H.* 2. and Brother of King *Richard*, succeeded, *viz.* *Anno* 1199. and he likewise followed the Examples of of his Brother and Father, in afforesting the Lands of his Subjects: So that the Forests were every where so much inlarged, that the greatest Part of the Kingdom was turned into Forests, the Boundaries whereof were so large, and the Laws so very severe, that it was impossible for any Man, who lived within these Boundaries, to escape the Danger.

7. And thus it continued till the seventeenth Year of his Reign, which was in the Year 1215.

8. At which Time this being a general Grievance to the People, several of the Nobility and Gentry petitioned the King, That all the new Afforestations made by him and his Predecessors, might be disafforested; and that he would likewise grant and confirm unto them such Liberties and Privileges in the Forests as were agreed amongst

themselves, and set down in certain Articles read to be exhibited to him.

9. The King seem'd unwilling at first, but afterwards condescended, and promised to grant the same; and for that purpose, the Petitioners assembled themselves in a Meadow called *Runing-Mead*, between *Windsor* and *Stanes*; and there the King met them on the 15th Day of *June*, in the eighteenth Year of his Reign, and finding it expedient to grant their Requests, he sealed and subscribed the said Articles, being, for the most part, the same which are now contained in the *Charta de foresta*, beginning thus:

10. *Johannes Dei gratia, &c. Rex, &c.* and dated thus: Given by our Hand in the Meadow call'd *Runing Mead*, or *Ryme-Mead*, between *Stanes* and *Windsor*, the 15th Day of *June*, in the eighteenth Year of our Reign. 4 *Inst.* 298. *Hollingshed*, 185. *B. Matt. Paris.* See the Records of the Tower, *Tempore Johannis*, and *Rayn. Wolfe*, 186. *A.* 10.

11. The King, at the same Time, not only granted their Petition, but gave Power and Authority to the Petitioners to choose certain grave and honourable Persons to see all things performed which he had granted.

12. And thereupon they chose for that purpose, the Earls of *Clare*, *Albermarle*, *Gloucester*, *Winchester*, and *Hereford*; also Earl *Roger*, Earl *Robert*, Earl *Marshal* the Younger, *Robert Fitz-Walter* the Younger, *Gilbert de Clare*, *Eustace de Vesey*, *Hugh Bigot*, *William de Mowbray*, the Mayor of *London*, *Gilbert de la Vale*, *Robert de Roos*, *John Constable* of *Chester*, *Richard de Percy*, *John Fitz-Robert*, *William Mallet*, *Jeoffrey de Say*, *Roger de Mowbray*, *William de Huntingfeild*, *Richard de Mountfychet*, and *William de Albeny*.

13. These Noblemen and Barons had several other Persons sworn to assist them in such Things

as they should appoint for the better accomplishing the said Grant.

14. And moreover the King by his Letters Patent, which were directed to the Sheriffs of every County, commanded them to see those Ordinances and Liberties, which he had granted and confirmed, to be diligently observed and kept; and he procured the Pope to confirm the same.

15. But before any Thing was done in pursuance thereof, King *John* died at *Newark Castle* in the County of *Nottingham*: And his eldest Son *H.* 3. who was then but 9 Years old, succeeded him, *viz.* in 1216. but nothing was done by him till the 9th Year of his Reign.

16. (At which the King keeping his *Christmas* at *Westminster*, assembled his Parliament there, and demanded Money for carrying on his Wars against *France*; and accordingly had the 15th penny in value of all the moveable Goods in the Kingdom) as well of the Spiritualty as the Temporalty, upon Condition that he would confirm the Liberties of his Subjects.

17. And therefore in the Charter, by which he confirmed the disafforesting all the new afforestations, 'tis expresly mentioned, that it was in consideration of a full fifteenth penny in value, of all the moveable Goods as aforesaid: And thus the King desiring to have the Money, condescended to the Requests of his People, and made and confirmed those two *Charters*, *viz. Magna Charta*, and *Charta de Foresta.*)

18. These *Charters* so made and confirmed in this Parliament, being in After-ages found to be very good and necessary for the People, have several Times been confirmed by succeeding Kings, and part of the Laws of this Kingdom, now in Use, depend thereon. See *Rotul. in Turr e, in perambulatione Foresta* 39 *Ed.* 1. and *Raym. Wolf. fo.* 207.

19. This King sent those Charters into every County to be proclaimed: The first Article of *Charta Forestæ* is thus, *viz. Imprimis omnes forestæ quas Henricus avus noster afforestavit, videantur per bonos & legales homines, & si Boscum aliquem alium quàm suum Dominicum afforestavit ad dampnum illius cujus Boscus ille fuerit, statim deafforestetur, & si Boscum suum proprium afforestaverit, remaneat foresta, salvà communiâ de Herbagio & aliis in eadem illis qui eam habere consueverunt.*

20. And likewise in the third Article of the said Charter of the Forest, there are these Words, *viz. Omnes autem bosci qui fuerint aforestati per Regem Richardum avunculum nostrum, vel per Regem Johannem patrem nostrum usque ad primam Coronationem nostram, statim deafforestentur, nisi sit Dominicus boscus noster.*

21. And for the better performing these two Articles, for disafforesting such Woods and Lands as were afforested by the aforesaid Kings; it was decreed by *H.* 3. That on a certain Day after *Easter* then next following, an Inquisition should be taken by a substantial Jury, for the dividing the *new Forests* from the *old*; so that all those Lands which had been made Forests since the Reigns of the said *Kings*, and likewise of this King *H.* 3. should be disafforested.

22. And thereupon, after *Easter*, one *Hugh de Novile* and *Bryan de Lisle* were sent forth as Commissioners to take those Inquisitions, as may be seen in the *Tower* in the Perambulation of Forests made by *H.* 3. by vertue whereof many great Woods and Lands were disafforested, assarted and improved into arable Lands by the Owners.

23. After the Charter thus made and confirmed, some of the new Afforestations were *perambulated*; and after such *Inquisitions* taken, and the certain extent of the Ground known by matter of Record, *viz.* What Woods and Lands were newly afforest-

ed

ed by any of the aforesaid *Kings* since the Coronation of *H.* 2. some of them were disafforested by the said King *H.* 3. but yet the greatest part remained still afforested during all his Reign.

24. After whose Death *Edw.* 1. sirnamed *Longshanks*, eldest Son of *H.* 3. succeeded, *viz.* 22 *November*, *Anno* 1273. who being often petition'd both by the Nobility and Gentry to confirm those Liberties which his Father had granted, did at last confirm the same.

25. And now, when all Things were confirmed according to their Petition, they delivered both those *Charters*, thus confirmed, to the Sheriffs of *London*, who read the same in a great Assembly of the People in St. *Paul's Church-yard*; and afterwards the Lords and Commons petitioned the King that *Perambulations* might be made of all the *new Forests*, that the same might be *disafforested* according to the aforesaid Articles.

26. By the Records in the *Tower* in the Reign of *Ed.* 1. it appeareth, That three *Bishops*, three *Earls*, and three *Barons* were appointed to make those *Perambulations*, who being Commission'd by the King under the *Great Seal* of *England* for that purpose, did accordingly *perambulate* the same: And after that was done, and *Inquisitions* taken as aforesaid, and returned into the *Chancery*, by which the King was ascertained which were *new* and which were *old Forests*; he caused all those which were the *old Forests* to be meered and bounded with unremoveable Marks, Meers and Boundaries, to be known by matter of Record for ever; and thus he divided the *new* from the *old*, which he caused to be likewise returned into that *Court* by Marks, Meers and Boundaries, to be known by matter of Record for ever.

27. And after all this was done, the King by Letters Patent under the *Great Seal* of *England*, reciting

citing the *Perambulations* so made and returned into the *Chancery*, did thereby grant and confirm the same, and that all such *new Afforestations*, as by those *Perambulations* were severed from the *old* to be disafforested, should remain so for ever; and that all Woods and Lands which were *ancient Forests* before any such *new Afforestations* made, should likewise remain and continue Forests still, and by such Marks, Meers and Boundaries as they were then returned and certified of Record.

28. And that the manner thereof may the better be understood, I have here set down two perfect Precedents, one for the *Forest of Waltham*, the other for the *Forest of Windsor*.

'Edwardus, Dei Gratia Rex Angliæ, Dominus
'Hiberniæ, & Dux Aquitaniæ, omnibus ad quos
'præsentes literæ pervenerint, Salutem. Sciatis,
'quod cum Communitas Regni nostri nobis con-
'cesserit *quintamdecimam* omnium bonorum suo-
'rum mobilium, quæ habebunt in Festo Sancti
'Michaelis proximo futuro, extunc taxandorum,
'quæ quidem quintadecima post hujusmodi taxa-
'tionem colligi debet, levari, & fideliter nobis
'solvi; Volumus & concedimus pro nobis & hære-
'dibus nostris, quod perambulationes factæ coram
'dilecto & fideli nostro Radulpho de Hengham
'& sociis suis ad hoc assignatis, per præceptum
'nostrum, de Forestis nostris in Comitatu Essex,
'de cætero teneantur & observentur per metas
'& bundas contentas in eisdem perambulationibus,
'quarum tenor de verbo ad verbum sequitur in
'in hunc modum;

'ss. Perambulatio Forestæ de Waltham in Co-
'mitatu Essex, facta apud Chelmesford, Die Ve-
'neris in Crastino Ascensionis Domini, Anno
'regni Regis Edwardi, filii Regis Henrici vicesi-
'mo octavo, coram Dominis, Radulpho de Heng-
'ham,

'ham, Willielmo Troſſel, Stephano de Graveſ-'end, & Willielmo de Sutton, Juſticiariis Domi-'ni Regis ad dictam perambulationem faciendam 'aſſignatis, *viz.* per Dominos, Robertum de Sanc-'to Claro, Hugonem de Blunde, Thomam de 'Maundevill, Walterum le Bande, Willielmum 'de Haningfield, Johannem Heron, Radulphum 'de Hemenhale, Willielmum de Horkely, Johan-'nem de Preers, Johannem de Sutton, Milites; 'Johannem Dowe, Johannem Malegraffe, Mat-'thæum de Branketree, Sewallum de Waleton, 'Edmundum de Badewe, Richardum de Clovil, 'Rogerum Bokſcyn, Richardum le Dukes, Ro-'bertum le Walies, Thomam de Septem fontibus, 'Warinum Code, Willielmum de la Rokele, Jo-'hannem de Slamondeſhey, Lucam Morel, & 'Thomam de Ulting, Juratos, qui inceperunt 'præd' perambulationem die prædicto, ad pon-'tem de Stratford vocatum le Bowe, ſub quo cur-'rit Ripa de Luye & ſic eundo in Hundred' de 'Becontree per regiam viam uſque Hyleford, & 'de Hyleford directè per eandem viam Regiam 'quæ ducit verſus Romford, uſque ad quandam 'crucem ſitam ad caput cujuſd' venellæ vocatæ 'Wytheſlane in villa de Havering, & ab illa cruce 'retornando verſus Auſtrum per hayam, quæ eſt 'diviſa inter terram Gilberti Godebold de feodo 'Abbatiſſæ de Barking, & terram Johannis Atte 'Withe de feod' de Havering, quæ haya eſt diviſa 'inter villas de Havering, & Dakenham, & ſic per 'illam hayam uſque ad foſſatum Johannis de Fran-'ſith, & Agnetis Attewithe de Dakenham, & 'ab illo foſſato uſque ad Regiam viam quæ ducit 'de Yleford uſque ad Monaſterium cornutum, ſi-'cut quædam aqua decurrit ex tranſverſo ejuſdem 'viæ, quæ aqua vocatur Wythedenbroke, & eſt 'diviſa inter Havering & Dakenham. Et ab illa 'aqua uſque ad quendam locum vocatum la Berwe,

'cum

'cum tota pecia terræ, in qua prædictus locus vo-
'catus la Berwe existit, sicut divisa se extendit in-
'ter villas de Havering & Dakenham usque ad
'quendam cursum aquæ vocatum la Borne, quæ
'aqua decurrit de quodam fonte vocato Havering-
'Welle usque ad quendam locum vocatum Daken-
'hambeem, & ab illo loco usque ad filum aquæ
'de Tamise, per quoddam fossatum vocatum
'Marke dike, inter Havering & Dakenham. Et
'sic per Tamisiam usque ad fletum vocatum Wa-
'deflet, extendens se usque ad quendam pontem
'vocatum Reynhambeem, quod fletum dividit vil-
'las de Havering & Reinham in Hundred. de
'Chafford, & ab illo ponte vocato Reinham-
'beem directè usque ad pontem vocatum Delle-
'bregge, sicut aqua decurrit, quæ est divisa inter
'Hundred' de Becontree & Chafford, & ab eo-
'dem ponte usque ad quendam alium pontem vo-
'catum Weldebornebregge semper per rivulum
'qui dividit villas de Havering & Welde Abbatis,
'& ab illo ponte per eundem rivulum usq; ad
'quandam divisam vocatam Markethorn, quæ di-
'vidit villas de Havering, Welle Abbatis & Nastock
'in Hundred' de Aungre & sic in Hundred' de
'Becontree remaneant integrè in Foresta villæ de
'Havering cum suis appendiciis, Wansteed, Ley-
'ton, Welcomestow, & Woodford. Et villæ de
'Stratford in Westham, Estham, Hyleford parva,
'Berking & Dakenham pro parte remanent extra
'Forestam, & pro parte remanent in Foresta, pro-
'ut superiùs per metas & bondas pleniùs dividun-
'tu, Et sic eundo à prædicta divisa de Markethorn
'semper per prædictum rivulum usque ad domum
'Roberti le Tanour de Nastock in Hundred' de
'Aungre, & ab illa domo usque ad messuagium
'Willielmi filii Hugonis de Nastock: Et sic deinde
'ad Hesiam, directè sicut itur ad domum Ed-
'mundi de Nastock, Et ab illa Hesia usque ad

messua-

‘ messuagium quoddam Henrici de Wickham de
‘ eadem, & ab illo messuagio usque ad quendam
‘ locum vocatum Frithstigele in eadem, & ab illo
‘ usque ad terram Johannis de Stodeley, & ab illa
‘ terra usque ad Ripam talliatam, & sic semper per
‘ eandem Ripam usque ad pont. vocat. Pyssingford-
‘ bregge per mediam Ripam & à dicto ponte per me-
‘ diam ripam usque ad quendam pontem vocatum
‘ Affebregge, & ab illo ponte eundo directè usque ad
‘ Ecclesiam de Theydonboys, & ab eadem Ecclesia
‘ usque ad messuagium Joh. de Russelep ex opposito
‘ messuagio Rectoris Ecclesiæ de Theydonboys:
‘ Et ab illo loco retornando per costeram Bosci
‘ dicti Rectoris, & Gilberti de Theyden, usque ad
‘ messuagium ejusdem Gilberti, & à dicto messua-
‘ gio aliàs retornando per Hayam dicti Gilberti,
‘ usque ad messuagium Johannis Sprige: Et sic ab
‘ illo messuagio per venellam jacentem ante mes-
‘ suagium prædictum vocatam Sprigeslane, usque
‘ ad domum Rogeri Artesfrythe: Et ab illa domo di-
‘ rectè ad domum Willielmi de Gardener in eadem
‘ villa sitam super costeram de Eppinghath, & ab
‘ illa domo retornando per divisam, quæ dividit
‘ dimidium Hundred' de Waltham, & Hundred' de
‘ Aungre, directé usque ad caput Bosci vocatum
‘ vetus Wintered: Et ab illo Bosco per Regiam
‘ viam quæ est divisa prædictorum Hundred' de
‘ Aungre & Waltham, extendentem ad Boscum
‘ vocatum Gernonneswood in villa de Theydon
‘ Garnon: Et ab illo Bosco usque ad quercum
‘ vocat. Mark-oake quæ est divisa inter terras Ab-
‘ batis de Waltham, & Roberti filii Walteri, &
‘ Willielmi Garnon: Et sic retornando per regiam
‘ viam, quæ extendit inter terras prædictorum Ab-
‘ batis de Waltham, & Roberti filii Walteri, di-
‘ rectè usque ad locum vocatum Reodegate, in vil-
‘ la de Welde, & sic in Hundred' de Aungre, re-
‘ manent integrè in Foresta, villæ de Loketon,
‘ Chige-

'Chigewell, Lamborn, & Stapleford Abbatis: Et
'villæ de Nostock & Theydonboys, pro parte,
'remanent in Foresta, & pro parte extra Fores-
'tam, prout superius per metas & bundas plenius
'dividuntur: Et omnes residuæ villæ in Hundred'
'de Aungre prædicto debent remanere extra Fo-
'restam: Totum dimid' Hundred' de Waltham
'remanet integre in Foresta, nihil excipitur: To-
'tum dimid' Hundred' de Harlow remanet extra
'Forestam, præter villatam de Hatfield Regis cum
'suis Appendiciis quæ integrè remanet in Foresta,
'eo quod est de antiquo dominico Domini Regis,
'simul cum Hamletto vocato la Walle, & Bosco vo-
'cato le Monkenwood cum suis pertinentiis: Totum
'Hundred' de Chelmsford remanet extra Fores-
'tam præter villatam de Writtel, quæ integrè re-
'manet in Foresta cum suis appendiciis, eo quòd
'est de antiquo dominico Domini Regis: Item in-
'cipiendum est apud Colecest' ad pontem voca-
'tum Northbregge, eundo per Regiam viam du-
'centem ad quandam crucem vocatum Mylande-
'crouche, sitam super caput cujusdem Breueræ
'vocatum Kingeswodeheth, & sic deinde ante mes-
'suagium Richardi Martin, usque ad quandam
'Hesiam ante messuagium W. Warin de Colecest',
'& sic eundo per fossatum dictæ Bruaræ usque ad
'quandam plateam vocat' Kingeswodhach, quæ
'est divisa inter villam de Horkeley & Kinges-
'wodheth: Et sic directè per fossatum Philippi
'Attehache usque ad messuagium W. le Herd de
'Horkeley quondam Edmundi Attehache, & sic
'per quoddam fossatum extendens inter Horkeley
'& Kingeswood usque ad quandam divisam, quæ
'dividit villam de Horkeley, Bexsted & Kinges-
'wod: Et ab illa divisa per quoddam fossatum,
'quæ dividit Bexsted & Kingeswod, usque ad
'quandam aliam divisam quæ dividit Boscum Rad.
'de Bexsted & Boscum Johannis le Breton: Et
'sic

' sic eundo per fossatum quod dividit Kingeswod &
' Boscum præd' Johan. le Breton usque ad fossa-
' tum parci de Lengham: Et sic per præd' fossa-
' tum usque ad locum vocatum Kingeswodebregge
' ad costeram dicti parci, & sic retornando per re-
' giam viam, quæ ducit versus Colecest', usque ad
' pontem vocatum Estbregge: Et à dicto ponte
' de Estbregge, usq; ad quand' port' Colecest'
' vocat' Estgate cum tota præd' villa Colecest'
' infra muros cum omnibus dominicis Domini
' Dom' Regis ad castrum suum Colecest' spec-
' tantibus: Et sic in Hund' de Lexeden, remanet
' integrè in Foresta villa de Myland' cum Bosco
' de Kingeswod cum suis appendiciis: Et dicunt
' etiam quod Hund' de Westodeleford, Estodele-
' ford, dimid' Hundred' de Frosschewel, & dimid'
' Hundred' de Clavering sunt integrè extra Fo-
' rest', & fuerunt à tempore quo non extat me-
' moria. Item dicunt quòd Hund' de Dunmow,
' Hengeford, & Laxeden, ex parte Boreali de la
' Stanstreet, quæ ducit de Storteford usq; Colecest',
' sunt extra Forest' de perquisito Albricii quon-
' dam Com' Oxon. Item dicunt, quod id quod
' est ex parte Australi de dicta Stanstreet in præd'
' Hund' de Dunmow, Laxeden, & Hengeford,
' debet remanere extra Forest' præter id quod su-
' perius nominatur in Hund' de Laxeden in villa
' de Colecest', & præter villatam de Felstede cum
' Bosco de Blakholehey cum suis pertinen. in
' Hundred' de Hengeford, quod quidem maneri-
' um de Felstede cum Bosco de Blakholehey præd'
' cum pertinentiis Abbatissa de Cadamo tenet de
' dono Will'i Regis Conquest' Angliæ, & tenere
' clamat adeo liberè, sicut iidem manerium &
' Boscus tenebantur tempore Ed. 2. Regis Angliæ;
' sed nihilominus dicimus quòd præd' manerium
' cum præd' Bosco cum suis appendiciis integrè
' remanere debent in Foresta. Item dicunt quod

' Hund'

'Hund' de Tendringe & Rochford integrè ſunt ex-
'tra Foreſtam, & fuerunt à tempore quo non ex-
'tat memoria. Item dicunt quod Hund' de Chaf-
'ford, Bordeſtable, Danuſeye, & dimid' Hund'
'de Wytham, dimid' Hund' de Thurſtable, & di-
'mid' Hund' de Weneſtr. totaliter debent eſſe
'extra Foreſtam ſecundum tenorem Magnæ Char-
'tæ de Foreſta, eo quod afforeſtata fuerunt poſt
'Coronationem Dom' H. Regis Avi Dom. H. Re-
'gis patris Dom' Ed. Regis nunc, & per Reges R.
'& J. Quæ quidem perambulatio præſcripta adeo
'aperte & evidenter facta eſt, ſecundum intellec-
'tum, & ſanas conſcientias noſtras, ut didicimus
'per Anteceſſores noſtros: Et Sacramentum pro-
'borum militum & virorum antiquorum fide dig-
'norum nunc ſuperſiſtentium & præmeditantium
'propter diuturnitatem temporis elapſi, adeo long'
'cujuſcunq; alterius perambulationis in com' Eſ-
'ſex factæ, & melius ac plenius ſuper perambula-
'tione præd' deſideraremus certiorari tam pro ſta-
'tu Dom. Regis quam populi ſui, Si idem Domi-
'nus Rex evidentias aliquas apertas, ſi quas habue-
'rit, nobis, ut cæteris de regno ſuo infra limites
'Foreſtæ ſuæ exiſtentibus per conſilium ſuum in
'ultimo Parliamento ſuo apud Weſt' promiſit &
'conceſſit, demandaſſe placuiſſet. In cujus rei Te-
'ſtimonium, huic præſenti perambulationi, nos
'præd' Jur. ſigilla noſtra appoſuimus, Datum apud
'Chelmsford die & Anno ſupradictis: Ita quod,
'quicquid per iſtas perambulationes ponitur extra
'Foreſtam remaneat extra Foreſtam, & reſidu-
'um remaneat Foreſta, ſecundum metas & bun-
'das præd' imperpetuum. In cujus rei teſtimoni-
'um has literas noſtras fieri fecimus patentes.
'Teſte me ipſo apud Lincoln', quartodecimo
'die Februarii, Anno Regni noſtri viceſimo
'nono.

30.

30. The other is the Process of Perambulation of the Forest of *Windsor*, made in the County of *Surrey*, at a Parliament held at *Westminster* in the first Year of the Reign of *Ed.* 3.

31. At which Parliament a Complaint being made by the Lords *Spiritual* and *Temporal*, and Commons of the Realm, That the *Perambulations* made in the Reign of King *Edward*, Grandfather of the *King*, and granted and confirmed by him, were not kept or observed, and that several *Perambulations* in some Forests were not made, but still remained to be made in the Reign of the King's Father; he therefore at their *Petition* granted, that those *Perambulations*, which were already made, should be confirmed for the Time to come, and those which were not made, should forthwith be done with all convenient speed; and as soon as made, that the same should be returned into the Court of *Chancery*, by certain *Meets* and *Bounds*, which he would confirm by his *Charter*, both for *himself* and for *his Heirs*, to be observed for ever.

32. And the King was graciously pleased to grant his *Charter* in Parliament, in every County to those who would *Petition* for the same.

33. Whereupon the Commonalty of the County of *Surrey*, who were aggriev'd in their Lands lying in the Forest of *Windsor*, petition'd to have the King's *Charter* under Seal; which they had accordingly, testifying his Pleasure as aforesaid, as it appears more plainly in the Exemplification of the said *Charter*, kept in the *Abbey of Chertsey*: And which is as followeth.

' 34. Edwardus Dei gratia Rex Angliæ, Domi-
' nus Hiberniæ, & Dux Aquitaniæ, omnibus ad
' quos præsentes literæ pervenerint, salutem: Sciatis,
' quod

'quòd cùm celebris memoriæ Dominus Ed. quondam Rex Angliæ, avus noster, dudum fideles suos assign. ad Perambulationes in forestis suis, tam citra Trentam quàm ultrà faciend', & postmodum quasdem perambulationes in aliquibus forestarum illarum sub certis metis & bundis in eisdem content', factas, & retornatas per literas suas patentes pro se & hæredibus suis concessiss. & confirmasset, cæteroque præcipisset per prædict. metas & bundas in perpetuum observari, perambulationibus hujusmodi tempore dicti Avi nostri in aliquibus forestis remanentibus faciend', ac Dominus Edwardus nuper Rex Angliæ Pater noster in Parliamento suo nuper apud Lincoln convocato ad supplication' Prælatorum, Comitum & Baronum, & communitatis regni sui, asserentium dictas perambulationes factas, observatas non fuisse juxta concessionem & confirmation' prædictas, & perambulationes hujusmodi alibi factas non fuisse, per literas suas patentes, quinto die Augusti, Anno regni sui decimo, concess. pro se & hæredibus suis, quòd prædict' perambulationes præd' per dictum Avum nostrum concessæ & confirmatæ, sicut præd' est, sub metis & bundis in dictis literis patentibus ipsius Avi nostri content' & specificat', teneantur & in perpetuum observarentur; promittens quòd fideles suos ad perambulationes in forestis in quibus tunc factæ non fuerunt, faciend' assignari faceret: Ita quòd perambulationes illæ fierent ante festum Natalium Domini tunc prox' futur' & quòd perambulationes illas, cùm factæ fuissent, & retornatæ, per literas suas patentes, quas in eisdem contigerit contineri, pro se & hæred' suis confirmaret, prout in his Literis patentibus, ipsius patris nostri super hoc confactis, pleniùs continetur: Ac etiam insinuatione Prælatorum, Comitum & Baronum & totius Communitatis regni nostri in instanti Parlia-

'liamento nostro apud Westmonast' convocato 'accepimus, quòd tempore dicti patris nostri, 'perambulationes prædict' per prædict' Avum no'strum, ut præmittitur, concess. & confirmatæ, non 'fuerunt observatæ, & quòd perambulationes hu'jusmodi non factæ, remanserunt faciend'; per 'quod nobis cum instantia supplicarunt, ut pe'rambulationes, per dictum Avum nostrum, ut 'præmittitur, concessas & confirmatas, confirma're & ratificare velimus; Ac etiam perambula'tiones, quæ nondum factæ sunt, fieri faceremus 'indilatè: Nos eorum supplicationi in hac parte 'favorabiliter annuentes, concedimus pro nobis & 'hæredibus nostris, quòd perambulationes præd' per 'præfat' Avum nostrum concessæ & confirmatæ, 'sub metis & bundis in dictis literis ipsius Avi nostri 'contentis & specificat', teneantur & in perpetuum 'observentur: Et volumus quod perambulationes, 'quæ in aliquibus forestis adhuc restant faciend' 'per fideles nostros ad hoc assignand' fiant, sub 'ea celeritate, quâ fieri poterunt, bono modo: 'Quas quidem perambulationes, cùm factæ fuerint '& nobis retornatæ sub metis & bundis quas in 'eisdem inveniri contigerit, per literas nostras pa'tentes pro nobis & hæredibus nostris confirmari '& approbari faciemus. In cujus rei Testimoni'um has literas nostras fieri fecimus patentes: Teste 'meipso apud Westm' xxiii die Martii, Anno 'regni nostri primo.

Per ipsum Regem & Cons'.

35. Afterwards the Commonalty of *Surrey*, who found themselves aggrieved, because the Perambulations were not made in the Forest of *Windsor* in that County, in the Reign of King *Edward*, that King's Grandfather, nor in the Reign of his Father, obtain'd a Commission from the King, that

the Perambulations should be made, which follow in these Words:

'36. Edwardus, Dei gratia Rex Angliæ, Dominus Hiberniæ, & Dux Aquitaniæ, dilectis & fidelibus suis, Tho' Tegorr, Johanni de Stonore, Johanni de Ifeild, & Johanni Dabnon, salutem: Sciatis, quod cùm in Parliamento nostro apud Westm' convocato, per Prælatos, Comites, & Barones, & communitatem regni nostri, Asserentes, quod perambulationes tempore Domini Ed. quondam Regis Angliæ Avi nostri, in forestis suis tam citra Trentam quàm ultra factæ, non fuerunt observatæ, nobis fuisset supplicatum, ut nos eas sic factas per dictum Avum nostrum concessas & confirmatas, juxta easdem concessionem & confirmationem in omnibus observari, & in forestis, ubi dictæ perambulationes remanent faciend', eas fieri, & factas in forma prædicta confirmari curaremus, Assignavimus vos, duos vel tres Vestrum, quorum vos præfat' Johannem de Stonore unum esse volumus, custod' forestæ nostræ citra Trentam, vel ipsum quem posuerit loco suo, & omnes forestar' de feodo, & viridarios de forestis nostris in Com' Surrey, ad perambulationem rectam per visum trium vel duorum vestrum, quorum vos præfat' Johannem Stonore unum esse volumus, & illorum in forestis nostris, in eodem in quibus dictæ perambulationes tempore dicti Avi nostri factæ non fuerunt, per sacr' tam militum quàm aliorum proborum & legalium hominum de eodem Com, per quos rei veritas melius sciri, & perambulationes illæ fieri poterunt, faciend', juxta tenorem Chartæ Domini Henrici quondam Regis Angliæ, proavi nostri, de foresta: Et ideo vobis mandamus, quod ad certos dies & locos, quos vos tres, vel duo

'duo vestrum, quorum vos præfat' Johannem de 'Stonore unum esse volumus, ad hoc providentes, 'præmissa faciatis in forma præd', ita quod perambulationes præd' fiant & nobis retorn' citra 'festum Natalis Domini prox' futurum. Mandavimus enim Vic' nostro Com' præd' quod ad certos dies & locos, quos vos tres vel duo vestrum, 'quorum vos præfat' Johannem de Stonore unum 'esse volumus, ei scire faciatis, venire faciat coram 'vobis, tribus vel duobus vestrum, quorum vos præfat' Johannem Stonore unum, &c. tam Milites, 'quàm alios probos & legales homines de Com' 'præd' per quos rei veritas melius sciri & perambulationes præd' fieri poterint sicut prædictum 'est, Et perambulationem illam distincte & aperte sic factam, nobis sub sigillis vestris, trium 'vel duorum vestrum, quorum vos præfat' Johannem de Stonore unum esse volumus, & sigillis 'eorum, per quos factæ fuerint, reportetis ante 'festum supradictum, ut eam confirmemus juxta 'concessionem nostram dictis magnatibus inde 'factam. In cujus rei Testimonium, has literas 'nostras fieri fecimus Patentes: Teste meipso apud 'Westmonast' xx die Martii, Anno regni nostri 'primo.

Per ipsum Reg. & Cons.

37. And because 'tis mentioned in the said Commission, That the Sheriff of *Surrey* should cause certain *good and lawful Knights and others of that County*, to come before the Commissioners on a certain Day and Place by them to be appointed for that purpose, to make the said Perambulation; therefore the King did issue forth a Writ out of the Court of Chancery, giving him Authority so to do, which is as follows:

'38. Edwardus, Dei gratia Rex Angliæ, Do-
'minus Hiberniæ, & Dux Aquitaniæ, Vic' Surrey
'Salutem: Sciatis, quod cum in Parliamento no-
'stro nuper apud Westm' convocato, per præfat'
'Comites, Barones, & Communitatem regni
'nostri asserentes, quod perambulationes tempore
'Domini Edwardi quondam Regis Angliæ, Avi
'nostri, in forestis suis tam citra Trentam quàm
'ultra factæ, non fuerunt observatæ, nobis fuisset
'supplicatum, ut nos eas sic factas per dictum
'avum nostrum concessas & confirmatas, juxta
'easdem concessionem & confirmationem in om-
'nibus confirmari & in forestis, ubi dictæ peram-
'bulationes remanent faciend', eas fieri, & factas
'in formâ præd' confirmari curaremus, assignavi-
'mus dilectos & fideles nostros Tho' Tregorr,
'Johannem de Stonore, Johannem de Iseild, &
'Johan' Dabnon, tres vel duos eorum, quorum
'præfat' Johannem Stonore unum esse volumus
'ad convocand' in præsentiâ eorundem Thomæ,
'Johan', & Johan', vel duorum illorum, quorum
'prefat' Johannem de Stonore unum esse volumus,
'custod' forestæ nostræ citra Trentam, vel ipsum
'quem posuerit loco suo, & omnes forestar' de
'feodo, & viridarios forestæ nostræ in Com' Sur-
'rey, ad perambulationem rectam, per visum
'eorum vel trium eorum quorum præfat' Johan-
'nem de Stonore unum esse volumus, in forestis
'nostris in Com' præd, in quibus perambulationes
'tempore dicti Avi nostri fact' non fuerunt, per
'Sacramentum tam militum quàm aliorum probo-
'rum & legalium hominum de Com' tuo, per
'quos rei veritas melius sciri, & perambulationes
'illæ fieri poterint, faciend' juxta tenorem Chartæ
'Domini Henrici nuper Regis Angliæ, proavi
'nostri, de foresta: Et ideo tibi præcipimus,
'quod ad certos dies & locos, quos iidem Tho'
'Johannes, & Johannes, tres vel duo eorum, quo-
rum

'rum Johannem de Stonore unum esse volumus,
'tibi scire faciant, venire faciatis coram eis, tribus
'vel duobus eorum, quorum præfat' Johannem de
'Stonore unum esse volumus, tot & tales, tam
'milites quàm alios probos & legales homines de
'Com' præd', per quos rei veritas melius sciri,
'& perambulationes præd' fieri poterint, sicut præ-
'dictum est, & Habeas ibi hoc breve. Teste
'meipso apud Westm' xx. die Martii, Anno regni
'nostri primo.

Per ipsum Regem & Cons'.

39. And because the Commissioners by this last recited Commission, are to call before them the *Warden of the Forests on this side Trent, or his Deputy,* in order to make a true Perambulation; therefore, by vertue of the said Commission, they sent their Writ, directed to the said *Warden* or his Deputy, injoining them to be, on a certain Day and Place, with the said Commissioners, to do the same; the Writ is as follows:

'40. Tho' Tregorr, Johannes de Stonore, Johannes de Iseild, & Johannes Dabnon, custod' forestæ Domini nostri Regis citra Trentam & ejus locumtenen' in Com' Surrey, salutem. Cum in Parliamento Domini nostri Regis nuper apud Westm' convocato, per Prælatos, Comites, & Barones, & communitatem regni, asserentes quod perambulationes tempore dicti Edwardi quondam Regis Angliæ, avi sui, in forestis suis, tam citra Trentam quàm ultra factæ, non fuerunt observatæ: Et eidem Domino Regi supplicatum fuisset, ut ipse eas sic factas per dictum avum suum concessas & confirmatas, juxta easdem concession' & confirmation' in omnibus observari, & in forestis, ubi dictæ perambulationes remanent faciend' eas fieri, & factas in formâ præd' 'confirmari curaret: Idem Dominus Rex assignavit nos, tres & duos nostrum, quorum Johannem Stonore unum esse vult, ad convocand' in præsentiâ nostrum, trium vel duorum nostrum, quorum Johannem de Stonore unum esse vult Custodem forestæ suæ citra Trentam, vel ipsum quem posuerit loco suo, & omnes forestarios de feodo, & viridarios forestarum suarum in dicto Com' Surr', ad perambulationem rectam per visum nostrum, trium vel duorum nostrum, quorum Johannem de Stonore unum esse vult, & illorum in forestis illis in eodem Com' in quibus perambulationes tempore dicti Avi sui factæ non fuerunt, per sacramentum tam militum quàm aliorum proborum & legalium hominum de eodem Com', per quos rei veritas melius sciri & perambulationes illæ fieri poterint, faciend' juxta tenorem Chartæ Domini Henrici quondam Regis Angliæ, proavi sui, de foresta: Et quia Dominus Rex nobis mandavit, quod convocari fac. custodem forestæ suæ citra Trentam, vel ipsum quem loco suo posuerit in dict' Com' Surr' ad perambulat' rectam faciend', nos pretextu istius mandati assignavimus diem essendi apud Certesiam, die Lunæ prox' post quindenam sancti Johannis Baptistæ ad incipiend' exinde ad dictam perambulationem faciend, Quem diem vobis assignavimus, ut vos ad diem præd' ibidem personaliter intersitis, vel ipse quem loco vestro posueritis, ibidem intersit: Ita quod dicta perambulatio per visum vestrum, nostrum, & aliorum ad hoc summon' rectè fieri possit, secundùm tenorem Chartæ Domini H quondam Regis Angliæ proavi Domini Regis, de foresta.

41. And because 'tis mentioned in this last Writ, That the *Foresters in Fee*, and the *Verderons* of the Forest in the County of *Surrey*, should appear at a certain

certain Day to make the Perambulation, the Commissioners issued forth a Writ to cite the said Officers to be there, and that they should summon the Inhabitants of that Part of the Forest which lay in that County, and where no Perambulation was made in the Reign of the King's Grandfather, That they should be there on the Day and at the Place appointed, to see that the Perambulation be made as it ought to be, as it appears by this Writ.

' 42. Thomas Tregorr, Johan' de Stonore, ' Johannes de Ifeild, & Johannes Dabnon, dilectis ' sibi forestariis de feodo, & viridariis forestæ Dom' ' nostri Regis in Com' Surrey, salutem: Cum in ' Parliamento Domini Regis apud Westm' con- ' vocat', per Prælatos, Comites, Barones, & Com- ' munitatem regni, asserentes, quod perambulatio- ' nes tempore Domini Ed. nuper Regis Angliæ, ' Avi sui, in forestis suis tam citra Trentam quàm ' ultra factæ, non fuerunt observatæ, eidem Do- ' mino Regi supplicatum fuisset, ut ipse eas sic ' factas per dictum Avum suum concess. & con- ' firmatas, juxta easdem concessionem & confir- ' mation' in omnibus observari, & in forestis, ' ubi dictæ perambulat' remanent faciend', eas fieri, ' & factas in formâ præd. confirmari curaret, idem ' Dom' Rex noster assign. nos, tres vel duos no- ' strum quorum Johan' de Stonore unum esse vult, ' ad convocand' in præsentiâ nostra, trium vel du- ' orum nostrum, quorum Johannem de Stonore ' unum esse vult, custodem forestæ suæ citra Tren- ' tam, vel ipsum quem posuerit loco suo, & omnes ' forestarios de feodo, & viridarios forestarum sua- ' rum in dicto Com' Surrey, ad perambulation' ' rectam per visum nostrum, trium vel duorum ' nostrum, quorum Johannem de Stonore unum ' esse vult & illorum in forestis suis in eodem Com' ' in quibus perambulationes dicti Avi sui factæ non 'fuerunt, per Sacramentum tam militum quàm 'aliorum proborum & legalium hominum de 'eodem Com' per quos rei veritas melius sciri, & 'perambulation' illæ fieri poterint, faciend' juxta 'tenorem Chartæ Dom' H quondam Regis Angliæ, 'proavi sui, de foresta, & quia Dominus noster 'Rex nobis mandavit, quod convocari faceremus 'omnes forestarios de feodo, & viridarios foresta-'rum suarum in dicto Com' ac etiam illos in fo-'restis suis in eodem Com' in quibus perambulat' 'tempore dicti Avi sui factæ non fuerunt, ad pe-'rambulationem rectam faciend', vobis mandamus 'ex parte Domini nostri Regis, quod apud Certe-'siam, die Lunæ prox' post quindena S. Johan' 'Baptistæ, personaliter intersitis, ad perficiend' 'exinde perambulat' illam faciend', ac etiam præ-'munire faciat. omnes illos in forestis Dom' Regis 'in eodem Com' commorantes, in quibus peram-'bulat' tempore dicti Avi sui factæ non fuerunt, 'quod tunc sint ibi ad diem præd' exinde perfici-'end' ut perambulat' illæ per visum illorum, no-'strum, & vestrum fieri posset competenter.

43. The Commissioners, the Sheriff of *Surrey*, the Warden of the Forests on this side Trent, the Foresters, Verderors, and other the Inhabitants within the Boundaries of the Forest, and many Knights and worthy Men, summoned by the Sheriff, did all appear at *Chertsey* on the Day appointed; and the Jury appearing, that is to say, *Henry Hastings*, and *Henry de Montforth*, Knights; *Robert le Doll*, *Henry de Sunnerbus*, *Will' Huse*, *John le Burres* the Elder, *Nicholas Bachiler*, *John Prodhoame*, *W. de Porkle*, *John* at *Stoket*, *Robert de Ditton*, *John de Kingsnode*; they were charged according to the Commission.

44. Thereupon one *Swinnerton*, *Warden* of the Forests on this side *Trent*, produced a Commission, and al-

alledged to the Jury, that he had an Inquest taken at *Lambeth* before certain Justices in the Reign of King *Ed.* the Grandfather of the present King, testifying, that the Place where they intended to make the Perambulation, was always a Forest, and pray'd the Jurors, That they would be advised on the Behalf of the King, concerning the same; and this was given in Evidence for the King, as it appears by a Copy of the said Verdict, as follows:

'45. Perambulatio facta in Com' Surrey, de 'foresta de Windsor, die Sabbati prox' post festum 'Sancti Georgii Anno regni Regis Ed. Octavo 'apud Lampeth coram Rogero Brainson, Johanne 'de Barwick, Radulpho de Hengham, Will. Inge, '& Johanne de Crokesse, in presentia Philippi de 'Say, Cleric' Justiciar' forestæ & forestariorum & 'viridariorum forestæ præd' per sacramentum Will', 'Annubesas, Johannis de Bourstow, Willi' de 'Bekewete, militum, Roberti de Doll, Rob' de 'Valeton, Willi' de Northwood, Johannis Prod-'home, Roberti Attesonde, Michael de Wiston, 'Richardi de Horton, Edmundi de Suteworth, '& Johannis de Farnham: Qui dicunt per sacra-'mentum suum quòd totus Comitatus Surrey fuit 'foresta tempore Henrici Regis proavi Regis nunc, 'unde idem Henricus obiit seisitus, & ita remansit 'foresta usque ad quartum diem Decembris Anno 'regni Regis Richardi primo qui tunc deforestavit 'quandam partem ipsius Comitatus per certas me-'tas quæ continentur in Charta ipsius Regis inde 'factâ, viz. inter Kanciam & aquam quæ dicitur 'Waye, & de monte de Guldedone quantum 'Com' Surrey durat versus meridiem & residuum 'Com' prædicti, scilicet incipiend' ad aquam de 'Waye, per montem de Guldedone quantum 'Com' durat' versus Aquilonem remansit & est 'foresta, & post ipsius Chartæ confectionem nihil

'affo-

'afforestatum vel occupatum fuit per ipsum Regem
'Richardum nec per Regem Johannem nec per
'aliquem alium, dicunt etiam quod non sciunt
'quod aliquid de Com' præd. afforestatum fuit
'per prædictum Henricum proavum Regis nunc.
'In cujus rei testimonium Jurat. sigilla sua appo-
'suer.

46. Thereupon the Commonalty alledged in Evidence for themselves against the King, That a Perambulation was made in the said County in the Times of *H.* Great Grandfather of the present King; by which it appeared, that the whole County of *Surrey* was disafforested, and produced a Copy of the Inquest then taken, and of the Perambulation then made as follows:

'47. Perambulatio facta in Com' Surrey, per sa-
'cramentum Johan. de Waltone, Gilberti Dabnour,
'Gilberti de Abingworth, Nicholai Malemeyns,
'Hamonis de Gatton, Roberti de Watnill, Tho'
'de Hurtmere, Walteri Outworth, Willi' de Wan-
'ton, Willi' de Insula, Johannes de Mikelham,
'& Johannis de Burstowne; Qui dicunt apud
'Brudford sunt divisæ inter Berks, Southampton,
'& Surrey, & tunc divisæ inter Berks & Surrey
'de Brudeford per viam quæ ducit de Fremely
'apud Wishemere & postea per crucem Rad. us-
'que Gomerichford per medium le Shete usque ad
'Horton, & de Horton per la Lee versus cursum
'aquæ, & inde juxta aquam quæ dicitur Sideway
'usque de Thornhul, de Thornhul usque ad Har-
'pesford, de Harpesford per aquam usque ad Jugg-
'feild, & de Juggfeild usque Lodertakehuch, ubi
'tres Com' conveniunt; viz. Surrey, Berks &
'Bucks. Et sic dicunt quod totus Comitatus Surrey
'fuit extra forestam sicut divisæ content' Southamp-

'ton, Berks and Surrey condonant die quo Dominus Hen. filius R. Johannis fuit coronatus.

48. And after the Commonalties produced in Evidence, the Copy of a Charter made by one *Alan*, late *Abbot of Chertsey*, and the Convent of the same place, to King *Henry*, the great Grandfather of our King, by which they granted certain Lands to that King to be within the Bounds of the *Forest*, notwithstanding the *Perambulation* before made by the said King *Henry*, as it more plainly appears by the Copy of the said *Grant* as followeth.

'49. Omnibus ad quos præsens scriptum pervenerit, Alanus Abbas de Chertesey, & ejusdem loci conventus, salutem æternam in Domino: Noveritis nos concessisse, quod non obstante perambulatione facta per præceptum Domini Henrici illustris Regis Angliæ, filii Regis Johannis, de foresta de Windsor in Com. Surrey, omnes terræ & Bosci, & omnia tenementa contenta infra metas & divisas subscriptas, remaneant ipsi Domino Regi & Hæred' suis, Foresta imperpetuum, viz. à ponte de Stanes per Regium chiminum, sicut se extendit per mediam villam de Egeham usque Harpesford, & de Harpesford usque la Knapp, & de la Knapp usq; Loderlakeshack, ubi cadit in aquam Tamisiæ, Ita quod omnes terræ & Bosci, & omnia tenementa infra metas præd' & omnes homines manentes infra easdem metas, ex concessione ipsius Dom' Regis erunt quieti de regardo, salva ipsi Dom' Regi venatione sua. In cujus rei Testimonium, præsenti scripto sigill' nostrum duximus apponendum, hiis testibus Domino S. Cantuariens. archiepiscopo, Domino E. London J. Bathon. H. Lincoln. R. Sarum. R. Dunelm. Cancellar. Domini Regis, R. Cicestriæ, & W. Oxon. Episcopis: Hugone de Burgo Jus-

'tic.

'tic. Domini Regis, Will. Mareschall. Radulpho
'fil. Nich. Godfr. de Grancombe, & multis
'aliis.

50. And as a farther Evidence, the Commonalty produced a Certificate of several Knights, testifying, That the said Abbot *Alan* and his Convent had made this *Grant* to King *Henry* after the *Perambulation* made by him; as it appeareth by the said Certificate in these Words.

'51. Omnibus ad quos præsens scriptum pervenerit, Gilbert' de Abingworth, Rob. de Watervil Wilh. de Insula, Nich. Malemciens, Johannes de Milkenham, Walter' de Cutteworth, salutem in Dom. Noveritis nos interfuisse & audivisse, ubi Alanus Abbas de Certesey, & ejusdem loci Convent' concesserunt Dom' nostro Hen' illustri Regi Angliæ, fil. Regis Johannis, & chartam suam inde fecerunt, quod non obstante perambulatione facta per præceptum ipsius Dom' Regis de Foresta de Windsor in Com' Surr', omnes terræ & Bosci & omnia tenementa contenta infra metas, & divisas subscript', remaneant ipsi Dom' Regi & hæred' Foresta imperpetuum, viz. à ponte de Stanes per Regium Chim', sicut se extendit per mediam villam de Egeham usque Harpesford, & de Harpesford usque la Knapp, & de la Knapp usque Loderlake, ubi cadit in aquam Tamisiæ; Ita quod omnes terræ & Bosci & omnia tenementa infra metas præd' & omnes Homines manentes infra easdem metas, ex concessione ipsius Regis, erunt quieti imperpetuum de Regardo, salva ibidem ipsi Domino Regi venatione sua. In cujus rei Testimonium præsenti scripto sigilla nostra duximus apponend', hiis Testibus, S. Cantuar' Archiepisc. Domino E. London. J. Bathon. H. Lincoln. Ro. Sarum. R. Dunelm. Cancellar'

'Do-

'Domini Regis, R. Cicestren. & W. Exon, Epi-
'scopis: H. de Burgo Just' Domini Regis, Wil'
'Mareschal, Rad', fil. Nich. Godfr. de Grand-
'combe, & multis aliis.

52. Which said *Perambulation*, so made in the Reign of King *Henry*, together with the Abbot's *Charter*, and the Certificate concerning the same, do now remain in the King's Treasure; and therefore the Commonalty were ready to vouch the Second if the Judges would permit.

53. But the Jury withdrew, after they had a Charge given, and consulted a long time amongst themselves, and then gave their Verdict in manner following.

'54. Qui dicunt super sacram. suum, quod tem-
'pore dicti Regis Edwardi Avi Domini Regis
'nunc, nulla perambulatio facta fuit in Forestis
'Com. de Surrey, & dicunt quod perambulatio
'faciend' nunc in Forestis illis, inchoanda est apud
'Waymouth, & abinde semper in longitudine
'Tamisiæ usque Loderlakeshache, ubi tres comit.
'conveniunt., viz. Surrey, Berks, & Bucks, &
'abinde usque Orientalem corneam parci de Wind-
'sor', Et abinde usque molendinum de Harpes-
'ford, Et abinde usque Thornhill. Et abinde usque
'Sydway, Et abinde usque Le Lee, Et sic usque
'Horton, Et abinde per medium Lashete usque
'Gomerichesford, Et abinde usque Rolnescrouch,
'Et abinde usque Wishemoredene, Et abinde usq;
'Brudeford, ubi tres Com' conveniunt, viz. Surr'
'Berks & Southampt. Et sic dicunt quod totus
'Com' Surr' est extra Forestam, & fuit tempore
'Regis H. proavi Dom' Regis nunc, sicut patet
'per quandam perambulationem factam tempore
'ejusdem Regis H. secundum tenorem Chartæ Re-
'gis H. de Foresta; Dicunt etiam, quod tempore

'Regis Edwardi Avi dicti Regis nunc, quædam in-
'quisitio capta' fuit apud Lampeth, coram Rogero
'Gravason, Joh. de Berewick, Radolpho de Heng-
'ham, Wil. Juge & Joh. de Crokesse, per procu-
'rationem Dom' Hug. le Despens. senioris homi-
'nibus Com' præd' non præmunitis, exceptis qui-
'busdam personis in inquisitione illa existen', vi &
'metu ejusdem Hugonis ad hoc ductis, ad bundas
'& metas in Forestis com. præd' faciend', qui nul-
'lam perambulationem nec equitationem in Fo-
'restis illis fecerunt, nec bundas nec metas in eis-
'dem posuerunt. In cujus, &c.

55. And because the *Inquisition* which was produced here in Evidence for the King against the Commonalty, was found by the aforesaid Verdict, the Judges would not make any *Perambulation* according to the Boundaries found by the Jury, without taking farther Advice and Direction from the King: And thereupon they appointed another Day for the Warden of the Forests on this Side *Trent*, and for the *Verderors*, and the *Jury*, and all other *Inhabitants* of the Forest, who were then attending, to appear at *Weymouth*, *viz.* on *Monday*, being the Feast of St. *Matthew* next ensuing. And in the mean time the Judges would be advised, and meet on the Day and at the Place appointed.

56. And on that Day they all met, *viz.* Sir *Thomas Tregor*, the *Verderors*, the *Jury* and the *Inhabitants* of the Forest: But neither the *Warden* of the Forest or his *Deputy* did appear, nor any of the *Foresters* who were summoned to attend on that Day.

57. At which Time and Place the Commonalty of *Surrey* produced the King's Writ directed to the aforesaid Judges and Commissioners, giving them Authority to make a *Perambulation* notwithstanding the aforesaid *Inquisition* taken in the Reign of

of King *Edward*, Grandfather of the King: And tho' the same was returned into the Court of *Chancery*, yet the King would not permit that *Perambulation* to be executed, before this other *Inquisition* should be taken and returned into that Court.

58. And thereupon this *Inquest* was taken by the Advice and Direction of the King, that Right and Justice might be done; as it appears by his following Writ, with a *non obstante*.

' 59. Edwardus, Dei Gratia, Rex Angliæ, Dominus Hiberniæ, & dux Aquit', dilectis, & fidelibus suis, Thomæ Tregorr, Johanni de Stonore, Johanni de Ifeild, & Johanni Dabnor, salutem: Cum nuper ad prosecution' Prælatorum, Comit' & Baronum, & communitatis Regni nostri Angl' nuper nobis in Parliamento nostro apud West' convocat' suggeren', perambulationes tempore Domini Edwardi quondam Regis Angliæ Avi nostri, in Forestis suis, tam citra Trentam quàm ultra factas, observatas non fuisse, & nobis supplicantium; ut nos eas per dictum avum nostrum sic factas, concessas, & confirmatas, juxta easdem concessiones & confirmationes observari, & in Forestis ubi dict' perambulationes rem' faciend', eas fieri, & factas in forma prædicta confirmari, curaremus, Assignavimus vos, tres & duos vestrum, quorum præfat' Johan' de Stonore unum esse volumus, ad convocand' in præsentia vestra, trium vel duorum vestrum, quorum præfat Johannem de Stonore unum esse volumus, custodem forestæ nostræ ultra Trentam, vel ipsum quem ponere vellet loco suo, Et omnes Forestar. de feod' & viridar. Forestarum nostr. in Com. Surrey ad perambulationem rectam per visum vestrum, trium vel duorum vestrum, quorum vos præfat. J. de Stonore unum esse volumus, & ill' in Forestis nostris in eodem Comitat. in quibus perambular. tempore

' pore dicti Avi nostri factæ non fuer', per sacram.
' tam militum quàm aliorum probor. & leg' homi-
' num de eodem Com', per quos rei veritas meli-
' us sciri, & perambulationes illæ fieri possunt, fa-
' ciend' juxta tenorem Chartæ Domini H. quon-
' dam Regis Angliæ, proavi nostri, de Foresta: Et
' vobis mandamus, quod ad certos dies & loca,
' quod vos, tres vel duo vestrum, quorum vos præ-
' fat. Joh. de Stonore unum esse volumus, ad hoc
' provideritis, præmissa faciatis in forma prædicta.
' Ita quod perambulationes illæ prædict' fierent, &
' nobis retorn' citra festum Nativitatis Domini,
' prout in literis vestris patent. inde vobis confect'
' plenius continetur: Ac etiam ex parte communi-
' tatis com' prædict' accepimus, quod licet vos in-
' quisit. super metas & bundas Forestar. in Com.
' prædicto, prætextu assignat. nostræ prædict. fece-
' retitis, perambulationes tamen juxta metas &
' bundas in inquisit. illa contentas, prætextu qua-
' rundam inquisit. tempore dicti Avi nostri de hu-
' jusmodi metis & bundis factar', ut dicitur, hu-
' cusque facere distulistis, & nobis sit supplicatum,
' ut super hoc remedium apponamus: Nos ea quæ
' in dicto Parliamento nostro sic concessa fuerunt,
' volentes executioni debitæ demandari, vobis
' mandamus, quod perambulationes in Forestis
' nostris in com. prædicto, juxta formam assign'
' nostræ præd. cum celeritate qua poteritis faciatis
' inquisit. tempore dicti Avi nostri inde, ut dicitur,
' factis non obstantibus, & easdem perambulationes
' sic factas, ad terminum præd, in Cancellaria
' nostra juxta formam assign. nostræ supradictæ re-
' torn. Nolumus faciend. executioni demandentur,
' antequam in Cancellar. nostra nobis retornarent.
' & visis inquisit. tempore dicti Avi nostri sic
' capt. ulrer. inde fiat, quod de consilio nostro ra-
' tionabiliter fore videmus faciend'. Teste meipso

'apud Stanhope, primo die Aug. An. Reg. nostri
'primo.

60. By vertue of which Writ the *Verderors* of the Forest in that County, the *Jury* and the *Inhabitants* of the said Forest made a *Perambulation* on the Day aforesaid, by the View of the King's Justices, without regarding the absence of the *Warden* of the Forests on this Side *Trent*, or his *Deputy*, for neither of them was there. The manner of which *Perambulation* was as followeth.

'61. Videlicet, Quod de Weymouth in longitudine Tamisiæ usque Stanesbridge: Et abinde in longitud' Tamisiæ usq; ad Lodershach, ubi tres Com' conveniunt Surr' Berks & Bucks, Et abinde dimittendo Com' Berk. à dextra parte usq; Stondhuldwel, & abinde usq; les Quelmes, & abinde usq; Orientalem partem corneram parci de Windsor', & semper in longitud' palatii ejusdem parci usq; ad molendinum de Harpesford: Et abinde per eundem palatium usq; Australem portam ejusdem parci, & abinde transmeando regiam viam usq; Wyndwygshal: Et abinde usq; interiorem portam de Bromhal: Et abinde usque Thornhul: Et abinde per viam quæ dicitur Sydway, in longitudine ejusdem viæ, & abinde usq; la Lee: Et sic usq; Horton, & abinde per medium la Shete per Gomericheford, quæ in antiquo tempore vocatur Bachetesford.

62. And they went no further that Day, but lay at *Backshete* that Night; and the next Day, being *Tuesday*, they went.

'63. A Gomerichford usque ad Rowelscrouch, & abinde declinando in dextra parte usq; Wishmorsden, & abinde usque Brudesfordbrigge ubi tres

'Com' conveniunt, viz. Surrey, Berks & South-
'ampton.

64. And the Judges in several places of this *Perambulation* caused Proclamations to be made, That no Man should *hunt* or commit any *Trespass* in the Forest under pretence of this *Perambulation*, until the same was returned into the Court of *Chancery*, and confirmed by the King and his Council.

65. And afterwards they made a Report of every Thing that they had done, according to the purport of the Commission first granted to them, and made a Return thereof under their Seals into the Court of *Chancery*, a long Time before the Day given for that Purpose: A Copy of which Record is as followeth:

'66. Perambulatio Forestæ Comitatus Surrey, 'juxta metas & bundas per inquisitionem captam 'coram Thoma Tregorr, Johan. de Stonore, Jo. 'de Ifeld, & Jo Dabnon, ad perambulationem il-'lam factam assignat', Anno Regni Regis Edwar-'di tertii à Conquest' primo, postea per visum 'præd' Joh. de Stonore, Johan. de Ifeld, & Johan' 'Dabnon.

'Dominus Rex mandavit Tho. Tregorr, Joh. 'de Stonore, Johan. de Ifeld, & Johan. Dabnon, 'breve suum in hæc verba.

'Edwardus, Dei Gratia, Rex Angliæ, Dominus 'Hiberniæ, & dux Aquit. dilectis, & fidelibus suis, 'Thomæ Tregorr, Johan. de Stonore, Johan. de 'Ifeld, & Johan Dabnon, salutem: Sciatis quod 'cum in Parliam. nostro nuper apud West. con-'vocat' per Prelatos, Comites, Barones, & Com-'munitatem Regni nostri, asserentes, quod per-'ambulationes tempore Domini Ed. quondam Re-'gis Angliæ, Avi nostri, in Forestis suis, tam ci-

'tra

'tra Trent. quam ultra factæ, non fuerunt observatæ 'nobis fuisset supplicatum, ut nos eas sic factas, 'per dictum Avum nostrum concessas, & confir'matas, juxta easdem concessionem & confirma'tionem in omnibus observari: Et in Forestis ubi 'dictæ perambulationes remanent faciend', eas fieri '& factas in forma prædict. confirmari curaremus, 'Assignavimus vos, tres vel duos vestrum, quorum 'vos præfatum Johannem de Stonore unum esse 'volumus, ad convocand' in præsentia vestra, 'trium vel duorum vestrum, quorum vos præfat' 'Johannem de Stonore unum esse volumus, custo'dem Forestæ nostræ citra Trentam, vel ipsum 'quem posuerit loco suo, & omnes Forestar. de 'feodo, & Viridarios Forestarum nostrarum in 'Com' Surrey, ad perambulationem rectam per 'visum vestrum, trium vel duorum vestrum, quo'rum vos præfat. Johannem de Stonore unum esse 'volumus, & illorum in Forestis nostris, in eodem 'Com. in quibus perambulat. dicti Avi nostri fac'tæ non fuerunt, per Sacr. tam militum quam alio'rum proborum & legalium hominum de eodem 'com. per quos rei veritas melius scir. & perambu'lationes illæ fieri poterunt, faciend', juxta teno'rem Chartæ Domini H. quondam Regis Angliæ, 'proavi nostri, de Foresta: Et ideo vobis manda'mus, quod ad certos dies & loca, quos vos, tres 'vel duo vestr. quorum vos præfat' Johannem de 'Stonore unum esse volumus, ad hoc providerit. 'peram' faciat' in forma præd. ita quod perambu'lat' præd. fiant, & nobis retorn. citra Fest' Nat' 'Dom' prox. futur. Mandamus etiam Vic. Com' 'nostri Surrey præd', quod ad certos dies & loca 'quos vos, tres vel duo vestr', quorum vos præfat' 'Johan' de Stonore unum esse volumus, ei sciri 'faciatis, venire faciat coram vobis, tribus vel duo'bus vestrum, quorum vos præfat. Johan. de Sto'nore unum esse volumus, tot & tales, tam milites,

T 2 'quam

'quam alios probos & legales homines de Com.
'præd: per quos rei veritas meliùs sciri, & per-
'ambulationes præd. fieri poterunt, sicut prædict-
'um est, & perambulationem illam distinctè &
'apertè sic factam, nobis sub sigillis vestris, trium
'vel duorum vestrum, quorum præfatum Johan.
'de Stonore unum esse volumus, & sigillis eorum,
'per quos factæ fuerunt, reportetis ante festum su-
'pradictum, ut eam confirmemus juxta concessio-
'nem nostram dictis magnatibus inde factam. In
'cujus rei testimonium has literas nostras fieri feci-
'mus patentes. Teste meipso apud Westm' primo
'die Martii, Anno Regni nostri primo.

68. By vertue of which Writ, the Judges commanded the Sheriff of *Surrey*, That he would cause to come before them at *Chertsey* on *Monday* next, after the Feast of St. *John Baptist*, as well Twenty four Knights, as other good and lawful Men of the said County, by whom the Truth of the Matter, and the *Perambulations* should be the better known and made, according to the Purport of the Writ: And they signified the Day of their Meeting both to the *Warden* of the Forests on this Side *Trent*, and to all the *Foresters* in Fee, and to the *Verderors* of the Forest in the said County, commanding them to be then and there present; and that the *Verderors* would summon all the *Inhabitants* of the Forest, where no *Perambulation* was made in the Reign of the King's Grandfather; that they likewise must be there to make a right *Perambulation* in manner aforesaid.

69. And afterwards, in the presence of the said Judges, came *John Swinton* Knight, whom *Thomas Wake*, Warden of the Forests on this Side the *Trent*, had made his *Deputy*, by Letters Patents, which he produced in these Words.

'70.

'70. *Thomas Wake*, Lord of *Lydel*, Justice of the 'Forests on this Side *Trent*, to all those to whom 'these Letters shall come, wisheth Health, *&c.* 'Know ye that we have instituted and ordained 'our good Friend *John Swinton* Knight, to be our 'Deputy in the said Forests, and to do every 'thing there in our Name, belonging to us to do: 'Wherefore we charge and command you in the 'Name of our Lord the King, that you attend 'our said Deputy in those Forests. In Witness 'of what we have done to the said *John*, we have 'hereunto made these our Letters Patents, to con-'tinue during Pleasure. Given at our Manor of '*Pynghe*, the 20th Day of *April*, in the first Year 'of the Reign of King *Edward* the Third, after 'the Conquest.

'71. Et Henricus de Stogton, Galfr' at Donne, '& Robertus de Immoworth, Viridar. Forestar. il-'larum veniunt, & testatum est per eosdem Viri-'darios, quòd non est aliquis Forestarius de feodo 'in Forestis prædict', alii tamen Forestarii, qui 'non sunt de feodo, scr. Robertus at Lake, & Ro-'bertus de Bifflete, & Thom. de Keneton, veniunt; '& similiter alii in Forestis p ædict' commorantes, 'viz. Rowlandus de Wicford, R. de Trottesworth, 'R, de Wike, W. de Withwel, Robertus de Cer-'teseye, Simon de Woodham, Thom. de Freme-'lesworth, Thom. de Hamme, Henricus de Bergh, 'Williel. de Brudnestone, Robertus de Kerswell, 'Gilbertus de Withewel, Stephanus de Froillebu-'rie, Robertus Myles, Thom. de Wonborne, Jo-'hannes de Watingford, Petrus Payne, Walter. at 'Church de Basseligh veniunt. & Vicec. Surrey ve-'nire fecit Henricum Huse, & Henr. de Monte 'forti, milites, Robertum le Doll, Henricum de 'Somerburie, Willielmum Huse, Johannem de

'Bures seniorem, Nicholaum de Bachilleu, Johan-'nem Prodehome, Willielm. de Porkle, Johannem 'at Stoker, Robertum de Ditton, & Johannem de 'Kingesnode, Jur'. Et postquam iidem jurati fue-'runt ad veritatem super præmissis dicendam, præ-'dictus Johannes de Swinerton suggessit eisdem Ju-'rat. quod tempore Regis Ed. Avi Dom. Regis 'nunc, capta fuit quædam inquisit. de metis & 'bundis Forestar. Com. prædict' coram quibus-'dam fidelibus ipsius Regis ad inquisit: illam capi-'end. assignat. quam inquisit. idem Johannes asse-'rit, ut intellexisset, in curia Domini Regis reror-'natam, & ab hoc requisivit eosdem Jurator. quod 'præd. inquisitio latere non debuit, ex parte Do-'mini Regis quod ipsi in inquisit. ista de prædictis 'metis & bundis faciend' circumspectè agerent, & 'porrex. quand. schedulam, formam illius inquisi-'tionis continentem: Et prædict' Jurator. habito 'inter eos diutino consilio dicunt per sacram 'suum, quod tempore Regis E. Avi Domini Re-'gis nunc, nulla perambulatio facta fuit in Forestis 'Com' Surrey, & dicunt quod perambulat. faciend. 'nunc in Forestis illis inchoanda est apud Way-'mouth, & abinde semper in longitudine Tamisiæ 'usque Loderlakeshache, ubi tres Com' conveniunt' '*viz*. Surrey, Berk. & Buck. Et abinde usque Ori-'entalem corneram parci de Windsor', & abinde 'usque molendinum de Harpesford, & abinde us-'que Thornhul, & abinde usque Sydway, & abin-'de usque la Lee, & sic usque Horton, & abinde 'per medium Lashete usque Gomerichesford, & 'abinde usque Rolnescrouch, & abinde usque 'Wishemorfedene, & abinde usque Brudeford, ubi 'tres Com. conveniunt, viz. Surr. Berk. & South. 'Et sic dicunt quod totus Com' Surr. est extra Fo-'restam, & fuit tempore Regis H. proavi Domin. 'Regis nunc, sicut pater per quandam perambula-'tionem factam tempore ejusdem Regis H. secun-

'dùm

'dum tenorem Chartæ ejusdem Regis H. de Fo-
'resta: Dicunt etiam, quod tempore Regis Ed-
'wardi Avi dicti Dom. Regis nunc, quædam inqui-
'sitio capta fuit apud Lampeth, coram Rogero
'Gravason, Johanne de Berwicke, Radolpho de
'Hengham, Will. Jugge & Joh. de Corkesley, per
'procurationem Dom. Hug. le Dispens. senioris
'hominibus Com' præd' non præmunitis, except'
'quibusdam personis in inquisitione illa existen', vi
'& metu ejusdem Hugonis ad hoc ductis, ad bun-
'das & metas in Forestis in Com' præd' faciend',
'qui nullam perambulationem nec equitationem in
'Forestis illis fecerunt, nec bundas nec metas in
'eisdem posuerunt: Et quia aliàs tempore Regis
'Ed. Dom. Regis nunc Avi capta fuit inquisitio de
'hujusmodi metis & bundis, prout liquet per in-
'quisitionem istam modo captam, & etiam ex dic-
'tis prædict. Johannis de Swinerton: Ideo præ-
'dictus Thom. Tregor & socii sui, perambulation.
'in Forestis prædict. juxta metas & bundas in in-
'quisitione ista modo capt. content', facere distu-
'lerunt, usque diem Lunæ in festo Sancti Matthæi
'apud Weymouth, ad interim consulend' & deli-
'berand', qualiter in hoc casu in præmissis sit fa-
'ciend'. Quem quidem diem præfixerunt præfatis
'Johanni de Swinerton, Viridar. Forestar. Jurator.
'& aliis de Forestis illis ibidem existen. ut præ-
'dictum est quod ipsi ibid. tunc interessent. Pos-
'tea ad diem illum prædict', Johannes de Stonore,
'Johannis de Iseld, & Johannes Dabnon, vene-
'runt ad locum prædict'. & Custos Forestæ Dom.
'Regis citra Trentam, nec ejus locumtenens, nec
'aliquis Forestarius Forestarum prædictarum, scili-
'cet, Viridar. Jurator. prædict. & alii in Fores-
'tis illis commorantes venerunt. Et super hoc
'Dom. Rex mandavit Thomas Tregor, & sociis
' tribus vel duobus eorum breve suum, quod
vocatur non obstante ut patet supra.

'Et ideo prædcti Viridarii, Jurator. & alii in
'Forestis prædict' commorantes, per visum præ-
'dictorum Johannis, Joh. & Johannis non expec-
'tata præsentia custodis Forestæ vel ejus locum-
'tenentis, ad prædict' perambulationes faciend'
'processerunt in hunc modum, viz. de Weymouth
'in longitudine Tamisiæ, usque Stanesbridge. Et
'abinde in longitudine Tamisiæ usque Loderlake-
'shacne, ubi tres com. conveniunt, viz., Surrey,
'Berk. & Buck. Et abinde dimittendo com. Berk.
'à dextra parte usque Stonyhelwel, & abinde usq;
'les Quelms, & abinde usq; Orientalem corneram
'parci de Windsor', & insuper in longitudine pa-
'latii ejusdem parci usque molendinum de Harpes-
'ford, & abinde per eundem palatium usq; Austra-
'lem portam ejusdem parci, & abinde transme-
'ando Regiam viam usque Windwingshul, & ab-
'inde usque interiorem partem de Bromhall, & ab-
'inde per viam quæ dicitur Sydeway in longitu-
'dine ejusdem viæ, & abinde usque La Lee, & sic
'usq; Horton, Et abinde per medium la Shete usq;
'Gomerichesford, & abinde usq; Rolnescrouche,
'& abinde declinando in dextra parte usque Wy-
'shemorseden, & abinde usque Brudefordesbridge,
'ubi tres com' conveniunt, videlicet, Surrey, Berk.
'& South. Et ita per prædictas metas & bundas
'facta est perambulatio Forestarum prædict' in
'Com' prædict'. Et præfat. Joh. & socii sui in
'diversis locis, ubi videbatur eis faciend', publicè
'proclamar. fecerunt, inhibent. omnibus & singu-
'lis ex parte Domini Regis, ne quis venaret seu
'aliquid malefaceret in prædict. Forestis, prætextu
'perambulat', antequam perambulatio illa per
'Dominum Regem & Consilium suum confirma-
'retur, prout in prædicto Parliamento ipsius Do-
'mini Regis fuit ordinat', sub pœna quæ incubue-
'rit.

72. And afterwards the Commons of the said County, (the King being at *Pomfret*) petitioned the Lord Chancellor, Sir *John Hotham*, then Bishop of *Ely*, in full Court, that he would see right done concerning this *Perambulation*, so returned by the Justices before him; and that the same might be confirmed by the King's Charter, according to the first Charter, which he granted for the Confirmation of the *Perambulations*, in the first Year of his Reign, in a Parliament then held at *Westminster*; which Charter was now produced, by which it did appear, that it was the King's Pleasure to confirm it.

73. And the said Lord Chancellor having called to his Assistance the most eminent Clerks of the *Chancery*, *viz.* *Henry de Celiff*, Sir *William de Harlestone*, Sir *Michael de Wath*, Sir *Thomas de Evesham*, Sir *Henry de Edenstow*, Sir *Hugh de Bourgh*, and Sir *Adam Brome*, and others: The said Inquisition was read in Court, and afterwards they consulted together what was best to be done in the behalf of the *King*; and at last they decreed, that the said *Commonalty* should sue out a Writ to summon the Constable of *Windsor-Castle* to appear before them in the Court of *Chancery* on a certain Day, to shew what he could say for the *King*, why the said *Perambulation* should not be confirmed.

74. And because the said Writ was sealed before *John de Lyle* (who was then Constable of the said Castle) came from *Pomfret*, and was delivered to the Chamberlain in full Court; and because the said Constable was then present, the Lord Chancellor told him, He might go and advise with the *King* if he had any thing to object why the said *Perambulation* should not be confirmed; and thereupon he had a Week's Time given him to speak with the

2 *King*

King and his *Council* at *Pomfret* concerning this *Affair*.

75. And thereupon the said *Constable* went and took Advice accordingly: And afterwards he came into the Court of *Chancery*, and then the Court asked him, If he had any Thing to say for the *King*: And he alledged in Court that an *Inquest* was taken at *Lampheth* in the Reign of King *Edward*, the Grandfather of the present *King*, of certain *Meets* and *Bounds* of the Forest of *Windsor*, in the County of *Surrey*, before certain good and lawful Men, deputed by the *King* for that purpose, which was produced before Sir *Thomas Tregor* and his *Companions* by *John de Swinerton*, Deputy *Warden* of the Forests on this Side *Trent*, and prayed that the Court would consider in the *King*'s Behalf.

76. The *Commonalty* alledged, That in the *Inquisition* of that *Perambulation* now returned before the Judges, there was no mention made of the said *Inquest*.

77. And afterwards the Lord *Chancellor* asked the *Constable* if he had any thing else to say for the *King*; who replied he had not: For which Reason he was at this Time dismissed, and required to appear on another Day, and that he would be well advised in the mean Time.

78. And now the *King* came out of the North into the West Parts of *England*, with the Lord Chancellor attending him: And the *Commonalty* still pressing this *Affair* until the *King* came to *Hayles*, and from thence to *Winchcombe*, at which Place the Court of *Chancery* was kept: And *Roger Mortimer*, Earl of *March*, and other Persons of Quality, sitting near the Lord Chancellor, the said *Commonalty* petitioned him for Justice, and if he pleased, to decree that the said *Perambulation* might be confirmed.

79. Whereupon the said *Chancellor* caused the said *Inquest* to be read before the aforesaid Earl of *March* and others, and they having consulted together, at last they told the *Commonalty* that the *Nobility* and the *King*'s Council would be the next Week at *Gloucester*, where King *Ed.* the *King*'s Father was to be buried, and then they would advise with the *King* and the *Peers* there present, that Right and Justice might be done.

80. And thereupon they were adjourned to *Gloucester*, and the *Commonalty* came afterwards from *Winchcombe* to *Chiltenham*, and from thence to *Gloucester*, and there they prosecuted this Business, and prayed that it might be confirmed.

81. The *King* and the *Nobility* then present, *viz. Henry de Lancaster* Marshal, *Edmond* Earl of *Kent*, *John* Earl *de Grane*, *Roger* Earl of *March*, and other Barons and Knights, being of the *King*'s Privy Council, caused the *Chancellor* to recite all the Proceedings in this *Affair*; and at last it was agreed, that the same should be confirmed according to the *King*'s Grant in Parliament; and the said *Chancellor* was commanded to deliver the same to the *Commonalty*; and thereupon another Day was appointed, because the *King* went from *Gloucester* to *Tewkesbury*, and from thence to *Worcester*, where he kept his *Christmas*.

82. And there the *Commonalty* prayed Execution as aforesaid, and the *Chancellor* ordered the Charter to be engrossed; and when it was written, he was ordered not to Seal it till the *King*'s Pleasure was known, and not without his *Warrant* for that purpose.

83. And the *Commonalty* having renewed their *Petition* on the *Friday* following, being *Christmas*-Day: And the *King*'s *Will* being known, and his *Warrant* obtained, the said *Charter*, which confirmed the *Perambulation*, was sealed on *Saturday*, being

St.

St. *Stephen's* Day, in a little House near the *Severn*, belonging to the Prior of *Worcester*, where the *Chancellor* on the same Day sealed all other *Writs*; and thereupon they having paid the *Fees* for the Seal, had their *Charter* confirmed, as it appears by the Exemplification thereof in the Words following.

'Edwardus, Dei Gratia, Rex Angliæ, Dominus 'Hiberniæ, & dux Aquitaniæ, omnibus ad quos 'præsentes literæ pervenerint, salutem: Sciatis, 'quod cum nuper in Parliamento nostro apud 'Westm. convocato, ad supplicationem Prælato-'rum, Comitum, Baronum, & Communitatis Reg-'ni nostri, per literas nostras patentes concess. 'quod perambulat. tempore Domini Ed. quondam 'Regis Angliæ, Avi nostri, in Forestis suis, tam ci-'tra Trentam quam ultra factæ, & per ipsum Avum 'nostrum concessæ & confirmatæ secund' metas & 'bundas in eisdem perambulat' contentas obser-'ventur imperpetuum & teneantur, & quod per-'ambulat' in Forestis, in quibus tempore dicti 'Avi nostri factæ non fuerunt, per fideles nostros 'ad hoc assign. fierent, sub ea celeritate qua fieri 'possent bono modo: Et quod nos perambulatio-'nes illas, cum factæ fuerint, & nobis returnatæ 'sub metis & bundis, quas in eisdem inveniri con-'tigerit, pro nobis & hæred. nostris confirmari & 'approbare faceremus, prout in literis nostris præ-'dict. pleniùs continetur, ac postmodum ad re-'quisitionem Commun. com. Surrey nobis sugge-'rent', quod perambulat. in Forestis nostris in eo-'dem Com. factæ non fuerunt, Volentes concessi-'onem nostram prædictam effectum mancipari, as-'signavimus dilectos & fideles nostros Tho. Tregor, 'Joh. de Stonore, Joh. de Iseild, & Joh. de Dab-'non, ad perambulationem rectam in Forestis no-'stris in eodem Com. in quibus perambulationes

'tem-

'tempore dicti Avi nostri factæ non fuerunt per sacram' tam militum quam aliorum probor' & legalium hominum de eodem com. per quos rei veritas melius sciri & perambulationes illæ melius fieri possent, faciend. juxta tenorem Chartæ Dom. H. quondam Regis Angliæ proavi nostri, de Foresta: Ac iidem Thomas, Johannes, Johan. & Johannes. perambulat. hujusmodi in eodem com. prætextu assignat. nostræ eis inde sic factæ, fecerunt, & eas nobis in Cancellar. nostram miserunt, in forma subscripta.

'Perambulatio Forestæ Comitatus Surrey, juxta metas & bundas, per inquisitionem inde captas coram Thoma Tregor, Joh. de Storiore, Joh. de Ifeild, & Joh. Dabnon, ad perambulationem illam faciend' assignat. Ac postea facta per visum prædicti Johan. Joh. & Johan. ac per sacram. H. Huse, Henrici de Monteforti, Militum, Ro. le Dol. Henrici de Somerbury, Will' Huse, Joh. de Bures sen, Mich. de Batchiller, Johan. Prodehome, Will' de Porkle, Joh. Stoket, Rob. le Ditton, & Joh. de Kingswood Jurat. qui dicunt, quod tempore dicti avi nostri nulla perambulatio facta fuit in Com. Surr. sed perambulatio faciend' in Forestis illis inchoanda est apud Waymouth, Et abinde semper in longitudine Tamisiæ usq; Loderlakeshach, ubi tres com. conveniunt, viz. Surr. Berk. & Buck. Et abinde usq; Orientalem cornetam parci de Windsore, & abinde usq, molendinum de Harpesford, & abinde usq; Thornhull, & abinde usq; Sideway, & abinde usq; la Lee, & sic usque Horton, & abinde per medium la Shete usq; Gomerishford; & abinde usque Rolnescrouch, & abinde usq; Wishemoresden, & abinde usque Brudeford ubi tres Com' conveniunt, *viz.* Surrey, Berk, & South. Et quod totus Com' Surrey est extra Forestam, & fuit tempore dicti Regis Henrici proavi nostri.

'Nos

'Nos perambulationem prædict. acceptantes, eam
'pro nobis & hæred. nostris, quantum in nobis
'est, ratificamus, approbamus, concedimus, &
'confirmamus, secundum metas & bundas prædic-
'tas imperpetuum observand': Salvo semper in
'omnibus jure nostro. In cujus rei testimonium
'has literas nostras fieri fecimus patentes. Teste
'meipso apud Wigorn. xxvi. die Decemb. Anno
'Regni nostri primo.

Per ipsum Regem & Cons.

85. And afterwards the said *Commonalty* attended the Chancellor to *Solybul* and *Ardern*, and there they had a Duplicate of the said Charter, the one was sealed with *green Wax*, which is kept in *Chertsey Abbey*, and the other was sealed with *white Wax*, which they kept themselves.

86. And because it was the King's Will that the Charter, confirming the said *Perambulation*, should be read publickly in the County, *Proclamation* was made, that it should be firmly kept according to the Boundaries, saving to himself Forty Days to hunt the Beasts out of the *Purlieus* into the *Forest*.

87. And for that Purpose he issued forth a Writ directed to the Sheriff of *Surrey*, the transcript whereof is as followeth.

'88. Edwardus Dei Gratia Rex Angliæ, Domi-
'nus Hiberniæ, & dux Aquit. vicec. Surrey salut'
'Cum nuper in Parliamento nostro apud Westm'
'convocato, ad supplicationem Prælatorum, Comi-
'tum' Baronum, & Communitatis Regni nostri,
'per literas nostras patentes concess. quod peram-
'bulat. tempore Domini E. quondam Regis Angl.
'Avi nostri in Forestis suis, tam citra Trentam
'quam ultra factæ, & per ipsum Avum nostrum
'concessæ & confirmatæ secund' metas & bundas
'in

' in eisdem perambulat. contentas observarentur
' imperpetuum, & tenerentur, Et quod perambul.
' in Forestis, in quibus tempore dicti Avi nostri
' factæ non fuerunt, per fideles nostros ad hoc
' assignatos fierent sub ea celeritate qua fieri
' possent bono modo: Et quod nos perambulatio-
' nes illas, cum factæ fuerint, & nobis returnatæ
' sub metis & bundis, quas in eisdem inveniri con-
' tigerit, pro nobis & hæredibus nostris confirmari
' & approbari faceremus, prout in literis nostris
' plenius continetur; Ac postmodum ad requisitio-
' nem Communitatis Com' Surrey nobis suggerent.
' quod perambulatio in Forestis nostris in eodem
' Com' factæ non fuerunt, Volentes concessionem
' nostram prædictam effectam mancipari, Assig-
' navimus quosdam fideles nostros ad perambulat'
' rectam in forestis nostris in eodem Com', in qui-
' bus perambulat' tempore dicti Avi nostri factæ
' non fuerunt, per sacramentum tam militum quam
' aliorum proborum & legalium hominum de
' eodem Com', per quos rei veritas melius sciri, &
' perambulat' illæ melius fieri possent, faciend', jux-
' ta tenorem Chartæ Dom' Henrici quondam Regis
' Angl' proavi nostri de foresta: Iidem fideles nostri
' perambulat' hujusmodi in eodem Com' prætextu
' assignationis nostræ inde eis factæ, fecerunt, &
' eas nobis in Cancellaria nostra miserunt: Ac nos
' per literas nostras patentes dictam perambulatio-
' nem acceptavimus, & eam pro nobis, & hæred'
' nostris, quantum in nobis est, ratificavimus, ap-
' probavimus, concessimus, & confirmavimus,
' secundum metas & bundas in dicta perambula-
' tione contentas imperpetuum observand': Salvo
' semper in omnibus jure nostro, prout in literis
' prædictis nostris plenius continetur: Tibi præci-
' pimus, quod literas nostras in pleno Com' tuo
' legi, & perambulationem dictam secundum me-
' tas & bundas in eisdem literis contentas publicè

'proclamari, & firmiter observari faciatis :-Salvis 'nobis quadraginta diebus à tempore dat. hujus 'brevis numerand', ad feras nostras in locis extra 'forestam perambulat' præd sic posit' existentes, 'ad forestam nostram effugand'. Teste meipso 'apud Wigorn. 26 die Decembris Anno regni 'nostri primo.

Per ipsum Regem & Cons'.

89. And because it was the King's Will that the Constable of *Windsor*-Castle should go about the Boundaries of the said Perambulation, and drive the Beasts out of the same into the Forests within the said forty Days, he, by another Writ, commanded him so to do, the transcript whereof is likewise as follows:

" 90. Edwardus, Dei gratia Rex Angliæ, 'Dominus Hiberniæ, & Dux Aquitaniæ, Consta-'bulario Castri nostri de Windsor, vel ejus locum-'tenenti, Salutem: Cum nuper in parliamento 'nostro apud Westm' convocato ad Supplicatio-'nem Prælatorum, Comitum, Baronum & com-'munitatis nostri regni per literas nostras patentes 'concess. quod perambulationes tempore Domini 'Edwardi quondam Regis Angliæ, Avi nostri, in 'Forestis suis tam citra Trentam quam ultra factæ, '& per ipsum Avum nostrum concessæ, & con-'firmatæ secundum bundas in eisdem perambula-'tionibus contentas observentur in perpetuum & 'teneantur, Et quod perambulationes in forestis, 'in quibus tempore dicti Avi nostri factæ non fue-'runt, per fideles nostros ad hoc assignatos fie-'rent, sub ea celeritate qua fieri possent bono 'modo: Et quod nos perambulationes illas, cum 'factæ fuerint, & nobis retornatæ, sub metis & 'bundis, quas in eisdem inveniri contigerit, pro 'nobis & hæredibus nostris confirmari & appro-

'bari

'bari faceremus, prout in literis nostris plenius 'continetur; Ac postmodum ad requisition. Com-'munitatis Com' Surrey nobis suggerent', quod 'perambulationes in Forestis nostris in eodem 'Com' factæ non fuerunt, Volentes concessionem 'nostram præd' effectum mancipari, assignavimus, 'dilectos & fideles nostros Tho' Tregorr, Johan' 'de Stonore, Johan' de Ifeild, & Johan' Dabnon, 'perambulationem rectam in forestis nostris in ad. 'eodem Com' in quibus perambulationes tempore 'dicti Avi nostri factæ non fuerunt, per sacramen-'tum tam militum quam aliorum proborum & 'legalium hominum de eodem Com', per quos 'rei veritas melius sciri, & perambulationes illæ 'melius fieri possent, faciend', juxta tenorem 'chartæ Domini Henrici quondam Regis Angliæ, 'proavi nostri, de Foresta: Ac iidem Thomas, 'Johannes, Johan' & Johannes, perambulationem 'hujusmodi in eodem Com', prætextu assign' no-'stræ eis inde sic factæ fecerunt, & eas nobis in 'Cancellariam nostram miserunt in forma sub-'scripta.

'Perambulatio Forestæ Comitatus Surrey juxta 'metas & bundas per inquisitionem inde captam, 'coram Tho' Tregorr, Johan' de Ifeild, Johan' 'de Stonore, & Johan' de Dabnon, ad perambu-'lationem illam faciend. assignat. Ac postea facta, 'per visum præd. Johannis, Johannis, & Johan', 'ac per sacramentum H. Huse, Henrici de 'Mounteforti, Militum, Rob. le Doll, Henrici de 'Somersbury, Willi. Huse, Johannis de Bures, sen. 'Mich. de Bachiler, Johannis de Prodehome, 'Willi' de Pokle, Johannis Stocker, Rob. de Dit-'ton, & Johannis de Kingswood, Jurat: Qui di-'cunt, quod tempore dicti Avi nostri nulla peram-'bulatio facta fuit in Com' Surrey, sed perambu-'latio faciend' in forestis illis inchoanda est apud 'Waymouth, Et abinde semper in longitudine

'Tamisiæ usque Loderlakeshach, ubi tres Com' conveniunt, viz. Surrey, Berks, & Bucks, Et abinde usque Orientalem Corneram parci de Windsor, Et abinde ad molendinum de Harpesford, Et abinde usque Thornhull, Et abinde usque Sideway, Et abinde usque le Lee, & sic usque Horton, Et abinde per medium la Shete usque Gomerishford, Et abinde usque Rolnescrouch, Et abinde usque Wishemoreseden, Et abinde usque Brudeford, ubi tres Com' conveniunt, viz. Surrey, Berks, & Southampton, Et quod totus Com Surrey est extra forestam, & fuit tempore dicti Regis Henrici proavi nostri.

'Ac nos perambulationes prædict' acceptantes, & eas pro nobis, & hæred' nostris, quantum in nobis est, ratificaverimus, approbaverimus, concesserimus, & confirmaverimus, secundum metas & bundas prædictas imperpetuum observand': salvo semper in omnibus jure nostro, prout in literis nostris præd. plenius continetur: Per quod præcepimus Vicecom. nostro com. præd', quod perambulat' prædict' secundum metas & bundas in eisdem literis nostris contentas faciat observari: Salvis nobis quadraginta diebus à tempore brevis nostri sibi inde directi numerand', ad feras nostras in locis extra forestam per perambulationes prædict' sic positis existentes, ad Forestam nostram effugand'. Vobis mandamus, quod feras nostras infra quadraginta dies à locis extra forestam sic positis, ad forestam cum omni celeritate, qua poteritis, effugari faciatis, Et talem & tantam diligentiam in hac parte apponatis, quod dampnum nobis de feris nostris ibidem per vestram negligentiam nullatenus generet. Teste meipso apud Wigorn, xxvi. die Decembris, Anno Regni nostri primo.

Per ipsum Reg. & Cons'.

91. By

91. By vertue of which Writ, after the said Charter was read and proclaimed in the County-Court, that the said Perambulation should be firmly kept, the Constable of *Windsor-Castle* drove the King's Beasts out of the Perambulation into the Forest, within the forty Days limited for that purpose; during all which Time the Men of *Surrey* behaved themselves in a peaceable manner, without committing any Trespass; and after the said forty Days were expired, they enjoyed the Franchises so granted and confirmed to them by the King as aforesaid.

92. And thus ended the Process of the Perambulation of the Forest of *Windsor*, in the County of *Surrey*, which was prosecuted in this manner till a Charter was made and confirmed by the King, according to that which he had before granted in Parliament to the Nobility and Commons of the Realm, to be kept and observed by himself and his Heirs for ever.

That the Purlieu, in some sort, is Forest still.

93. By these Precedents it appears, in what manner the new Afforestations were disafforested by these *Perambulations*, and how they began: for all such Woods and Lands which were afforested by King *Henry* 2. King *Richard* 1. or King *John*, and were afterwards disafforested and severed by these Perambulations from the old Forests, they were and are still called *Purlieus*, but very corruptly; for they are properly *Purlieus* which are Lands disafforested by *Perambulations*.

94. But yet the same were not so absolutely disafforested to every Man; for by *Charta de forestâ*, *Artic.* 1. it was granted, That if the King had afforested any other Woods than his own, *ad damptium illius cujus Boscus ille fuerit, statim deafforestetur*; so

so that the *Purlieu* was disafforested only *quoad illos*; and no other Man was to take the Benefit thereof, but those who were the proper Owners of such Woods or Lands: And notwithstanding the disafforesting, they may suffer their Lands to continue as part of the Forest still, if they intend to have Common there.

95. This appears by the Statute of 33 *Ed.* 1. *cap.* 5. So that the Disafforestation was made only for the Owners of those Lands, and for their Benefit, and not generally to give Liberty to any Man to hunt the Wild Beasts and spoil the *Vert*.

96. For if these Beasts should escape out of the Forest into the *Purlieu*, the King hath a Property in them still against every Man, but against the Owners of the Woods and Lands in which they are; and such Owners have a special Property in them *ratione loci*, but yet so that they hunt them fairly with Dogs or Greyhounds, and not forestall them in their Return towards the Forest again.

97. And for this purpose the King hath Officers in the *Purlieu*, called *Rangers*, who are to look after the Beasts of the Forest, and to drive them out of the *Purlieus* into the Forest; which shews, that though they are in the *Purlieus*, yet the King hath still a Property in them, for otherwise the *Rangers* have no Authority to drive them out.

98. *Anno* 7. *H.* 6. Justice *Cockeine* was of Opinion, That if a *Hart* stray out of the Forest, the King's Foresters may pursue and make Proclamation in the next Towns, that no Person should hunt or kill it; which likewise proves, That though the Wild Beasts are out of the Forest and in the *Purlieus*, yet the King hath still a Property in them.

99. Therefore the *Purlieu*, as to some purposes, is Forest still, *viz.* for the King's Wild Beasts to have their free Recourse therein, and safe Return

to

to the Foreſt, without any Hurt or Deſtruction, other than by the Owners of the Lands in the *Purlieu* where they ſhall be found, and that only to hunt and chaſe them back again towards the Foreſt, without any foreſtalling, as aforeſaid.

100. The Caſes 13 *H.* 7. *fo.* 10. *placito* 14. and *Paſch.* 7 *H.* 6. *fo.* 36. *placito* 41. and *Hill.* 13 *H.* 7. *fo.* 16. *placito* 14. prove, That though a Man may preſcribe to hunt Wild Beaſts in his *own Land*, yet a Preſcription is not good to hunt the *King's Wild Beaſts*, though they are in his *own Land*, *viz.* thoſe which eſcape out of the Foreſt into the *Purlieus.*

How and for whom the Purlieu is free to hunt in.

101. But though the *Purlieu* be Foreſt ſtill to thoſe who have neither Woods nor Lands of Freehold therein of the yearly Value of 40 *s.* yet thoſe who have Lands there of that Value, might keep *Greyhounds* there by the Statute of 13 *R.* 1. *cap.* 13. 4 *Co.* 303, 304. 43 *Ed.* 3. *fo.* 8.

102. But this Qualification is now altered by ſubſequent Statutes (which may be ſeen in Title *Dogs*;) and thoſe who are now qualified to keep Dogs by theſe Statutes, and who have Woods or Lands in the Purlieus, finding any Wild Beaſts there, may *hunt* them towards the Foreſts, becauſe they have a Property in them, as aforeſaid, *ratione ſoli*, and if they begin the Courſe in their own Lands, they may follow the Chaſe through any Man's Grounds whatſoever.

13. But if the Beaſt return towards the Foreſt, they muſt not foreſtal him with Dogs or any manner of Engine whatſoever; for that is prohibited by *the Aſſiſes of Woodſtock*, *Anno* 30. *H.* 2. *Artic.* 13. upon pain of a Year's Impriſonment, and the Offender to be fined at the King's Pleaſure.

104. So that the *Purlieu*, to some purposes, is free to some Men to *hunt* there: But it was the Opinion of *Noy*, Attorney-General, That such *hunting* is only by Toleration, without any manner of Right; for a Man cannot prescribe to hunt in a *Purlieu*, because a *Purlieu* itself began within time of Memory; and there is no Statute which gives a Purlieu-Man any such Authority, for he is only to keep the Deer out, but cannot kill them though they are in his own Grounds. *Jones*'s *Rep.* 275.

15 But 'tis plain, there must be no forestalling; for, by the aforesaid *Assises*, *Anno* 20 *H.* 2. 'tis ordained, *viz. Item Rex præcipit, quòd nullus de cætero chaceat ullo modo ad capiendum feras per noctem infra forestam, neque extra, ubicunque feræ frequentant, vel pacem habent aut habere consueverunt, sub pænâ imprisonament' unius Anni, & faciendo finem & redemptionem ad voluntatem suam, & quòd nullus sub eadem pænâ faciat aliquam forstallationem feris suis vivam vel mortuam inter forestam suam & boscos vel alia loca per ipsum vel progenitores suos deafforestat'.*

106. By this it appears, that all manner of *forestalling*, either with Dogs or any Engine whatsoever, is utterly forbidden in the *Purlieus*, and the Punishment is particularly declared against those who offend therein; and though a *Purlieu*-Man hath a Property in the Beasts, *ratione soli*, against every Man but the King, yet 'tis but a Conditional Property; that is, if he kill the Beast without forestalling, and in hunting it fairly with his Dogs, in such Case 'tis his own; but if the Beast once recover the Forest, though it be only *filum forestæ, viz.* the List or Brink of the Forest, before the Dogs fasten, then 'tis absolutely the King's or the Owner's of the Forest.

107. And yet in some case a Purlieu-Man may enter the Forest; *viz.* If the Dog fastens on the Deer before he recovers the Boundaries thereof, and

and by the Force and Strength of the Beast is drawn into the Forest; and the Beast kill'd there: In such case the *Purlieu*-Man may enter by reason of the *first Property* which he had *ratione soli*, and by the Pursuit and Possession which he had by the fastening of his Dog, and may take and carry the Deer away.

108. But 'tis to be observed, That a Purlieu-Man must hunt his own *Purlieu* himself, and with no other Company than his own servants, and not otherwise; for he cannot licence any other Person or Persons to hunt there, because the Authority which he hath himself, is only conditional; 'tis a Licence of Profit which is strict and cannot be deputed to another.

109. This appears in *Ashton*'s *Case*, *Mich.* 18 *Ed.* 4. *fo.* 14. *viz.* If a Man hath a Licence to kill a Buck in a certain Place, and to dispose of it at his Pleasure, his Servant cannot justify the doing it by his Command, because the Licence goeth strictly to him to whom it was given, and no other.

110. Neither may a *Purlieu*-Man hunt or kill a Deer out of Season, though 'tis found in his own *Purlieu*, because that would be a double Trespass to the Forest, *viz.* to kill a Deer good for nothing, and when 'tis not able to run.

111. And if he doth hunt in his own *Purlieu*, and his Dogs pursue the Chase towards the Forest, he must recal them before they enter therein, for otherwise he will be a Trespasser, if the Deer is killed in the Forest.

112. This appears in 43 *Ed.* 3. *fo.* 8. *placito* 23. *viz.* If a Hunter call back his Dogs before they enter the Forest, in such Case, if they enter and kill the Beast there, the Owner of the Dogs shall not be a Trespasser, if he do not enter the Forest himself, nor meddle with the Beast so killed.

113. Therefore, that a Purlieu-Man may the better remember in what Manner he may hunt in his Purlieu, he must observe,

1. That he begin the Chase in his own *Purlieu.*
2. That he do not forestall, *&c.*
3. That before his Dogs enter the Forest, he call them back.
4. That he do not follow his Dogs into the Forest, except they fasten on the Deer first, and are then drawn into the Forest, and the Deer killed there.
5. That he do not hunt with any more in Company, than with his own Servants.
6. That he do not kill a Deer out of Season.

When and how often a Purlieu-Man may hunt, &c.

114. But a Purlieu-Man must not hunt at all times and seasons, nor in what manner he will; for then the Purlieus would soon destroy the Forests; for which Reason the antient Usage and Policy of the Forest-Laws have always prohibited these Men to hunt contrary to any of the following Rules.

115. §. 1. A Purlieu-Man must not hunt in his own Purlieu in the *Night-time*; this is prohibibited by the 13th Article of *Assisa de Woodstock*; that is, He must not hunt there after the setting of the Sun, nor until the rising of the same; and the Reason is, because the King's Wild Beasts may not be disturbed in their feeding in the Forest; for 'tis impossible for any Man to hunt in the Purlieus in the Night-time, without it be *ad Terrorem ferarum quæ sunt infra forestam*; for though the Dogs may not follow the Beasts out of the *Purlieus* into the

the Forest, yet the Noise and Fright of the Deer which are driven into the Forest, will disturb the Quiet of those which are there, it being the Nature of those Beasts to feed in the Night-time, and to rest in the Coverts all Day; and therefore the hunting them at that Time is prohibited.

2. He must not hunt on the *Sunday*, for that is a Day appointed for the Rest both of Man and Beast, and for the Service of God, and not for Sports; 'tis a Day in which all profitable Business is forbidden by the Statute of 1 *Eliz.* though it tends to the publick Good, and much more *hunting*; and for that Cause 'tis not accounted *Dies juridicus*, that is, a Day in any Court at *Westminster*, or elsewhere. See *Dyer*, *fo.* 168. *placito* 17.

3. He must not hunt in the *Fence-Month*, because of disquieting the Deer which are then ready to *fawn*, or for fear of killing the young *fawns* which are not able to run.

4. He must not hunt oftner than *three Days in a Week*, lest, by often hunting, he disquiet the Beasts in the Forest, or fright them from their Pasture or Places where they usually frequent; for the Laws of the Forest prohibit all things which are *Ad terrorem ferarum Forestæ Domini Regis*; and therefore a Man may not build a new Mill in the Forest without Leave.

5. He must not hunt in the Purlieu with any other Company but his *own Servants*, because his Interest in hunting is only a Conditional Licence of Profit, which goes strictly to him to whom 'tis given, and not to any other; and 'tis likewise clear in Law, That he who hath a Licence or an Interest of *Profit*, may justify for *himself and his Servants*; but he who hath

a Licence or Interest for *Pleasure*, cannot justify for his Servants, though he may for himself; but he who may justify for his Servants, cannot justify for any other Person. *Hill*, 13 *H*. 7. *fo*. 13. *placito* 2. Besides, the Laws of the Forest do not allow a multitude of People to assemble themselves together to hunt in the Purlieus, because that is likewise *Ad terrorem* of the Beasts in the Forest.

6. He must not hunt within *forty Days* next after the King's hunting in the Forest, because the Beasts frighted out of the Forest, may have Liberty in that Time to return; for they did not come into the Purlieus of their own accord, but were frighted, and took Shelter there: And the Laws of the Forest intend, That if they are not disturbed, they will return within that time, or that the Rangers will drive them back; and 'tis for this Reason that, in every Grant of a Purlieu of such Lands which were disafforested, there is always an Exception of forty Days reserved for the Return or driving back the Deer to the Forest, as may be seen before in the Precedent of *Windsor* Forest.

7. As he may not hunt forty Days *after*, so he must not hunt in the Purlieus forty Days *before* the King's hunting in the Forest, because, during that Time, the Beasts are not to be disquieted, that the King may have a full View of them.

8 He must not (after Notice given) hunt in the Purlieus when any Forester is serving a Warrant in the Forest, to hinder him from such Service.

9. He must not hunt with any manner of forestalling; neither shall he make any Salteries

or

or Leaping Places where the Deer may leap into the Purlieu, and cannot return.

10. He may not hunt a Deer out of Season, though 'tis found in his own Purlieu, because they are not able then to run, and are worth nothing when caught; and therefore he must not hunt a Deer of *Antler* in the Winter, nor *Does* in the Summer.

116. All these Things have been taken for Law ever since Purlieus were first made, and have been used and executed for Law by all the Justices in Eyre, and Learned Men and Judges, that have given any Charges in their *Iters* of the Forest, as it appears in all the Charges of the said Justices ever since the Time of *William* Lord *Vesey*.

117. The Offenders likewise, and those who were Trespassers in hunting in the Purlieus contrary to any of those Ordinances, have been punished for the same; as it appears by *the Assises and Iters of the Forest of Waltham*, in the Reign of *Ed.* 2. and *Ed.* 3. which are now to be seen in Mr. *Anger*'s Office in the *Exchequer*; and if there had been no such Ordinances, the Forests would not have continued so long as they have done.

118. Upon the whole Matter, a Purlieu-Man must *utere suo ut alienum non lædas*; he may hunt in the Purlieu, so that he doth not disturb the Deer in the Forest.

119. 'Tis a sorrowful thing to see so many stately Forests which were formerly accounted Ornaments of the kingdom, to be now destroyed, partly because the true Meets and Boundaries of them are not known, by reason whereof, that which was really Forest is now Purlieu; and partly because the Abuses done therein are suffered to continue without any Punishment; for they now hunt in the Purlieus as they please, and pursue

their

their Chase into the very Forests, and kill and carry away any Deer there; by which Means they have almost destroyed *Waltham*-Forest.

How and where Offences, done in a Purlieu, are to be punished.

120. The Offences committed in the Purlieus, contrary to the Laws and Ordinances aforesaid, are accounted Offences of the Forest, because they are Injuries and Wrongs done to the Wild Beasts there; and such Offences are to be presented by the *Rangers* at the next Court of Attachments to be holden for the Forest adjoining to the Purlieu, or else at the next Court of *Swanimote* or *Justice-Seat*, which shall first happen to be kept for the said Forest, to the end that all such Trespassers and Offenders in the Purlieu may be punished according to the Quality of their Offences, after a lawful Trial at the Court of *Swanimote* before the *Foresters*, *Verderers*, *Regarders*, *Agistors* and other Ministers of the Forest, in such sort as by the Laws and Ordinances thereof is ordained and appointed.

121. After such Tryal had and Conviction of the Offenders and Trespassers in the Purlieus, they are to be bound with good Sureties to the Good Behaviour of the Forest, until the next Justice-Seat which shall be holden for the said Forest; and then they are to appear there, and to be punished according to the Direction of the Lord Chief Justice in Eyre, either by Imprisonment, Fine or Ransom.

The Difference between a Forest, a Purlieu, and Land which never was Forest.

121. All the Woods and Lands which are within the Regard of the Forest, are subject to the Charge and

and Laws thereof, as well in respect of the Owners of the Woods and Lands which are therein, as of any other Person whatsoever; for they may not fell their Woods within the Regard, without the King's Leave, nor improve their Lands, nor hurt or chase the Wild Beasts there, without some Warrant or Authority from the King.

122. Those who have Woods or Lands within the *Purlieus*, are without the *Regards* of the Forest, and are therefore absolutely free from the Charge or Laws thereof in respect of *felling their Woods*, or converting their Lands into Tillage, or otherwise improving the same to their best Advantage or Profit; but yet those Lands are not absolutely free to them from all manner of Charge of the Forest, because the Wild Beasts may have recourse therein, when they escape out of the Forest, and are not to be disturbed by any Man but the Owner of the Lands where they are.

123. But that which was never Forest or Purlieu, and by consequence never disafforested, is absolutely free, and there the King's Wild Beasts have no manner of Privilege, neither are there any *Rangers* or other Officers appointed to hunt or drive them back to the Forest out of such Grounds; so that if they are not very near the Boundaries of the Forest, any Man who is qualify'd to keep *Greyhounds* or *Dogs*, may hunt and chase them, so that he doth not forestal them in returning to the Forest.

124. *In Itinere Windsor*, *Jones's Rep* 275. Mr. Attorney *Noy* argu'd, That Purlieu-Men might keep out the Deer, but could not kill them though they were in their own Grounds, and that their hunting there is only by Toleration; they cannot prescribe to hunt, because no Purlieu is by Prescription; and by the Statute-Law they have no such Authority. *Jones's Rep.* 275.

Pur-

Purpresture.

See { *Nusance*, 9, 20.
Appendix, Ch. Forestæ, 4, 12.
Appendix, Assisæ Forestæ, 4 }

1. THE Word *Purpresture* is taken for any thing which a Man hath wrongfully incroached on another, and by Inclosure or Usage hath appropriated to himself.

2. 'Tis called by Mr. *Glanvill*, *Lib.* 9. *cap.* 11. *fo.* 71. *Purprestura*, which is a Word of Art, for 'tis not *Latin*, but derived from the *French* Word *Pourpris*, which signifies, to take from another, and to inclose for himself; and that which the *French* call *Pourpris*, the *Latinists* call *Conseptum*, which signifies an *Inclosure*.

3. This is a Trespass so very injurious to the *Vert and Venison* in the Forest, that if there were not severe Laws to prohibit it, and likewise to punish the Offenders, all Forests would, in a little time, be destroyed; for as a *Waste* therein is one Means to decay it, *viz.* by cutting down the Woods and Coverts, and an *Assart* by utterly destroying them and converting the Land where they grew to Tillage; so *Purpresture* is likewise another effectual Means to destroy it, by building and new erecting Houses and other Inclosures therein.

4. For if every Owner of Lands in the Forest might build as many Houses there as he pleased, it would in a short time, be so full of People and Houses, that the Wild Beasts would be frighted out of the Forest; and therefore, at first, Forests were made where they were few or no Inhabitants, and afterwards, by the special Licence and Favour

of

of the King, some few People were suffered to dwell there; and so, in process of Time, the Inhabitants increased, but still they were to have Leave from the King to dwell there.

5. When some Forests were made, the Kings who made them, pulled down, not only Houses, but Churches in those Places, that the Wild Beasts might rest there undisturbed: And if this could be lawfully done, then, by the same Law, they might forbid all those who are Owners of Lands in the antient Forests to build any Houses there without the Leave of the King, or his Chief Justice in Eyre, because new Erections, and increasing dwelling-Houses in the Forests are,

1. *Ad terrorem ferarum*, for the sight of many Houses would terrifie the Deer.
2. *Ad nocumentum Forestæ*, because the People and the Inhabitants would destroy the *Vert*.
3. *Ad superonerationem Forestæ*, for by the encrease of Houses and Inhabitants, the Forest of Necessity would be surcharged.
4. *Ad exilationem ferarum*, because the multitude of People and their Dogs would drive the Deer out of the Forest.

6. Therefore nothing can be more hurtful to a Forest than *Purprestures*, and the conniving at one causes many more; so that where *Forests* are well governed, there must be special Care taken to suppress all manner of *Purprestures*, for if they are tolerated, the Forests in a short Time would be destroyed.

What is a Purpresture in the Forest.

7. A *Purpresture* in the King's Forest is any *Building*, or *Inclosure*, or using any *Liberty* or *Privilege* there without Warrant so to do.

8 *In Libro rubro Scaccarii, titulo accidentibus*, there is this Clause, *viz. Quod purprestura sit interdum per negligentiam Vicecomitis, vel ministrorum Regis, vel per continuationem in longa tempora, vel bellicam tempestatem, ut qui habitant prope fundum Coronæ, vel adjacent, aliquam eorundem portionem sibi usurpent, & suis portionibus ascribant: Cum autem per lustrantes Judices per sacramentum legitimorum virorum compertum fuerit, appretiantur, & Vicecomiti traduntur, unde seorsim respondeat, & hanc dicimus purpresturam, vel occupationem injustam.*

9. (Now, tho' this Clause seems rather to prove what is *Purpresture* at Common Law, than by the *Forest-Law*; yet it seems plain, that to make any Encroachment on the King without Warrant or good Will, is a *Purpresture* at Common Law, and so 'tis likewise by the *Forest-Law*.)

10. And Mr. *Hesket*, *fo.* 10. tells us, That if a Man incroach unto himself any Thing to which he hath no Right, that is a *Purpresture*.

11. But this seems to be a little too general, for the Meaning must be, If he take *any Thing* (that is) any *Land*, *Liberty*, or *Jurisdiction*, by Incroachment from another, and possesseth it as his own, and that wrongfully; this is a *Purpresture*.

12. With this agreeth Mr. *Glanvil*, who was a Judge here in the Reign of *H.* 2. in his Book of *The Laws and Customs of* England, *viz. Lib.* 9. *cap.* 11. *fo.* 71.

13 *Dicitur autem purprestura vel porprestura propriè, quando aliquid super Dominum Regem injustè occupatur, ut in Dominicis Regis, vel in viis publicis obstructis,*

2 *vel*

vel in aquis publicis transversis a recto cursu, vel quando aliquis in Civitate super Regiam plateam aliquid ædificando occupaverit: Et generaliter, quoties aliquid fit ad nocumentum Regii tenementi, vel Regiæ viæ, vel Civitatis, placitum inde ad Coronam Domini Regis pertinet.

14. In the *Assises of Lancaster, Anno* 12 *Ed.* 3. *fo.* 6. it was adjudged in the general Eyre of that Forest, That no Man may inclose any Ground in the Forest *ad nocumentum ferarum*, and that such an Inclosure is a *Purpresture*; and tho' he hath a Licence to inclose, it must not be done, *cum alta haya & fossato, nec cum alto palatio*: For if he doth, 'tis *contra assisam Forestæ*.

15. It was there likewise adjudged, That if a Man *build* a House in a Forest without Licence, tho' 'tis on his own free Land, 'tis a *Purpresture*: And the Judgment is, *Quod ipse in misericordia, & quod clausum prædictum prosternetur.* And if the Land, on which such *Purpresture* is made, is granted to another, both the Grantor and Grantee shall be amerced.

16. So by the Claim of the Abbot of *Merival, Anno* 12 *Ed.* 3. *in the Assises of Pickering and Lancaster*, it appeareth, That no Man may *build* any Houses or low Houses within the Regard of the Forest: And so it was also there adjudged in the Case of the Prior of *Lancaster, Anno* 12 *Edw.* 3. *fo.* 9.

17. Now the Abbot claimed, by a *Grant* from the King, that he might make *omnimodum commodum suum in Foresta, sine assartando, & sine ædificando, modis omnibus*: By which *Grant* it appears, That it was excepted to *Assart* or *build* Houses there; therefore he might do neither.

18. *Anno* 7 *Eliz. Dyer fo.* 246. *plac.* 45. It was resolved by the Majority of all the Judges of *England*, and by the Queen's Council at *Serjeants-Inn*,

in the presence of the Earl of *Sussex*, then Lord Chief Justice in Eyre of all her Forests on this Side *Trent*, That the building any House within the several Soil or Waste of any Man in the Forest was a *Purpresture*, and an Annoyance to the Forest and Game; and the Person was either to be fined or to pay a certain Rent, if the same was suffered to be continued: But it was at the Judgment and Discretion of the Chief Justice in Eyre, either to fine the Person or to pull down the Building.

19. The aforesaid Chief Justice in Eyre was *Learned* in the Laws himself, and yet he called to his *Assistance* the Judges and the Queen's Council, who assembled at *Serjeants-Inn* in *Fleetstreet*, and gave their Opinions as aforesaid; and my Lord *Dyer* was then Chief Justice of the Common Pleas, who reported this Case, so that 'tis Law, being so solemnly resolved.

20. *Anno* 2 *Car.* 1 *Christian Smith* and others being presented for *building Cottages* upon the Waste of the Manor of *John Gale* in *Windsor Forest*; it was agreed, That if a Lord of a Manor will suffer poor Men to build *Cottages* upon his Waste, tho' he take no Rent for them, yet they shall be fined, and the Lord of the Manor shall pay the *Fines*: And if the Manor descends or is conveyed to another after the building such *Cottages*, and the Person hath received any small Rent for the continuance of those *Cottages*, he shall pay the *Fines* because he upholds them.

21. But in this Case, the *Cottages* being built before *Gale* purchased the Manor, and he having never received any Rent, it was ordered, That the poor Men who dwelt in them should continue there during their Lives, and afterwards to be pulled down. *Jones Rep.* 272.

22. In the same Year one *William Matthews* was presented for *continuing* a *Cottage* built on the King's Waste in the said Forest of *Windsor*; and he producing a Licence from the Earl of *Nottingham*, late Chief Justice in Eyre to inclose and build there, *Noy, the Attorney General*, said, That the Licence might excuse the first Trespass in *Building*; but that the Chief Justice might now reseise it, and let it to any other who will give more Rent, and he was fined 5 *s.* and a higher Rent set. *Jones Rep.* 276.

23. In the same *Iter* Sir *Sampson Darrel* was fined 5 *l* for *building* a *Windmill* in the Forest on his own Ground. *Jones's Rep.* 293.

24. And at the same Time one *Thomas Brown* was presented for *building* a *Brickwall*, and thereby straitening the Highway in the Forest. In this Case Mr. Attorney *Noy* said, That the Court could not set a Rent to be paid for it, unless there had been an *Inquisition, per ministros Forestæ, si sit competens passagium*: For if it be not, then 'tis a *Nusance*, in which the Subject is so far interested, that the King cannot dispense with it. *Jones's Rep.* 277.

25. At the same *Iter Mr. Attorney* said, That if the Lord Chief Justice in Eyre will grant a Licence to *erect* a Cottage in the Forest, or to make any Inclosure, and reserve a Rent for it for ever, it must be done *sedente Curia*, otherwise it may be pulled down: But if it is granted in Court, and the Rent set, then 'tis good for ever. *Jones's Rep.* 277.

How many sorts of Purprestures there are.

26. There are Four sorts of *Purprestures*.

Purprestures { 1. Against the King.
2. Against the King and the Publick.
3. Against the King and a common Person.
4. Against a common Person only.

27. (1.) *Purpresture against the King*, is where a Man doth new *erect* or *build* any Dwelling-House, or other House in the Forest without Licence, and in a Place where there never was any House before, tho' the same is in his own Ground; this is a *Purpresture* against the *King*, and not against any other Man, because 'tis no Incroachment upon any Body but only upon the King's Forest.

28. (2.) *Purpresture against the King and Publick*, is where a Man *builds* a new House or Mill on the *King*'s Highway or Waste in a Forest; or if he *build* it in his own Land, if 'tis an hindrance of the Common Passage of the People.

29. (3.) *Purpresture against the King and a Common Person*, is where a Man hath Land inclosed, lying in a Forest, and adjoining to the Waste of a Lord of a Manor, and the Owner incroacheth on that Waste, by removing a Hedge and taking in part of it, and so wrongfully enlarging his own Ground: For 'tis a *Purpresture* against the King to inclose Land in the Forest which never was inclosed before; and 'tis a *Purpresture* against the Lord of the Manor wrongfully to inclose any Part of his Waste Ground.

30. (4) *Purpresture against a Common Person alone*, is where a Man hath an ancient Dwelling-House, or other House in the Forest, and by enlarging it he incroacheth upon the Lands of his Neighbour: In this Case he alone hath the Injury done to him; for it being an ancient House, it might stand

in the Forest, and the *King* hath no wrong by this *Incroachment*.

31. So that where a Man doth wrongfully incroach any Thing to himself in a Forest, either upon the *King* or upon any other Person, or doth take upon himself any *Jurisdiction* or *Franchise* there, without any lawful *Warrant*; these are *Purprestures*: As for Instance,

32. If a Man keeps a *Fair or Market* there, without Prescription or a lawful Grant from the King; or if he inclose any of the King's Waste Soil, or build any *Hogsty* or *Hovel* on such Waste, or on the Waste of any other Man in the Forest, these are *Purprestures*.

The Forfeiture and Punishment of those who commit Purprestures on the King's Lands.

33. The Punishment in this Case is to be committed without *Bail* until he hath paid a Fine to the King, which Fine is not certain but Arbitrary, at the Will of the Chief Justice.

34. This appears *in Assisa Forestæ*, *Anno* 6 *Ed.* 1, and by *Glanvil*, *Lib. cap.* 11. *fo.* 72. *viz. Et qui per Juratam ipsam, aliquam hujusmodi fecisse Purpresturam convictus fuerit, in misericordia Domini Regis remaneat de toto feodo quod de eo tenet, & quod occupavit reddat.*

35. The Law intendeth a very grievous Fine should be set on him who makes a *Purpresture* on the *King's Lands*, for 'tis an Aggravation of the Offence, and therefore the Fine should be proportioned to the Crime; and the Place on which the *Purpresture* was made, is to be surrendered to the King to whom it doth rightfully belong.

The Punishment of him who commits a Purpresture in his own Land.

36. The Punishment in this Case is, That the Offender be committed until he is delivered by *the Pledges*: This is for the *first Offence*, by the Assises of the Forest aforesaid.

37 For the *second Offence*, he shall be committed until he is delivered by *twelve Pledges*.

38. And for the *third Offence*, he shall be committed until he pay a Fine to the King; and in this Case the Offender is not *bailable* by Law, but only *ex gratia* of the Lord Chief Justice in Eyre, who is obliged by no certain Rules, but may set an Arbitrary *Fine*, according to the quality and quantity of the Offence.

39. And 'tis to be observed, That the Judgment is Twofold, even for every *Purpresture* which a Man makes on his own Lands in the Forest, *viz.* *to pay a Fine* to the King, and that the *House be pulled down*, or to pay a *Rent*, if continued; but this is at the Discretion of the Chief Justice in Eyre.

40. And because every *Purpresture* in the Forest is *finable at Discretion*, according to the quantity and quality of the Offence; therefore 'tis necessary, that in all Indictments or Presentments for the same, there be a sufficient certainty in these Particulars following.

1. Who made the Purpresture, in what manner and when the same was done.
2. Where the Ground lies in which it was made, and in whose Tenure it is, and what quantity the same doth contain, and what it was worth by the Year.
3. Whether the Purpresture was made on the Soil and Inheritance of the King or of a common Person.

4. In

4. In whose Fee the same is, in what Parish, and who hath the Inheritance.

The difference between Purprestures and Assarts.

41. There have been some Opinions, that *Purpresture* is properly on the Lands *of the King*, but *Assarts* may be made on the Lands of *any Person*: And this was the Opinion of Mr. *Treberne* and Mr. *Archer* in their Readings on the Forest-Laws.

42. But this seems to be a Mistake, not only upon the Authorities before mentioned, but by the Words and Meaning of *Charta de Foresta*, *Artic.* 4. by which 'tis enacted, That all Men who have *Woods* in the Forest shall enjoy them in such manner as they did at the Coronation of *H.* 2. And 'tis further enacted, That they shall be pardoned for all *Purprestures*, viz. *Quod habeant boscos suos, & quod quieti sint imperpetuum de omnibus purpresturis vastis & Assartis*, which shews that *Purprestures* may be made on their own Lands as well as *Assarts* and *Wastes*.

43. So likewise in the *Assises of the Forest*, *Artic.* 4. and in *Rastal. Abr.* 21. *Si quis inventus fuerit in Dominico Regis assartando vel purpresturam faciendo, corpus debet protinus retineri; sin autem extra Dominicum infra Rewardum, debet poni per sex plegios, & si alias inveniatur debet duplicare eius plegios, &c.*

44. Here the Law is clear, viz. That *Purprestures* and *Assarts* may be committed in the *King's Lands*, for which Offence there is a particular Punishment appointed, different from the Punishment which is to be inflicted on those who make *Assarts* and *Purprestures* on the Lands of other Men: So that the difference of the Punishment plainly shews that *Assarts* and *Purprestures* may be made on other Mens Lands, and not only on the King's.

45. But the true difference between *Assarts*, and *Purprestures* is, That *Assart* is the converting any Coverts in the Forest into Arable; but *Purpresture* is a wrongful incroaching of a new Thing either upon the King or a Common Person.

46. Upon the whole Matter, 'tis a *Purpresture* for a Man to build any House in the Forest, altho' on his own Land: And upon the Conviction of the Offender, the Judgment is, *Ideo ipse in misericordia & clausus prædictus prosternetur*; *Assisa Lancast. fo.* 6.

47. And if he who maketh a Purpresture, grants over his Lands where the Purpresture was made, both he and the Grantee shall be fined. *Fol.* 6.

48. They are likewise bound to *pull down the Buildings*, at or before a certain Day for that purpose appointed, or otherwise to pay a yearly *Rent* to the King for the continuance of them: But I do not find that any Man hath been bound to the Good Behaviour in the Forest for making any *Purpresture* there.

49. In *Windlesham* in the Forest of *Windsor* there were several Cottages and Inclosures made in the King's Soil: And afterwards the King sold the Manor; and the Question was, Whether this had dispenced with the *Purprestures*? And Mr. Attorney *Noy* argued, That it had not, but that the Grantee must be now fined for the *continuance* of them, and that they must be pulled down if he would not agree to pay a new *Rent* for them; for otherwise the King's Grant would be taken by implication to continue a Wrong in the Forest, which he never intended; And therefore the Lord of the Manor was fined, and a new Rent set on the Houses. *Jones's Rep.* 277.

Ranger.

Ranger.

See *Purlieu*, 97, 120.

BEcause the *Purlieus* were once Forest, and great store of Deer and other wild Beasts continued there after they were disafforested; therefore it was very necessary for the King to have some particular Officers there, to have a care to preserve the wild Beasts therein, for otherwise the Forests might be destroyed by the *Purlieus*.

2. Therefore immediately after the disafforestaon by the Perambulations, there were certain Officers appointed for that Purpose called *Rangers*, who are no Officers of the Forest, as *Regarders* are, to take charge of the *Vert*; but they are Officers of or to the Forest, tho' not *within* the Forest, and they have no Charge of the *Vert*, but only of the *Venison* which cometh out of the Forest into the *Purlieus*, and which they are to drive back again without destroying the same.

3. There are some of the King's Forests which were never enlarged by any new Afforestations, and by consequence such Forests have no *Purlieus*, and therefore there are no *Rangers* there.

4. And in such Case the *Foresters* may pursue and follow the Deer which get out of the Forests and drive them back, which they cannot do where there are *Purlieus* and *Rangers*, unless they follow them with fresh pursuit within their View. *Pasch.* 7 *H.* 6, *fo.* 36. *Placito* 41. *Hill.* 13 *H.* 7. *fo.* 16. *Placito* 14.

By

By whom made, his Office, Oath and Authority.

5. A *Ranger* is made by the King's Letters Patent, who alloweth to every one of them a yearly Fee or Pension of 20 or 30 *l.* payable out of the *Exchequer*, and a Fee-Deer, both red and fallow, out of the Forest.

6. His Office consists in ranging and walking about the *Purlieus*, to drive the wild Beasts safely into the Forests; and in presenting all Offenders and unlawful Hunters, and what Trespasses they have done in the *Purlieus*, and in their Walks; So that his Office and Authority consists in three Things.

7. (1.) *Ad ambuland. quotidie per terras deafforestatas, ad vidend. audiend. & inquirend. tam de malefactis, quam de malefactoribus in Balliva sua.*

8. (2.) *Ad refugand' feras Forestæ, tam veneris quam chasiæ, de terris deafforestatis in terras afforestatas.*

9. (3.) *Ad præsentandum omnes transgressiones Forestæ in terris deafforestatis factas, ad proximas curias illius Forestæ tentas.*

10. And to the Intent that every *Ranger* should be the more careful to execute his Office according to the Laws, he must be sworn. The Form of his Oath is;

The OATH.

YOU shall truly execute the Office of a Ranger in the Purlieus of Windsor *upon the Borders of the King's Forest of* Windsor. *You shall rechase, and with your*

your Hounds drive back again the Wild Beasts of the Forest, as often as they shall range out of the same Forest into your Purlieus. You shall truly present all unlawful Hunting and Hunters of wild Beasts of Venery and Chase, as well within the Pourallees as within the Forest, and those and all other Offences you shall present at the next Court of Attachments or Swanimote, which shall first happen. So help you God, &c.

11. In this Oath is contained the whole Office of a *Ranger*; and he is so called, because they range or walk thro' the Forest: In *Latin* 'tis called, *Ordo*, *Striga*, or *Series*, which signifies an *Order*, *Row*, or *Range*. The *French* say *Va de Range*, which signifies to go up and down in Order.

12. And because a *Ranger* is specially deputed and appointed by the King to walk in the *Purlieus*, according to the Laws and Orders prescribed to him for that purpose, and which he is sworn to observe, therefore he is properly called a *Ranger*.

Regarder.

See
- *Boundaries*, 17.
- *Chief Justice*, 23.
- *Dogs*, 22, 33, 34, 50, 53.
- *Forest*, 32.
- *Forester*, 44.
- *Nusance*, 10.
- *Officers*, per totum.
- *Presentment*, 19, 20.
- *Appendix*, Charta Canuti, 2, 7.
- *Appendix*, Charta Forestæ, 5.

1. BY the Laws of *Canutus*, *Canon* 2. it appeareth, That there were certain Persons who did

did then execute the same Office, which *Regarders* do at this Day.

2. They were in number sixteen, and were called *Mediocres homines*; and by the *Danes*, *Young Men*: Their Business was to take the Care and Charge upon themselves, *tam viridis quam veneris*.

3. But those Officers were quite worn out, and none left in the Forests, when *H.* 2. came to the Crown, neither did the Foresters or Woodmen take any regard thereof, insomuch that the *Woods* were very much destroyed; and there was little or no Venison in the Forests.

4. Therefore it was ordained by the *Assises of the Forest* made in his Reign, in these Words.

5. *Item Dominus Rex præcipit quod in quolibet comitatu in quo habet venationem, ponantur duodecim Milites ad custodiend. Venationem suam & viridem in Foresta: Et quatuor Milites ponantur ad agistandum boscos suos.*

6. And these Knights were called *Regarders*, which Name they took from their Office, because they were *agere curam custodiendi viridis & veneris*, *viz.* to regard the safe keeping and preserving the *Vert* and *Venison*.

7. In those Days this Office was given only to *Knights*, but now any good and lawful Man may be appointed by the King to execute the same.

8. A *Regarder* is an Officer of the King's Forest, who is sworn to make the Regard thereof, as the same hath been used to be made in former Time; and also to view and inquire of all the Offences of the Forest, as well as *Vert* of *Venison*, and of all Concealments of any Offences or Defaults of the Foresters, and of all other Officers of the Forest, concerning the Execution of their Office.

How

How many Regarders there must be in a Forest.

9. By the Assises of the Lord *William Vesey*, *Anno* 15 *Ed.* 1. it appeareth, that there must be twelve Regarders of the Forest, *viz. Quia evidenter constat Justiciario itinere suo, quod tam magna oneratio regardatorum est in Foresta prædicta, quod non est sustinenda propter magnum Domini Regis damnum. Provisum est, quod de cætero in Foresta non sint nisi tantum dict' duodecim Regardatores, Et quod illi Regardatores faciant regard' per totam Forestam quoties Assisa Forestæ voluerit, &c.*

10. These are the same Officers which are called *Duodecim milites*, by the *Assises* of *H.* 2. and of Necessity there must be so many; therefore if any of them are sick or dead, there must be others chosen to make that number, otherwise there cannot be any Regard made in the Forest; for if any under that number should make a certificate of their Inquisition, 'tis not a sufficient Charge against any Offender, because it appeareth by matter of Record, that it was not made by the whole number of Twelve, as it ought; for it must be intended there are always so many Regarders in every Forest, who are bound by the Laws thereof, to view all the Trespasses done therein; and 'tis not sufficient for any under that Number to *View*, but they must all do it; and they must all certify it as their Presentment or Verdict, like a Jury at Common Law; if eleven are agreed on a Verdict, 'tis not good if one disagree.

How and in what manner the Regarders are made.

11. A Regarder may be made by Letters Patent by the King, or by any of his Justices of the Forest in the General Eyre, or at such time as the Re-

Regard is to be made by vertue of the King's Writ, directed to the Sheriff of the County, commanding him to summon the whole Regard of the Forest to make their Regard there as usual; and in such case, if any is dead or sick and cannot appear, then the Sheriff shall, in his *County-Court*, choose so many as will make up the Number Twelve to serve in their Places; the Form of which Writ is as follows. *Co.* 4 *Inst.* 291, 292.

'12. Georgius Dei gratia Magnæ Britanniæ, 'Franciæ, & Hiberniæ Rex, Fidei Defensor, &c. 'Vic. Essex, salutem: Præcipimus tibi quod sine 'dilatione convenire facias omnes Forestarios & 'Regardatores ad regardum faciendum in Balliva 'tua ante adventum Justiciariorum nostrorum de 'Foresta: Et locis Regardatorum qui mortui sunt, 'aut infirmi, alios eligi facias, Ita quod duodecim 'sint in Foresta, & nomina eorum imbrevientur: 'Et Forestarii dictos duodecim Milites electos ducent per totam Ballivam suam ad videnđ. omnes 'transgressiones quæ exprimuntur in Scripto Capi-'tulor. quæ tibi mittimus, & quod hoc non omittas 'pro aliqua re: Et quod dicti Milites jurent quod 'facient Regardum sicut solet & debet fieri: Et 'quod ibunt sicut Forestarii eos ducent ad præ-'dictam Forestam videndam: Et si Forestarii no-'luerint vel nescíverint eos ducere, vel aliquod fo-'forisfact. voluerint concellare, ipsi milites non 'omittent propter illos quin forisfactum illud vi-'deant, & imbreviari faciant: Et hoc pro nulla 're omittant. Et quod regardum illud fiat citra 'tale Festum. Teste, &c.

13. Before the Chief Justice in Eyre holds his General Sessions, he usually causes this Writ to be made and sent to the Sheriff of the County where the Forest is, and where the Justice-Seat is to be kept;

kept; together with an Abstract of all such Matters which the Regarders are to inquire into.

14. By vertue of which Writ the Sheriff summons all the Regarders and Foresters to meet at a certain Day, and at a certain Place for that Purpose by him appointed; and when they meet he declares to them the Purport of the Writ, and gives them a Charge to inquire of all such Matters as are contained in the said Abstract; and if any of the Regarders are dead or sick, and cannot appear to make the Regard, the Sheriff shall choose others to make up twelve in Number to serve in their Places.

15. The *Regarders* thus chosen must be sworn by the Sheriff in the County-Court, and that by vertue of the Writ, *viz. Et dicti Milites jurent quod facient Regardum sicut solet & debet fieri*: The Form of the Oath is as follows:

16. *YOU shall truly serve our Sovereign Lord the King in the Office of Regarder of the Forest of* Waltham; *you shall make the Regard of the same Forest in such manner as the same hath been accustomed to be made; you shall range throughout the whole Forest, and through every Bailiwick of the same, as the Foresters there shall lead you, to view the same Forest: And if the Foresters will not or do not know how to lead you to make the Regard or Range of the Forest, or that they will conceal from you any thing that is forfeited to the King, you yourselves shall not let for any thing, but you shall see the same Forfeiture, and cause the same to be inrolled in your Roll; you shall inquire of all Wastes, Purprestures and Assarts of the Forest, and also of Concealments of any Offence or Trespass in the Forest, either in Vert or Venison, by any Officer of the same Forest. And all these things you shall, to the uttermost of your Power, do;*

So help you God.

17.

17. If a Regarder is made by Letters Patent to fill up the Number of twelve, they cannot, *ex officio*, make the Regard without such Writ directed to the Sheriff, because, by the Authority of the Writ, he must swear the Regarders as aforesaid; and they cannot by Law make the Regard of the Forest, though they are twelve in Number, until they are all sworn; for if they do, their Proceedings are void.

18. But when once they are elected and sworn, they may hold their Regard according to the Assises of the Forest *once in three Years*, *ex officio*, without any new Writ, Precept or Command.

19. It likewise appeareth, by the Statute *de Ordinatione Forestæ*, made *Anno* 34. *Ed.* 1. *fo.* 11. That where a Regarder is dead or sick, or by any other Means hindered that he cannot attend the *Swanimote*, then the Lord Chief Justice in Eyre, or his Deputy, may appoint another in his Place; otherwise the Indictments in that Court cannot be found by all the Officers of the Forest as they ought.

20. Therefore such Appointment is of Necessity, to make up the full Number of Twelve to supply the Place *pro hac vice*; but if a Regarder is *dead*, and another appointed in his Place, as before mentioned, he shall continue Regarder still; 'tis otherwise where he is *sick*, or hinder'd by any other Means; then such Appointment of another to serve in his Place, is only at the Court. *Hesket*, *fo.* 24.

21. By *the Laws and Customs of the Forest*, there are three sorts of Regarders:

22. (1) Those who are made by the King's Letters Patent; and in such case the Grant is sometimes for Life, and sometimes in Fee. 4. *Inst.* 291.

23. (2) Those who are made by the Chief Justice in Eyre, or by the King's Writ to the Sheriff,

as aforesaid; and such are only *durante beneplacito*, *viz.* during the King's Pleasure.

24. (3) Those who are made for the present Service of the *Swanimote*, or to serve at some other Time in the Absence of them who are not able to attend, or are sick; and those are *Pro hâc vice tantum.*

Of the Office and Duty of a Regarder.

25. *In Charta de Foresta*, *Artic.* 15. 'tis thus enacted, *viz. Regardatores nostri eant per forestam ad faciendum Regardum, &c.* And by the *Assises* in the Reign of *H.* 2. it appeareth, That the Regard of the Forest ought to be made by the Regarders, Foresters and Woodwards; *viz. Milites, forestarii & Woodwardi debent intentè inquirere in itinere suo quis habuerit aliquod ingenium ad malefaciend' Domino Regi in feris suis.* Such Knights or Regarders were made at first to controul the other Officers of the Forest.

26. Their Office is to see and inquire whether any Surcharge is made in the Forest, either by the Foresters or others; and they have Authority to appoint as many Foresters as they shall think convenient to look after the Forest.

27. They must go through the whole Forest every third Year to make their Regard, and to inquire of all Offences in *Vert* and *Venison*, and of all Concealments of any such Offences by any Officer of the Forest; which Regard, in former Days, was called, *Visitatio nemorum.*

28. They must go through the whole Forest with the *Foresters* and *Woodwards* to survey all the *Assarts*, *Wastes* and *Purprestures*, and all the Faults; they must inquire who made the same, and who doth hold the Land where such Trespasses are made; and if 'tis sown with Corn, then they are

to inquire whose Corn it is, and how often it hath been sown since it was made *Assart*, *Waste*, or *Purpresture*, and how much 'tis worth to be sold, and in whose Fee the same is, and to what Town it doth belong; and having made Inquiry into all the Particulars before mentioned, then they are to write in a Roll all the antient *Assarts*, *Wastes* and *Purprestures*, and other Defaults which they have found; and they are likewise to write in another Roll all such which they have found to be newly made; and if the Foresters will not go with the Regarders to make this View and Inquiry, they may go without them.

29. They shall survey all the old and new Purprestures, and value them severally by themselves, and set down the same in the Rolls of the Forest, and in what Place they were made, whether in Woods, Plains, Heaths, Waters, Lands, Pools, Hedges or Ditches, or in any other Place in the Forest; and all such Defaults shall be written in a Roll by themselves.

30. They are to survey all the Woods which are wasted in the Forest, as well those which are antient, as those which are new, and have been made since the 2d Year of *Ed.* 1. for in most of the King's Forests there are certain Woods, which belong to the Crown; and the King hath the Regard of all the Woods and Waste Grounds, and other Lands which are afforested, and within the Boundaries of the Forest, as well of those which are not his own, as those which are.

31. And sometimes it happens that there are Woods within the Boundaries, which are no part of the Forest; as for Instance, *Wallwood* in *Essex* was within *Waltham* Forest, and yet not any part of the Forest, nor within the Regard thereof; but all such Woods which are parcel of the Forest, are within the Regard thereof, and if within the Boundaries,

daries, and yet no part of the Forest, there 'tis out of the Regard.

32. And this is the Meaning of the *Assises*, *Artic.* 3. & 4. *viz. Si quis inventus fuerit extra domitiicum boscum infra Rewardum, &c.* and so there is a plain Difference between *infra & extra Rewardum forestæ.*

33. In surveying the Woods they are to see what manner of Trees have been felled, as *Oaks, &c.* since the last Regard, and upon Inquiry and View they are to certify the Number and the Damage which hath been done to the Woods; and in like manner they are to do of all Lopping of Trees, and Destruction of Underwood.

34. They are to view all the Hedges and Fences for fencing the King's Woods or Lands, and whether they are kept in sufficient Repair; and if not, then who is in Fault, and to what Damage of the King that the Fences are not kept repaired, and whether 'tis the Cause why the Lands or Woods lie open or common.

35. They are to survey all Forges and Mines for finding out Metal in whomsoever's Fee the same is in the Forest, as well in the Woods or Lands of the King, as of any other Person; and what Rents and Customs they pay for the same, and to whom; and all Ports and Creeks of the Sea, where any Ships or Boats do or may arrive, to carry away any Timber-Wood or Underwood out of the Forest; and in whose Tenure or Occupation the same is or are, and by whom brought thither, and in whose Fee the same was done.

36. They are to inquire, who doth keep any Bows or Arrows, Cross bows, Guns, Hounds or any other Engines, to hunt or destroy the Deer, &c.

37. And when they have made their Inquiry and find any Offences done and committed in the Forest, they are to write the same fairly on a Roll,

and bring it either to the *Court of Attachments*, or *Swanimote*; at the first of which Courts all the Officers of the Forest ought to assemble every forty Days; and all such Matters as are so found by the Regarders, they are to *certify* under their Hands and Seals there, and likewise *present* the same under their Hands and Seals unto the Lord Chief Justice in Eyre, at the next General Eyre or Sessions of the Forest, which is to be holden every Third Year; and 'tis necessary the Regarders should make their Regard before such Sessions is holden, which must be done by vertue of the King's Writ, as aforesaid, for they cannot do it without.

38. But there are several other Officers employed to make the Regard besides these Regarders, and those are the *Foresters* and *Woodwards*, and other Persons who are Owners of Woods and Lands in the Forest; and if any Man hath a Regard in Fee, and hath likewise Foresters in Fee belonging to the same; in such Case the Foresters or Regarders of any other Regard cannot enter or do any thing therein, because 'tis out of their Jurisdiction, and in the Charge of another.

39. But in such case, the Chief Warden of the Forest, and the King's Foresters and Regarders, may survey the same, and make the Regard thereof, being within the Bounds and Limits of the King's Forest, though there are particular Officers for that Place.

40. This appears *in Assisa forestæ*, in the Reign of *H* 2. *viz. Quod omnes illi qui habent boscos infra metas forestæ ponant idoneos forestarios in boscis eorum de quibus, &c.*

41. And note, That a Man cannot be a Regarder for any Forest, but for the King's only; and no man can take upon him the Office of a Regarder in the King's Forest, without he hath a lawful Title to it.

42. The

42. The Words *in Charta de Foresta* are, *viz. Regardatores nostri eant per forestam, ad faciendum Regardum, &c.* from which it may be inferred, That they are not to do or certify any thing concerning their Office, without first viewing the same.

43. Therefore 'tis said, *Eant per Forestam*; that is, They must go through the whole Forest, and through every Bailiwick thereof, to see and inquire of the Trespasses and Offences there.

44. In the following Words, *viz. Ad faciendum Regardum*, it appears for what Cause they are to go through the Forest, and therein the whole Office of a Regarder is comprehended, which consists in these Particulars;

45. *Ad* { *Videndum.* | *Imbreviandum.* ; *Inquirendum.* | *Certificandum.*

1. They are to certify nothing but what they have *seen*, and this must appear in the Certificate itself, otherwise the Presentment is not good; neither shall the Offender be charged upon such a Presentment, but the Regarders shall be amerced for their insufficient Certificate.

'Tis like the Return of a Sheriff in an Action of Waste, where the Words *Accessi ad locum vastatum* are left out, 34 *H.* 6. or like the Presentment of a Coroner, where the Words *Super visum Corporis* are omitted.

But if the Regarders set forth in their Certificate, That they did go through the Forest, and that they did *view* the Trespasses which they certify and present, when in truth they did not; yet such Presentment and Certificate is good, because a Man cannot, by Law, traverse the Return or Certificate of a sworn Officer.

And 'tis not sufficient, that the *View* of a few of the Regarders be certified; but it must be the whole Number of Twelve, and they must certify the same as their Verdict.

2. *Ad Inquirendum*, *viz.* The Regarders must go through the Forest, not only to *see* and *view* the Trespasses done in the Forest, but also to *inquire* out the Certainty of every Offence, and to learn the Truth of all such Matters as shall be delivered to them in Charge.

3. *Ad Imbreviandum*; *viz.* To inroll and enter the View and Inquisition which they have made; so that when they have gone through the Forest, and have viewed the Trespasses and Defaults, and have inquired into the Truth of every thing given them in Charge; then they must cause all those Defaults to be enter'd and written fairly in a Roll of Parchment, in which Inrollment Four Things are to be observed.

1. What the Offence is.
2. When it was done.
3. Where it was done.
4. By whom.

4. *Ad Certificandum*; The Inrollment being thus made, there can be no Execution or Punishment done to the Offenders until the Regarders have made their Certificate thereof unto the Lord Chief Justice in Eyre, at his Justice-Seat.

46. But before they make such Certificate to the Chief Justice in Eyre, they must present their Inquisition at the *Swanimote*, before the other Officers of the Forest, to the Intent that the Offenders may be indicted there according to the Ordinance

of

of the Forest, *Anno* 34 *Ed.* 1. for if 'tis certified to the Chief Justice before the Offenders are indicted there, then they may *traverse* the *Presentment* or Certificate, because the same was not *Præsentat' per forestarios, & duodecim Juratores, & convict. per Viridarios.*

47. Next after the Words *in Charta forestæ* before-mention'd, *viz. Regardatores nostri eant per forestam ad faciendum Regardum*, there are these Words which follow; *viz. Sicut fieri consuevit tempore primæ Coronationis Regis Henrici Avi nostri, & non aliter.* Which Clause imports, That this Branch of the Statute did not ordain any new Thing, but was only made in Affirmance of the Law and Usage of the Forest in the Time of *H.* 2. *viz.* That the Regard was to be made according to *the Assises and Customs of the Forest* used in his Time; and therefore it will be necessary to shew in what Manner that was.

48. §. The Inquiry and Presentment of all Articles must be every Third Year; for so it appears by the *Assises* of *H.* 2. *cap.* 10, 17. and then the Regard is to be made but only within the Boundaries of the Forest; for they ought not to inquire or present any thing that is done out of the Bounds, nor out of the Precinct of the Regard within the Forest: And this likewise appears by the same *Assises*, *cap.* 10, 17. for 'tis there mentioned, *viz. Those who have Woods out of the Regard of the Forest where the Wild Beasts usually rest and take Shelter, or those who have Woods or Lands in the Forest, and have the Privilege that they shall be out of the Regard, the same shall not be impeached for any Cause.*

49. But yet in such Case, those who have that Privilege ought to have a *Woodward* to look after their Woods, who must be sworn to *the Assises of the Forest*, that is, to preserve the *Vert* and *Venison*. *Hesket*, *fo.* 26.

49. And if the Regarders do inquire or make Presentment of any thing done in such privileged Place, it may be avoided by pleading this Matter specially; for he shall never be punished upon such a Presentment, if the Truth of it appear by Matter of Record in the Justice-Seat.

50. The same Law if the Regarders will present any Thing which is not specified *in capitulis de Regardo fiendo*, which are always sent to the Sheriff together with the Writ before mentioned, when the Regard is to be made.

51. As for instance, if they present that *J. R.* hath agisted his Woods or Lands before the King's Hedge-rows in the Forest were agisted, or that he hath taken any Pannage contrary to the Assises of the Forest: Such a Presentment is void without any Plea, if it appears unto the Court by Matter of Record, comprised in the very Presentment, that the Offence therein mentioned is not what was given them in Charge to present or inquire into.

52. So where Regarders are chosen by Writ to the Sheriff, and afterwards make the Regard without a new Writ *within three Years, viz.* voluntarily, and of themselves, *every Year*; Such Regard and all Presentments against any Person whatsoever are void, and the Party against whom 'tis made, may discharge himself by Plea.

53. But such a Presentment made by Regarders once elected and chosen, altho' they made their Regard every *fourth Year* or *fifth Year*, that is good and sufficient in Law, and shall bind the Party, tho' such Presentment and Regard was not by any command directed to the Sheriff; because when they are once elected by Writ and sworn, then they may hold their Regard according to the Assises of the Forest *every third Year, ex officio*, without any Writ, Precept or Command.

54.

54. *In Itinere Windsor, Jones's Rep.* 275. Mr. Attorney *Noy* moved, That the several Regarders might be fined, *Quia minùs plenè præsentaverunt & imperfectè*; whereupon every Regarder of *Battel's Bailiwick* was fined 5 *l.* and every Regarder of *Finchamsted Bailiwick*, 5 *l.* and every Regarder of *Fine's Bailiwick* 10 *l.*

The difference between infra Regardum Forestæ *and* infra metas Forestæ.

55. In the Ordinances of the Forest made *Anno* 6 *Ed.* 1. which may be seen in *Rastall. Abr. Stat. Titulo Forest.* 21. are often found these Words, *viz. Infra Regardum* and *infra metas Forestæ*, and sometimes *in Foresta* generally.

56. Now there is a great difference between these Words; for a Thing may be done *infra metas Forestæ*, and yet it may be *extra regardum*; but not *è converso*; for a Thing cannot be done *infra Regardum Forestæ*, but it must of necessity be *infra metas Forestæ*.

57. As for Instance, in the Third *Article of the said new Ordinances*, 'tis mentioned, *Si quis inventus fuerit extra Dominicum boscum & infra rewardum prosternens quercum, &c.* there the Words *infra Rewardum* must be taken to be *infra metas Forestæ*.

58. But in the Fifth Article, the Words are, *Si quis attachiabilis fuerit contra vadios & plegios debet distringi per catalla sua infra metas Forestæ invent.* In this Case, the Offender may have Cattle distrainable *infra metas*, and yet *extra Rewardum*; as if such Cattle were remaining in certain Woods or Grounds exempted by the King's Grant from the Charge of the Forest; so that tho' they are *infra metas*, yet they are *extra Rewardum*.

59. And there are many Precedents of such Exemptions; for in the Reign of *Ed.* 1. when *Hugh* De-

Despenser was Chief Justice in Eyre of all the King's Forests *ultra Trentam*, when the Perambulations were made there, it appeared by the Claims and Charters in several *Iters*, that there were many Woods within the Limits and Bounds of the Forest, which were exempted out of the Regard.

60. And I have seen the like of several Forests on this Side *Trent*, in the Time of *Ed.* 1. when *Adam de Valentia*, Earl of *Pembroke*, was Chief Justice in Eyre of all the Forests *citra Trentam. In Libro Glasconiæ, fo.* 81.

61. So it may happen that some Woods may be within the Bounds of the Forest, which are no part thereof; as for Instance, *Wellwood* in *Essex* was within the Forest of *Waltham*, and yet no part thereof, nor within the Regard of that Forest; and so *Havering* Park is *infra metas Forestæ de Waltham*, but out of the *Regard* thereof, and not any part of that Forest.

62. If a Wood belonging to a Manor is *infra metas* and *extra Regardum Forestæ*, in this Case, by the Assises of the Forest, the Lord of that Manor must claim it thus, *viz. Gilbertus de Acton clamat tenere boscum suum de Trovisdale pertinen. ad manerium suum de Chad. extra Regardum Forestæ, viz. illum boscum qui est ex parte Boreali*, and recite all the Limits and Boundaries thereof.

63. But all such Woods and Lands, which are *Part* of the Forest, are within the *Regard*; and all which are within the Bounds, and yet no part of the Forest, are out of the Regard: And this is the meaning of those Words in the Ordinances and Assises of the Forest; and this Distinction was taken in the Case of Sir *John Bynn*, reported by *Bridgman*.

64. In a *Quo Warranto*, for using Liberties and Privileges therein mentioned in his Manor of *Colwick*, being within the *Metes* and *Bounds* of the

King's Forest of *Sherwood*, and within the *Regards* of the said Forest.

65. The Defendant in his Plea, did acknowledge the Manor to be within the *Metes* and *Bounds* of the Forest, but did not answer whether it was within the Regards or not; for it might be within the *Metes* and *Bounds* of the Forest, and yet not within the Regards; as if the Manor had been disafforested by *Charta de Foresta*, because it belonged to a Subject and not to the King, it might still be *within* the *Metes* and *Bounds* of the Forest, and not within the Regards; for by the disafforesting it was made *Purlieu*, and not subject to the Regards and Laws of the Forest as to the Owner of the Manor: So if the King had granted that this Manor should be free of Regards, or out of the Regards, yet it is still within the *Metes* and *Bounds* of the said Forest.

69. *In Itinere Windsor. Jones's Rep.* 289. Mr. Attorney *Noy* said, That to be out of the Regard of the Forest, is to be quit and discharged of the Fees due to Foresters, and that was all.

Rolls of the Forest.

See { *Agistment*, 14. *Regarder*, 29, 45. *Appendix*, *Assis. Foreste*, 21. }

1. THE Presentments of Offences in the Court of *Attachments*, and the Indictments upon such Presentments in the Court of *Swanimote*, must be entered on the respective Rolls of the said Courts; and being sealed with the Seals of the Verderors, are to be kept by them till the

the next Justice-Seat, and then they are to present the same to the Lord Chief Justice in Eyre.)

2. And if any Forester, Verderor, or other Officer of the Forest, who hath the Custody of such Rolls, neglect or refuse to bring in the same on the first Day of the next Justice-Seat; then the Person so neglecting or refusing, his Heirs, Executors, or the Tenants of their Lands, in what County soever the same are, shall be thus punished, *viz.* There shall go forth a Precept directed to the Sheriff of that County where the Lands are, commanding him, *Quod expulsis uxore & liberis seisiri faciat omnes terras & tenementa quæ fuerunt ipsius, &c. in balliva sua. Ita quod de valore eorundem per annum respondeat præfat. Justiciar', &c. nisi tenentes terræ & tenementorum ipsius prius venerint ad rotulos suos & alia memoranda prædicta dictum Iter tangentia reddenda, &c.*

3. The Fact contained in these Rolls, and of which the Party is convicted, cannot be traversed; but a Pardon or Release, or any other subsequent matter, so as 'tis not contrary to the Fact, may be pleaded, tho' it was before the Conviction. And this was the Lady *Villars*'s Case, who was indicted and convicted by the Verderors, for cutting Trees in the Forest without Warrant: And she pleaded a Grant of those Lands in the Forest, by vertue whereof she felled the Trees; and this was held a good Discharge of the Presentment of the Verderors. *Kellew.* 66. But it was otherwise in one *Gibbon*'s Case, who being convicted of the like Offence, pleaded the like Plea, *viz.* a Grant of the Lands and the Trees there growing; but did not alledge, that the Lands were *within the Forest*; so that he could not fell them without Licence from the King, or the Chief Justice of the Forest. *Jones* 347.

4. And if such Rolls of the Forest or Memorandums are lost; then by the *Assises of the Forest*, the

the said Officers, their *Heirs*, *Executors* or *Tenants*, may pray the Justices of the Forest, that they may be admitted to pay a Fine to the King. And in such Case the Entry is thus, *viz. Et admittuntur ad finem dimid. Marcæ, &c.*

5. But if it happen that the Rolls are burnt or destroyed by the Enemies, that will not be any Excuse by the Laws of the Forest, tho' it may be so at Common Law: *Quia judicia Forestæ & assisament. ejusdem seorsim, ab aliis Regni judiciis secernunt, & solius Regis arbitrio vel ejusdem familiar. ad hoc specialiter deputati subjiciunt*: And therefore in this Case, the Officer shall make his Fine for the same, or otherwise his Lands shall be seised.

6. And the like Law, if *Agistors* fail of their Rolls and Accompts; and so likewise if the Verderors make Default in bringing in their Rolls and Indictments concerning the Forest at the next Justice-Seat, they shall be amerced and distrained by their Lands to bring in the same.

7. In the Retorn of the Writ of Summons to a Justice-Seat to be held for the Forest of *Pickering*. 4 *Inst*. 310. 'tis thus amongst other Things returned.

8. *Bernardus de Burgh qui obiit fuit Viridarius in Foresta illa, & Alexander de Burgh filius ejus & hæres venit & reddidit Rotulos suos tam de viridi quàm de venatione tangen. Forestam istam de tempore prædicto.*

9. And my Lord *Coke* tells us, that the Law of the Forest is, That if a Verderor die, his Heir is to bring in the Rolls of his Ancestor's Time; which if he do, then the Entry is in Form as above-written.

10. *Bernardus de Burgh viridar' venit & reddidit rotulos suos tam de viridi quàm de venatione tangent' istam Forestam, &c. Guilielmus Ward viridar' non venit ad rotulos suos redd': Ideo præceptum est vicecom' seisire omnes terras & tenementa sua, &c. Postea venit*

præd

præd' Guilielm' & petit admitt' ad finem faciend' die Martii, &c. & quoad rotulos suos dicit quod furati fuerunt ab eo per quosdam Malefactores, & petit quod possit admitti ad finem faciend' cum Domino Rege in hac parte, & admittitur pro fine 100 s. Intratur Foresta Pick. 8 Ed. 1. coram Justiciar. Itineran.

11. Johannes Kilmington nuper Custos Forestæ istius dicit quod præd. feræ acciderunt in Morina quorum corpora putrida fuerunt suspensa super quercus, & de hoc vocat record' rotulorum viridariorum, &c.

12. Forestarii venerunt & dicunt pro seipsis & omnibus aliis Forestar. istius forestæ, Quod ipsi forestarii nunquam fuerunt onerati de aliquibus Rotulis, seu indictament' tangentibus forestam. Et quod omnes Rotuli & Indictament' remanent penes viridar', &c. Et hoc parati sunt verificare per ministros, &c. Qui quidem ministri ad hoc jurat' hoc idem testantur, &c.

Scotale.

See { *Charge in Chief Justice*, 20. *Forester*, 28, 29, 30, 31. *Appendix*, Ch. Forestæ, 7. }

1. SCotale is where any Officer of the Forest keeps an Ale-house, and by *colour of his Office*, causeth Men to come to that Ale-house in the Forest, there to spend their Money for fear of his Displeasure.

2. 'Tis prohibited by *Charta de Foresta, cap.* 7. *viz. Nullus Forestarius vel Bedellus de cætero faciat Scotellas, &c.* And the Offence is to be inquired *per duodecim juratores* at the *Swanimote*, and also at the general Sessions of the Forest; and if the Officer is attainted, he is to be punished and put out of his Office.

3. The

3. The like Law, if a Forester or other Officer of the Forest keeps a *Gaming-house* or *Ale-house* on any certain Day to sell Ale, and by *colour of his Office*, causeth the People to come thither and spend their Money.

4. The Prohibition *in Charta de Foresta* aforesaid, *viz. Nullus de cætero faciat Scotellat, &c. nisi per visum & Sacramentum duodecim Regardatorum*, doth imply, That in some Cases *Scotales* may be lawful, and may remain and continue to this Time, *viz.* if they are found and presented upon the View of the Regarders, and upon their Oaths, when they make the Regard of the Forest, that such *Scotales* had a lawful Beginning, which must be either by *Prescription*, *Grant* or *Tenure*; so that it may appear the Thing was lawfully done, and by right and good Title to the same, and not newly and wrongfully exacted on the People by *colour of the Office* of any Forester or other Minister of the Forest.

Sheep-Silver.

THis is an antiquated Service now turned into Money, which is paid in respect that antiently the Tenants washed the Lord's Sheep; as in some Places the Lords have now *Plough-Silver* and *Sheep-Silver*, which is likewise turned into Money and the Service spared. *Jones's Rep.* 280.

Staff-herding, See Common, 71.

Steward. } See { Bail, 7. Forest, 32. Swanimote, 17, 18.

Summons. See Chief Justice, 21.

Swanimote.

See { *Agistment*, 29, 32.
Charge in Chief Justice, 22.
Fence-Month, 4.
Presentment, 4, 5, 6, 8.
Venison, 6.
Appendix, in Charta Canuti, 10.
Appendix, Ch. Forestæ, 8.
Appendix, Assisa Forestæ, 22.
Appendix, Ordinatio Forestæ, 2.

1. THis Word is derived from the *Sax.* Speing *Minister* and Mote, which is *Curia*; so that 'tis properly a Court of the *Ministers* of the Forest, and called *Swanimote*, because 'tis but a Preparative to the Justice-Seat. 4 *Co.* 239.

2. Our Ancestors had several compound Words ending in *Mote*; thus, *Halimote*, which signified a Court Baron; *Folkemotes* were the Courts held in *London*, where all the *Folk* or *People* of the City did complain against the Mayor and Aldermen for Misgovernment. *Portmote* is ever in a *Haven Town*, for 'tis the Court of the *Port* or *Haven*; and the *Swanimote* is the Court within the Forest, to which all the Freeholders do owe Suit and Service.

The Verderors are Judges of this Court, and not the Chief Warden or his Deputy.

3. It was the Opinion of my Lord *Coke* in 2 *Bulst.* 295. That a Subject may have a *Swanimote*. And in 4 *Inst.* 289. he tells us, That the Pleas in that Court are called *Placita Forestæ*, but that the Verderors are the proper Judges there.

4. 'Tis true, Mr. *Hesket*, *fo.* 34. mentions, That the Chief Warden of the Forest, or his Lieutenant may sit there, but I know not by what Authority, for he is no *Judicial Officer*; if he was, he cou'd not make a *Deputy*, of which there are many Instances in the Common Law.

5. The Chief Justice in Eyre is a *Judicial Officer*, and yet he may make a *Deputy*, but that is by vertue of the Statute of 32 *H.* 8. *cap.* 35. which gives him Power to make a *Deputy* to execute his Office; and this may be done by Writing under his Hand and Seal, and likewise under the Seal of his Office, and not otherwise: So that before the making this Statute, 'tis plain he had no Authority to make a *Deputy*.

6. But there is no Statute which gives the *Chief Warden* of the Forest any Power to make a *Deputy*; there is a Statute which shews that he is not a *Judicial Officer*, *viz.* The Statute of 1 *Ed.* 3. *cap.* 8. which recites, That several People have been undone by the *Chief Wardens of Forests*; and then it enacts, That no Man shall be imprisoned for *Vert* or *Venison*, unless taken *in the Manner*, or an Indictment found against him; and then the *Chief Warden* of the Forest is to discharge him upon Bail to appear at the next Eyre; and if he refuse, the Party may issue forth a Writ out of *Chancery*, directed to him to bail him till that Time; which shews that he is a *Ministerial* and not a *Judicial Officer*, and therefore the Writ is directed to him, and the Reason is given by the Statute, *viz.* because the *Chief Warden* may not be a *Justice*, nor have any Record; so that neither he or his *Deputy* are *Judicial Officers*, and by consequence cannot be Judges of any Court.

7. But the same Statute likewise mentions, That the Names of the *Bail* shall be delivered to the

Verderors, because they are proper Judges of this Court.

How often the Swanimote shall be held in a Year, and what Officers and others are to attend.

8. Before the making of *Charta de Foresta*, there was not any certain Time limited for the holding the Courts of the Forest; and therefore the *Chief Wardens* and *Foresters* kept the Courts of *Swanimote* as often as they would, and compelled the Inhabitants of the Forest to attend those Courts, till at last this became a very great Oppression.

9. For these Courts were so frequently held, that the People could not constantly attend, and several Fees were exacted from those who could not, and so their Appearance was excused.

10. To remedy which Inconveniency, it was provided by that Statute, That *nullum Swanimotum de cætero teneatur in Regno nostro nisi ter in Anno, viz.* Fifteen Days before *Michaelmas*, when the Agistors of the King's Woods do meet to take Agistments; and about the Feast of St. *Martin* in the *Winter*, when the said Agistors receive the Pannage: And to those two Courts of *Swanimote* the *Foresters, Verderors, Agisters, and none other*, shall come, or shall be compelled by Distress. The third *Swanimote* shall be kept fifteen Days before the Feast of St. *John Baptist*, when the *Agisters* meet to fawn the Deer, and the *Foresters and Verderors, and none other*, shall come to to this Court, and if they fail, shall be compelled by Distress.

11. But this Law is now altered by the Statute of 34 *Ed.* 1. called, *Ordinatio forestæ, cap.* 1. and likewise several Years after that, *viz.* in the beginning of the Reign of King *Ed.* 3.

12. The Words *in Ordinatione forestæ* are, That Presentments of Offences in *Vert* and *Venison* shall

be made in the next Swanimote, before the *Foresters*, *Verderors*, *Regarders*, *Agistors*, and other Ministers of the same Forest, &c. and that Indictments made in any other manner shall be void.

13. So that now it appeareth by this Statute, That notwithstanding the Negative Words in *Charta de forestâ*, the *Foresters*, *Verderors*, *Regarders*, *Agistors*, and other Ministers of the Forest, are to come to this Court, and also Freeholders and all other honest and lawful Men of the Forest; for otherwise the Indictments there made are void.

14. And the Reason is, because the Indictments must be found by all the Officers of the Forest; therefore they must all be present; and if any of them are dead, or by Sickness, or any other Means, are disabled or hinder'd in coming to this Court, the Chief Justice of the Forest, or his Deputy, shall constitute others in his or their room, that the Indictments may be made by All; and this is according to *Ordinatio Forestæ*, 34 *Ed.* 1. *cap.* 2.

15. Then by the other Statute, *viz.* 1 *Ed.* 3. *cap.* 8. it appears, That the *Freeholders*, and other good and lawful Men of the Forest, must be present at this Court to make Inquests and Juries there; for, by the Words of this last Statute, the Presentments must be made *per Sacramentum tam Militum quam aliorum proborum & legalium hominum de partibus vicinioribus ubi*, &c. This is also proved by the Statute of 7 *R.* 2. *cap.* 3.

16. So that though by *Charta de foresta* 'tis enacted, That only Three Sorts of Officers shall come to the *Swanimote*, *viz.* The *Foresters*, *Verderors* and *Regarders*, & *nulli alii per districtionem*, yet the *Woodwards*, and all other the Officers of the Forest, and all the Freeholders dwelling therein, and the Four Men and the Reeve of every Village in the Forest, must come to the Swanimote, and give

their Attendance there; and in Default thereof, shall be amerced, and the same to be estreated to the Chief Warden of the Forest, to levy it by Distress.

17. By the Words in *the Ordinance of the Forest*, *cap.* 1. *viz. Ac aliis earundem forestarum Ministris*, are meant *Stewards* of the *Swanimote*; and such should be learned Men, especially in the Laws of the Forest. 6 *Ed.* 1. *cap.* 22.

18. It appeareth by *the Assises of the Forest*, *cap.* 22. That there ought to be a Steward at every Swanimote; the Words are, *Quod homo attachiatus pro ramis caesis, placitum illud pertinet ad Swanimotum coram Seneschallo, &c.*

19. By the Statutes before mention'd, 'tis plain, That all Offences in the Forest against *Vert* or *Venison*, are to be presented at the next *Swanimote*, and 'tis there mention'd in what Manner; *viz. Coram Forestariis, Viridariis, Regardatoribus, Agistatoribus, & aliis earundem forestarum ministris, & si in alio modo fiat indictamentum, pro nullo penitus habeatur*; and if the Jury find the Presentment true, then the Offender is convicted by Law, and shall not *traverse* the Indictment.

20. And generally all Offences in the Forest are there to be presented, and 'tis usual for the *Steward* to give in Charge these Offences following:

Concerning:
- *Acorns*, gathering them in Forest, and selling them in the Market.
- *Agistment*; What Agistments have been taken in to the Hurt of the Deer.
- *Assarts* newly made; In what Place, and by whom. *Dyer*, 7 *Eliz.* 24. *b.*
- *Browse*; If any Warden of the Forest, or his Deputy, or any Forester, have cut *Browse* for his own

own Advantage, and the Value thereof.

Concerning
- *Burning Heath*, *Fern* or *Ling* in the Forest or Towns adjoining.
- *Church-Ways* in the Forest streightened, and by whom.
- *Crabs* growing in the Forest, gathered, and what Quantity.
- *Deer* killed without Warrant, and by whom, and what Deer, and in whose Walk.
- *Dogs*; Those who do not take them up passing through the Forest, but suffer them to kill the Deer, the Names of the Men, and what Deer kill'd; and all Borderers keeping strange Greyhounds and Dogs, not qualified to keep them.
- *Extortions* by Officers of the Forest.
- *Fawning-time*; If any Person come into the Forest at that Time to *common* Sheep, not being sworn to preserve the Game.
- *Fences*; Whether well made and repaired to save the King's Covert.
- *Foresters*; If there are more than usually have been, and who they are, and who made them.
- *Fox*, killed in the Forest without Warrant.
- *Goats*; Whether any in the Forest; for they are not *commonable*.
- *Hares*; Whether any killed in the Forest without Warrant.
- *Hawks-Eggs*; If taken out of the Forest, and by whom.
- *Herons-Eggs*; If taken out of the Forest, &c.

Concerning

Hogs; If any in the Forest not ring'd the Number and Price, for they are forfeited.

Those who have a Grant to put in a certain Number, and agist more than the Number, and the Price of them.

Not ringed and taken in the Forest since the last Sessions, the Number and Price; for they are forfeited to the King, being not commonable.

Hogsty; If built in the Forest without Licence, and by whom.

Hunting the King's Deer within seven Miles of the Forest, either forty Days before or so many Days after the King's hunting.

Inclosing any part of the Forest, and thereby inlarging his own Ground; inclosing the Purlieus, or streightning the Forest.

Meers; Carrying away or removing any Meer, Stones, or other Metes, Marks or Boundaries of the Forest.

Mills; Whether any new built in the Forest, or the old Mills not repaired, and the Damage in either Case.

Mines; Whether any Person hath digged in the Forest for Mines, without Licence.

Nets; Whether any kept in the Forest, by whom, and who hath set any, where and when; for 'tis unlawful, though no Deer are killed.

Par-

Concerning

Pannage; If those who have Woods in the Forest, drive their Hogs out of those Woods into the Forest.

Partridge-Eggs; Whether any taken out of the Forest, and by whom.

Pheasants Eggs; If taken out of the Forest.

Pounding any Cattle out of the County.

Purlieus; Those who hunt there oftner than three times in one Week, or before Sun-rising, or after Sun-set, or with more in Company than their own Servants, or in the Fence-Month, or forestall the Deer in returning to the Forest.

Purprestures; If any are newly made where, what, and by whom.

Salteries; If any made in Parks or Purlieus.

Sheep; If any taken the third time since the last Sessions, the Number and Value; for they are forfeited.

Sheep-House, If any built in the Forest.

Suit and *Service*; Those who owe any, how much behind, and on what Days.

Surcharge in the Forest, and by whom, and with what Cattle, or otherwise.

Timber cut down and employed to his own Use, and the Value thereof.

Trees; Whether any fell'd in the Forest, and by whom.

Concerning

Vert; Felling Oaks or other Trees in the King's Wood, and carrying them away, the Price of the Horses, Carts and Trees, and if any felled, then by what Authority.

Waifs and *Strays*, If any since last Court.

Ways; If any are streightned in the Forest, where, and by whom.

Warrants, To have Trees, and more are taken without View of the Verderors, or more Deer than mention'd in the Warrant, and what Deer, and what Season.

Wood; If any felled, or any manner of Underwood, and where, by whom, and the Price thereof.

21. Likewise the *Regarders* are to present at the next Swanimote after their Regard, what Mastiffs are kept in the Forest unexpeditated.

22. And all Offences in the Purlieus are to be tried in this Court, but no Judgment shall be given in any Case, or Execution awarded there, for that must be reserved to the Justice-Seat. 4 *Inst* 289.

23. Lastly, In this Court enquiry must be made *desuper venatione forestariorum & aliorum ministrorum forestæ, & de eorum oppressionibus populo illatis*; and may convict them, but not give Judgment.

24. And all who are indicted in this Court, and in these Words, *Quod sunt Communes Malefactores de venatione Domini Regis in forestâ*, may be outlawed.

Venison.

See *Presentment*, 12.

1. VEnison is a general Word for any *Beast of Forest or Chase*; 'tis called in *Latin*, *Venatio*, and no other Word is used either in *Charta de forestâ*, or in *Ordinatio forestæ*, to express *Venison*; 'tis deriv'd from *Venor*, which signifies to *hunt*; and in a general Sense, it signifies every Wild Beast, either of the Forest or Chase, which is taken by hunting, and as well those which are not eaten for *Venison*, as those which are.

2. That which is accounted *Venison* for the Goodness of the Meat, as *Red* and *Fallow Deer*, is more properly called *Ferina*, and in this Sense 'tis used by *Virgil*,

Implentur veteris Bacchi pinguisque Ferinæ.

3. The *English* Word *Venison* is derived from the *French Venaison*, which comes from their Verb, *Venir*, which likewise signifies, to *hunt*; and in old *English* 'tis called, *Venson*, and not *Venison*; but I know not why. In *Budæus* there are these Verses:

Non est inquirendum unde venit Venison.
Nam si forte furto sit sola fides sufficit.

4. *Vert* and *Venison* are the two greatest Ornaments of every Forest, the later of which is a Word of Art proper only to Beasts of Forest, or of Chase, for no other are called *Venison.*

5. This appears *in Charta de foresta*, in these Words: *Præterea, singulis quadraginta diebus per totum annum conveniant Forestarii & Viridarii, ad videndum attachiamenta de Foresta, tam de viridi, quam de*

de venatione, where the Word *Venatio* is taken for any Beast of Forest or Chase.

6. And in in the same Charter 'tis appointed, That *Nullus Constabularius, Castellanus, vel Ballivus, teneat placita de Foresta, sive de Viridi, sive de Venatione*: There likewise the Word *Venatio* must be understood, the killing, hunting or chasing any Beast of Forest or Chase; so that all the Pleas of the Forest are, *vel de Viridi, vel de Venatione.*

7. So in *Ordinatio forestæ*, made *Anno* 34 *Ed.* 1. *Artic.* 1. the Words are, *Imprimis ordinavimus pro nobis & hæredibus nostris, quod de transgressionibus in forestis nostris, de viridi & venatione de cætero factis, Forestarii infra quorum Ballivas hujusmodi transgressiones fieri contigerint, præsentent easdem ad proximum Swanimotum, coram, &c.*

8. In which Paragraph all the Trespasses in the Forest are comprehended by the Words, *de Viridi & Venatione*; and there the Word *Venatio* must be understood of every Beast meant or intended to have privilege in the Forest, and those are Beasts of Forest and Chase.

9. And in the same *Ordinance of the Forest, Artic.* 5. where mention is made of the King's Pardon, 'tis in these Words, *viz. De transgressionibus de Viridi & de Venatione*; by which is understood, every Trespass in hunting any Beast of the Forest, whether they are Beasts of the Chase or of the Forest.

10. The Word is likewise used *in Charta de foresta, Artic.* 10. *Si quis captus fuerit, & convictus de captione venationis nostræ*: There the Word *Venatio* is used for every Beast of the Forest and Chase.

11. And in the same Charter, Article 16. *Sed quilibet Forestarius de feodo attachiet placita de foresta, tam de viridi quam de venatione*: By which it appears, That all Attachments and Pleas of the Forest are either of *Vert* or *Venison*; therefore the

Word

Word *Venatio* comprehends every Beast in the Forest which hath any Privilege there.

12. And in this Sense the Word *Venaison* is taken by the *French* Authors, *viz.* For every Beast of Forest or Chase. *Pierius, in Lib. Venery.*

Of the general and special Signification of the Word Venison.

13. In the general Acceptation of the Word, 'tis taken for any Wild Beast kill'd in hunting, and which are not Beasts of Forest or Chase, as *Squirrels, Goats, &c.* And *Hollingshed*, in his Description of *England, Pag.* 206. tells us, That, in the *East Countries*, the *Bear* is hunted, which is excellent *Venison.*

14. So that both the Words, *Venatio* and *Ferina*, in a general Sense, are taken for any Wild Beasts killed in hunting; but the Foresters and Forest-Lawyers do not take *Venatio* in that Sense, but only in a more restrained Sense; for such Beasts which are privileged in the King's Forests, and are therefore called, *Beasts of Forest*, or, *Beasts of Chase*, and no other.

15. Likewise the Word *Venison*, in a restrained Sense, is taken, by the Common People, for nothing else but the *Flesh of Red and Fallow Deer*, because that is usually eaten for *Venison.*

16. And though other Beasts of Forest and Chase are accounted *Venison* by the Foresters and others, because they make Sport in *Hunting*; yet because they are not *eaten*, therefore they are not accounted so by some Men.

17. 'Tis for this Reason that *Budeus* tells us, *Venison* is Two-fold, *viz.* Some Wild Beasts are accounted *Venison* for the Delicacy of their Flesh to be eaten, and others for the Sport and Pleasure which

which they make in *hunting*, and which are not eaten when killed.

18. *Præsentatum est per forestarios, &c. quod Gulielmus Fishborn est Communis Malefactor Venationis Domini Regis ubique in foresta illa & malefactoribus consentiens.*

Verderor.

See
Bail, 5, 6, 8, 9.
Attachment, 38.
Distress, 1, 2.
Dogs, 38.
Forest, 32.
Nusance, 11.
Officer, 5.
Presentment, 4, 7.
Rolls, 1.
Swanimote, 3.
Appendix, in Charta Canuti, 1, 6.
Appendix, Assisa Forestæ, 21.

1. A Verderor is a *Judicial Officer* of the King's Forest, chosen by his Writ in the full County in which the Forest is, and sworn to keep the Assises or Laws thereof; and also to view, receive and inroll the Attachments and Presentments of all manner of Trespasses of the Forest of *Vert* and *Venison*. 4. *Inst.* 291, 292.

2. He is called, in *Latin*, *Viridarius*, which is derived *à Viridi*, *Vert*, or *green Hue*, for his Office is principally concerned in looking after the *Vert* or *Green*, and to see it preserved.

3. The

3. The Definition above-mention'd may be explained by shewing,

1. In what Manner a Verderor is chosen.
2. The Form of his Oath.
3. The Extent of his Office.

4 (1) Upon a Certificate made to the King in his Court of Chancery, That *T. Barefoot*, one of the Verderors of the Forest of *Waltham*, is dead; he thereupon grants the Writ, *de Viridario Eligendo*, directed to the Sheriff of the County where the Forest is, thereby commanding him, in his full County, to choose another: The Writ is thus:

'5. ss. Georgius Dei gratia Magnæ Britanniæ, 'Franciæ & Hiberniæ Rex, Fidei Defensor, &c. 'Vic. Essex salutem. Quia Tho' Barefoot nuper 'unus Viridariorum nostrorum Forestæ nostræ de 'Waltham mortuus est, ut accepimus, ideo tibi 'præcipimus quòd si ita est, tunc in pleno Com' 'tuo de assensu ejusdem Com' loco prædict' Tho' 'Barefoot eligi facias unum alium Viridar' qui 'præstito sacramento prout moris est, extunc ea 'faceret & conservaret quæ ad officium Viridarii 'pertinent in Foresta prædictâ, tamen eum eligi 'facias qui melius sciat & possit officio illi intendere, & nomen ejus nobis scire facias: Teste, &c. 'F. N. B. 164.

The Form of his OATH.

6. (2) *YOU shall truly serve our Sovereign Lord the King in the Office of a Verderor in the Forest of* W. *You shall, to the uttermost of your Power, do the best you can for the Profit of the King so far as it doth appertain to you to do; you shall preserve the antient Rights and Franchises of the Crown; you shall*

not conceal from his Majesty any Rights and Privileges, nor any Offence in Vert or Venison, nor any other Thing: You shall not withdraw or abridge any Defaults, but shall endeavour your self to manifest and redress the same. And if you cannot do that of your self, you shall give Knowledge thereof to the King or to his Justice of the Forest. You shall deal indifferently with all the King's Liege People: You shall execute the Laws of the Forest, and do equal Right and Justice, as well unto the poor as to the rich, in that appertaineth unto your Office: You shall not oppress any Person by colour thereof, for any Reward, Favour, or Malice: All these Things you shall to the uttermost of your Power observe and keep: So help you God.

7. By the said Writ it appears, That a *Verderor* is to be chosen in full County by the Freeholders in the same manner as a *Coroner*; that when he is chosen, the Sheriff must give him the *Oath*; and when he is sworn, the said Sheriff must make his Return on the Writ, that by vertue thereof he hath caused an Election to be made, *&c.* and that *T. B.* is chosen, *&c.* which he must certify to the Court of *Chancery*: And in this manner, and no otherwise, a *Verderor* is made, as appeareth by the Ordinance of the Forest, made *Anno* 34 *Ed.* 1. *fo.* 11. *F. N. B.* 164.

8. (3.) The Person thus chosen ought to be an Esquire, or Gentleman of good Estate and Learned in the Laws of the Forest; and because he is chosen in the same manner as a *Coroner*, so in some respects their Office is alike; for as a *Coroner* is to make Inquest *super visum Corporis*, and upon the Oath of twelve Men, how and in what manner the Person was killed: So a *Verderor*, upon Notice given, is to view the Deer which are killed or hurt, and to take an Inquisition *per quatuor villatos propinquiores*

fe-

forestæ, how and by whom they were killed. *Assisa forestæ, Artic.* 7.

9. But his whole Office consists — *Ad* — *Videndum. Inquirendum. Recipiendum. Imbreviandum. Judicandum. Certificandum.*

1. He is to *view* the *Vert* and *Venison*; this appeareth in *Assisa Forestæ, Artic.* 3. *viz. Si quis inventus fuerit extra dominicum boscum, & infra Rewardum prosternens quercum sine visu aut liberatione Forestarii aut Viridarii, debet attachiari per quatuor plegios, & per visum Viridar. debet quercus appreciari, & in Rotulo Forestar. & Viridarior. nomina pleg. imbreviari:* And tho' a Man may fell Trees in his own Grounds for necessary Boots by the View of the *Verderors*, they ought to present what was felled, and that it was by *View*, that it may appear on Record. *Jones's Rep.* 295.

2. By *Assisa Forestæ, Artic.* 21. the Verderors ought to make *Inquisition* of all Trespasses in the Forest, as well as of those which concern *Vert* or *Venison.*

3. They ought to *take Inquests* of such Offences and Trespasses.

4. And by the Assises of the Forest they ought to *Inroll* them, and likewise their View and Price of all Trees felled.

5. His Office is likewise to *Judge* of Offences and Trespasses committed in the Forest, as in *Vert*, where the value is under 4 *d.* And by the Assises of *Lancaster* and *York, fo.* 11. the Entry is, *Præsentatum est per Forestarios & convictum per Viridarios:* By which it appears, that the Office of a Verderor is a *Judicial Office.*

6. So

6. So that his Office being to *view and receive* the Attachments of the Foresters, and to Inroll them in his Rolls; it followeth that the *Verderors* are to certifie those Rolls to the Justices of the Forest, at their next General Sessions or Eyre: *Assisa Forestæ, Artic.* 21.

7. *In Itinere* for the Forest of *Dean*, *An.* 10 *Car.* it was held by the Judges in Eyre, That where a Man is convicted of a Fact entered in the *Verderors* Rolls, it cannot afterwards be traversed; but the Defendant may plead any Collateral Matter, as a Pardon or a Release, or any other Thing precedent or subsequent to the Conviction; so that 'tis not directly contrary to that Fact of which he hath been convicted.

8. As in the Lady *Villars's* Case before mentioned; she was indicted and convicted by the *Verderors*, for cutting Trees in the Forest without Warrant: She pleaded a Grant to her of certain Lands *there*, and so justified the felling the Trees growing on those Lands: And this was held a good Discharge.

9. But in one *Gibbon's* Case, who was convicted for the same Fact; he pleaded a Grant of the *Lands and Trees* growing thereon; but did not set forth in his Plea, that the Lands were *within the Forest*, as the Lady *Villars* did; and therefore he could not cut Trees without the King's Leave. *Jones's Rep.* 347. *Kellew* 66.

10. If a *Verderor* is discharged from his Office by the King's Writ to the Sheriff upon a false Suggestion made, he may have a Commission out of the *Chancery* to inquire into the same, and to certify such Inquisition into that Court; or the Justices of the Forest may certify to the Court under their Seals, that the Suggestion is false: And in such Case a *Supersedeas* shall issue to the Sheriff not to remove

the

the *Verderor*, or if he is removed, then to restore him to his Office as before. *F. N. B.* 164.

11. A *Verderor*, and other *Ministers* of the Forest, are exempted from attending the *Assises*, or to be sworn of *Juries* there; for if he is summoned by the Sheriff, he may have a Writ by vertue of the Statute of 34 *Ed.* 1. by which they are exempted from all manner of Attendance there. *F. N. B.* 167. *a.*

12. There are usually in every Forest of the King four *Verderors*, and they are the Judges of the Court of *Swanimote*, and Directors of all the other Officers of the Forest in their Course; and therefore when that Court is held, one of them gives a Charge, which may be seen in Title *Fence-month*.

In clameo Burgens' de Scarborough, coram Dno. Willi Vesey Judiciar. Forestæ.

13. *Et quia Viridarii præd. nihil responderunt de transgr. venationis factis in foresta præd' hoc Anno, Ideo committuntur Prisonæ, Et educti venerunt & fecerunt finem per* 111 l.

14. *Abbas de Whitby clamat habere Viridarios suos proprios de libertate sua de Whitby eligend. de cætero in pleno Comitatu Eborum. prout moris est, ad responsiones & præsentationes faciend. de transgressionibus quæ amodo fieri contingent de viridi & venatione infra metas forestæ de Whitby, coram Justiciarius Domini Regis itiner. ad placita forestæ in partibus illis & non alibi, sicut Viridarii forestæ Domini Regis hujusmodi responsion. & representationes facere debent & consueverunt.*

Vert.

See { *Attachment*, 36.
Chief Justice, 9, 17.
Charge in Chief Justice, 1.
Nusance, 8, 16.
Prescription, 20.
Presentment, 12.
Regarder, 5, 6, 8.
Appendix, Charta Canuti, 21.
Appendix, Assisa Forestæ, 1, 2, 21.
Appendix, 1 Ed. 3.

1. THE Word *Vert* is derived *à Viriditate*, which signifies *Greenness*: The *French* call it *Verd*, and 'tis every green Tree in the Forest, which together with *Venison*, are the principal Ornament thereof; and therefore the Forest-Laws are very strict to preserve the *Vert*; for where that is plentiful, the *Venison* is likewise preserved; and nothing so much defaces the Forest as to cut down the *Covert*, which is the *Vert*; and for this and other Causes the Laws provide to preserve it with great care.

2. For 'tis the Nature of the Wild Beasts to frequent the *Coverts* and great *Woods*, where in the Winter they are sheltered from the Cold, and in the Summer from the Heat; and when they are hunted, they run thither for Protection.

3. The *Coverts*, *Woods*, and *Trees* in the Forest, especially those which are accompted *Vert*, bear several *Fruits* which serve to feed the Wild Beasts in the Winter, when there is very little Pasture for them elsewhere; for then they feed on Acorns, Haws, Sloes, and the like; and when such Fruits

are

are not sufficient, then those who have the Charge of them cut down the Branches of Trees (which is called Browse wood) to feed them: So that the *Vert* is not only a Shelter, but the Food of the Deer.

4. The *Vert* is preserved *propter decorem*, for 'tis a pleasant prospect for a Prince to see stately Trees, which grace the Forest; and Kings have often come thither, not only for the sake of Hunting, but to refresh themselves with such delightful Prospects. This we find *in Libro Rubro Scaccarii, viz. Quia in forestis penetralia Regum sunt, & eorum maxima deliciæ; ad has quidem venandi causa, curis quandoque depositis accedunt, ut modica quiete recreentur illic, seriis simul ac multis curiæ tumultibus omissis, in naturalis libertatis gratiam paulisper respirent, unde fit ut delinquentes in ea soli Regiæ subjaceant Animadversioni.*

5. It was a Question soon after the making of *Charta de foresta*, what should be accompted *Vert* by the Forest-Laws: Some were of Opinion that it was Trees which bore *Fruit* to feed the Deer, and that nothing else was *Vert*. But this Matter was cleared in the Reign of *Ed.* 1. *Rastall Abr. Stat.* Tit. *Forest* 41. who made this Law, *viz. Sciendum est quod omnes Arbores fructum non portantes, & hæ quæ fructum portant per totum annum, & fraxinus si antiqua fuerit in Foresta & in arabili, hæc existimabunt Viridia; quia Rex est in seisina:* Where the Words *Omnes Arbores* must be understood as well Underwood as Trees. *Hill.* 20. *H.* 6. *fo.* 22. 11 *H.* 4. *fo.* 32. *Case* 59.

6. So that *Vert* in general, is every *Tree*, *Underwood*, *Bush*, and such like, growing in a Forest, and bearing green Leaves, which may cover or feed the Deer.

How many Sorts of Vert there are, and the Punishment for cutting it.

7. (1.) There are two Sorts of *Vert* in every Forest, *viz.* *Over-Vert*, which the Lawyers call *Hault Bois*, and this is great Wood and Trees, as well those which bear no Fruit, as those which do, and old *Ashes* and *Hollies*, *&c.*

(2.) *Nether Vert*, which the Lawyers call *Sous Bois*, and that is properly all manner of *Underwood*, and all *Bushes*, *Thorns*, *Gorse*, and the like; and some are of Opinion, That *Fern* and *Heath* are *Nether Vert*; but that is a Mistake. *Fleetwood fo.* 4. *Hesket*, *fo.* 39.

8. However, 'tis not lawful for any Man to burn or destroy *Heath or Fern* in the Forest, because by the Assises, *&c.* 'tis accompted Covert for the Deer.

9. The Forest Lawyers make another Division of *Vert*, *viz.* *Special Vert*, which is every Tree and Bush in the Forest bearing Fruit to feed the Deer, as *Pear-trees*, *Crab-trees*, *Haw-thorns*, *Black-thorns*, and the like; and 'tis called *Special Vert*, because the Offence in destroying it is more severely punished than the destruction of any other *Vert*, according to the quantity thereof, as may be seen hereafter

10. And this *Special Vert* may be either *Over* or *Nether Vert*, or both if it bear Fruit, for nothing is accompted *Special Vert*, but such which beareth Fruit to feed the Deer, unless 'tis in the King's Woods.

11. It was adjudged in the Assises of *Pickering*, *Anno* 8 *Ed.* 3. That to cut down *Lignum Viride* or *Ramos Virides* in any Forest is an Offence finable; and he who selleth *Underwoods*, *Thorns*, *Elder-Trees*, *Boughs*, or *Lignum Siccum vel Ramos Siccos*, *vel* bu-

hujusmodi, is likewise a Trespasser in *Vert*, and finable.

12. *Hollinshead*, who was a Clergy-man and a Writer of our *English* History, *fo.* 153, tells us, That before the making *Charta de Foresta*, *viz.* *Anno* 10 *R.* 1. That King did constitute *Hugh* and *Gervas Nevil* and *Hugh Walley*, Justices Itinerants of his Forests, and commanded them to assemble the Prelates, Nobility and Freeholders, together with the Reeve, and four substantial Men of every Town or Village, to hear what he had given them in Charge concerning the Ordinances of the Forest, amongst which this was one, *viz.* That he who offended in cutting down Woods or Bushes, or in any other way destroying the same, should be fined: And this is Law to this Day, for it was not altered by *Charta de Foresta*, nor by any other subsequent Statute.

13. 'Tis true by the new Ordinances of the Forest, made *Anno* 6 *Ed.* 1. there are some new Offences made in *Vert*, *viz.* by cutting down *House-boot* or *Hedge-boot* within their own Woods, but no alteration was made of the Punishment, for these are Offences finable as those were before.

14. But the Punishment for killing Deer in the Forest, was altered by *Charta de Foresta*; for before that Law, a Trespasser in this Case was to lose either his *Eyes*, *Genitals* or *Life*; but this was taken away by that Statute, *viz.* *Nullus de cætero amittat vitam, vel membra pro venatione nostra.*

What is Vert in the King's Woods.

15. The King hath in every Forest some Woods of his own, and every Tree which grows therein, whether great Wood or small Wood, or whether it beareth Fruit or not, is accounted *Special Vert*.

16. And it was so accounted by the *Charter of the Forest*, granted by *Canutus*, *Canon* 28. *Bosco nec subbosco nostro sine Licentia primariorum Forestæ, nemo manum apponat, quod si quis fecerit, reus sit fractionis Regalis chaceæ.*

17. And as every Tree in the *King's own Woods* is special *Vert*, so 'tis privileged in a particular Manner; and therefore the Offenders in the *King's Vert* are more severely punished than those who offend in the *Vert of other Men.*

18. For whoever cuts *Bushes* or *Thorns* in the Forest and in the *King's Woods*, and carries them away with Cart and Horses, they are all to be seised to the King's Use; for both Cart and Horses are forfeited, and the Offender shall be likewise fined to the value of the Wood.

19: So if he carry away the *Vert* only on Horseback, he forfeits the Price of the *Vert*, and his Horse shall be seised to the King's Use.

20. Every small Tree or Bush growing on the *King's Land* in the Forest is *Special Vert*; so called, because the Offenders therein are more specially punished in manner as aforesaid, of which there are many Precedents in the Assises of *Pickering*, *Anno* 2 *Ed.* 3. and this is one.

21. *Præsentatum est per Forestarios, & convictum per viridarios, quod Humfredus Taber cepit undecim virides quercus infra Dominicum, precii cujuslibet* 1 *d & cariavit illas cum uno plaustro & sex Bobus ad sexdecim solid. pretii cujuslibet* 2 *s.* 8 *d. unde tenentes terræ & tenementorum Rich. de S. viridarii istius forestæ, ad cujus manus pretium præd. devenit, respondeant, & similiter pro forisfactura ejusdem, undecim solidos.*

22. By which Precedent this Difference may be observed, *viz.* That in every Presentment against an Offender in *Vert* in the *King's Woods*, 'tis said to be *infra Dominicum*; and in such Case the Cart

4 and

and Horses, or any other Thing drawing or carrying away such *Vert*, is forfeited to the King.

23. And the same Difference is taken in the Constitutions of the Forest, *Anno* 6 *Ed.* 1. concerning *Vert* in the *King's Woods*, where in every Branch or Article which relates to this Offence, you will find these Words, *Infra Dominicum*, and where they are omitted it concerns the *Vert* in *other Mens Lands*, and not in the King's.

What shall be Vert in the Woods of a Common Person.

24. The *Vert* of Common Persons is both the great Wood and Under-wood, called *Over and Nether Vert*; but there is no *Special Vert* out of the King's Woods, but such Trees which bear Fruit to feed the Deer. This appears by the Laws of *Canutus*, *Canon.* 29.

Si quis verò ilicem, aut arborem aliquam quæ victum feris suppeditat, sciderit, præter fractionem Regalis Chaceæ, emendet Regi viginti solidos.

25. And in the new *Ordinances* of the Forest, made *An.* 6 *Ed.* 1. *Si quis inventus fuerit extra Dom. Bosc. & infra Regardum, prostern. quercum sine visu vel liberatione Forestarii aut Viridarii, debet attachiari per quatuor plegios, & per visum Viridariorum debet quercus appretiari, & in Rotulo Forestar. & Viridar. nomina plegiorum imbreviari.*

26. So that an Oak, which beareth Acorns to feed the Deer, shall not be felled, tho' it grow in a Man's Freehold, without the Delivery of the Foresters and Verderors.

27. The same Law of every Tree which beareth Fruit; which Trees are called *Special Vert* for another Reason, *viz.* Because the Laws of the Forest do more specially regard the Preservation of them than of any other *Vert*; so that in the *King's Woods*, every Tree whatsoever is *Special Vert*; but

in the Woods of a *Common Person* 'tis otherwise, for no Tree is *Special Vert* there, unless it beareth Fruit to feed the Deer.

28. Now in some Cases, those Trees which are not *Special Vert*, and which grow on a Man's Freehold in the Forest may be cut down without Licence, *viz*. Such which stand scattering, and not together in great Numbers; and where the felling them doth not damnify any great Covert, tho' such cutting is still a Trespass in *Vert*, yet *de minimis non curat Lex*.

29. But where they stand together in great Numbers, there the cutting them without Licence is punishable, because the King by his Prerogative may use such Coverts to shelter his Wild Beasts, *Nec interest cujus sunt nemora sive Regis sive Procerum*; as it was adjudged in *Fithborn*'s Case, *in Assis. Lancastr: Anno* 8 *Ed*. 3. for his Beasts must have free Recourse there, and for that Reason the Woods must not be destroyed.

30. If any Man offend in cutting down *Vert* in the Forest, and *dieth* after 'tis presented; yet the King shall be answered for this Trespass either by the *Heirs* of the deceased or by the Tenants of his Lands. *Assis. Pickering, fo.* 22.

Warrants.

See { *Hunting*, 10.
Licence, per totum.
Purlieu, 108, 109. }

1. A Man may have a Right or Interest to have Yearly a Fee-Deer in a Forest, and this by Prescription; as belonging to his Office of Deputy-Warden or Verderor, *&c.*

2. And

2. And where ſuch Deer have been always taken, the Foreſter, who is to ſerve it, is to take Notice of them as good Warrants, and muſt ſerve them accordingly, as he likewiſe is bound to ſerve all lawful Warrants.

3. Now in this Caſe, he who is to have the Deer muſt give Notice to the Foreſter or Keeper, when and where he will have the Deer delivered, and deſire him to execute the Warrant accordingly.

4. And if after ſuch Notice, he refuſe or neglect to ſerve the Warrant, then the Perſon who is to have the Deer may enter into the Walk of ſuch Foreſter or Keeper with Servants to hunt, kill, and carry away the ſame, and juſtify the doing it, becauſe 'tis a *Warrant of Profit*, otherwiſe he could not hunt with his Servants.

5. For he who hath an Intereſt or Right to have the principal Thing, may uſe the neceſſary means to come to it: As for Inſtance, If I have a Grant of all the Trees growing in *Alton Woods*; by this Grant I have an Intereſt in them, and therefore I may enter into the Wood and cut and carry away the Trees thro' the Ground of the Grantor, and juſtify the doing it. *Perkins*, *fo.* 23. *Fitz.* Tit. *Bar*, 237.

6. *In Mich.* 13 *H.* 7. *fo.* 10. an Action of Treſpaſs was brought againſt the Defendant for hunting in a Park; who pleaded, That the Plaintiff being the Owner of the ſaid Park gave a Buck to *B.* and he as a Servant of the ſaid *B.* and by his command came with him to the Park to hunt and kill the Buck: By vertue whereof he entered, *&c* and there did kill the ſame, as it was lawful for him to do. And the Court held this to be a good Juſtification; by which it appears, That where a Man hath an Intereſt or Right to have a Deer, he may juſtify both for himſelf and *Servants* to kill and carry away. *Hill*, 13 *H*, 7. *fo.* 13. *placito* 2. like Caſe.

7. For

7. For where a Man hath a *Right*, and the Forester or Keeper refuses to deliver it; in such Case, if he could not justify the necessary Acts and Circumstances to come at that Right, he would be without Remedy; and therefore if the Forester or Keeper complain of such hunting and taking the Deer, either before the Justice in Eyre, or any other Officer of the Forest, the Person, by pleading, may justify it; for 'tis no Offence or Breach of the Laws of the Forest, the Words being, *Si quis ceperit feram sine Warranto in foresta, corpus suum arrestetur, &c.* From which it may be inferr'd, That he may take Deer, if he hath a good Warrant. *Assisa forestæ, Artic.* 10.

8. The Validity of every Warrant must be determined in the Justice-Seat; at which Time the *Chief Forester* must give an Account of all Deer which have been killed by Warrant; and for those Warrants which have been served, and not good, the Forester shall be punished. *Itin. Pick. fo.* 6.

Warren.

See { *Chase*, 13. *Forest*, 39. *Inclosures*, 7. *Prescription*, 21, 22, 23.

1. A *Warren* is a Place privileged for Beasts and Fowls of *Warren* only; and those are the *Hare*, *Coney*, *Pheasant*, and *Partridge*: 1 *Inst.* 233. and those Warrens which are in Forests, are either by *Grant* or *Prescription*.

2. If by the King's *Grant*, then the Words are, *Quod ipse & hæredes sui habeant liberam Warrenam in omnibus dominicis terris suis in* N. *in Com'* B. *dum tamen feræ illæ non sint infra metas forestæ nostræ, ita quod*

quod nullus intret terras illas ad fugandum in eis, vel aliquod capiend' quod ad Warrenam pertinet.

3. And this is called, a *free* or *Charter Warren*; and every such *Charter* would be very uncertain by the Words, *Quod ad Warrenam pertinet*, if it was not certainly known what were Beasts and Fowls of Warren; and therefore, in the Register in the Writ of Trespass for hunting in a Warren, 'tis averred, That the Trespass was done therein taking or driving away those Beasts or Fowls which are Beasts and Fowls of Warren, which, as *Budæus* tells us, are such which may be taken by long-wing'd Hawks; and those are the *Hare*, the *Coney*, the *Pheasant*, and the *Partridge*. *Reg.* 93. 69. *Lib. Int.* 585. *Tit. Hunting*, 2, 3. *Mich.* 3 *H.* 6. *fo.* 28. *Hill.* 34 *H* 6. *fo.* 34 *F. N. B.* 86, 87.

4. *Warren* may be by *Prescription*, but not without the help of an Allowance in Eyre, and then a Grant is supposed: *Jones*, 272. This was Sir *Richard Harrison's* Case, *in Itinere Windsor*, *fo.* 280. who prescribed to have a Warren in that Forest; but it not being allowed in Eyre, he was fined 10 *s.* and ordered, that the Warren should be destroyed.

5. In *Pascha* 5 *Jacobi*. All the Judges were assembled to resolve certain Questions concerning Forests and Chases, and amongst other Resolutions reported by my Lord *Coke*, 12 *Rep.* 22. this was one, *viz.* That he who hath any Freehold in a *free Chase*, may have a *Warren* there, either by Grant or Prescription; and he who hath such a *Warren* may keep Conies, and may lawfully build a convenient Lodge in his Inheritance there to preserve the Game; and if he hath the *Warren* by *Prescription*, he may not make Cony-burrows, but in such Places where they usually were made; but if by *Grant*, then he may make them where he will.

6. And because *Conies* are the most common Beasts of *Warren*, therefore several Laws have been made

made to preserve them; and particularly the Statute of 1 *H.* 7. *cap.* 7. prohibits hunting in *Warrens* with *painted Faces*, or other Disguises in the *Night-time*, which was commonly done in those Days.

7. If the Offender, in such case, is taken, and being brought before a Justice of Peace, and, upon Examination, denieth or concealeth the Hunting, 'tis Felony; but if he confesseth, then 'tis only finable at the next Sessions. 2 *Rolle's Rep.* 133.

8. But then, upon such Confession, he may be bound to his Good Behaviour with Sureties, or he may be committed by the Justice, because it might happen that he may not be found if any *Concealment* should be afterwards proved against him.

9. By the Statute of 3 *Jac.* 13. 'tis enacted, That if a Man enters wrongfully into any *Ground inclosed*, and *per Statute* 23 *Car.* 2. *cap.* 25. Though 'tis *not inclosed*, and where *Conies* are usually bred, and there chaseth, taketh or killeth them, he shall be committed for three Months, and afterwards pay treble Damages to the Owner of the *Warren*, to be assessed by the Justice, before whom the Party is convicted, and must find sureties for his Good Behaviour for Seven Years.

10. He who *kills* or *takes* Conies in the *Night-time*, upon the *Borders* of Warrens, must pay to the Party grieved what the Justice shall think fit, before whom he was convicted; and shall likewise pay any Sum not exceeding 10 *s.* to the Overseer of the Poor of the Parish where the Offence was committed, for the Use of the Poor People there; or otherwise must be sent to the House of Correction for any Time not exceeding one Month.

11. The Manner of Conviction is appointed by these Statutes, *viz.* Either by the Confession of the Offender, or by the Oath of one sufficient Witness, made before a Justice of the Division, &c. within a Month after the Offence committed.

12. The

12. The Party may appeal from such Conviction to the Sessions, whose Determination shall be final.

13. It hath been a Question, Whether a Man could kill Conies feeding in a *Common*, and by that Means destroying it? It was agreed, That the Commoner had no other Remedy; and yet it was formerly held, That he could not kill them, because the *Property of the Soil* was in the Lord of the Manor; and so long as his Conies were on his own Ground, though they are *feræ Naturæ*, they may be properly called, *Cuniculos suos*; for the *Commoner* hath no manner of Property in them, either *ratione soli*, or otherwise; he hath nothing to do with the Land, but to put in his Cattle to Common there; and therefore he could not kill the Conies. 4 *Leon* 7.

14. But the Law is otherwise; for no Man can tell whose Conies they are when in a *Common*: And because they are *feræ Naturæ*, the Lord hath no Property in them when out of the *Warren*; and therefore the Commoner may kill them, for he hath no other Remedy to preserve his Common from them; he cannot have an Action on the Case, because that would create Multiplicity of Actions, which the Law will not suffer. 2 *Cro.* 195. *Cro. Car.* 388.

25. 'Tis true, in *Hyndley* and *Wilkinson*'s Case, the Plaintiff did recover in such an Action; but upon a Writ of Error brought, that Judgment was reversed. *Jones*'s *Rep.* 356. *Cro. Car.* 387. 1 *Roll. Abr.* 405.

16. In the Case of *Grisell* and Sir *Thomas Leigh*, it was resolved, That if a Man is seised of a Manor, and the Tenants have Right of *Common* in the waste Ground there, and the King grants, that the Lord of that Manor shall have a *Warren* in such a Part thereof; yet he cannot put in Conies in the

Waste,

Waste, to prejudice his Tenants in their Commons there: This was in an Action of Trespass. *Jones's Rep.* 12. *Winch.* 16.

Waste in Forests.

1. WASTE is derived from the *French*, *Gaster*; in *Latin*, *Vastare*, and it properly signifies a Spoil and Destruction in the *Coverts* and Pastures of the Forest.

2. To fell or cut down any *Woods* which grow scattering, or any thick Covert in the Forest, though on a Man's own Inheritance, yet if done without Licence of the Chief Justice in Eyre, or View of the Foresters, 'tis *Waste*.

3. There is a great Difference between *Waste* at Common Law, and *Waste* by the Laws of the Forest, I mean in respect of the Persons by whom 'tis punished; for at Common Law, no Man is punishable in an Action of Waste, but he who hath a particular Estate in the House or Land, as Tenant for Term of Years, or for Life, and he is punishable only by him who hath the *Inheritance*; but by the Forest-Laws, if he who hath the Inheritance doth make Waste in the Forest, he is punishable by the King, and by no other Person.

4. There is a Difference likewise between *Destruction* and *Waste* in a Forest; for every *Destruction* of the Covert is *Waste*, and perpetually so; but every *Waste* is not *Destruction*; for a Man may fell his Woods and destroy the Covert for a time, and by preserving the Fences, the same may be Coverts again.

5. But if the Owner of such Woods is negligent, or doth not sufficiently preserve the *Fences*, after his Woods are so felled without Licence, that they

may

may grow again, and that, in a short time, this is Waste.

6. This Difference between *Destruction* and *Waste*, is warranted by *the Assises of Woodstock, Artic.* 1. in the Reign of *H.* 2. in these Words; *viz. Defendit Dominus Rex quod nullus donet, vel vendat aliquod ad destructionem Bosci sui, vel ad Vastum si sit infra forestam Regis, &c.* where, by the Disjunctive *Vel*, it appears, That *Destructio* and *Vastum* are different Offences.

7. So that though the Fences are preserved after the Woods are cut that they may grow again; yet this is *Waste*, but no *Destruction*, because the Woods are not quite destroyed, but may grow, being preserved from the Cattle.

8. Like the Case in *Mich.* 20 *H.* 6. *fo.* 1. *placito* 5. If Tenant for Life cut down and sell them, 'tis Waste, though they grow again: So 'tis by the Forest-Law, If a Man cut down Covert in the Forest without Licence, 'tis Waste, though it grow again.

9. But if a Man hath a *Licence* to sell Woods which are Coverts in a Forest, and he selleth them, but doth not make *Fences* to preserve the Sprouts, so that they are eaten and destroyed by the Cattle that they never grow again; this is *Waste* and *Destruction*; and so it is if he sell them at unseasonable Times, and they die and grow no more.

10. There is also some Difference in the Manner of pleading; for, in an Action of *Waste*, at Common Law, 'tis said, *Quod idem, R. B fecit Vastum venditionem & Destructionem, &c. ad exhaereditationem ipsius, W. N.* but in an Indictment against the Defendant for destroying the Covert in a Forest, 'tis said, *Quod Johannes Melsa de Preston, &c. succidit Boscos suos de Trowesdale infra forestam de Pickering, sine Warranto Domini Regis, ad Vastum &*

De-

Destructionem cooperti ejusdem forestæ, & ad exilaonem ferarum Domini Regis. Assisa Pickering, fo. 24. *In libro Intrationis, fo.* 16. *Tit Waste,* 1.

11. But if the Coverts are quite destroyed, so that they cannot grow again, then the Form of the Indictment is, *Quod Johannes Melsa vastavit & & destruxit Boscos & Coopertum ejusdum forestæ in Trovesdale, &c. ad Destructionem ejusdem Bosci & Cooperti imperpetuum, & ad magnam exilationem ferarum Domini Regis. Assisa forestæ de Pickering, fo.* 25, 26. Both which Precedents shew, that a *Waste* and *Destruction* in a Forest are different Things.

12 And as at Common Law 'tis *Waste* for a Lessee for Years, willingly, to suffer a Meadow to be drowned, which makes it barren and full of Rushes; or if he convert Meadow into Arable, the same is likewise *Waste* by the Forest-Law. *Mich.* 20 *H.* 6. *fo.* 1. *placito* 5.

13. So if the People of a *Township* commit Waste in the *green Hue* of the Forest, the whole Town shall be fined, *viz. de Villata de D.* 5 *l.*

The Forfeiture and Punishment of those who commit Waste in a Forest.

14. He who commits Waste, either by felling Trees, or destroying any Covert or Wood, is to be fined by the Chief Justice in Eyre, and the whole Wood or Place so wasted, shall be seized for the Use of the King; and so it shall remain till the Owner hath paid the Fine; and if the Offender dieth before any Presentment be made of the Offence, yet the *Heir* shall be fined, and the Land seized till he pay the Fine. *Anno* 8 *Ed.* 3. *Assisa Pickering, fo.* 22.

15. The like Law when the *Waste* in a Forest is done by plowing any Meadow; but in these

Cases

Cases the Land is not forfeited, 'tis only to be seised, and so continue till the Offender hath paid a Fine.

16. Now this Fine is neither certain, nor altogether arbitrary, because the Number of Acres contained in the Place wasted, are mention'd in the Indictment or Presentment; and usually the Chief Justice in Eyre doth assess the Fine according to the Number of those Acres; and not only the Number, but the Value of such Acres wasted, is likewise set forth in the Indictment; in which Indictment these Things are specially to be considered:

1. Who made the Waste.
2. What manner of Waste it was.
3. When it was done.
4. Where the Ground is in which it was done.
5. In whose Tenure it was at that Time.
6. What Number of Acres it doth contain.
7. What every Acre is worth to be sold.
8. Whether it is Waste or Destruction, or both.
9. In whose Fee it is, and in what Parish.
10. Whose Inheritance it is.

17. 'Tis Waste to cut down Trees in a Forest; and if the King pardons *Transgressions*, this doth not pardon the Waste; and so it was adjudged in Sir *Walter Titchburne*'s Case, *in Itinere Windsor*, *Jones's Rep.* 279.

Woods in Forests.

See { *Boundaries*, 35, 36.
Charge in Chief Justice, 68, 69, 70, 71, 72, 73, 75.
Prescription, 2, 3. 5, 9.
Purlieu. 121, 122.
Purpresture, 41.
Regarder, 30, 31, 32, 33.
Vert, per Totum.
Waste, per Totum.
Appendix, Ch. forestæ, 3, 4.
Appendix, Assisa forestæ, 3, 6.
Appendix, Ordinatio forestæ, 4.
Appendix, Stat. 1 Ed. 3.

1. 'TIS necessary, that there should be Woods in every Forest, both to *shelter*, and, at some Times, to *feed* the Deer; and therefore the Laws of the Forest have, in a particular Manner, provided for the Preservation of the Trees and Coverts there.

2. But they make some Difference between *Woods* and *Coverts*; for where the Trees grow scattering, and at such a Distance that they do not touch one another, such Places are properly called Woods.

3. *Coverts* are those Woods which are *Thickets*, and full of Trees touching one another, which, in *Latin*, are called, *Impeditissimæ Sylvæ*; and *Cicero* calls it, *Latibulum*, and sometimes *Dumetum*; *Budæus* calls it *Umbraculum*; and the old Foresters call it *Covert*; for as they call *Vert*, *à Viriditate*, so likewise by the Word *Covert*, they understand alll those Trees and Woods which grow thick together, deriving the Word from the *French Couvert*, which signifies a Covering or Hiding-place for the Deer.

4. Un-

4. Under this Title may be comprehended those Woods and Coverts which properly belong to the *King*, as growing on his *own Lands* in the Forests, and those Woods and Coverts which grow on the Lands of any of his *Subjects* there.

5. As concerning Woods and Trees growing on the *King's own Lands* in his Forests, some Questions were made in the Reign of King *James*, between the Earl of *Nottingham*, then Justice in Eyre of all his Forests, and the Earl of *Dorset* then Lord Treasurer of *England*, about the Disposal of such Trees; and all the Judges of *England* were assembled by the King's Command, who, upon Conference amongst themselves, and a mature Deliberation, resolved these four Points following, and relating to Woods and Trees:

1. That the Justices in Eyre, and the King's Officers in the Forest, have Charge of *Venison*, *Vert* and *green Hue*, for the Maintenance and Preservation of the King's Game; and of all manner of *Trees* for *Covert*, *Browse* and *Pannage*; but when there is Occasion to sell Woods in the Forest, or Timber for the King's Use, it must be taken and sold by Authority under the Great Seal, or Exchequer-Seal, by the View of the Forester, that it may not be taken in Places inconvenient for the Game; but the Justices in Eyre, or any of the King's Officers in the Forest, cannot sell or dispose of any Wood in the Forest, without Commission; and so the Exchequer and the Foresters have *divisum imperium*, the one for the Profit, and the other for the Pleasure, of the King.

2. That, regularly, neither the Court of Exchequer, nor any of the King's Officers, can dispose of the King's Timber or Woods; but

it ought to be done by Commission, and for his best Profit.

3. That every Man in his *own Woods* in the Forest, may take *House-bote* and *Hay-bote*, by the View of the Foresters: And the King's Farmers, who have Authority, by their Leases, to take Timber by View, *&c.* may take the same accordingly; and so may the Freeholders by *Prescription*; and also Copyholders who, by Custom, have used to take *House-bote, &c.* they may take the same by View of the Foresters or others, according to the Custom. 1 *Ed.* 3. *Stat.* 2.

4. It was resolved, That no Officer of the Forest could claim *Wind-falls*, or Dotard-Trees by *Prescription* for their Fees, because they were once parcel of the King's Inheritance; but they ought to be sold by Commission for the Benefit of the King. *Itin. Pickering*, 8 *Ed.* 3. *Rot.* 30. in the Case of *William de Persey*, and *Petronilla* his Wife.

Upon this Resolution of the Judges, the following Order was made by the Court of Exchequer:

The Order of the Exchequer about Woods and Trees in the King's Forests.

'6. WHereas heretofore some Question hath 'been mov'd between the Lord Trea'surer of *England*, and the Warden and Chief 'Justice, and Justice Itinerant of all the King's Fo'rests, Chases, Parks and Warrens on this side *Trent*, 'what apperteineth to each of their Offices and 'Places concerning the dealing with, and disposing 'of Woods, Trees and Coppices within his High'ness's Parks, Forests and Chases, which being, 'by his Majesty, referred to the Consideration and 'De-

Determination of his Judges and Barons, they have resolved concerning the same, by one uniform Assent, as followeth:

'ſſ. That as the Lord Treasurer of *England* for the Time being, and Court of Exchequer, have the only ordinary Power under the King, to deal therein, so far forth as it concerns the Inheritance and Profit of the Crown, as in the Sale of Woods, Trees and Coppices, and such like; so, in like manner, it concerns the Warden and Chief Justice, and Justice Itinerant of all the King's Forests, Chases, Parks and Warrens, and their Ministers, to deal therein so far as it may concern the Preservation and Maintenance of the Game, in respect of the Shades, Coverts, Pannage, and such like, for the Deer; and therefore it was resolved by all their Opinions, That the Lord Treasurer of *England*, and Court of Exchequer, may not sell any Woods or Coppices within any the King's Parks, Forests or Chases, (except Wind-falls, Root-falls, and meer dead and sear Trees) without the Privity and Allowance of the said Warden, and Chief Justice, and Justice Itinerant within whose Jurisdiction it is; nor may cut down the dead and sear Trees, nor carry them or Wind-falls, or Root-falls away, but at fit Times, and by the View of such as have Charge of the Game; so that the same may be seen to be done at fit and convenient Times; and that no Trees, other than those which are dead, and sear, and meerly Wind-falls and Root-falls, may be thrown or taken away without the Privity and Allowance of the Warden and Chief Justice, and Justice Itinerant of his Majesty's Parks, Forests or Chases.

'And for the Warden and Chief Justice and Justice Itinerant, and the Keepers and other Ministers of Parks, Forests and Chases belonging to 'the King, they may not cut down any Trees for 'new Paling or Railing, or for repairing of Lodges 'without the Warrant and Allowance of the Lord 'Treasurer of *England* for the time being; but 'Timber needful for mending small Defects in old 'Pales or Rails broken, so as the same do not ex'ceed two or three Timber Trees in any one Fo'rest, Park or Chase in any one Year, they may 'be permitted to take off Trees in Places fit, with'out making any Waste thereof, or any Spoil or 'Prejudice to the King's Inheritance, acquainting 'the King's Surveyor of his Woods therewith, 'who is to see, that the same hath been accord'ingly well employed; and needful Browse also 'in fit Places and seasonable Times, the Keepers 'may take for the Deer, not cutting down the 'Limbs or great Boughs of the Trees. And there'fore 'tis ordered by this Court, That from hence'forth, where it shall be thought requisite to fell 'any of the King's Woods or Coppices within 'any Parks, Forests or Chases, that a Writ or 'Commission in Nature of an *Ad quod damnum*, 'shall be directed to the Warden and Chief Jus'tice, and Justice Itinerant within the Forests, in 'whose Government the same is to be done, to in'quire and certify what number of Trees and Cop'pices may be sold; and in what Places, to the 'least prejudice to the King's Game: And that up'on the Return thereof, the Sale shall be made of 'such Trees and Coppices, as upon true Certifi'cate shall be thought fit to be sold: And in like 'manner 'tis ordered, That for the new Paling 'and new Railing and new Building of Lodges, in 'any Place in or about any of his Majesty's Parks, 'Forests, or Chases, and the great Repairs of 'old Pales, Rails, or Lodges in or about the same, 'that it is to be done upon Certificate from the 'Warden, and Chief Justice, and Justice Itine-

'rant

'rant, and the Surveyor of his Majesty's Woods, 'within whose Jurisdiction it is, by a Warrant 'from the Lord Treasurer of *England* for the 'Time being.

8. *Concerning Woods and Coverts which grow on the Lands of any Subject in the King's Forests*, they must not be cut down without *View of the Forester*, and Licence of the Chief Justice in Eyre, tho' they grow on his own Freehold; and so it was adjudged in the Reign of *Ed.* 1. *Fitz. Abr.* Tit. *Trespass*, 239.

9. The like was ordained, *Anno* 1 *Ed.* 3. *ca.* 2. *viz. That every Man who hath Woods of his own in any Forest, may take them without being attached by any Officer of the Forest, so that he do it by the View of the Foresters.* And the Reason is, because they know the Want or Plenty of other Coverts near it; but they cannot Licence any Man to cut down Wood; for that must be done by the Lord Chief Justice in Eyre, and no Man else can do it but the King.

10. *Anno* 9 *&* 10 *Eliz. Plowd. Com. fo.* 332. in a Case concerning the felling Woods in *Waltham* Forest, *Wray*, Chief Justice, was of Opinion, That if a Manor in the King's Forest escheats to him, and afterwards he grants the same to another in Fee; the Grantee hath not that Liberty which the King had in the Manor concerning the Forest; for notwithstanding the Grant, the King's Deer must feed there still; neither can the Grantee cut down Woods which are in the Forest without Licence of the Justice in Eyre; for that is a Thing collateral to the Soil, and Things of Prerogative, or Liberties which are collateral to the Soil, will not pass by a *Grant* thereof.

11. By which Case it appears, That a Man who hath Lands in the King's Forest must hold them

subject to the Laws thereof, unless they are exempted by some good Title; for the wild Beasts must be preserved there, which cannot be done without Coverts to rest and abide in; and therefore the King hath a Prerogative over the Woods of every Man within the Forest, so that they may not be felled without the Licence of the Chief Justice of the Forest.

12. Neither can any Man cut his own Woods in a Forest for necessary *Boots*, without *View of the Foresters*: This appears by the new Ordinances of the Forest, made *Anno* 6 *Ed.* 1. *Artic.* 6. *in Rast. Abr. Stat.* Tit. *Forest* 21. *viz. Libertatis autem House-boot & Hay-boot, fiat prout Boscus pati potest in statu quo est, & non ad exigentiam petentis, nec potest aliquid dare nec vendere de Bosco sine Warranto Domini Regis.*

13. But my Lord *Coke*, 4 *Inst.* 298. tells us, That a Man may prescribe to take and cut down Timber Trees in his own Woods in a Forest, without the View of the Forester, notwithstanding the Ordinance of 34 *Ed.* 1. and notwithstanding the Statute of 1 *Ed.* 3. *cap.* 2. because that Ordinance is no Statute; and the Act of 1 *Ed.* 3. is but in Affirmance of the Common Law; and that a Man may prescribe against all Statutes, which are only Declarative *antiqui juris*, and not introductory *novi juris*.

14. 'Tis true, the Chief Justice *Richardson* and Mr. Attorney *Noy*, *in Itinere Windsor*, *Jones* 271. held, That a Man cannot prescribe against a Negative Statute; and therefore a Prescription to fell Wood in a Forest without Foresters, could not be good, except it was with the help of an Allowance in Eyre: And in such Case the Court must intend a *Grant* upon which the first Allowance was made.

15.

15. But Mr. *Attorney* was of Opinion, That a *Prescription* for *House-Boot* and *Hay-boot* might be good without View of the Foresters, because of the Necessity of such *Boots*; and it may not be convenient at all Times to seek after the Foresters: Besides the Negative Words of this Statute, *viz. Nec potest aliquid dare vel vendere de bosco sine Licentia Regis*, do not extend to those Cases.

16. But he was of Opinion, That *per visum* only was not good, for it ought to be *per visum & allocationem Forestariorum & Viridariorum*: For if it be *per visum*, omitting the other Word *allocationem*; then if a Forester is required to come and view the Place, and he refuse to come, the Person might cut down the Woods without View, which is contrary to the Laws of the Forest, and for this, one *Leicester*'s Case was cited in the Dutchy. *Jones Rep.* 275.

17. This Opinion is contrary to Sir *Thomas Palmer*'s Case, 5 *Rep.* 25. where it was held, That there is no material Difference between the Words *per visum*, and the Clause *per visum & allocationem Forestariorum*; for in both Cases upon a Request, and Refusal made, the Party may take the Thing without View or Delivery.

18. *In Itinere Windsor*, *Jones* 275. the Inhabitants of *Egham*, *&c.* prescribed to cut down their *Coppices* in that Forest at Pleasure: And in the same *Iter*, the Tenants of the Manor of *Bray*, which was *antient Demesne*, prescribed to sell their Woods at Pleasure, without View of the Foresters, notwithstanding the Negative Words in the Statute before mentioned. And to maintain this *Prescription*, their Counsel argued, That there was a manifest Difference between a Negative Statute declaratory of the Common Law, and the like Statute introductory of a new Law; for against the last no *Prescription* is good; but where the Statute is Negative, but

only

only declareth the old Law, there no Alteration is made; and therefore a *Prescription* may be as well against it as against the Common Law, which is the Reason a Man may prescribe to hold a Leet more than twice in a Year, tho' the Statute *de Magna Charta* is in the Negative, *viz.* That a Leet be held only twice in a Year.

And they cited a Case in 8 *Ed.* 3. *Itinere Pickering*, *Co. Lit.* 115. wherein *Thomas Wake* of *Lidham*, prescribed to cut Wood without View, and Issue was joined on that Prescription; and so is *Gilbert de Acton's* Case there.

19. And likewise *Henry Piercy's* Case in the same *Iter*, where the Lord of the Manor of *Seymour* claimed to cut his Wood without View; and Issue was likewise joined upon that Prescription and found for him, and afterwards allowed in the *King's Bench*.

20. And another Case, *Hill.* 19 *Ed.* 1. *Rot.* 58. between a Prebendary of *Chichester* and the Earl of *Arundel*, where Issue was joined upon the like Prescription.

21. And lastly a Case, *Anno* 6 *Eliz.* reported by the Chief Justice *Popham*, That a Prescription to cut down Wood without View was good.

22. To which Mr. Attorney answered, That a Prescription to cut down Wood, *&c.* was not good, because there can be no such Prescription since the Stat. of *Charta de Foresta*: For in *Artic.* 4. 'tis enacted, That all Wastes done after that Time, without the King's Licence, shall be punishable.

23. He agreed, That a Prescription to cut down Wood in a *Chase* without View, *&c.* might be good, because Chases are not within that Statute of *Charta de Foresta*: and so it was resolved, *Anno* 6. *Jac.* *Jones* 276. but he disallowed the Difference taken by my Lord *Coke*, between a Negative Statute introductory of a new Law, and where 'tis declaratory

tory of the old Law; and therefore he cited a Case, 20 *H.* 6. That tho' the Statute *de sylva cædua* is only declaratory of the old Law, *viz.* That Tithes ought not to be paid of Timber-Trees; yet that Statute being in the Negative, a Prescription to have Tithe of Timber is not good.

24. As to the Case, 8 *Ed.* 3. and *Piercy*'s Case, they were adjudged *in Itinere Pickering*, and therefore did not come up to the Cases in Question; because *H.* 3. gave the Forest of *Pickering* to his Son *Edmond* Duke of *Lancaster*; and so that Forest was out of the Crown, and in the Possession of a Subject when the Statute *de consuetudinibus & Assisis Forestæ* was made; and when a Forest is in the Hands of a Subject, any Man may cut his Woods there at Pleasure.

25. As for that Record cited 19 *Ed.* 1. between a Prebendary of *Chichester* and the Earl of *Arundel*; the Prescription was to fell Woods in a *Chase*, and the Statute *de Cons. & Assisis Forestæ*, relates only to Forests, and doth not extend to Chases.

26. And as for the Case, *Anno* 6 *Eliz.* reported by the Chief Justice *Popham*, that was likewise a Prescription to fell Wood in a *Chase*, whereof the King was seised in Right of his Dutchy of *Lancaster*: and no Man can shew any such Prescription to be good, except in the Cases of *Chases* as aforesaid, or those which have been adjudged in the *Iters of Pickering* Forest.

27. And he argued, That no Liberty in a Forest could be good by Prescription, which went either to the Destruction of the *Vert* or *Game*, unless they could shew an Allowance of it in a former Eyre, except only in the Case of *Common*, which is an equitable *Prescription*; and upon the Matter 'tis of Common Right, for 'tis reasonable, that since the Deer have fed on the Owners Grounds,

Grounds, that they should have *Common* in the plain Places of the Forest.

28. But *Popham*, Chief Justice, was of another Opinion, as 'tis reported by my Lord *Coke*, 12 *Rep. fo.* 23. *viz.* he cited one *St. Leger*'s Case in the *Exchequer*, who prescribed to cut Wood in the Forest of *Hay*, in the County of *Hereford*, and it was adjudged in the Time of the Chief Baron *Bret*, That such a Prescription to cut Wood in a Forest, growing on his own Inheritance, is good, altho' it was against the Ordinance of 43 *Ed.* 1. because that was only a Declaration of the Common Law, and it might be tolled by Custom. 2 *Ed.* 2. Tit. *Trespass*, *fo.* 9.

Ed. 1. *Trespass* 239. *Plow. Com. Dyer* 72, 322. *Ed*, 4. *cap.* 7. For, *consuetudo ex rationabili causa usitata privat Communem Legem.*

29. The Franchise of the Forest consists in *Vert* and *Venison*; now he who prescribes to have any profit in the Freehold or Inheritance of another, ought to make his Prescription in such manner as not utterly to exclude the Owner, and so must he who makes any Claim out of the Lands of another.

30. As for instance, in 2 *Co. fo.* 155. 'tis reported, That all the Judges of *England* were assembled by the King's Command in *Serjeants-Inn*, to confer of Matters concerning his Forest of *Leicester*, which he had in Right of his Dutchy of *Lancaster*; and it was by them resolved, That the Owners of Woods, growing in the Forests or Chases of a *Common Person*, and not of the *King*, may cut them down at their Pleasure, without Licence or View of the Forester; but yet so as they leave sufficient *Vert* there for the Deer.

31. The like Resolution was made in *Easter-Term*, 5 *Jac.* 12 *Rep. fo.* 22. in a Case concerning the same Forest, and likewise in a Case concerning the Forest of *Bowland* in *Warwickshire*, *viz.*

That

That the *Owners of any Freehold in free Chases*, and which are not Forests, may cut their Timber and Wood growing there, without any View or Licence of any Person whatsoever: But if he cut so much, that there is not sufficient left for the *Covert* and to maintain the King's *Game*, he shall be punished at the Suit of the King.

32. And so if a *Common Person* hath a *Chase* in the Soil of another, the Owner of that Soil cannot destroy all the *Coverts*, but ought to leave sufficient *Covert* and *Browse-wood* as usual.

33. The Lord of a Forest may by his Officers enter into any Man's Wood growing within the Regard of his Forest, and cut down *Browse-wood* for the Deer in Winter. *Assisa Pickering*, *fo.* 19.

34. And if any Man make Charcoal of *Browse-wood* in the Forest he is finable. *Assisa Pickering*, *fo.* 10. and if he make Title to it by *Prescription*, but doth not make his Claim the first Day of the *Justice-Seat*, he shall answer the value of the Coals to the King.

How Men may cut down Woods on their own Lands in the King's Forests.

35. Where a Man hath Woods in the King's Forest, and hath no such Prescription, as before mentioned; yet the Law affords him a Remedy and Means to fell his Wood and Timber there, so as it be no prejudice to the Game, but that sufficient is left standing.

38. And in order thereunto he must petition the King, who will cause a Writ of *Ad quod damnum* to be directed to the Chief Warden of the Forest, or to his Deputy, in these Words,

'Georgius, Dei gratia, Magnæ Britanniæ, Franciæ, & Hiberniæ Rex, fidei Defensor, &c. Dilecto

'tecto & fideli suo A. B. Custodi Forestæ suæ ci-
'tra Trentam, salutem: Mandamus vobis, quod
'per sacramentum tam Forestariorum quam Viri-
'dariorum Forestæ nostræ de W. quam aliorum,
'proborum & legalium hominum de partibus illis,
'per quos rei veritas melius sciri poterit inquiratis,
'si sit ad dampnum seu nocumentum Forestæ nostræ
'prædict' aut alicujus alterius si concedamus R. B.
'quod ipse arbores in Bosco suo de M. qui est in-
'fra metas Forestæ nostræ præd', succidere, & eas,
'quo voluerit, cariare, ac commodum suum inde
'facere, & solum illud postmodum assartare & in
'culturam redigere, ac parvo fossato & bassa Haia
'secundum assisam Forestæ, includere, & illud sic
'assartatum, in culturam redactum & inclusum te-
'nere possit sibi & hæredibus suis in perpetuum,
'necne; Et si sit ad dampnum seu nocumentum
'dictæ Forestæ nostræ, aut alicujus alterius, tunc
'ad quod dampnum, & quod nocumentum Forestæ
'nostræ prædictæ, & ad quod dampnum & quod
'nocumentum alicujus alterius, & qualiter, & quo
'modo, & quantum Boscus ille continet in se per
'numerum acrarum & quantum quælibet acra per
'se valeat per annum in omnibus Exitibus; &
'quantum Boscus ille distat a cooperto Forestæ il-
'lius; & si sit ibi frequens reperium ferarum no-
'strarum necne, & inquisitionem inde distincte &
'aperte nobis, &c.

38. This Writ may be seen in the Register, *fo.* 257. upon the Return thereof, the King doth Licence the Party to fell the Woods. 4 *Inst.* 298.

39. But first the Chief Warden of the Forest or his Deputy will cause the Foresters, Verderors and other lawful Inhabitants in the Forest, near the place where the Woods are growing, to inquire and certify to the King in his Court of *Chancery*, these Ten Particulars following.

40. (1.)

40. (1.) Whether the cutting down the Wood will be any hurt or annoyance to the King's Forest.

(2.) Whether it will be to the hurt or annoyance of any other Person.

(3.) What hurt it will be to the King's Forest.

(4.) What hurt it will be to any other Person.

(5.) How and in what manner it will be a hurt to the King's Forest.

(6.) How and in what manner it will be a hurt or annoyance to any other Person.

(7.) How many Acres of Wood it doth contain.

(8.) How much every Acre is worth by the Year.

(9.) How far 'tis distant from any other Covert of the Forest.

(10. Whether the wild Beasts of the Forest do frequent that Wood or not.

41. And then when the Foresters, *&c.* have viewed the Place, and made *Inquisition* as aforesaid, and certified the same to the Court of *Chancery*, or to the Chief Justice in Eyre, if it appear by the said Certificate that the Wood may be conveniently cut down without any damage to the King's Forest or to any other Person, the Lord Chief Justice of the Forest may grant to the Owner of the *Wood* a *Licence* to fell the same.

42. But before he hath such *Licence*, he must come before the Chief Justice, and there be bound in a *Recognizance* to the King in a certain Sum of Money, with *Condition*, that after the same is felled, and during the space of seven Years following, he shall fence and keep the same with sufficient Hedg-

ing and ditching, so that it may be well preserved from the Deer or any other Cattle during all that Time.

43. But to avoid this Charge and Trouble, the Lord Chief Justice in Eyre may take a shorter Course, *viz.* He may grant a Warrant under his Hand and Seal of Office, directed to the Foresters in the same manner, and in the like Words as the Writ, *Ad quod damnum*, before mentioned; and in *Itinere Windsor*, the Court gave a Licence to one *Halsted* to fell Timber in his own Ground in the Forest, to repair a Bridge. *Jones's Rep.* 274.

44. And where the Lord Chief Justice grants such a Warrant for felling Woods, upon an Inquisition and Certificate to him, the Owner must fence them in manner as aforesaid, that they may grow to be Woods and Coverts again; for he who hath such a Licence, must not destroy the Woods, except he hath a special Licence so to do; *viz.* To assart the Place, and turn it into Tillage according to the Writ, *Ad quod damnum*, before recited.

45. In which Writ the Words are, *Parvo fossato & bassâ Haiâ secundùm assisam forestæ includere*: But that must be intended of Fences and Inclosures of such Lands which were once Woods, and afterwards assarted and made Tillage: And in such case it must be inclosed only with a small Ditch and a low Hedge; but where 'tis to be preserved as *Wood-Land* still, it may be inclosed with great *Ditches*, and high Hedges, to keep the Deer out. *Per Stat.* 22 *Ed.* 4. *cap.* 7.

46. But though a Man may cut his Woods for necessary *Boots*, by *View of Foresters*, and by vertue of such a Warrant or Licence from the Chief Justice in Eyre; yet the Officers ought to present it at the next Court of *Attachments*, *viz.* How much was fell'd; and that it was done by the *View of the Foresters*, that it may appear on Record: This was the

the Opinion of Mr. Attorney *Noy*. *In Itinere Windsor*, *Jones*, 295.

47. *In eodem Itinere Jones Rep.* 297. One *Oakley* was presented for suffering several great Oaks to stand to the Destruction of all the *nether Vert*: the same Attorney *Noy* held, That though a Man could not fell his Timber or Wood without Licence, yet he was of Opinion, that the Law would not compel him to fetch a Licence, and by consequence, that the Court could not punish him for letting his Oaks stand.

48. Upon the whole matter, a Man may take Estovers in his own Woods by the *View of the Forester*; but they must not take any thing for their View; and if they do, 'tis Extortion. *Jones's Rep.* 277.

49. *Anno* 8 *Car*. One *Moor* was presented *in Itinere Windsor*, for suffering three Roods of Wood to be spoiled with Cattle, who came and shewed to the Court, That the Fence through which the Spoil was made, belonged to another to make; and so the Spoil was in his Default: But Mr. Attorney *Noy* argued, That it being in the Forest, he whose Wood is in danger of being spoiled, ought to request the other to make the Hedges; and if he refuse, then he must do it himself, and bring an Action on the Case against the other who ought to have done it; and therefore, for this Offence, *Moor* was fined 40 *s*. *Jones's Rep.* 277.

50. *In eodem Itinere*, One *Rapley* being presented for cutting unlawful *Browse-wood*, alledged, That he cut it by the King's Command, being an Under-keeper in the Forest of *Windsor*, and was ordered by the King to sell it, and to buy Hay for the Deer in a hard Winter: To which the Court reply'd, That though the King is to be obeyed, yet there is a legal way to have his Commands put in Execution; and therefore, not having the

Woods viewed where the *Browse* might best be spared, and not procuring a Licence in an orderly Method, he was fined 10 *s.* *Jones's Rep.* 279. But a Lord of a Forest may enter, by his Officers, into any Man's Woods growing in the Regard thereof, and cut down *Browse-Wood* in the Winter for the Deer. *Assis. Pick. fo.* 19. 'tis called, *Cablicia. Itin. Lanc fo.* 172.

51. So likewise one *Clifton* being presented for selling and carrying away seven Timber Trees, alledged to the Court, That they were felled to repair some *Bridges* which the King was to repair, and the Lops were sold to pay for the Workmanship; all which was affirmed by the Verderors, and yet for the undue way of taking the Trees, he was fined 5 *s.* *Jones's Rep.* 279.

52. In the same *Iter*, several of the Tenants of *Warfeild* being presented for cutting their Woods *without Licence*, desir'd that their Offences might be respited until Mr. *Nevil*, who was Lord of that Manor, came of Age, who was then the King's Ward, and had put in a Claim to discharge himself and his Tenants from all Fines by reason of any Offences.

53. Mr Attorney reply'd, That as to all Lands which, by Office, appeared to be in the King's Hands by reason of the Wardship, the Ward should receive no Prejudice, but that should be respited; and as for the other Lands, it was unreasonable that the Tenants should continue unpunished, unless they could make it appear, that the Ward had such a Franchise; and so divers of them were fined. *Jones's Rep.* 288.

54. If a Man fire any dry Oaks in a Forest, he is punishable by *Assisa Forestæ*.

55. If any Forester take Money for *Bark*, his Lands shall be seised for the Money. *Itin. Lanc. fo.* 7.

56. If any take Hawks, or destroy Eyries of Hawks in the King's Woods, he shall be fined.

57. At every Justice-Seat the Number of *Trees* which have been given away by *Warrant*, must be presented, and all *Windfalls* in the Forest since the last Court. *Itin. Lanc. fo.* 3. 8. and this is usually done by the Chief Forester. *Assis. Pick. fo.* 7, 18.

58. *Ministri forestæ præsentant quod Johannes de Aslaby cepit infra dominicum quatuor quercus pretii* 4 *d. Et dimissus fuit per viridarios manucaptoribus usque ad istam Assisam: Qui modo non venit. Ideo ad judicium de manucaptoribus & præd. Johan respondeat domino Regi de pretio præd. & pro forisfacturâ ejusdem* 4 *s.*

59. *Et quod Humfridus Tober cepit undecim quercus virides infra dominicum pretii cujuslibet* 1 *d. & cariavit illas cum uno plaustro & sex bobus quæ appretionat. viz. Plaustrum ad* 6 *d. & Boves ad* 16 *s. pretii cujuslibet* 2 *s.* 8 *d. unde Tenentes terræ & tenementorum Richardi de S. viridarii istius forestæ, ad cujus manus præd. devenit respondeant, & similiter pro forisfacturâ ejusdem* 11 *s.*

60. *Item præsentant quod Prior de Maldon cepit* 11 *plaustra Spineti in B. infra dominicum pretii* 11 *d. & per Viridar. dimissus fuit per manucaptores usque ad Assisam istam, &c. Qui modo venit, &c. Et super hoc convictus oneratur erga Dominum Regem de pretio præd. & pro forisfacturâ ejusdem* 11 *s.*

61. *Item quod Robertus Scalby cepit unam viridem quercum, &c. pretii* 1 *d. unde tenen. Viridar. respond. de pretio præd. & pro forisfactura* 6 *d. ad quorum manus pretium & forisfactura præd. devenerunt.*

62. The Paragraphs before-mention'd are Forms of Entries in *the Assises of Pickering, Anno* 8 *Ed.* 3. And in the same *Assises, fo.* 15, 17, 19. and in *the Assises of Lancaster, fo.* 9. it appeareth, That *William* Earl of *Warren*, by Deed, granted to the Abbot of *Furneaux*, that he and his Successors might take, within his Forest of *Lancaster*, *Maeremium, &c.*

Quæ ad usus suos sunt necessaria, & nominatim ad piscar' suam de Lancastr. faciend, quicquid eis ad hoc opus fuerit. By vertue whereof, the Abbot claimed Timber, both for his Messuage of *B.* and for his Piscary; and that he had enjoyed the same by the Word *Maeremium* ever since the Grant, and that without the View of the Foresters; and the Usage being found by the Jury, his Claim was allowed.

63. If a Wood is surrounded with the Forest, but yet out of the Regard thereof, the Owner must make his Claim in these Words: *Gilbertus de Acton clamat tenere Boscum suum de Trovesdale pertinen' ad manerium suum de B. extra Regardum forestæ, viz. Illum boscum qui est ex parte Boreali, &c.* and so express the Limits, *&c.*

Estovers.

64. If a Man hath Estovers allowed for making a Hedge, which Hedge would have lasted Two Years, but is burned in the first Year; in this Case, *per Assisas Forestæ*, he shall not be allowed new *Estovers*; and if he take more Estovers than he ought at one Time, they shall be seised, and the Party fined. *Itin. Pick. fo. 3.*

65. If he who hath *Estovers* in a Forest, make *Hurdles* of them, and sell those Hurdles, he is punishable.

66. *Ministri forestæ dicunt quod Tho. Wake, & omnes ill. &c. à tempore quo non extat memoria hominum habuerunt, &c. liberatione boscum in Communibus boscis suis pro se, &c. ad quodlibet attachiamentum & hoc sufficientiam bosci.*

67. *Præsentat' est quod Johan' Lancastriæ cepit tres quercus in foresta istâ; Qui venit & dicit quod eas habuit ex liberatione forestariorum pro Estoveriis suis, &c. Et quia hoc testatam est per Rotulos viridariorum esse verum Ideo dictus Johan. inde eat, &c.*

68. *Et quia inspectis Rotulis Viridar. istius forestæ nihil compertum est de pretio corticum trium quercuum præ-*

prædict' Ideo ipsi liberantur prisonæ, & ducti finem fecerunt cum Domino in hac parte dimid. marcæ.

Woodward.

See { *Common*, 34, 42.
Forest, 32, 34.
Officer, 5.
Regarder, 25, 28, 38, 48.
Swanimote, 26.
Appendix, Assisa Foresta, 12. }

1. A Woodward is an Officer of the Forest whose Charge is to look after the Woods and *Vert* there, his very Name denotes his Office, and he is often mentioned in *the Assises and Ordinances of the Forest*.

2. *In Assis. & Consuetudinibus Forestæ, Anno 6. Ed. 1. Artic. 12. viz. Si Woodwardus viderit Malefactores in custodiâ suâ vel bestiam mortuam, debet monstrare capitali Forestario, vel Viridario.*

3. Mr. *Manwood* infers from this Article, That a *Woodward* may *monstrare*, but he cannot *attachiare*; that is, he may present Offenders, but cannot attach them.

4. But if he had considered the Article immediately preceding in the same *Assises*, I cannot imagine how he could be of that Opinion, *viz.* Artic. 11. *Si quis viderit aliquos Malefactores infra Metas Forestæ aliquam feram capere vel asportare, debet illos capere secundùm posse suum.*

5. Now the Words, *Si quis viderit Malefactores, &c.* are general, and extend as well to *Woodwards* as to *Foresters*, or any other Ministers of the Forest: 'Tis true, if a *Woodward* see *Bestiam mortuam*, he is commanded by that Article, *Monstrare*

eam Capitali forestario; but if he see *Malefactores in Custodiâ suâ*, it may be impossible for him *monstrare eos Capitali Forestario*, because they may be gone before he finds the Forester; therefore it seems plain by those Laws, that he may attach them.

6. This Officer ought to appear at every Justice-Seat, and when he is call'd, he must present his *Hatchet* to the Lord Chief Justice in Eyre. *Jones's Rep.* 266.

7. He is likewise to appear at every Court of *Attachments*, and there to present all Offences done within his Charge.

8. *In Itinere Windsor*, *Jones's Rep.* 280. Mr. *Reston* claimed the *Woodwardship* of all the King's Woods in *Cokeham* and *Bray*, by vertue of a Grant from King *James* I. *Habendum officium præd. unacum omnibus & omnimodis boscis vocat.* Windsor *&* Fee-Trees *in boscis præd. vel in eorum aliquo cum omnibus aliis proficuis, &c. dicto officio aliquo modo debitis, consuetis, pertinen. sive spectan. &c. in tam amplis modo & forma prout aliquis alius dictum officium habuit, &c.*

9. It was adjudged, that he had no Title to the *Fee-Trees* by this Patent, because he had made no Title to the Office of *Woodward* by *Prescription*; for he doth not say that it was an antient Office, or that there were any Fees belonging to it; and without such an Averment, *viz.* of what did *antiently* belong to the Office, this Grant is very uncertain, for it doth not shew what Fees he shall have, the Words being, *Unà cum vadiis & feodis eidem Officio spectan'*, without any Averment, that those Fees which he claimed, did belong to his Office; and then the subsequent Words, *viz. In tam amplus modo & forma prout aliquis officium præd. habuit*, only relate to such Fees which any Grantee *licite habuit*, and not to those which he took wrongfully.

10.

10. And the Attorney-General *Noy* affirmed, That Mr. *Reston* could not *prescribe* to this Office, because there was no *Woodward* in those Places before the Reign of *H.* 8. but admitting the Patent to be good (which it was not in point of Law) he desired, that the Fact might be inquired into by the Ministers of the Forest, how this Office had been used by the Patentee, *viz.* Whether he or his Deputy-Woodward, or any of his Servants had fell'd any Trees without Warrant, or had otherwise misbehaved themselves in not presenting Abuses; for these and such like Offences are Causes of Forfeiture of his Office.

11. And it being found, that Mr. *Reston* or his Under-Woodward, had destroyed, or suffered to be destroyed, several Woods committed to their Custody and Charge, Judgment was given, That the Office of *Woodward* was forfeited upon finding this Abuse. *Jones's Rep.* 280.

12. In the Case last mentioned, the Lord Chief Justice *Richardson* disliked the Penning the Patent, because the Fees were not granted till after the *Habendum*, and not mentioned in the *Premisses*; and that there are many Cases to prove, that nothing will pass by the *Habendum* which is not named in the *Premisses*.

13. And moreover, that upon avoiding this Grant, the Spoils made by the Woodward were to be answered to the King; and then Inquiry was to be made, what Horses and Carts had carry'd away the Wood and Timber; for they are all forfeited, the Timber being the King's *own*, and growing on his *demesne Lands*: But Judgment was given as aforesaid.

14. If a *Subject* hath any Wood in a Forest, and his *Woodward* should neglect to appear at the Justice-Seat, his Wood shall be seised into the King's Hands,

and so remain till 'tis replevied by the Owner, and till he hath paid a Fine.

15. If an Owner of Woods in the Forest appoint and makes a *Woodward* in his Woods, where there was not such Office before, 'tis finable. *Assis. Pick. fo.* 8. And if he make a Woodward where there was usually one before, and that Woodward doth not appear at the Justice-Seat, the Wood is to be seised; and if he doth not replevy it in a Year, then *remaneat in manibus Dom. Regis imperpetuum*; and upon this Replevy, he is to be fined for not having a *Woodward*. If the King hath a Wood of his own in the Forest, and make a Lease of Years of it, the Lessee must provide a *Woodward*. *Jones's Rep.* 266.

16. *Ministri Forestæ dicunt quod cum contigerit quod Woodwardus præd. Prioris Sancti Johan' de Jerusalem non veniet ad Attachiamentum Forestæ prout alii Woodwardi diversorum Dominorum in Foresta veniunt, tunc ipse Woodwardus semper consuetus est ibidem amerciari, & Amerciamentum inde ad opus Dom' Regis Levari, sicut & de aliis Woodwardis qui non veniunt & fuerunt amerciati.*

17. The Office of a *Woodward*, and the Bark of Trees felled in the Forest, was claimed, as appertaining unto a Manor, and adjudged accordingly.

A P-

APPENDIX.

Charta de Foresta, OF CANUTUS, a *Dane,* and King of this Realm; granted at a Parliament holden at *Winchester, Anno Dom.* 1016.

Incipiunt constitutiones CANUTI *Regis, de Foresta.*

' HÆ sunt sanctiones de foresta, quas ego ' Canutus Rex cum consilio primario-' rum hominum meorum condo & fa-' cio, ut cunctis regni nostri Angliæ ' Ecclesiis & pax & Justitia fiat, & ut omnis delin-' quens secundùm modum delicti, & delinquentis ' fortunam patiatur.

' 1. Sint jam deinceps quatuor ex liberalioribus ' hominibus qui habent salvas suas debitas consuet. ' quos Angli *Pægened*, appell. in qualibet regni mei ' provincia constituti, ad justitiam distribuend. ' una cum pœna merita & materiis forestæ cuncto ' populo meo, tam Anglis quam Danis, per totum ' regnum meum Angliæ quos quatuor primarios ' forestæ appellandos censemus.

This is the first Constitution made by *Canutus*, but my Lord *Coke* bids us beware of the whole; *viz.*

This shews the Jurisdiction of the Court of *Swanimote*, where the *Verderors* are Judges to convict the *Regarders* and *Foresters* of any Offence; for there their Causes are to be *judicatæ & decisæ*; but they are not to be punished by that Court: 'Tis true, if the Verderors offend, they are to be punish'd by the King or by his Chief Justice in Eyre, in the Justice-Seat, *ne scelus aliquod remaneat inultum.*

'11. Habeant hi quatuor unam regalem potestatem (salvâ nobis nostrâ presentiâ) quaterque in Anno generales forestæ demonstrationes & viridis & veneris forisfactiones quas *Muchehunt* dicunt, ubi teneant omnes calumnias de materia aliqua tangente forestam, eantque ad triplex judicium quod Angli *of Gangfordel* dicunt. Ita autem acquiretur illud triplex judicium: Accipiat secum quinque & sit ipse sextus & sic jurando acquirat triplex judicium, aut triplex juramentum. sed *purgatio ignis* nullatenus admittatur nisi ubi nuda veritas nequit aliter investigari.

There were Three sorts of Tryals formerly used in *England*, one was *Purgatio ignis*; and Two other by Water; and those were called, by the old Writers, *Triplex judicium.*

The *Purgatio ignis* was admitted to none but the Nobility, and to such who were Free-born; the Manner was thus;

Sf. The Party accused was to go certain Paces with a hot Iron in his hand, which sometimes weighed a Pound, and then it was called, *Single* or *Simplex Ordelium*; sometimes three Pounds, and then it was called, *Triplex Ordelium*; or he was to walk Bare-foot upon red hot Plough shares; and, in either case, if he was not burnt or scorched, he was adjudged innocent; but if otherwise, he was then condemned of the Fact for which he was accused.

Our

Our Hiſtories mention, That *Emma*, the Mother of King *Edward* the Confeſſor, was accuſed of the Death of her Son; for which ſhe was adjudged by *Robert*, then Archbiſhop of *Canterbury*, to this Tryal; and was led blindfold by two Men to paſs over nine Plough-Shares red hot; which ſhe did Barefoot, without any hurt. *Grafton's Chron. pag.* 180.

The other two Tryals were *per aqnam*, and thoſe were for Men of ſervile Condition; one of which Tryals was *per aquam frigidam*, and then the Accuſed was thrown into ſome Pond, River or great Veſſel of cold Water, and if he continued under the ſame for ſome time, without ſtruggling for Life, he was then acquitted; but if he laboured for Breath ſoon after he was thrown in, then he was condemned as guilty.

The Tryal *per aquam calidam* was, to thruſt his Arm up to the Shoulder into a Veſſel of hot Water, and if he had no hurt he was acquitted, otherwiſe was condemned.

Theſe Tryals were long before the Conqueſt, and were continued till the Reign of King *John*, but were totally aboliſhed by Act of Parliament in the Reign of *H.* 3. They were called in *Saxon*, Ordæle, which ſignifies *Expers Criminis*, whereof the Defendant being arraigned and pleading not guilty, it was a proper Queſtion then to ask him, how he would be tried? becauſe there were ſeveral ſorts of Tryals in thoſe Days, *viz.* By Ordeal, which was called, *Judicium Dei*, and by the Country, which was by *Jury*.

We ask the ſame Queſtion now, which is very improper, becauſe there is but one Manner of Tryal now uſed, and that is by *Jury*: And the Anſwer of the Criminal is as improper, *viz.* to ſay, That he will be try'd by God and his Country, when

when the Tryal, which in those Days, was called, *Judicium Dei*, is now abolished.

'Liberalis autem homo *i. e. Pegen*, modo crimen 'suum non sit inter majora, habeat fidelem homi-'nem qui possit pro eo jurare juramentum, *i. e. Fo-'rathe*: Si autem non habet, ipsemet juret, nec 'pardonetur ei aliquod juramentum.

When a Man had another to swear for him, this was called, *Forathe*.

'13. Si Advena vel Peregrinus qui de longinquo 'venerit sit calumniatus de foresta, & talis est sua 'inopia ut non possit habere plegium ad primam 'calumniam, qualem nullus Anglus judicare potest: 'Tunc subeat captionem Regis, & ibi expectet 'quousque vadat ad judicium ferri & aquæ: Atta-'men si quis extraneo vel Peregrino de longo ve-'nienti, sibi ipsi nocet si aliquod judicium judicaverit.

'14. Quicunque coram *primariis hominibus* meis 'forestæ in falso testimonio steterit & victus fuerit, 'non sit dignus in posterum stare aut portare testi-'monium, quia legalitatem suam perdidit, & pro 'culpa solvat Regi decem solidos quos *Dani* vocant '*Halfe-bang*, alias *Hals-bang*.

'15. Si quis vim aliquam primariis forestæ meæ 'intulerit, si liberalis sit amittet libertatem & omnia 'sua, si villanus abscindatur dextra.

'16. Si alteruter iterum peccaverit reus sit mor-'tis.

'17. Si quis contra autem cum primario pugna-'verit, in placito emendet secundum pretium suf 'ipsius, quod Angli *Pere* & *Pite* vocant, & solvat 'primario 40 solid.

'18. Si pacem quis fregit ante mediocrem forestæ, 'quod dicunt *Getbbreche*, emendet Regi decem 'solidos.

'19.

' 19. Si quis mediocrium aliquem cum irâ per-
' cusserit, emendetur prout interfectio feræ regalis
' mihi emendari solet.

' 20. Si quis delinquens in foresta nostra capie-
' tur, pœnas luet secundum modum & genus de-
' licti.

' 21. Pœna & forisfactio non una eademque erit;
' liberalis (quem Dani *Ealderman* vocant) & illibe-
' ralis, Domini & servi, noti & ignoti, nec una
' eademque erit causarum tum civilium tum crimi-
' nalium ferarum forestæ & ferarum regalium, ve-
' neris & viridis tractatio; nam crimen veneris ab
' antiquo inter majora, & non immerito numera-
' batur: Viridis vèro (fractione chaceæ nostræ re-
' galis excepta) ita pusillum & exiguum est, quod
' vix ea respicit nostra constitutio: qui in hoc
' tamen deliquerit sit criminis forestæ reus,

' 22. Si liber aliquis feram forestæ fugerit, sive
' casu, sive præhabita voluntate, ita ut cursu celeri
' cogatur fera anhelare, decem solidis Regi emen-
' det; si illiberalis, dupliciter emendet; si servus,
' careat corio.

' 23. Si verò harum aliquot interfecerit, solvat
' dupliciter & persolvat, sitque pretii sui reus con-
' tra regem.

' 24. Sed si Regalem feram, quam Angli *Stag-*
' *gon* appellant, alteruter coegerit anhelare, alter
' per unum Annum, alter per duos careat libertate
' naturali: Si vero servus pro utlagato habeatur,
' quem Angli *Frendlesman* vocant.

' 25. Si vero occiderit, amittet liber scutum li-
' bertatis, si sit illiberalis careat libertate; si servus,
' vitâ.

' 26. Episcopi, Abbates, & Barones mei, non
' calumniantur pro venatione, si non regales feras
' occiderint, & si regales, restabunt rei Regi pro
' libito suo, sine certa emendatione.

27.

'27. Sunt aliæ (præter feras forestæ) bestiæ quæ
'dum inter septa & sepes forestæ continentur,
'emendationi subjacent: Quales sunt capreoli,
'Lepores, & Cuniculi. Sunt & alia quamplurima
'animalia quæ quanquam infra septa forestæ vivunt, & oneri & curæ mediocrum subjacent, forestæ tamen nequaquam censeri possunt, qualia sunt Equi, Bubali, vaccæ, & similia, Vulpes & Lupi, nec forestæ, nec veneris habentur, & proinde illorum interfectio nulli emendationi subjacet: Si tamen infra limites occiduntur fractio sit regalis Chaceæ, & mitius emendetur. Aper vero quanquam forestæ sit, nullatenus tamen Animal veneris haberi est assuetus.

'28. Bosco nec subbosco nostro sine licentia primariorum forestæ nemo manum apponat, quod si quis fecerit, reus sit fractionis Regalis Chaceæ.

'29. Si quis vero ilicem vel arborem aliquam qui victum feris suppeditet sciderit, præter fractionem regalis Chaceæ, emendet Regi viginti solidis.

'30. Volo ut omnis liber homo pro libito suo habeat Venerem sive viridem in planis suis super terras suas, sine Chaceâ tamen: Et devitent omnes meam, ubicunque eam habere voluero.'

By this Law it appears, That before that Time, all Wild Beasts, though out of the Forest, belonged to the King; for otherwise there had been no occasion for him to grant, that every Freeman might take them on his Lands at pleasure.

But my Lord *Coke* is of a contrary Opinion, and tells us, That if *Canutus* made any Law about this Matter, it was thus:

'§. Præterea autem concedo ut in propriis ipsorum privilegiis quisque tam in agris quam in 'sylvis excitet agiterque feras autem meas ne venentur cum pœna præcipio.

Which Law differs from the other in these Respects, *viz.* It extends to Woods as well as Plains; and by this Law a Man may *hunt*, but cannot by the other. 4 *Inst.* 320.

'31. Nullus mediocris habebit nec custodiet Canes quos Angli *Greyhounds* appellant. Liberali vero dum genuscissio eorum facta fuerit coram primario forestæ, licebit, aut sine genuscissione dum remoti sunt à limitibus forestæ per decem Milliaria: Quando vero propius venerint, emendet quolibet Miliare uno solido. Si vero infra septa forestæ reperiatur, dominus canis forisfaciet & canem & decem solidos Regi.

'32. *Velteres* vero, quos *Langeran* appellant, quia manifestè constat in iis nihil esse periculi, cuilibet licebit sine genuscissione eos custodire. Idem de canibus quos Ramhunds vocant.

'33. Quod si casu inauspicato hujusmodi canes rabidi fiant, & ubique vagantur negligentia dominorum, redduntur illiciti, & emendetur Regi illicitis, &c. Quod si intra septa forestæ reperiantur talis, exquiratur herus, & emendet secundum pretium hominis medioeris, quod secundum legem Merimorum est ducentorum solidorum.

'34. Si canis rabidus momorderit feram, tunc emendet secundum pretium hominis liberalis, quod est duodecies solidis centum. Si vero fera Regalis morsa fuerit reus sit maximi criminis.

These are the Constitutions of *Canutus* concerning the Forest, very barbarously translated out of the *Danish* Language into *Latin*. This *Canutus* was King of *England*, *Anno* 1018. about 49 Years before the Conquest.

Charta de Foresta, Anno 9 H. 3.

ALL Forests which King *Henry*, our Grandfather, afforested and made, shall be viewed by good and lawful Men; and if he hath made Forest of any other Wood more than of his own Demesne, whereby the Owner of the Wood hath Hurt, We will that forthwith it be disafforested. And if he hath made Forest of no Mens Woods but his own, then We will that it remain Forest still: Saving the Common of Herbage, and of other things in the same Forest to them which before were accustomed to have the same.

2. Men that dwell out of the Forest, from henceforth shall not come before the Justices of our Forest by Common Summons, unless they be impleaded there, or be Sureties for some other that were attached for the Forest.

3. All Woods which have been made Forests by King *Richard* our Uncle, unto our first Coronation, shall be forthwith disafforested, unless it be our Demesne Woods.

4. All Archbishops, Bishops, Abbots, Priors, Earls, Barons, Knights, and other our Freeholders, which have their Woods in Forests, shall have their Woods as they had them at the time of the first Coronation of King *Henry* our Grandfather, so that they shall be quit for ever of all Purprestures, Wastes and Assarts made in those Woods after that Time, until the beginning of the second Year of our Coronation. And those that from henceforth do make Purprestures without our special Licence, or waste, or assart the same, shall answer unto us for the same wastes, Purprestures and Assarts.

5. Our Regarders shall go through the Forest to make their Regard, as it hath been accustomed at

the Time of the First Coronation of King *Henry* our Grandfather, and no otherwise.

6. The Inquiry or View for lawing of Dogs being within our Forest, shall be made, from henceforth, when the Regard is made, that is to say, every third Year; and then it shall be done by the View and Testimony of honest men, and not otherwise. And he whose Dog is not then found expeditated, shall be amerced, and shall pay for the same, 3 s. And from henceforth no Ox shall be taken for lawing of Dogs; and such lawing shall be done by the Assise commonly used, that is to say, That three Claws of the Fore-foot shall be cut off by the Skin. But from henceforth such lawing of Dogs shall not be done, but in the Places where it hath been accustomed from the Time of the first Coronation of the said King *Henry* our Grandfather.

7. No Forester or Beadle from henceforth, shall shall make Scotale, or gather Garb, or Oats, or any Corn, or Lamb, or Pig; nor shall make any gathering, but upon the Sight and upon the Oath of the twelve Regarders, when they shall make their Regard. So many Foresters shall be assigned to the keeping the Forests, as reasonably shall seem sufficient for keeping of the same.

8. No Swanimote from henceforth shall be kept within this our Realm but thrice in the Year; First, the 15th Day afore St. *Michael*, when that our Gistakers of our Woods come together to take Agistment in our Demesne Woods; and about the Feast of St. *Martin* in Winter, when that our Gistakers shall receive our Pannage. And to these two Swanimotes shall come our Foresters, Verderors, Gistakers, and none other, by Distress. The three Swanimotes shall be kept in the beginning of 15 Days before the Feast of St. *John Baptist*, when that our Gistakers do meet to fawn our Deer:

 And

And at this Swanimote shall meet our Foresters and Verderors, and none other by Distress. Moreover, every 40 Days throughout the Year, our Foresters and Verderors shall meet to see the Attachments of the Forest, as well for green Hue as for Hunting by the Presentment of the Foresters, and afore them attached. And the said Swanimotes shall not be kept but within the Counties in which they have been used to be kept.

9. Every Freeman may take Agistment in his own Wood, within our Forest at his pleasure, and shall take his Pannage. And also we do grant, That every Freeman may drive his Swine freely, and without Impediment, through our Demesne Woods, for to agist them in their own Woods, or else where they will. And if their Swine tarry one Night and lie within our Forest, there shall be no Occasion taken thereof whereby he may leese any of his own.

10. No Man from henceforth shall lose neither Life nor Member for killing our Deer; but if any Man be taken therewith, and convict for taking of our Venison, he shall make grievous Fine, if he hath any thing whereof to make fine; and if he have nothing to leese, he shall be imprisoned a Year and a Day, and after the Year and Day expired (if he can find sufficient Sureties) he shall be delivered, and if not, he shall abjure the Realm.

11. Whatsoever Archbishop, Bishop, Earl or Baron, coming to us at our Commandment, passeth by our Forest, it shall be lawful for him to take and kill one or two of our Deer, by the View of the Forester, if he be present, or else he shall cause one to blow an Horn for him, that he seem not to steal our Deer: And likewise they shall do in returning home from us.

12. Every Freeman from henceforth, without Danger, shall make, in his own Wood, or in his Land,

Land, or in his Water which he hath within our Forest, Mills, Springs, Pools, Marl-Pits, Dykes or arable Ground, without inclosing the arable Land, so that it be not to the Annoyance of his Neighbours.

13. Every Freeman shall have, within his own Woods, Airies of Hawks, Sparrow-Hawks, Falcons, Eagles and Herons; and shall have also the Honey that is found in his Woods.

14. No Forester from henceforth (which is not a Forester in Fee) paying to us Farm for his Bailiwick, shall take Chiminage: But a Forester in Fee, paying us Farm for his Bailiwick, shall take Chiminage, that is to say, for Carriage by Cart, the Half-year, 2 d. and for another Half-year, 2 d. for a Horse that beareth Loads, for half a Year, an Half-penny, and for another Half-year, an Half-penny; and but of those only that come as Merchants through his Bailiwick, by his Licence, to buy Bushes, Timber, Bark, Coal, and in another Place to sell it again, where they will at their Pleasure; but for no other Carriage by Cart, Chiminage or Toll shall be taken: Nor Chiminage shall not be taken but in such Places only where it hath been used to be taken. Those who bear on their backs, Brush, Bark or Coal to sell, though it be their Living, shall pay no Chiminage to our Foresters, except they take it within our Demesne Woods.

15. All that be outlawed of Trespass within our Forest since the Time of King *Henry* our Grandfather, unto the first Year of our Coronation, shall come to our Peace without Let; and shall find to us Sureties, that from henceforth they shall not trespass unto us within our Forest.

16. No Constable, Castellain or Bailiff, shall hold Plea of the Forest, neither for green Hue, nor Hunting; but every Forester in Fee shall make

Attachments for Plea of Forest, as well for green Hue as Hunting, and shall present the same to the Verderors of the Provinces. And when they be inrolled and inclosed under the Seals of the Verderors, they shall be presented to our Chief Justices of our Forest, when they shall come thither to hold Plea of Forest, and before them they shall be determined.

Trespassers in Parks. Stat. Merton, Cap. 11. Anno 20. H. 3.

Concerning Trespassers in Parks and Ponds, it is not yet discussed, for the Lords demanded the proper Imprisonment of such as they should take in their Parks and Ponds; which the King denied, wherefore it was deferred.

Westm. 1. Cap. 20. Anno 3 Ed. 1.

It is provided also for Trespassers in Parks and Ponds; That if any be thereof attainted at the Suit of the Party, great and large Amends shall be awarded according to the Trespass, and three Years Imprisonment; and after shall make Fine at the King's Pleasure (if he have whereof) and then shall find good Surety, that after he shall not commit the like Trespass; and if he have not whereof to make Fine, after three Years Imprisonment, he shall find like Surety; and if he cannot find like Surety, he shall abjure the Realm. And if any guilty thereof be Fugitive, and have no Land or Tenement sufficient, whereby he may be justified, so soon as the King shall find it by Inquest, he shall be proclaimed from County to County; and if he come not, he shall be outlawed. It is provided also and agreed, That if none do sue within a Year and a Day for the Trespass done, the King shall have

have the Suit. And such as be found guilty thereof by lawful Inquest, shall be punished in like manner in all points as above is said. And if any such Trespasser be attainted that he hath taken tame Beasts or other things in his Parks by manner of Robbery in coming, tarrying or returning, let the Common Law be executed upon him, as upon him that is attainted of open Theft and Robbery, as well at the Suit of the King as of the Party.

Assisa & Consuetudines Forestæ, Anno 6. Ed. 1.

1. IF any Forester shall find any Man attachable for Vert in the Forest, first he shall attach him by Two Pledges, if they be to be found; if not, he shall be brought to the next Town where they may be found; and if he be afterwards found, he shall attach him by Four Pledges; and if the third Time, he shall be presented before the Verderors, and be put by eight Pledges; after the third Attachment, his Body shall be attached and retained, that he may remember what thing Vert is.

2. It is to be known, That all Trees not bearing Fruit, and those which bear Fruit at any time in the Year, and an Ash, if be old, shall remain in the Forest; and in the arable Land they be all Vert, because our Lord the King is in Possession of them.

3. If any Man shall be found felling an Oak within the Demesne-Wood, and within the Regard of the Forest, without the View or Delivery of the Forester or Verderor, he shall be attached by Four Pledges; and by the View of the Verderor, the Oak shall be praised, and the Names of the Pledges

ſhall be written in the Roll of the Foreſters and Verderors.

4. If any Man ſhall be found in the King's Demeſnes, aſſarting or doing Purpreſture, his Body ſhall be forthwith retained, but if without the Demeſnes, within the Regard, he ſhall be put by Six Pledges, and if he be afterwards found, he ſhall double his Pledges, if the third Time, he ſhall retain his Body.

5. If any Man ſhall be found attachable, contrary to his Sureties and Pledges, (that is, after he hath given Sureties not to treſpaſs in the Foreſt, and is afterwards found treſpaſſing there) he ſhall be diſtrained by his Cattle found within the Bounds of the Foreſt; but if he have none, his Body ſhall be detained until he have done that which he ought: and if his abode be without the Bounds of the Foreſt, his Name and the Name of the Town whence he is, ſhall be inrolled.

6. But Delivery of Houſe-bote and Hay-bote ſhall be made as the Wood may ſuffer the ſame to remain in the State in which it is, and not at the Requeſt of the Demandant, neither may he give or ſell any thing of the Wood without the King's Warrant.

7. If any Deer be found dead or wounded, there ſhall be an Inquiſition made by four of the next Villages to the Foreſt, which ſhall be written in the Roll; the Finder ſhall be put by Six Pledges, and the Fleſh ſhall be ſent to a Spittle-Houſe, if, by the Teſtimony of the Verderors and the County, there be any nigh: But if there be no ſuch Houſe near, the Fleſh ſhall be given to the Poor and Lame, the Head and Skin ſhall be given to the Poor of the next Town; and the Arrow, if there be any found, ſhall be preſented to the Verderor, and inrolled in his Roll.

All

All this must be intended of such Deer which are not sweet or fit to be eaten by the better Sort of People; for if a principal beast is found newly killed, 'tis not intended by this Statute, that it should be given to an Hospital; and if such Beast is dead, 'tis the King's Deer, for so it was when alive, and the Property is not altered by the killing, and in such Case the Justice of the Forest may dispose it at at his Pleasure.

8. If any Greyhound or Mastiff be found running to do any Hurt, the Forester shall retain them and present them in the Presence of the Verderors, and send them to to the King, or to the Chief Justice of the Forest.

9. If any Mastiff be found upon any Deer, and shall be expeditated, he whose Mastiff he is, shall be quit of the Deed; but if he be not expeditated, the Owner of such Mastiff shall be guilty, as if he had given it with his own Hand; and he shall be put by Six Pledges, whose Names shall be written, and also what kind of Dog it was.

10. If any Man take a Deer in the Forest, without Warrant, his Body shall be arrested wheresoever he be found within the Bounds of the Forest; and when he is taken he shall not be delivered without special Command of the King, or Chief Justice of the Forest.

11. If any see any Misdoers within the Bounds of the Forest to carry away any Deer, he shall do what he may to take him; and if he cannot, he shall levy Hue and Cry, and if he do not so, he shall remain in the King's Mercy.

12. If any Woodward shall see Misdoers within his Wardship, or shall see a dead Wild Beast, he shall shew him to the Chief Forester or Verderor; and if he does not, and the Forester of our Lord the King find such a Fault in his Wood within the

Pre-

Precinct of the Regard, that Wood shall be taken into the King's Hands, by the King's Command, or of his Chief Justice, and the Woodward is to be attached by Four Pledges.

13. If any Man shall have a Wood near unto the Demesne Wood of our Lord the King, it is lawful for him, after the Demesne Hedges are agisted, to have, in the Time of Pannage, so many Swine as the Wood may suffer, by the View of the Foresters, Verderors, Regarders and Agistors, and other lawful Men; and this shall be done of the Profit of Swine.

14. Know ye, That in Time of Pannage, when the Agistment ought to be made, the Foresters, Verderors and Agistors ought to crave the Assent of the Justices of our Lord the King's Forest, and seek their Good Will; and the Agistment shall be made as well within the Demesne Hedges, as without; and the Agistment shall be made according to their Commandment and Tenor of their Letters, which Letters he shall have before the Justices of the Forest, in the next Circuit. And it is commanded, That hereafter be taken for every Hog, as much as may be to the Use of the King for Pannage, *viz.* 1 *d.* or 2 *d.* but of little Pigs, no more than before.

15. If any Man of another County put, or willingly suffer, his Cattle to go within the Bounds of the Forest, the Forester may retain the Cattle by Sureties and safe Pledges, which if he cannot do, by the Testimony of the Verderors, he shall shew the Sheriff of the County thereof, that he may make Distress until he find Pledges; if the Sheriff do it not, the Forester shall shew it to the Justices.

16. No Mower shall bring with him a great Mastiff to drive away the Deer of our Lord the King.

King, but little Dogs to look for things without the Coverts.

17. Of these which claim to have Privileges, as Dogs unlawed, and Greyhounds, within the Bounds of the Forest, there shall be nothing done to them without our Lord the King's Warrant, or his Justices.

18. A Wood remaining in the Hands of our Lord the King, by one Year and a Day, it is in the King's Pleasure, except it be recovered by the Judgment of the Justices.

19. All the Bounds of the Forest are wholly the King's.

20. It is lawful for the Abbot of the Borough of St. *Peter* to hunt, and to take Hares, Foxes and Martens within the Bounds of the Forest, and to have unlawed Dogs, because he hath sufficient Warrant thereunto.

21. When Verderors have taken an Inquest, one shall set to his Seal, and the other keep the Roll; and so from time to time till the coming of the Justice: Then the first Day he and all the Ministers shall present the Roll, or else they shall be amerced, and Mainpernors that Day shall be proferred for the Forest, or else they shall incur a Seisure.

22. A Man attached for cutting Boughs, that Plea appertaineth to the Swanimote, before the Steward. And a Man attached for felling an Oak in the Demesne of the King or of any other Man, it belongeth to be tried before the Justice; and if he do it to any Man in the Night-time, he shall be imprisoned.

23. A Man attached to the Swanimote for green Hue, and not presented at the Swanimote, at another time the Presentment shall not hurt him, but shall be taken as a Fault in the Forester for the Con-

Concealment; and he that is attached, shall go quiet by Assise.

24. If a Forester do agree unto an Offence in the Demesne Woods of the King, the King shall take from him his Chief Office, if the Keeper be living: And because the King's Wood is wasted, at every Iter of the Justice of the Forest, they shall pay the King half a Mark.

Anno 21 Ed. 1. Placita Parliament. 134. de Malefactoribus in Parcis.

'UT Malefactores in Forestis, Chaceis & Parcis & Warrenis de cætero plus timeant intrare & malefacere quàm consueverunt, Dom. Rex ad Parliamentum suum post Pascha Anno Regni sui vicesimo primo, ad instantiam magnatum regni sui concessit & firmiter extunc præcepit observari: Quod si quis Forestarius, Parcarius aut Warrenarius in Balliva sua Malefactores aliquos invenirent in Balliva sua vagantes ad damnum ibidem faciend. & qui Forestario, Parcario aut Warrenario post clamorem & Hutesium levatum ad pacem Regis standum recto reddere noluerint, immo malitiam suam persequendo & continuando & pacem Regis diffugiendo fugam fecerunt, & vi & armis se defenderent, licet Forestar. Parcar. aut Warrenar. illi seu alii quicunque ad Pacem Dom. Regis existentes, & in comitava Forestariorum, Parcariorum & Warrenariorum illorum venientes, ad tales Malefactores sic inventos arrestandum seu capiendum; aliquem seu aliquos hujusmodi Malefactorum interfecerint, non propter hoc occasionentur coram Dom. Rege aut justic. suis quibuscunq; aut aliis Ballivis Domini Regis, seu aliorum quorumcunq; infra libertatem aut extra; nec propter hoc amittant vitam aut membrum, aut etiam pœnam subeant, immo fir-

'mam

'mam pacem Dom. Regis inde habeant, sed bene
'caveat Forestarius, Parcarius, Warrenarius, &
'alii quicunq; ne occasione contentionis, discordiæ,
'contumeliæ, aut alicujus malevolentiæ seu odii
'præhabitorum aliquibus per Ballivas suas transeuntibus
'malitiosè imponant quod causâ malefaciend.
'in Ballivis suis intrant, cum hoc non fecerint nec
'ipsos vagantes ut malefaciant, nec malefacientes
'invenirent, nec causa mmalefaciendi quærentes &
'sic eos occidant: Quod si fecerint, & de hoc
'fuerint convicti, fiat de morte sic interfectorum
'prout aliorum ad pacem Dom. Regis existentium,
'& prout de jure, & secundum consuetudinem
'Regni fuerint faciend.

Statute, Anno 33 Ed. 1. cap. 5.

WHereas certain People that be put out of the Forest for the Purlieu, and, by the Great Men, have made Request to our Sovereign Lord the King, at his Parliament, That they might be acquitted of their Charge and of the Things that the Foresters demand of them, as they were wont to be. Our Sovereign Lord the King answered; First, That where he had granted Purlieu, that he was pleased it should stand in like Manner as it was granted, albeit the Thing were sued and demanded in an evil Point. Neverthelest he willeth and intendeth, That all his Demesne Lands, wheresoever they be, that have been of the Crown, being returned by way of Escheat or otherwise, shall have Estate of free Chase and free Warren, and in such Manner shall be saved and kept to his Use for all manner of Escheats, and for all manner of Things that pleaseth him. And in right of them that have Lands and Tenements disafforested for the said Purlieu, and such as demand to have Common within the Bounds of Forests, the

Intent and Will of Our Sovereign Lord the King is, That from henceforth, where Purlieu is, they may claim to be quit of Charge of the Forests. And whereas the King's Beasts cannot have their Haunt and Repair upon the Forest Ground as they had so long as they were within the Forests, that such Folk shall not have Common nor other Easement within the Bounds of the Woods, nor of the Lands the which remain in Forest. But if any of them that be disafforested by the Purlieu, would rather be in the Forest as they were before, than to be out of the Forest as they now are, it pleaseth the King very well, That they shall be received thereunto, so that they shall remain in their antient Estate, and shall have Common and other Easement as well as they had before. Whereupon our Sovereign Lord the King willeth and commandeth, That his Justices of the Forests on this side *Trent*, and beyond *Trent*, in like manner, shall keep and hold and cause to be kept and holden straitly, the aforesaid Points within their Liberties.

Anno 33 Ed. 1. Placita Parliament. 279.

WHereas several People have been put out of the Forest by the Perambulations; and by the King's Grant have petitioned this Parliament, That they might be discharged of all those Things which were formerly demanded of them by the Foresters; The King answered, That after he had granted the Perambulations, it was his Pleasure, that it should be as he had granted, and as it ought to be, without demanding any thing, or, at least, he intended it so; but that all his Demesne Lands, whether they were those which were antiently in the Crown, or which came by way of Escheat, or in any other Manner, should be free Chases and free Warrens, and should

should be held and kept as such for his own Use, and all the Woods therein, in such manner for ever after as he pleased.

And as concerning the Right of those whose Lands and Tenements were disafforested by the said Perambulation, and who claimed Common within the Bounds of the Forest, it was his Pleasure and Intention, That since, after the Perambulation, they claimed to be dischatged of several Duties; and since the King's Beasts could not now repair to those Lands as formerly, they being now out of the Forest by the Perambulation, therefore they ought not to have any Common or any other Easement within the Boundaries, or in the Woods or Lands which are in the Forests; But if those who have been disafforested by the Perambulation had rather be again within the Forest than without, as they are now, it is the King's Pleasure that it should be so, and that they shall enjoy their former Estates and Commons, and other Privileges in the Forests as usually they have done; wherefore the King commands the Justices of the Forest, both of this side and beyond *Trent*, that they keep and observe, or cause to be kept and observed, these Things in their Bailiwicks, and in this Manner.

Ordinatio Forestæ, made *An.* 34. *Ed.* 1.

1. FIrst, we have decreed for our selves and our Heirs, That of Trespasses hereafter to be done in our Forests of green Hue and Hunting, the Foresters within whose Bailiwicks such Trespasses shall happen to be committed, shall present the same at the next Swanimote, before the Foresters, Verderors, Regarders, Agistors, and other Mi-

Ministers of the same Forest; and upon such Presentment there before the Foresters, Verderors, and all other Ministers aforesaid, by the Oath as well of Knights, as of other honest Men, of the nearest Parts where the Trespass so presented shall be done, not suspected, by whom the Truth of the Matters may be fully inquired of; and the Truth so inquired of, the Presentments shall be solemnly affirmed and sealed with their Seals, by the common Agreement and Assent of all the Ministers aforesaid; and if the Indictment be made otherwise, it shall be void.

2. And if it happen, that any of the said Foresters, Regarders, or other Ministers of the same Forest to die, or by Sickness, or by any other Means to be hinder'd, by reason whereof, he cannot be present at such Swanimote, immediately the Justice of the Forest, or his Lieutenant, shall put another in his Place, so that the Indictment may be made by all in Form aforesaid; and that the Officers which are to be placed, be placed as hitherto it hath been accustomed to be done, saving the Verderors which shall be appointed by Election, and by our Writ. And we will, that none of the aforesaid Ministers hereafter be put in any Assises, Juries or Inquests to be taken within the Forests.

3. And if any Surcharge be found of the Foresters, or other, which have to do as Ministers of the Forest, such Surchargers shall be amoved, and shall be imprisoned according to the Discretion of the Justice of the Forest, or his Lieutenant. And they also by whom they were placed there, shall be punished likewise at our Pleasure. And at every Swanimote it shall be inquired of the Surcharge of the Foresters and other Ministers of the Forest, and of their Oppressions brought upon our People, and they shall make thereof Amends, and shall be

punish'd as above is express'd. And as concerning those Persons which, since the Time that the Forest was disafforested, have committed Offences in Vert and Venison within the Forest, to disafforest the same; and that the Sentence of Excommunication was publish'd against the same Offenders, though the same, by our good Will, should not have proceeded; which Sentence the Pope himself afterwards revok'd, and which Grants and disafforesting, for certain Causes, we do revoke and make void. For we will, That those Offenders be pardoned, except those Offences which are committed in that Part which doth remain still Forest; so that the Hedges and Ditches that were made in the mean time, shall be thrown down and removed, and utterly avoided; saving unto us our Rents, which we will have to remain according to the Assises of the Forest.

4. The Wood which is cut and fell'd, shall be removed, and the Wood standing shall remain in the Forest; and if, by chance, any such Wood yet standing be sold, it shall remain in the Forest, and the Seller shall satisfy the Buyer according to the Quantity of the Portion of the Wood standing in the Forest, and so of Wood sold in the mean time, and even as he shall take of the same Buyer.

5. We will also, That the Justice of our Forest, or his Lieutenant, in the Presence of our Treasurer, and by his Assent, have Power to take Fines and Redemptions of them which are indicted of Trespasses commited in the Forest; before this time, not inquired of in the Justices Circuit.

6. We will moreover, That they which have had Common of Pasture in the Forest, before Perambulation made, and they which afterwards were deny'd in the Forest, and they which have been letten of the said Common by the Perambulation aforesaid, shall have their Common of Pasture,

from henceforth, in the Forest, as largely and freely as they were wont to have before the Perambulation aforesaid; saving our Rents in Form aforesaid." *Teste apud W.* 28 *Maii.*

Statutes made in the Reign of *Ed.* 3.

Anno 1 *Ed.* 3. *Cap.* 8.

WHereas divers People be disinherited, ransomed and undone by the chief Keepers of the Forest on this side *Trent*, and beyond, and by other Ministers, against the Form of the Statute of the Great Charter of the Forest, and against the Declaration made by King *Ed.* Son of King *Henry*, in Form following, that is to say: We will and grant, for us and our Heirs, That for any Trespass done in the Forest, of Vert and Venison, that the Foresters in whose Balliwick such Trespass shall be committed, shall present the same Trespasses at the next Swanimote, before the Foresters, Verderors, Regarders, Agistors, and other Ministers of the same Forest: And that such Presentment be made before the said Foresters, Verderors, Regarders and Agistors, and other Ministers aforesaid, as well by the Oaths of Knights, as by other discreet and lawful Men, and not suspicious of the Parties joining near where such Offences shall be presented, and where the Truth may best and most clearly be known; and the Truth perfectly known, then such Presentments by the common Assent and Consent of all the said Ministers, shall be solemnly written, and with their Seals insealed: And if any Indictment be in any other Manner made, the same shall be void. And therefore because the Chief Wardens of the Forest have not observed the

the ſame hitherto, it is agreed and ordain'd, That henceforth no Man ſhall be taken nor impriſoned for Vert or Veniſon, unleſs he be taken *with the Manner*, or elſe indicted after the ſame Form before ſpecified; and then the Chief Warden of the Foreſt ſhall let him to mainpriſe till the Eyre of the Foreſt, without any thing taken for his Deliverance. And if the ſaid Warden ſhall not do ſo, he ſhall have a Writ out of the Chancery, which hath been in old time ordained for ſuch Perſons indicted to mainpriſe till the Eyre. And if ſuch Warden, after he hath received the Writ, do not incontinently deliver ſuch Perſons indicted to Mainpriſe, without taking any thing, then the Plaintiff ſhall have a Writ out of the Chancery to the Sheriff, to attach the ſaid Warden to be before the King at a certain Day, to anſwer wherefore he hath not replevied him that is ſo taken. And the Sheriff (the Verderors being called to him) ſhall deliver him that is ſo taken by good Mainpriſe in the Preſence of the Verderors; and ſhall deliver the Names of the Mainpernors to the ſame Verderors to anſwer in the Eyre of the Juſtices. And if the Chief Warden be thereof attainted, the Plaintiff ſhall recover his treble Damages, and the ſaid Warden to be committed to Priſon, and ranſomed at the King's Will. And from henceforth it ſhall be written to them as to the Chief Wardens of the Foreſt, becauſe they may not be Juſtices, nor to have any Record.

Note, Taken *with the Manner*, in the laſt Statute mentioned, is in 4 Sorts for Veniſon, *viz. Stable-ſtand*, *Dog-draw*, *Bloody-Hand*, and *Back-bear*. And 2 Sorts for Vert, *viz.* Cutting it, and carrying it away.

Anno 1 *Ed.* 3. *Cap.* 2.

Every Man that hath any Wood within the Forest, may take House-Boot and Hay-Boot within his said Wood, without being attached for the same by any Officer of the Forest, so that he do it by the View of the Foresters.

By the Statute of 1 *Ed.* 3. *cap.* 8. before mentioned, it appears, That the Chief Warden of the Forest is not a *judicial* but a *ministerial* Officer, because, by that Statute, if he refuse to bail an Offender in *Vert* or *Venison*, the Party grieved shall have a Writ out of Chancery, directed to the said Warden to bail him; which Writ, if he do not immediately obey, then the Party shall have another directed to the Sheriff to apprehend the Warden himself.

Anno 3 *Ed.* 3. *Cap.* 1.

That the great Charter of the Liberties, and the Charter of the Forest be observed and kept in every Article: And that the old Perambulations of the Forest in the Time of King *Ed.* Grandfather to the King, that now is, be from henceforth holden in like Form as it was then ridden and bounden: And thereupon a Charter to be made to every Shire where it was ridden and bounden; and in such Places where it was not bounden, the King will, that it shall be bounden by good Men and lawful, and that a Charter be thereupon made as aforesaid.

Anno 25 *Ed*. 3. *Cap*. 7. *Stat*. 5.

No Forester nor Keeper of Forest or Chase, nor none other Minister, shall make or gather Sustenance, nor no other Gathering of Victuals, nor other thing, by Colour of his Office, against any Man's Will, within their Bailiwick nor without, but that which is due of antient Right.

Anno 7 *R*. 2. *Cap*. 3.

NO manner of Jury shall be, from henceforth, compelled by any Minister of the Forest, to travel from Place to Place out of the Places where their Charge is given to them against their Gree, nor by Malice, nor by Menace, or other Duress, constrained to say their Verdict of a Trespass done in a Forest otherwise than their Conscience will clearly inform them; but they shall say their Verdicts upon their Charge in the Places where the Charge is given them, as above is said.

Anno 7 *R*. 2. *Cap*. 4.

That no Man be taken or imprisoned by any Minister of the Forest, without due Indictment or by Manovery, or Trespassing, in the Forest, or elsewhere; nor shall not be constrained to make any Obligation or Ransom to any Minister of the Forest, by any manner against their Gree and the Assise of the Forest: And if any do against this Ordinance in any point, and thereof be attainted, he shall pay to the Party damnified, their double Damages, and Fine and Ransom to the King for his Offence.

Anno 22 *Ed.* 4. *Cap.* 7.

IF any of the King's Subjects, having Woods of his own, growing in his own Ground, within any Forest, Chase or Purlieu of the same, within this Realm of *England*, shall cut or cause to be cut, the same Wood or part thereof, by Licence of the King or his Heirs, in his Forests, Chases or Purlieus, or, without Licence, in the *Forest*, Chase or Purlieu of *any other Person*, or make any Sale of the same Wood: It shall be lawful to the same Subject, Owner of the same Ground whereon the Wood so cut did grow, and to other such Persons to whom such Wood shall happen to be sold, immediately after the Wood so cut, to coppy and inclose the same ground with sufficient Hedges able to keep out all manner of Beasts and other Cattle out of the same Ground for the Preservation of their young Spring: And the Hedges so made, the said Subjects may keep them continually by the space of seven Years next after the same Inclosing, and repair and sustain the same as often as it shall need within the same seven Years, without suing of any other Licence of the King, or of his Heirs, or other Persons, or any of their Officers of the same Forests, Chases and Purlieus.

Note, Two Things are to be observed upon this Statute, *viz.* 1st, That a common Person might have a Forest, which appears by these Words in the Statute, *viz.* If any one cut Wood in the King's Forest, with his Licence, or in the *Forest* of *any other Person*, without Licence, he may inclose the Ground on which the Wood did grow, &c.

2d, This Statute being made in the Negative of the Common Law, shews, That before it was made, a Man could not inclose his own Grounds where he had cut any Wood in a Forest, without Leave from the King, or some Officer of the Forest; but now he might not only inclose it, but keep it inclosed for seven Years, without any manner of Leave from any Person whatsoever.

Anno 32 H. 8. cap. 13. *The Statute for the Drift of Forests, and what Beasts are not Commonable in the Waste of the Forests.*

NO Commoner or Commoners within any Forest, Chase, Moor, Marsh, Heath, Common, or Waste Ground, nor any Officer or Officers of or within any of the said Forests or Chases, nor any other Person or Persons whatsoever he or they be, at any time after the last Day of *March*, which shall be in the Year of our Lord, 1543. shall have or put to Pasture, into or upon any such Ground, Forest, Chase, Moor, Marsh, Heath, Common or Waste Ground, any *Stoned Horse* or Horses, being above the Age of *Two Years*, and not being of the Altitude and *Height* of *Fifteen Handfulls*, to be measured from the lowest part of the Hoof of the Fore-foot, unto the highest part of the Wither, and every *Handfull* to contain *Four Inches* of the Standard, to pasture, feed, or be in or upon any of the said Forests, Chases, Commons, Moors, Marshes, Heaths, or Waste Grounds, within any of the Shires and Territories of *Norfolk, Suffolk, Cambridge, Bucks, Huntingdon, Essex, Kent, South Hampshire, North-Wiltshire, Oxford, Berks, Worcester, Gloucester, Somerset, North-Wales, South-Wales,*

Wales, *Bedford*, *Warwick*, *Northampton*, *Yorkshire*, *Cheshire*, *Staffordshire*, the County of the City of *York*, the Town and Liberties of *Glocester*, the County of the Town of *Kingston upon Hull* the County Palatine of *Lancaster*, the Counties of *Salop*, *Leicester*, *Hereford* and *Lincoln*, or within any of them; nor shall put to feed or pasture any *Stoned Horse* or Horses, being above the said Age of two Years, and not being of the Altitude or *Height* of *Fourteen Handfuls*, to be measured, as aforesaid, within or upon any *like Ground* or Grounds, as been above written, lying or being in *any other Shire* of this Realm, nor within any of them, upon pain of *Forfeiture* of the said *Horse* or Horses which shall be found in or upon any such Ground, Forest, Chase, Moor, Marsh, Heath, Common or Waste Ground, at any time after the said last Day of *March*, which shall be in the Year of our Lord, 1543. contrary to the Form of this Statute.

And that it shall be lawful to every Person and Persons that shall find any such Horse or Horses contrary to the Form of this Statute, to seize the same in Manner and Form following; that is to say, The Person or Persons so finding any Horse or Horses contrary to this Act, in any Forest, Chase, Common, Moor, Marsh, Heath, or Waste Ground within the said Shires, or other Limits aforesaid, or in any of them, shall first go unto the Keeper or Keepers of the same Forest or Chase, or to his Deputy or Deputies, or to the Constable, Bailiff, Headborough, Bursholder or Tithing-man, of any Township next adjoining unto the said Place where the said Horse or Horses shall be; and shall command or require him or them, in the King's Behalf, to go with him or them to bring every such Horse or Horses as he or they shall think to be there feeding, or going contrary to this Statute, to the next Pound; and there the said Horses to be measured by any of the same Officer or Officers in the Presence of three other honest Men, to be named and appointed by the said Officer; and if it be so found, that the same Horse or Horses be contrary to this Act, that then it shall be lawful to every such Person and Persons that shall so challenge and seise the same, to take and retain the same Horse or Horses, and every of them, to his own Use, as his proper Goods and Chattels for ever, without Let, Interruption Vexation, Suit or Trouble of the Owner or Owners of them or any of them, or any other Person or Persons.

And it is further Enacted by the Authority aforesaid, That if any of the said Keepers, their Deputy or Deputies, Bailiffs, Constables, Headborougs, Bursholders or Tithing-men, or any of the said three other honest Men which shall be required to be at the said Measuring of the said Horse or Horses, as is aforesaid, do refuse to do as is aforesaid, or else do not truly measure such Horse and Horses; that then every such Bailiff, Keeper, Deputy or Deputies, Constable, Headborough, Bursholder and Tithing-man, and the said three honest Persons to be named as aforesaid, and every of them, not doing, or refusing to do his or their Duty in the Premisses, shall forfeit 40 *s.* for every time so refusing to do, or not doing as is aforesaid, the one half thereof to the King, and the other half thereof to the Party that will sue, *&c.* in which Action no Essoin, *&c.*

Provided always, That this Statute shall not extend to any *Stoned Horse* or Horses that shall happen once in every Year after the said last Day of *March*, to break, escape or go out of any several Pasture or Ground against the Will and Mind of the

the Owner or Possessor of such Horse or Horses, into any of the said Forests, Chases, Moors, Marshes, Heaths, Commons, or Waste Grounds, so that the said Horse or Horses so breaking, escaping or going out, do not remain or abide in the said Forests, Chases, Moors, Marshes, Heaths, Commons or Waste Grounds, or any of them, by the space of four Days next after sufficient and open Notice and Knowledge given at the Dwelling-house of the Owner of the said Horse or Horses, or after any Publication thereof made upon a Sunday or other Festival Day, in the Parish-Church where the Owner or Possessor of such Horse doth dwell.

And be it Enacted, *&c.* That all Forests, Chases, Commons, Moors, Marshes, Heaths and Waste Grounds, within this Realm of *England* and *Wales*, and the Marches of the same, and every of them, shall be driven at the Feast of St. *Michael the Archangel* next coming, or within fifteen Days then next after, and so yearly to be driven by the Lords, Owners or Possessors of the said Forests, and Chases, or by the Officers of the same, and by the Constables, Headboroughs, Bailiffs, Bursholders and Tithing-men, within whose Offices, Precincts and Limits the Commons, Moors, Marshes, Heaths and Waste Grounds, being out of the Forests and Chases, be or lie, upon pain of 40 *s.* to be forfeited to our Sovereign Lord the King, by every of the said Officers, Bailiffs, Constables, Headboroughs, Bursholders and Tithing-men, as often and at every time as the said Drift shall be omitted or left undone, or not effectually done, within fifteen Days after the said Feast of St. *Michael* the Archangel, as is aforesaid.

And it shall be lawful also to the said Lords, Owners and Possessors of the said Forests and Chases, by by their Officers of the same, and to the Constables, Bailiffs, Headboroughs, Bursholders and Tithing-men, and every of them, within the Limits of their Offices, to make like Drift of the said Forests, Chases, Commons, Moors, Marshes, Heaths and Waste Ground; at any other Season and Time of the Year whensoever, and as often as they shall think meet and convenient.

And furthermore, be it enacted, That if, in any of the said Drifts, there shall be found any *Mare*, Filly-fole, or Fole, or Gelding that then shall be thought not able to bear Foles of reasonable Stature, or not able nor like to grow to be able to do profitable Labours by the Discretion of the Drivers aforesaid, or of the more Number of them, then the same Driver or Drivers shall cause the same unprofitable Beasts, and every of them, to be killed, and the Bodies of them to be buried in the Ground, or otherwise bestowed, as no Annoyance thereby may come or grow to the People there near inhabiting or thither resorting.

And it is further enacted, &c. That the Justices of Peace in every their Riding, and other Place, in their Quarter-Sessions to be kept and holden by vertue of the King's Commission of the Peace to them directed; and all Stewards of Leets and Law-Days, shall have Authority, by this Act, to inquire of all Defaults, Contempts, Omissions and Offences contrary to the Effects above written, and every of them; and all Presentments thereof to be found in any of the said Leets and Law-Days, shall be certified by the Steward or Deputy-Steward, or Court-holder of the same Leet or Law-Day, in the next General Sessions of the Peace to be holden in the County where such Presentment shall be found or had, or unto the *Custos Rotulorum* of the same Shire, within forty Days next after the

Pre-

Presentment made; which Justices of the Peace, in their Quarter-Sessions of the Peace, shall have Power and Authority by this Act, to hear and determine every such Presentment before themselves found, or in any of the said Leets or Law-Days, to be presented and certified as is aforesaid, as well by Examination as otherwise: And if any such Steward, Deputy-Steward, or Court-holder aforesaid, imbezil or conceal any such Presentment, or do not certify the same as is before written, every of them so offending shall forfeit and lose for every such Offence, 40 s. the one half of every such Forfeiture, and of every other the Forfeitures afore-written, to be to the King, and the other half to the Person or Persons that will sue for the same before the said Justices of Peace in their said Quarter-Sessions, by Bill or Information, which Justices shall have full Power and Authority, by virtue of this Act, to hear and determine every such Offence as well by Examination as otherwise, as is before-mentioned.

And be it further enacted, &c. That no Person or Persons after the Feast of St. *Michael* the Arch-angel next coming, shall have or put to Pasture any Horse, Gelding or Mare infected with Scab or Maunge, in, to, or upon any of the said Forests, Chases, Moors, Marshes, Heaths, Commons, Waste Grounds, or Common Fields, upon pain to forfeit, for every Horse, Gelding or Mare so infected, pasturing in any of the said Grounds, Ten Shillings; which Offence shall be inquired and presented before the Steward in every Leet as other Common Annoyances be: And the Forfeiture therefore to be to the Lord of the said Leat where the said Offences shall be presented.

Provided always, That this Act or any thing therein contained, shall not extend or be

p:e-prejudicial to any Person or Persons having any *Stoned Horses* under the Heights and Altitudes above-mentioned, for or concerning the having or putting any of the said Horses to feeding in or upon any Common or other Waste Grounds where any Mares or Fillies be not used or suffered to be fed, pastured or kept.

This Statute doth not extend to the Fens in *Ely*, nor to the Counties of *Cambridge*, *Huntingdon*, *Northampton*, *Lincoln*, *Norfolk* and *Suffolk*; so that the Horses there kept in Commons, *&c.* are not under thirteen Hands high, 8 *Eliz.* *cap.* 8. Nor to the County of *Cornwal*, 21. *Jac. cap.* 28.

Scabbed or infected Horses shall not be put in Commons, in pain to forfeit 10*s.* to the Lord of the Leet.

Anno 32 H. 8. cap. 35. *That the Justice in Eyre may make a Deputy.*

From henceforth all and every Justice and Justices of the King's Forests, Parks and Chases within this Realm, which now be, or hereafter shall be, by their Writing, sealed with their Seal of Office, shall make, assign, depute and appoint as many Deputy or Deputies, for the exercising of the same Office of the Justice or Justices of the Forests, as to such Justice or Justices, from time to time, shall be thought convenient: Which Deputy and Deputies so appointed, shall have like Power and Authority to do and execute all things concerning the King's Forests, Parks and Chases, and all other things concerning the Office and Offices of the Justices of the Forests, to all Intents and Purposes, and in as large and ample Manner and Form as the same Justice or Justices might

might or may lawfully do or execute by the Laws of this Realm, and as though the same Justice or Justices were there personally present in his or their own Person or Persons.

By the Common Law, before the making this Statute, the Justice of the Forest being a Judicial Officer could not make a Deputy; but by this Law he was enabled to make one in Manner as thereby directed.

Anno 17 Car. 1. cap. 16. *An Act about the Boundaries, &c. of Forests.*

WHereas by an Act of Parliament, made in the First Year of the Reign of the late King *Ed.* 3. it is ordained, That the old Perambulation of the Forest, in the Time of King *Ed.* 1. should be, from thenceforth, holden in like Form as it was then ridden and bounded; and in such Places where it was not bounded, the King would, that it should be bounded by good Men and lawful.

And whereas for many Ages past certain *Meets*, *Meers*, *Limits* and *Bounds* of Forests have been commonly known and observed in the several Counties wherein the said Forests lie.

And whereas of late divers Presentments have been made, and some Judgments given, whereby the said *Meets*, *Meers*, *Limits* and *Bounds* of some of the said Forests have been variously extended, or pretended to extend beyond some of the said *Meets*, *Meers*, *Limits* and *Bounds* so commonly known, and formerly observed, to the great Grievance and Vexation of many Persons having Lands adjoining

to

to the ſaid *Meets*, *Meers*, *Limits* and *Bounds* ſo commonly known and formerly obſerved.

And whereas, of late time, ſome Endeavours or Pretences have been to ſet on foot Foreſts, in ſome parts of this Realm, and the Dominion of *Wales*, where, in truth, none have been or ought to be, or at leaſt have not been uſed of long Time: For Remedy thereof, may it pleaſe your Majeſty, That it may be declared and enacted by Authority of Parliament.

And be it delared and enacted by the King's moſt excellent Majeſty, and the Lords and Commons in this Parliament aſſembled, and by the Authority of the ſame, That from henceforth the *Meets*, *Meers*, *Limits* and *Bounds*, of all and every the Foreſts reſpectively, ſhall be, to all Intents and Purpoſes taken, adjudged, and deemed to extend, no farther reſpectively, than the *Meets*, *Meers*, *Limits* and *Bounds* within the ſeveral Counties reſpectively wherein the ſaid Foreſts lie, were commonly known, reputed, uſed or taken to be the *Meets*, *Meers*, *Limits* and Bounds of *the ſaid Foreſts* reſpectively, in the Twentieth Year of the Reign of our late Sovereign Lord King *James*, and not beyond, in any wiſe, any Perambulation, or Perambulations, Extents, Surveys, Judgments, Records, Decrees, or other Matter or Thing whatever, to the contrary notwithſtanding.

And that all and every the Preſentments ſince the ſaid 20th Year made, and all and every other Preſentment and Preſentments, and all and every Judgment and Award upon or by Reaſon or Pretext of any ſuch Preſentment or Preſentments, and all and every Perambulation and Perambulations, Surveys, Extents, and other Act and Acts, at any time heretofore had or made, by which the *Meets*, *Meers*, *Limits* and *Bounds* of the ſaid Foreſts,

rests, or any of them, are or are pretended to be farther extended than as aforesaid; and also all and every Presentment of any Person or Persons at any *Justice-Seat*, *Swanimote*, or Court of Attachments, for or by reason or by colour of any Act or Acts whatsoever, done or committed in any place without or beyond the said *Metes*, *Meers*, *Limits* or *Bounds* respectively, so commonly known, reputed, used or taken as aforesaid; and all and every Fine and Fines, and Amerciament and Amerciaments upon, by reason or colour of any such Presentment or Presentments, shall be, from henceforth, adjudged, deemed and taken to be utterly void and of no Force or Effect, any Law, Statute, Record or Pretence whatsoever, to the contrary notwithstanding.

And be it further enacted by the Authority aforesaid, That no Place or Places within this Realm of *England*, or Dominion of *Wales*, where no such *Justice Seat*, *Swanimote*, or *Court of Attachments*, have been held or kept, or where no *Verderors* have been chosen, or *Regard* made within the space of *Sixty Years* next before the First Year of his Majesty's Reign, that now is, shall be at any time hereafter, judged, deemed or taken to be *Forest*, or within the Bounds or Meets of Forest. But the same shall be, from henceforth for ever hereafter, disafforested, and freed and exempted from the Forest-Laws; any Justice-Seat, Swanimote or Court of Attachment held or kept within or for any such Place or Places at any time or times since the beginning of his Majesty's said Reign; or any Presentment, Inquiry, Act or Thing heretofore made, or hereafter to be made or done, to the contrary notwithstanding.

Provided also, and be it further enacted by the Authority aforesaid, That for the better putting

into

into Certainty all and every the *Meets*, *Meers*, *Bounds* and *Limits* of all and every the Forests, as aforesaid, the Lord Chancellor or Lord Keeper of the Great Seal of *England*, for the time being, shall, by vertue of this Act, upon Request of any of the Peers of this Kingdom, or of the Knights and Burgesses of the Parliament, or any of them, grant several Commissions under the Great Seal of *England*, to Commissioners to be nominated respectively by the said Peers, Knights and Burgesses, or any of them, to inquire of and find out, by Inquests of good and lawful Men, upon Oath, and by the Oaths of Witnesses to be produced at the said Inquests, and by all other lawful Means, all and every the *Meets*, *Meers*, *Bounds* and *Limits* of the said Forests respectively, which were commonly known to be their Meets, Meers, Bounds and Limits respectively, in the said 20th Year of the Reign of our late Sovereign Lord King *James*, and to return the Inquests so taken into the Court of Chancery. And that all and every the Sheriffs and Bailiffs of and in every County wherein any such Inquests shall be so to be taken, and all and every the Verderors, Foresters, Rangers, and other Officers of the Forests respectively, where any such Officers be, shall be assistant and attendant to the Execution of the said Commissions, according as by vertue of the said Commissions respectively they shall be commanded; and where no such Officers are, or where such Officers be, if they or any of them shall refuse or neglect such Assistance and Attendance, as aforesaid, then the said Commissioners shall and may proceed without them in the Execution of the said Commissions.

And be it further enacted by the Authority aforesaid, That the Forests whereof the Meets, Meers, Limits and Bounds shall be so returned and certified by vertue of any the said Commissions as aforesaid, from henceforth, shall not extend, nor be extended, nor be deemed, adjudged or taken to extend, any farther in any wise than the Meets, Meers, Limits and Bounds that shall be so returned and certified; and that all Places and Territories that shall be without the Meers, Meets, Limits and Bounds so returned and certified, shall be, and are hereby declared to be, from thenceforth free to all Intents and Purposes, as if the same had never been Forest, or so reputed; any Act or Acts, Matter or Thing whatsoever, to the contrary notwithstanding.

Provided, and be it further enacted by the Authority aforesaid, That all and every the Grounds, Territories or Places which have been or are disafforested, or mentioned to be disafforested, in or by any Letters Patent, Charters or otherwise, since the said twentieth Year of the Reign of our said late Sovereign Lord King *James*, shall be excluded and left out of the Meets, Meers, Limits and Bounds of the Forests, which are to be inquired of, returned and certified by vertue of the said Commissions, or any of them respectively; and shall be and are hereby declared and enacted to be utterly disafforested, free and exempt to all Intents and Purposes, as if the same had never been at all Forest, or so reputed: Any Thing in this present Act contained, or any other Act, Matter or Thing whatsoever, to the contrary in any wise notwithstanding.

Provided nevertheless, and be it enacted, That the Tenants, Owners and Occupiers, and every of them, of Lands and Tenements which shall

be

be excluded and left out of the Meets and Meers, Limits or Bounds of the Forests, to be returned and certified by vertue of any of the said Commissions, shall or may use and enjoy such Common or other Profits and Easements within the Forests, as antiently or accustomably they have used and enjoyed: Any Thing in this present Act contained, or any Act or Ordinance made in the 33d Year of King *Edward* the First, or any Custom or Law of the Forest, or any other Matter or Thing to the contrary thereof notwithstanding.

THE TABLE.

A.

B.

C.

Case

E.

Ex-

G. **Game**

G.

H.

Except

L.

M.

rence

N.

O.

S.

Statutes *relating to Forests.*

Tryal.

War-

Lightning Source UK Ltd.
Milton Keynes UK
UKHW012242110219
337137UK00006B/1005/P

9 780267 914630